IMAGINING BOSNIAN MUSLIMS IN CENTRAL EUROPE

AUSTRIAN AND HABSBURG STUDIES
General Editor: Howard Louthan, Center for Austrian Studies, University of Minnesota

Before 1918, Austria and the Habsburg lands constituted an expansive multinational and multiethnic empire, the second largest state in Europe and a key site for cultural and intellectual developments across the continent. At the turn of the twentieth century, the region gave birth to modern psychology, philosophy, economics and music, and since then has played an important mediating role between Western and Eastern Europe, today participating as a critical member of the European Union. The volumes in this series address specific themes and questions around the history, culture, politics, social and economic experience of Austria, the Habsburg Empire, and its successor states in Central and Eastern Europe.

Recent volumes:

Volume 32
Imagining Bosnian Muslims in Central Europe: Representations, Transfers and Exchanges
Edited by František Šístek

Volume 31
More Than Mere Spectacle: Coronations and Inaugurations in the Habsburg Monarchy during the Eighteenth and Nineteenth Centuries
Edited by Klaas Van Gelder

Volume 30
Estates and Constitution: The Parliament in Eighteenth-Century Hungary
István M. Szijártó

Volume 29
Antisemitism in Galicia: Agitation, Politics, and Violence against Jews in the Late Habsburg Monarchy
Tim Buchen

Volume 28
Revisiting Austria: Tourism, Space, and National Identity, 1945 to the Present
Gundolf Graml

Volume 27
Empty Signs, Historical Imaginaries: The Entangled Nationalization of Names and Naming in a Late Habsburg Borderland
Ágoston Berecz

Volume 26
Men under Fire: Motivation, Morale and Masculinity among Czech Soldiers in the Great War, 1914–1918
Jiří Hutečka

Volume 25
Nationalism Revisited: Austrian Social Closure from Romanticism to the Digital Age
Christian Karner

Volume 24
Entangled Entertainers: Jews and Popular Culture in Fin-de-Siècle Vienna
Klaus Hödl

Volume 23
Comical Modernity: Popular Humour and the Transformation of Urban Space in Late Nineteenth-Century Vienna
Heidi Hakkarainen

For a full volume listing, please see the series page on our website: http://berghahnbooks.com/series/austrian-habsburg-studies.

IMAGINING BOSNIAN MUSLIMS IN CENTRAL EUROPE
Representations, Transfers and Exchanges

Edited by František Šístek

First published in 2021 by
Berghahn Books
www.berghahnbooks.com

© 2021, 2026 František Šístek
First paperback edition published in 2026

All rights reserved. Except for the quotation of short passages
for the purposes of criticism and review, no part of this book
may be reproduced in any form or by any means, electronic or
mechanical, including photocopying, recording, or any information
storage and retrieval system now known or to be invented,
without written permission of the publisher.

Library of Congress Cataloging-in-Publication Data
Names: Šístek, František, editor, author.
Title: Imagining Bosnian Muslims in Central Europe : representations, transfers and exchanges / edited by František Šístek.
Description: New York : Berghahn Books, 2021. | Series: Austrian and Habsburg studies ; volume 32 | Includes bibliographical references and index.
Identifiers: LCCN 2020018001 (print) | LCCN 2020018002 (ebook) | ISBN 9781789207743 (hardback) | ISBN 9781789207750 (ebook)
Subjects: LCSH: Muslims—Bosnia and Herzegovina—Public opinion. | Muslims—Europe, Central—Public opinion. | Muslims—Balkan Peninsula—Public opinion. | Bosnia and Herzegovina—Ethnic relations. | Europe, Central—Ethnic relations. | Balkan Peninsula—Ethnic relations.
Classification: LCC DR1674.M87 I459 2021 (print) | LCC DR1674.M87 (ebook) | DDC 305.6/9708991839043—dc23
LC record available at https://lccn.loc.gov/2020018001
LC ebook record available at https://lccn.loc.gov/2020018002

British Library Cataloguing in Publication Data
A catalogue record for this book is available from the British Library

EU GPSR Authorized Representative
LOGOS EUROPE, 9 rue Nicolas Poussin, 17000, LA ROCHELLE, France
Email: Contact@logoseurope.eu

ISBN 978-1-78920-774-3 hardback
ISBN 978-1-83695-393-7 paperback
ISBN 978-1-80758-773-4 epub
ISBN 978-1-78920-775-0 web pdf

https://doi.org/10.3167/9781789207743

Contents

Acknowledgements		vii
Introduction *František Šístek*		1
Chapter 1.	The 'Turkish Threat' and Early Modern Central Europe: Czech Reflections *Ladislav Hladký and Petr Stehlík*	28
Chapter 2.	The Muslims of Bosnia and Herzegovina between Millet and Nation *Božidar Jezernik*	42
Chapter 3.	Ambivalent Perceptions: Austria–Hungary, Bosnian Muslims and the Occupation Campaign in Bosnia and Herzegovina (1878) *Martin Gabriel*	63
Chapter 4.	Sleeping Beauty's Awakening: Habsburg Colonialism in Bosnia and Herzegovina, 1878–1918 *Clemens Ruthner*	76
Chapter 5.	The Portrayal of Muslims in Austro-Hungarian State Primary School Textbooks for Bosnia and Herzegovina *Oliver Pejić*	92
Chapter 6.	Towards Secularity: Autonomy and Modernization of Bosnian Islamic Institutions under Austro-Hungarian Administration *Zora Hesová*	104
Chapter 7.	Under the Slavic Crescent: Representations of Bosnian Muslims in Czech Literature, Travelogues and Memoirs, 1878–1918 *František Šístek*	121

Chapter 8.	Divided Identities in the Bosnian Narratives of Vjenceslav Novak and Rebecca West *Charles Sabatos*	145
Chapter 9.	Austronostalgia and Bosnian Muslims in the Work of Croatian Anthropologist Vera Stein Erlich *Bojan Baskar*	155
Chapter 10.	The Serbian Proverb *Poturica gori od Turčina* (A Turk-Convert Is Worse Than a Turk): Stigmatizer and Figure of Speech *Marija Mandić*	170
Chapter 11.	From Brothers to Others? Changing Images of Bosnian Muslims in (Post-)Yugoslav Slovenia *Alenka Bartulović*	194
Chapter 12.	Exploring Religious Views among Young People of Bosnian Muslim Origin in Berlin *Aldina Čemernica*	214
Chapter 13.	The West, the Balkans and the In-Between: Bosnian Muslims Representing a European Islam *Merima Šehagić*	225
Conclusion	*František Šístek*	236
Index		243

Acknowledgements

This book represents the final result of the research project entitled 'Střední Evropa a balkánští muslimové: vztahy, obrazy, stereotypy' [Central Europe and Balkan Muslims: Relations, Images, Stereotypes], coordinated by Ladislav Hladký (Institute of History, Czech Academy of Sciences, Brno) and František Šístek (Institute of History, Czech Academy of Sciences, Prague). The project was generously supported by the Czech Academy of Sciences research framework Strategy AV21 – Top Research in the Public Interest in 2017, more specifically by the research programme for social sciences and humanities entitled 'Europe and the State: Between Civilization and Barbarity'.

I greatly appreciate the scholarly advice of Ladislav Hladký and his organizational contribution during the research phase of the project. I would like to thank my colleagues and friends who took part in our research project at various stages, especially the active participants of our seminars and international conference, for their ideas and support. I especially wish to thank all the collaborators on this volume for their hard work and patience. Bojan Baskar (University of Ljubljana) and Clemens Ruthner (Trinity College, Dublin) read parts of the work-in-progress, and provided me with valuable feedback at the right time. My special thanks go to copywriter and translator John Spence for his professional and meticulous proofreading of the manuscript at several stages of the work. I am also indebted to the two anonymous reviewers commissioned by the publisher for their positive assessment of the volume, and their comments and suggestions. At Berghahn Books, I would like to thank senior editor Chris Chappell and editorial assistant Mykelin Higham for their cooperation and readiness to answer all my questions.

For the cover of this book, the photographer and photography historian Pavel Scheufler (Prague) has kindly granted us permission to use an image from his unique collection of photographs from the Austro-Hungarian period. The photo was taken in the town of Cazin in north-western Bosnia, probably in 1906, by Rudolf Bruner Dvořák (1864–1921), an important yet (for much of the twentieth century) nearly forgotten figure of Central European photojournalism who served as the official photographer to the Habsburg heir to the throne, Archduke Franz Ferdinand, from 1891 until the Sarajevo Assassination of June 1914.

Rudolf Bruner Dvořák travelled extensively throughout Central and South East Europe, and he visited the Bihać and Cazin regions repeatedly in the early years of the twentieth century after his sister married a local judge of Czech origin serving in Bihać in the Austro-Hungarian administration of the province. His photographs (most of them still not properly restored) provide rare glimpses into Bosnian Muslim small-town and rural life in the seemingly idyllic early years of the twentieth century. The famous photographs documenting the immediate aftermath of the assassination of Franz Ferdinand and his wife Sophia in Sarajevo, which triggered the First World War and shook the world and its certainties forever, were taken by Rudolf's brother and closest collaborator Jaroslav.

INTRODUCTION

František Šístek

The main purpose of this book is to highlight the importance of the rich encounters, transfers and exchanges between the peoples of Central Europe and the Muslims of Bosnia and Herzegovina for the development and transformations of modern Bosnian Muslim identity and its representations from the nineteenth century until the present. It also provides evidence of how the history of relations with the Bosnian Muslims shaped attitudes and policies towards Muslims and Islam in general in the Habsburg Empire, among its various peoples, and also in the post-Habsburg successor states of the region. The representations and conceptualizations of the Bosnian Muslims, constructed by Central European authors and observers of various national and social backgrounds, did not remain without effect on the Bosnian Muslims themselves, their self-conceptualizations, and the wider process of 'reordering the universe' in the radically different post-Ottoman era and the turbulent twentieth century. From the Central European perspective, the autochthonous Slavic Muslims of Bosnia and Herzegovina represented the closest Muslim population, a rare outpost of the Orient on European soil. The occupation of the Ottoman province of Bosnia and Herzegovina, with its relatively sizeable Muslim community, by the predominantly Roman Catholic Austria–Hungary in 1878 set the scene for a series of unique policies and modernization efforts with the aim of pacifying, controlling, accommodating and modernizing the Bosnian Muslim society, especially Muslim elites and institutions. Partly as a legacy of Habsburg colonial rule over Bosnia and Herzegovina (1878–1918), but also because of geographic proximity and other factors, namely the influx of refugees as a result of the war in Bosnia and Herzegovina (1992–95), the peoples of Central Europe and the Bosnian Muslims have maintained intense contacts and ties in the twentieth and twenty-first centuries.

This collective monograph devotes considerable attention to representations and conceptualizations of the Bosnian Muslims and their development from the nineteenth century onwards. The peoples of Central Europe played an important (indeed in many ways a pioneering) role in the real as well as discursive discovery of the Slavic Muslims of Bosnia and Herzegovina. Until the end of the twentieth century, when the war in Bosnia and Herzegovina was receiving global attention that generated a wave of similarly global academic and media interest, a significant part of what could be termed general (European or Western) as well as scholarly knowledge about Bosnia and Herzegovina and its Muslims arguably originated in Central Europe, or was filtered and channelled through Central European sources and interpreters. Bosnia and Herzegovina has often been conceptualized in a somewhat patronizing way as 'our' (Habsburg, Central European, Slavic) piece of the Orient, and its Muslims increasingly as 'our' (European, secular, tolerant) Muslims rather than exotic aliens and hereditary enemies of Christendom. Since the nineteenth century, Central European authors and observers – officials, diplomats, travellers, scholars, journalists, artists and tourists – have produced a wide range of representations and conceptualizations of Bosnian Muslims. Apart from the mainstream, Habsburg, or common Central European discourse on the Bosnian Muslims, this book pays special attention to specific national discourses on the Bosnian Muslims developed within the Habsburg Monarchy and its successor states (e.g. Czech, Slovene, Croatian).

Far from celebrating the self-proclaimed Habsburg 'civilizing mission' and the results of the cultural work achieved by Austria–Hungary, this collective volume presents a more critical and ambivalent but hopefully also a more balanced view of the complex history of transnational encounters between the peoples of Central Europe and the Muslims of Bosnia and Herzegovina. It provides representative samples of different types of Central European contributions to conceptualizations and representations of Bosnian Muslims, and it discusses the formative influence of Habsburg imperial policies on education and the transformation of Islamic institutions, as well as the very recent experiences of Bosnian Muslims as immigrants in Central European countries and the ongoing reinterpretations of Bosnian Muslim identity within the context of contemporary debates on the integration and coexistence of Muslims in Europe.

This volume represents the final outcome of a larger research project that focused on multiple links between Central Europe and Balkan Muslims from the nineteenth century until the present, including not only the Bosnian Muslims but also the Albanians, Turks, and other Muslim groups of the Balkan peninsula. The project was supported by the Czech Academy of Sciences research framework Strategy AV21 – Top Research in the Public Interest, more precisely in 2017 by the research programme for social sciences and humanities entitled 'Europe and the State: Between Civilization and Barbarity'. The output of our particular research project, entitled 'Střední Evropa a balkánští muslimové: vztahy, obrazy, stereotypy' [Central Europe and Balkan Muslims: Relations, Images, Stereotypes], coordinated by Ladislav Hladký (Institute of History, Czech Academy of Sciences, Brno) and František Šístek (Institute of History, Czech Academy of Sciences, Prague), included several workshops, public presentations, and an interdisciplinary conference.

Ladislav Hladký and I first conceived the idea of an international and interdisciplinary research project focusing on the links between Central Europe and the Balkan Muslims as the European migration crisis of 2015 and 2016 was reaching its peak. Due to its geographical position, the Czech Republic remained practically unaffected by the refugee flows coming from the Middle East via the so-called Balkan route; however, the country's public space was literally swept by a tide of anti-refugee hysteria and Islamophobia. Most alleged sightings of suspected dark-skinned aliens and Islamic radicals by concerned citizens, the defenders of Christian values and patriots, resulted in grotesque police manhunts against grossly wrong targets, who in the end turned out to be football players of African origin, Bulgarian workers from a local factory, and even chimney sweeps. Despite its irrational causes and proportions, the wave of xenophobia was skilfully instrumentalized by a significant segment of the political class, including leaders of mainstream political parties and the Czech Republic's top political representatives, and further augmented by the alarmist media, often owned or indirectly controlled by the very same politicians. Meanwhile, voices of reason appeared as well. As in other countries, experts frequently stressed the fact that Islam and the Muslim world are far from homogeneous and monolithic, and that there are many ways of practising and thinking the Muslim identity. After discussions with other colleagues researching, in one way or another, the past and present of Balkan Muslim societies, we were convinced that there was a strong need for a more intense exchange of ideas and experiences, for cooperation and coordination in the face of the irrational avalanche of lies, prejudice and outright racism. The best answer we could think of, apart from individual civic activism, was the intensification of research on the Muslims we know best, namely the Balkan Muslims, who for centuries have lived literally next door, and increasingly also in Central Europe itself.

Scholars dealing with the Balkan Muslims, their links and exchanges with the lands and peoples of Central Europe, and their representations in this area, often work with similar material, face similar problems, and raise similar questions. The existence of multiple languages in Central and South Eastern Europe, however, complicates the picture: many sources, and a significant portion of older as well as recent academic output, are available only in the national languages of the region rather than in English. Research on the Balkan Muslims and their relations with Central Europe has been further burdened by the prevalence of old-fashioned attitudes, partiality, inconsistency, and the relatively slow penetration of fresh methodological approaches and concepts. These tendencies, primarily with regard to particular national academic milieux, have already received critical attention from some Central European scholars. In a text dealing primarily with German-speaking authors from the late Habsburg period, the historian Christian Promitzer laments the lack of major scholarly works on the topic, despite the fact that the period in question represented a formative era for the acquisition of knowledge about the Balkans. While some literature on the topic does indeed exist, mostly addressing the German-speaking countries together (thus underplaying the imperial, multinational and multilingual context of the Habsburg Balkan experience), Promitzer maintains that 'its level of elaboration remains positivist, and tends to treat the respective authors in uncritical, affirmative terms' (Promitzer 2015: 198). Focusing on a different but sufficiently close national milieu in the same period, the Turcologist Jitka Malečková comes to similar conclusions in her recent article on Czech representations of Bosnian Turks (Muslims). She notes, among other things, the absence of the Western framework of colonialism, imperialism and Orientalism in the studies of Czech attitudes towards the Ottoman Empire and Balkan Muslims during the late Habsburg period: 'Leaving aside older critiques of Czech capitalist expansion . . . , mainstream Czech historiography does not pay attention to Czech colonial ambitions. Orientalism is mostly mentioned in value-free descriptions of nineteenth-century Czech art'. She further expresses 'the need to examine the Czech relationship with Muslim Others within the context of societies that lacked overseas colonies' (Malečková 2018: 16).

Another problematic perspective regarding Central European attitudes towards the Balkan Muslims re-emerged in the 2010s, though it may have never completely disappeared. It was probably most evident during the centenary of the Islamgesetz (Islam Law) of 1912, the law that recognized freedom of worship and regulated the religious needs of the Islamic community in late Habsburg Austria, but which was symbolically replaced in 2015 with a contemporary version of the Islamgesetz (see Hafez 2014; Fillafer 2016; Skowron-Nalborczyk 2016; Kropáček 2017; Rexhepi 2019). Its adoption practically coincided with the European refugee crisis, the related wave of Islamophobia and, on a brighter note, with increasing interest in the accommodation of Islam and the integration of Muslims in Europe. In public discourses, journalistic accounts, and sometimes even in the academic community, some voices suggested that the Habsburgs and the peoples of Central Europe in general knew how to handle the Muslims, presumably unlike the current generation of regional politicians and unlike Brussels and all the other usual culprits. This is certainly not our position: the authors of this volume refuse and problematize the self-proclaimed civilizing mission of the Habsburg Empire in the Balkans, as well as other related ideas such as the presumed leading Czech role in the process of the awakening, cultivation and modernization of the South Slavs, the civilizational superiority of the Slovenes (or Croats) above the backward Yugoslav southerners, and so on. On a more general level, we are trying to avoid hegemonistic, exclusivist and paternalistic discourses rooted in the hierarchical mental mapping of Europe, which tend to ascribe a privileged position to Central Europe *vis-à-vis* the Balkans, with their less developed, less fortunate, and allegedly somehow less European populations (see Todorova 1997: 140–60). A conference called 'Central Europe and Balkan Muslims: Relations and Representations', which took place at Vila Lanna in Prague in October 2017 as part of our research project, revealed a relative richness and variability of research on Bosnian Muslims (Bosniaks), who received considerably greater attention from our group of scholars of different disciplines than other Muslim populations of South Eastern Europe. This imbalance partly reflects the current state of research priorities in Central Europe, characterized by a relatively stable interest in Bosnia and Herzegovina and its Muslims, with most attention being focused on the formative experience of Habsburg rule (1878–1918) and the post-Yugoslav era (1992–present). This interest can also be attributed to the shared history of coexistence under the common roof of the Austro-Hungarian Empire (as well as Yugoslavia in the case of the Slovenes, Croats and Serbs), to specific national traditions of research rooted in the (post-)Habsburg and or Slavic and Slavophile contexts, to the relative geographic proximity and accessibility of Bosnia and Herzegovina, and, last but not least, to an increased presence of Bosnian Muslims in Central Europe following the wars of Yugoslav succession in the 1990s. The results of new and innovative research on various aspects of Bosnian Muslim historical and contemporary experiences with Central Europe, and the rich representations of Bosnian Muslims in literature, scholarly works, textbooks, paintings, proverbs, songs, journalistic accounts, political discourses and the media, which are reflected in the individual chapters compiled in the present volume, hopefully justify our decision to narrow the focus of this book to the Muslims of Bosnia and Herzegovina, their links and exchanges with Central Europe, and their representations in this area.

Central Europe and Bosnian Muslims: Delimitation and Terminology

It is certainly not the intention of this book to contribute to the already plentiful conceptualizations of Central Europe, let alone debates about its proper delimitations or discussions of its allegedly specific character, whether rooted in the region's exceptional cultural traditions, unique historical experiences, precarious geopolitical position, inimitable coffeehouse culture, or elsewise. Our definition of Central Europe is primarily practical and relatively flexible when it comes to perceived limits of the region, which are notoriously difficult to define. For the purpose of this volume, Central Europe primarily, but not exclusively, corresponds to the historical region of the late Habsburg Empire and its imperial legacy. In our view, during its first post-Habsburg century, the core of this space, characterized by numerous similarities and shared, parallel, and overlapping traditions and practices at different levels of life (from politics to popular culture), roughly corresponded to the present-day nation states of Austria, Hungary, the Czech Republic, Slovakia, Slovenia and Croatia. Relations between these lands and their peoples with Bosnia and Herzegovina and its Muslims have been relatively extensive, as are the resulting representations and conceptualizations of the Bosnian Muslims in the various national milieux and languages of this space. The long-term academic interest in Bosnia's history and present is reflected in the considerable number and variety of scholarly texts published by authors originating from or working in the successor states of the Habsburg Monarchy (see the selected but representative bibliography *Forschungsliteratur zu Bosnien-Herzegowina* in Ruthner and Scheer 2018: 539–60).

Apart from the core area of the late Habsburg Monarchy, we have also included material from Croatia and Serbia. This might raise some eyebrows: are not the Croats, let alone the Serbs, supposed to belong to the Balkans rather than to Central Europe? The Serbs and Croats have indeed enjoyed a special position *vis-à-vis* the Muslims of Bosnia and Herzegovina. The Serb, Croat, and Bosnian Muslim (Bosniak) ethnic spaces, histories, and national discourses have been intensely intertwined and overlapping, especially in the territory of Bosnia and Herzegovina itself (Okey 2011). From the nineteenth century onwards, the process of collective self-conceptualization of the Bosnian Muslims, with its successive reinterpretations, has developed as a result of a complex interplay of the Croat and Serb national discourses. By way of cultural transfers, some representations, conceptualizations and stereotypes of Bosnian Muslims generated in the Serb and Croat milieux also influenced the ways the population was imagined by those peoples of Central Europe living further afield.

Since the break-up of Yugoslavia and the establishment of Croatian independence in the early 1990s, there have been serious attempts to do away with the unwelcome Balkan identity, which is too closely associated with the shared but recently repudiated Yugoslav history and the supposedly Balkan Serbs as the negatively conceived Other in contemporary Croatia. In official discourses, Croatia has been conceptualized primarily as a Central European (or at best a Central European and Mediterranean) country (Luketić 2013); however, for the purposes of this volume, the treatment of the Croats as Central Europeans should not be understood as a pledge of support for discourses that construct the Central European identity of the Croats at the expense of their neighbours, but rather as an acknowledgment of their position in particular historical contexts. The territory of the present-day Republic of Croatia was, in its entirety, an integral part of the late Habsburg Empire. As subjects of the Habsburg Empire, the Croats played an important role in the Austro-Hungarian (semi-)colonial enterprise in Bosnia and Herzegovina after 1878, while their political and cultural elites developed their own images and visions of the Bosnian Muslims beginning in the early days of the Croatian national awakening in the first half of the nineteenth century (Baskar 2008: 70–73; Stehlík 2013; Stehlík 2015). Along with other South Slavs, the Bosnian Muslims and Croats spent the greater part of the twentieth century as citizens of the Yugoslav state. Despite the recent history of hostilities, ethnic unmixing, and ongoing nationalist antagonisms after Yugoslavia's collapse, the Croats and Bosniaks continue to be closely intertwined in many ways.

Similar arguments can be made in the case of the Serbs. Despite the core of the modern Serbian state developing on the fringes of the Ottoman Empire, and the nascent Serb national discourses being strongly influenced by authors and traditions from the post-Ottoman territories, including not only present-day Serbia but also Montenegro and other areas (see the chapter by Marija Mandić in this volume), it would be a mistake to exclude the Serbs from our conception of Central Europe. Before 1918, large numbers of Serbs lived along the southern borderlands of the Habsburg Empire, from Dalmatia and Croatia in the west and the present-day Serbian province of Vojvodina to eastern Banat in modern-day Romania. Novi Sad, Sremski Karlovci, and other towns and cities in southern Hungary represented radiant centres of Serb national life during the late Habsburg Monarchy. The River Danube, which in many ways epitomizes the myth of Central Europe, also played the role of the vital axis and artery of the Serb national revival and the subsequent process of mass ethnic homogenization (Roksandić 1991: 66–80). There are many good reasons to include both Serbs and Croats in a book on Central Europe and the Bosnian Muslims rather than exclude them as impure or incomplete Central Europeans simply because they can be simultaneously ascribed to alternative imagined regions such as the Balkans, South Eastern Europe and the Mediterranean (Bjelić and Savić 2002). After all, overlapping of imperial legacies, ethnic spaces, and territorial concepts has been the rule rather than the exception in Central and South Eastern Europe.

Most contributions gathered in this volume focus on Habsburg and post-Habsburg Central Europe; however, the Habsburg legacy obviously cannot remain the only defining factor one hundred years after the demise of the old empire and three decades after the fall of the Iron Curtain. In fact, it seems that the myth of Central Europe has already lost much of the glamour and appeal it held at the peak of its popularity in the 1980s and 1990s. As a result of postsocialist transformations, globalization, and the process of European integration, the idea of a specific Central European historical and cultural identity does not always seem to correspond to current realities. The postcommunist states of Central Europe joined the European Union in 2004, nine years after Austria. Croatia followed in 2013. Once in the EU, the notion of a specific Central European identity became progressively blurred in the complex world of new, pragmatic and temporary allegiances and alliances. Its symbolic capital seemed largely spent after the dream of a return to Europe finally came true, but it soon gave way to a dull, grey, everyday reality that did not quite match the original expectations of catching up with the West. Since the global financial crisis (2009) and the European refugee crisis (2015), the countries of Central Europe have gained increasing notoriety for the anti-immigrant, Islamophobic, and nationalist stands of their political leaders. In the meantime, the considerable importance of Germany for contemporary Central (and South East) Europe has become even more obvious than before. Whether it is fully or partly *Mittel* European or predominantly West European remains an eternal academic question; however, Germany indisputably performs the role of an economic engine of Europe and often epitomizes the EU and its policies in popular imagination across the continent. This has become most evident in the case of the great European refugee crisis that culminated in 2015 and 2016, and in the attitudes towards immigration and the integration of newcomers, especially those of Islamic faith and/or Muslim cultural origin. In Austria, Hungary, the Czech Republic, Slovakia, and the post-Yugoslav states, Germany (rather than Austria) plays an important role in internal debates, politics, and popular imagination in many topics, and is regarded both as a model worthy of emulation by some and as a negative example that must be avoided at all costs by others. While we might erect a discursive fence between Central Europe and Germany for a number of reasons and practical considerations, this cannot change the fact that much of Central Europe lives in Germany's shadow; therefore, we have also included some contributions based on material from Germany in the closing part of the volume dedicated to the post-1989 period and up to the present.

This collective monograph focuses on the Bosnian Muslims, their interactions with the peoples and states of Central Europe, and the representations of them that have developed in the region. A short terminological clarification is needed at this point. We have opted for the term 'Bosnian Muslim' instead of the term 'Bosniak'. Since 1993, the appellation 'Bosniak' has denoted the South Slavic nation (*narod*) previously officially recognized under the ethnonym 'Muslim' (*Musliman*) in late socialist Yugoslavia. When spelled with the lower-case 'm', as in 'musliman', the term was reserved for Islamic religious identity regardless of ethnic background (Bringa 1995: 10; Bougarel 2001: 112–13; Bougarel 2015: 10). The term 'Bosniak', denoting modern national rather than confessional identity, is appropriately employed in several contributions in this book focusing on the post-Yugoslav period; however, some chapters focus on earlier periods prior to the start of the process of modern ethnic homogenization, when prenational identities were the norm across the region (Detrez 2013: 13). The term 'Bosniak' would represent an ahistorical projection if used in inappropriate contexts. On the other hand, the term 'Bosnian Muslim' remains relatively flexible, as it can be fairly accurately used for the Ottoman era, for the nineteenth and twentieth centuries, and also for the present, especially in cases when the focus is primarily on religious identity. Another reason for the term 'Bosnian Muslim' being more accurate for our purposes is that the present volume does not focus on the Bosniaks as a national group in their entirety, living not only in Bosnia and Herzegovina, where they represent the most numerous of the three main ethnic groups, but also as ethnic minorities on the territory of the neighbouring states of Serbia and Montenegro, and even in the more distant Kosovo.

Throughout the volume, the full name Bosnia and Herzegovina is used rather than the hyphenated version Bosnia-Herzegovina or the abbreviated form BiH (derived from the original South Slavic name Bosna i Hercegovina). Bosnia and Herzegovina was the official appellation of the province under Habsburg rule (1878–1918). From 1945 until 1992, Bosnia and Herzegovina was the official name of one of the six republics that together comprised the socialist Yugoslav federation. Since 1992, Bosnia and Herzegovina has again been the official name, this time of an independent and internationally recognized state; nevertheless, Herzegovina and Bosnia remain two distinct historical and geographical regions, albeit closely intertwined. At the time of the Ottoman conquest of this part of the Balkan peninsula in the fifteenth century, there was already a distinction between 'the king's lands' (Bosnia proper) and 'the duke's lands' (Herzegovina): 'In their usual conservative fashion, this division was retained by the Ottomans' (Heywood 1994: 29). In the last decades of Ottoman rule at the end of the nineteenth century, as Edin Hajdarpašić explains, 'Bosnia was the name of the larger province that absorbed the south-eastern region of Herzegovina after it was reorganized several times and disbanded in 1865, later resulting in the official designation of the land as Bosnia-Herzegovina; the name Bosnia was a common shorthand for the entire region' (Hajdarpašić 2015: 6). Both regions, inhabited by a similarly mixed population composed of Christian Orthodox (Serbs), Roman Catholics (Croats) and Muslims (Bosniaks), have mostly been governed together and treated as one land in modern times. For practical reasons, the full name of the province/republic/state of Bosnia and Herzegovina is often shortened to Bosnia. This trend has also been evident in much scholarly literature, whether dealing with the past (the 'history of Bosnia') or present ('postwar Bosnia') of this territory (e.g. Malcolm 1996; Bieber 2006). In this book, we have tried to use the full 'impractical' name whenever possible, but to pay attention to cases where regional distinctions between Herzegovina and Bosnia are expressed.

However, even staunch opponents of the tendency to use the term Bosnia as a substitute for the name of the entire country acknowledge the fact that, in some cases, deviations from the ideal do make sense as 'it would indeed be difficult and impractical to speak of a "Bosnian-Herzegovinian language" or a "Bosniak-Herzegovinian people"' (Ančić 2015: 23). For these reasons, we have, throughout this volume, used the term 'Bosnian Muslims' rather than 'Bosnian-Herzegovinian Muslims' or 'Bosnian and Herzegovinian Muslims' for all the inhabitants of Bosnia and Herzegovina of Muslim faith and family background. The term Bosnian Muslims has been well established in recent scholarly literature and popular discourse. There are other practical reasons in modern times to treat the Bosnian

Muslims as one population. With due respect to the specificity of Herzegovina and its inhabitants, similar regional differences in historical development, geography, dialect, and what is commonly perceived as differences in 'mentality' in the emic perspective, can also be encountered within Bosnia proper – for example, between people from the Krajina region in the north-west and the Drina valley in the east.

In the present volume, the appellation 'Muslim' is used not only *sensu stricto* as a description of believers and practitioners of Islam of Bosnian and Herzegovinian origin but also in a more general sense for people of Bosnian Muslim family and cultural backgrounds, including agnostics and atheists who have been relatively numerous in Bosnian society since the Second World War as a result of the processes of secularization under socialist Yugoslavia. Labelling an atheist a 'sociological Muslim' may not be the most fortunate choice imaginable, but it has commonly been used in daily life in Bosnia and Herzegovina and, for practical reasons, in much scholarly literature also.

Many of the authors in this volume do in fact put more emphasis on various aspects of the religious rather than the national identity of the Bosnian Muslims in different periods of their modern development. Before the occupation of Bosnia and Herzegovina by Austria–Hungary in 1878, Bosnian Muslims tended to be overwhelmingly perceived in Central Europe as a local variety of Turk. Not only in the writings of observers from beyond the region (e.g. Rataj 2002) but also among the locals, the term 'Turk' was predominantly used in order to denote the Islamic religious identity in general, basically as a regional synonym for the term 'Muslim'. Similarly, the term 'Latin' was popularly deployed for Roman Catholics, and 'Serb' (*Srbin*) for adherents of Christian Orthodoxy in the Western Balkans, including Bosnia and Herzegovina, before the process of modern ethnic differentiation and homogenization (see the chapter by Božidar Jezernik in this volume). Under the rule of the predominantly Roman Catholic Habsburg Empire (1878–1918), the Slavic Muslim population of the newly acquired provinces was primarily perceived, organized and controlled with regard to its Islamic religious identity (see the chapter by Zora Hesová in this volume). Meanwhile, the question of national consciousness among the Bosnian Muslims and indeed the entire population of the provinces, including the Christian Orthodox (Serbs) and Roman Catholics (Croats), was steadily gaining in importance during the Austro-Hungarian era (Mujanović 2018; Babuna 2018; Džihić 2018). The Habsburg administration seriously experimented with its own nation-building project, the goal of which was the creation of a common Bosnian identity (*bošnjaštvo*) that would simultaneously transcend the previous religious divides, uproot the nascent processes of Serb and Croat national homogenization among Orthodox and Catholic Christians of the provinces, and, finally, ensure the lasting political loyalty of the newly homogenized mass of the Slavic citizens of Bosnian nationality (Donia 1981; Kraljačić 1987; Velikonja 2003;

Hladký 2005; Okey 2007). However, the religious identity of the Bosnian Muslims arguably remained more important in practical policies, conceptualizations and representations of this population before 1918 than their nascent and ambivalent ethnic identity. Even some of the contributions in this volume that deal with the post-1989 period, including the present, address Bosnian Muslims in the religious sense. Of course, the choice of this perspective does not mean that we are trying to deny or diminish the importance of the ethnic differentiation, national homogenization, or nationalism in Bosnia and Herzegovina, which have all received attention from numerous authors in recent decades.

Concepts and Themes

This interdisciplinary volume has brought together historians, anthropologists, and political and literary scholars. Most of them come from and are institutionally based in countries of Central and South Eastern Europe. As is usually the case, the individual chapters are characterized by their focus on diverse problems through different methodological approaches. In the following section, we will briefly highlight several major concepts and themes of this book.

The concept of 'Orientalism', as defined by Edward Said (Said 1978; Said 1993), has been sufficiently well known and debated in academic circles for four decades. As such, the concept is used by different authors throughout the book, although it generally refers to a certain perspective characteristic for visual and textual representations rather than a full acknowledgement of the existence of the monolithic and hegemonic Western discourse on the (Middle Eastern) Orient as originally conceived by Said himself. The specific features of Habsburg Orientalism, its discourses, practices and agents have recently been analysed elsewhere (Heiss and Feichtinger 2013; Gingrich 2016; Feichtinger 2018). Johann Heiss and Johannes Feichtinger maintain that it is not possible to speak of a single and uniform Habsburg Orientalist discourse. They distinguish between two distinct imaginary Orients: the first is distant, represented primarily by the Ottoman Empire and the Turks, while the second is located closer to home and epitomized by Bosnia and Herzegovina and the South Slav populations of the Western Balkans in general. In addition, a variety of Orientalist discourses with particular features developed in the multilingual Habsburg Empire (and the new Balkan nation states to the south-east) in non-German languages and national milieux. Some of the following chapters provide glimpses into these generally lesser-known Orientalist discourses vis-à-vis the Bosnian Muslims and the Balkans (especially Croatian, Serbian, Slovene and Czech).

The concept of frontier Orientalism has been gaining increasing currency in academic circles across Central and South Eastern Europe (Sabatos 2020). The term appeared for the first time in a conference paper by the anthropologist Andre

Gingrich (Gingrich 1998). Gingrich defines frontier Orientalism as a 'systematic set of metaphorical figures and mythological explanations' (Gingrich 1998: 119). Unlike Edward Said, who was primarily concerned with elite forms of academic, literary and political discourse in the West, Gingrich's idea of frontier Orientalism is derived from his analysis of Austrian popular discourses, namely the folk and public culture, and particularly that of Eastern Austria as the region most directly affected by the Habsburg–Ottoman wars before the Siege of Vienna in 1683 turned the fortunes decisively in favour of the Habsburg Monarchy. Numerous traces of this turbulent history are still memorialized in the public space and collective memory across Austria and the region in general (see also Sutter Fichtner 2008). Gingrich distinguishes between two discursive figures: that of a bad (hostile and threatening) Muslim, represented in the past by the Turk and increasingly replaced today by the Arab, and the good Muslim, incarnated in the Bosnian Muslim (Gingrich 1998: 107): '[T]he bad Muslim refers to early modernity; he is associated with a direct threat to "our" physical and cultural existence. . . . The good Muslim Oriental, on the other hand, refers to late colonialism. Here, the Muslim is no longer a dangerous rival but is transformed into a loyal subject. The good Oriental exists on this, "our", side of the frontier' (Gingrich 1998: 117–18).

The concept of frontier Orientalism has recently been applied by different authors to material from other regions that for centuries constituted the wider borderlands of empires and zones of conflict and exchange between the Habsburgs and the Ottomans. In their chapter on the Turkish threat and its memory in the present-day Czech lands, Ladislav Hladký and Petr Stehlík reach the conclusion that frontier Orientalism cannot properly reflect the Czech (or more precisely the Moravian) case due to the fact that south-eastern Moravia, let alone the rest of the Bohemian Crownlands, was not directly affected by the Habsburg–Ottoman wars (although it did in fact suffer from incursions of smaller, irregular advance units of the Ottoman army). In his chapter on representations of Bosnian Muslims in Czech language sources during the late Habsburg era, František Šístek maintains that the term does indeed adequately capture the essence of the standard set of images of the Turk (Muslim) in Moravian folklore and tradition, despite the fact that direct military encounters between the two empires took place in nearby Lower Austria and Hungary. Writing about the images of Bosnian Muslims in the literary work of nineteenth-century Croatian author Vjenceslav Novak, Charles Sabatos analyses the relationship between Central European frontier Orientalism, Western Orientalism, and Balkanism as defined by Maria Todorova (Todorova 1997). In her chapter on the changing perceptions of Bosnian Muslims in post-Yugoslav Slovenia, Alenka Bartulović speaks, in turn, of the framework of Yugoslav Orientalism, where varieties of frontier Orientalism mixed with ideologically constructed and nurtured memories of underprivileged rayah.

The term 'Balkanism' as defined by Maria Todorova in her influential book *Imagining the Balkans* (Todorova 1997) describes a spatialized, largely negatively prejudiced discourse about the Balkans and its inhabitants. She maintains that Balkanism 'is not merely a subspecies of Orientalism' and should be understood as a phenomenon that developed independently of Orientalism (ibid.: 8, 20). Despite strong stereotypical associations with violence and backwardness, the Balkans are considered to be an integral part of Europe; their inhabitants, therefore, represent internal Others, Europeans from a periphery rather than essentially different, non-European Others, such as the primarily Muslim inhabitants of the Middle East as seen in Western imagination. Another feature that distinguishes Balkanism from Orientalism is 'the absence of colonial legacy (despite the often-exploited analogies)' (ibid.: 20). Todorova defines the Balkans primarily as a historical and cultural legacy of the Ottoman Empire: in territorial terms, therefore, the Balkans are, more or less, identical to the old Turkey-in-Europe. Bosnia and Herzegovina, under Ottoman control until the Austro-Hungarian occupation of 1878 (and formally until annexation three decades later), certainly qualifies as a Balkan country and an object of Balkanist discourse as analysed by Todorova. The authors of the present volume have paid relatively limited attention to Balkanism in their particular contributions, with the exception of those chapters devoted to the analysis of representations in literature and other texts in a narrower sense. This can primarily be attributed to the overall focus of our volume on the colonial legacy of the Habsburg Empire, which succeeded the Ottomans in Bosnia and Herzegovina. Despite analogies and overlaps with neighbouring regions, Bosnia and Herzegovina also represents a unique case of a colonial experience in the classical sense in the Balkans, consisting of a direct domination and exploitation by a major European power of the time. The process of de-Ottomanization under late Austria–Hungary, linked with a perceived need for Europeanization and modernization but taking into account the existence of a large Muslim population, displayed specific features distinguishing Bosnia and Herzegovina (and its Muslims) from the fate of the Ottoman territories that became part of the new Christian national states and were subjected to other, usually more pronounced, anti-Ottoman and anti-Muslim nation-building projects (Šístek 2016: 30–34). In this volume, the focus on Bosnian Muslims, a group more closely linked with the perceived Oriental legacy and the Islamic world than most other Balkan populations, inevitably increased the attention our authors devoted to Orientalist representations and their derivations.

Another useful concept that has become increasingly common in the past few years, especially among historians and anthropologists, including several of the authors of this volume, can be attributed to the historian Edin Hajdarpašić and his monograph on nationalism and political imagination in Bosnia and Herzegovina from the late Ottoman period until the First World War (Hajdarpašić 2015). In his analysis of national narratives relating to Bosnian Muslims in the observed period and debates over their national identity, which included not only Bosnian Muslims themselves but also Serbs and Croats, Hajdarpašić explores the figure of the '(br)other'. This concept, echoing the term 'frenemy' best known from popular psychological discourses, integrates both binary perspectives characteristic for the ambivalent discourse on the Bosnian Muslims and their position in South Slavic identity struggles. According to particular needs and demands, they could be conceptualized both as hostile Oriental Others as well as brothers of their fellow South Slavs, the Serbs and Croats. Again, as in the previously cited works of Austrian specialists who have discovered similar discursive figures of the bad, alien, faraway Muslims versus the good, 'our', close-to-home Muslims based on their research on Austrian material, differentiation of this type eventually opens space for representations of the Bosnian Muslims as our, good Muslims: 'Within the proliferating nineteenth-century debates over the meanings of South Slavic brotherhood, the "Turks" occupied particularly conspicuous roles. Some Serbian and Croatian national activists tried to distinguish between the Turks (meaning non-Slavic Ottoman rulers) and "our" Turks (meaning Bosnian Muslims)' (Hajdarpašić 2015: 203). This approach obviously enabled the discursive and symbolic integration of the Bosnian Muslims in the framework of the South Slavic ideology and the later Yugoslav state-building projects, culminating in the period of officially promoted brotherhood and unity under socialist Yugoslavia.

The concept of a '(br)other' fittingly captures the Serb and Croat attitudes in the particular temporal and spatial context analysed by Edin Hajdarpašić and arguably also in many of the later Serb, Croat, Yugoslav, post-Yugoslav and Bosniak discourses. As some authors of this volume have shown, it can also be meaningfully applied to other Slavic nations living further afield such as the Slovenes and Czechs, and their attitudes to Bosnian Muslims and potentially to other fellow Slavs. Despite the greater geographical distance and relatively lower intensity of contacts with the Bosnian Muslims in comparison with the Serbs and Croats, the common Slavic identity provided a sufficiently powerful stimulus and opportunity for the development of similar discourses on Otherness and brotherhood vis-à-vis the Muslim population of Bosnia and Herzegovina. The chapter by František Šístek on representations of Bosnian Muslims in Czech sources under Habsburg rule – largely the same period covered by Hajdarpašić – reveals a number of similar strategies in the twists and turns of Czech conceptualizations of the Bosnian Muslims. Alenka Bartulović, in her chapter on the changing attitudes towards Bosnian Muslims in post-Yugoslav and post-socialist Slovenia, applies the term '(br)other' to Slovene perspectives on Bosnian Muslims from the 1980s until the present. The brotherhood in question is linked with experiences of common life in former Yugoslavia, in its demise, and in the newly independent Slovenia. In many ways, this is the story of the rise of the South Slavic brotherhood in reverse (from brothers to Others).

This book represents, among other things, a new contribution to the existing literature on representations of the Bosnian Muslims, Bosnia and Herzegovina, and the Balkans in general (e.g. Todorova 1997; Goldsworthy 1998; Hadžiselimović 2001; Jezernik 2004; Ruthner 2018). The multitude of faces of the elusive figure of the Bosnian Muslim in Central European sources testifies to a rich history of representations, transfers and exchanges, and, without a doubt, to a long-term fascination with the exotic, with the perceived Oriental world, and, on a more general level, with everything that contrasted most with one's own experiences, social norms and cultural expectations. (It has repeatedly and perhaps rightly been pointed out that of the three main ethnoreligious communities of the country, the Muslims of Bosnia and Herzegovina have attracted disproportionate attention in comparison with that devoted to their Christian Orthodox Serb and Roman Catholic Croat neighbours and fellow citizens.) On the pages of this book, the reader will have a chance to observe a long procession of successive images of the Bosnian Muslims: Bosnian Muslims cast as renegades, traitors of the ancestral faith who converted to Islam (*poturice*), enemies of their fellow Christian South Slavs and collaborators with their Ottoman and later Habsburg occupiers and oppressors; Bosnian Muslims as descendants of the medieval aristocracy and the heretical Bogomils; Bosnian Muslims as anachronistic relicts of another time, whose further survival in modern Europe is hard to imagine; Bosnian Muslims as potential converts to Christianity; Bosnian Muslims as 'ours' (Habsburg, Slavic, Yugoslav, European, white), as good Muslims as opposed to the bad, foreign, Asiatic Turks and Arabs; the fanatical and brave as well as passive and decadent Bosnian Muslims; Bosnian Muslims as loyal citizens of a secular state; Bosnian Muslims as real or potential Islamic radicals and terrorists; Bosnian Muslims as Slavic brothers; Bosnian Muslims as Orientals, as peasants from the Balkan South, *gastarbeiters* (guest workers), economic migrants and war refugees; as people of exemplary religious tolerance and even as members of the white race, who today can quietly integrate in the increasingly racist West, unlike the less fortunate Muslims of non-European origin.

The contributions gathered in this volume provide the reader with a diachronic, longue durée perspective from the early modern times until the present. The book places special emphasis on Habsburg rule over Bosnia and Herzegovina (1878–1918), its self-proclaimed civilizing mission, and the legacy of this key period for the Bosnian Muslims and for the development and transformations of their representations in general. From a geographical point of view, we can imagine the space that is observed in this book as an axis, with its starting point in Bosnia and Herzegovina. Apart from this land that represents (among other things) both the real and the symbolic homeland of the Bosnian Muslims, individual chapters cover topics dealing with Croats and Serbs as their compatriots sharing the same homeland and or immediate neighbours, with their more distant Slavic brothers (as they were conceptualized in the nineteenth century – namely the Slovenes and Czechs), with Austria and its complex conundrum of imperial experiences and their postimperial reflections, and, finally, as we progress in time and space, also briefly with Germany and the wider European context of debates on Islam, immigration and integration in the early twenty-first century.

Note on Contributions

In the opening chapter on Czech reflections of the Turkish threat in the context of early modern Central Europe, Ladislav Hladký and Petr Stehlík first provide a summary of the role of the Bohemian lands in the Habsburg–Ottoman military conflicts. Thus far, the significant and long-term financial and military contributions of the Bohemian lands to the defence of the Habsburg Monarchy against Ottoman expansion have not received sufficient attention in English-language scholarly literature. The second part of their chapter analyses the changing representations of the Turk in Czech (Bohemian) discourses between the sixteenth and eighteenth centuries. Despite certain specific features that can be attributed to the fact that the Bohemian lands were spared the direct effects of the devastating military conflicts between the two empires, these discourses can, in fact, be regarded as variations on a wider transnational discourse on the topic, with its more or less characteristic tropes well known from other regions and national milieux (e.g. Bartulović 2010). The authors believe that the wider Central European discourse on the Turk – often indistinguishable from the wider discourse on Muslims in general – preconditioned and influenced the formation of later representations of the Bosnian Muslims in the Habsburg Monarchy. Therefore, their chapter serves as a specific prologue to the other contributions, which provide rich evidence of the uneasy transformation of the traditional negative image of the Turk into a more nuanced or even positive image of a Bosnian Muslim. Finally, Hladký and Stehlík underline the fact that the historical role of the Bohemian lands in the Habsburg–Ottoman military conflicts has failed to assume a prominent place in the Czech collective consciousness. Despite a considerable wave of Islamophobia after 2015, linked with the European refugee crisis, attempts at instrumentalizing the memory of the wars against the Ottomans have been marginal and underdeveloped in the contemporary Czech Republic.

In his chapter, Božidar Jezernik paints a broad picture of the development of Bosnian Muslim collective identities, from the prenational, primarily religious, and regional sense of belonging characteristic for the Ottoman Empire and the process of nationalization accelerated during the Austro-Hungarian period through to identity debates in the interwar Yugoslav kingdom. Jezernik's text is based on a rich selection of period sources, comparing and contrasting a plenitude of successive voices over centuries, those of outside observers as well as natives. The long existence of the millet system ('millet' is characterized as a confessional nation), both as a central concept and a practical tool of collective identity and identity politics during much of the Ottoman era, had a lasting effect on the subsequent process of nationalizing collective identities during the Habsburg period. Jezernik believes that 'the inhabitants of Bosnia and Herzegovina adopted the term "*nacija*" (nation) simply as a translation of the old term "millet"'. He further underlines the interconnectedness of the process of nationalization in which the Bosnian Muslims often reacted to impulses and perceived threats from their nationally more awakened fellow Christian citizens. The pressure to accept either Serb or Croat national identity resulted in the growth of a distinct collective consciousness among the Bosnian Muslims in interwar Yugoslavia.

In the introductory part of his chapter on ambivalent perceptions of the Bosnian Muslims in the Austro-Hungarian German-language press during the occupation campaign of 1878, Martin Gabriel paints the conquest of the Bosnian vilayet by the invasion army under the command of General Josip Filipović in an uncompromising light as a violent, brutal and bloody affair. In the German-language press of the Dual Monarchy, the Muslim enemy fighters were portrayed as barbarians and savages waiting for the first opportunity to cut off heads, limbs and other body parts. An Austrian provincial paper quoted by the author argued that 'a more brute, inhuman people as the local Turks can hardly be imagined'. The starkly negative, stereotypical representations of the Bosnian Muslims arguably reached its peak during the occupation campaign and its aftermath (see the chapter by František Šístek in this volume for a related discussion on Czech perceptions following the occupation). Images of the Muslim populace, especially the Muslim insurgents, overemphasized their Islamic religious identity at the expense of social, national, economic, and other possible motives for their armed resistance. The depictions of Bosnian Muslim insurgents and bandits closely resembled, Gabriel reminds us, the old images of the cruel Turk based on the memories of the Habsburg–Ottoman wars transmitted through collective memory (see the chapter by Ladislav Hladký and Petr Stehlík in this volume on Bohemian/Czech and wider Central European conceptualizations of the Turkish threat). Such representations were, however, gradually replaced by more nuanced images, whose production was linked with a new state policy emphasizing the necessity of mutually advantageous cooperation with Muslim elites in the service of the smooth pacification and integration of the provinces into the Habsburg economic and political realm.

In his chapter, Clemens Ruthner provides a summary of the debates on the colonial or semi-colonial character of Habsburg rule over Bosnia and Herzegovina (1878–1918), and offers several plausible answers. Ruthner asks 'to what extent the colonial paradigm is applicable to this particular historical case', and summarizes the related discourses on the nature of Habsburg rule. The author underlines the ambivalent character of colonialism: military conquest, political domination and economic exploitation, as opposed to the modernization and growth of civil society. The key question of how the four decades of Habsburg rule should be assessed, he claims, still remains. Is it in terms of the self-proclaimed civilizing mission, or within the paradigm of European colonialism at the turn of the twentieth century? Ruthner states his belief that 'the k. u. k. intermezzo from 1878 to 1918 can be considered a kind of Austrian quasi colonialism'. He recommends the postcolonial approaches to Habsburg Central Europe as a middle way between the extremes of Habsburg myth and the nationalist discourses of self-victimization. 'The only reason others hesitate to call Bosnia and Herzegovina a colony is that it is not separated from its "motherland" by a large body of saltwater but lies at the peripheries of Europe', concludes Ruthner.

Education, especially the introduction of interconfessional education, which had no precedent in the modern history of the occupied lands, proved to be one of the most important early challenges of the self-proclaimed Habsburg civilizing mission in the newly acquired Balkan colony. In his chapter devoted to the portrayal of Muslims in Austro-Hungarian state primary school textbooks for Bosnia and Herzegovina, Oliver Pejić underlines the fact that Croatian models played a crucial role in the implementation of interconfessional education in Bosnia and Herzegovina. In the first, pro-Croat phase of the occupation (1878–82), textbooks imported from neighbouring Croatia, which were written primarily for Croats and thus from a Roman Catholic perspective, proved offensive to many Muslims in Bosnia and Herzegovina for their perceived anti-Islamic and anti-Turkish content. Following the Magyarization of the provincial administration after 1882 under the supervision of the Austro-Hungarian joint minister of finance and chief administrator of the Condominium of Bosnia and Herzegovina, Benjámin Kállay, the provincial government again sought inspiration in Croatia, but this time in an experiment with interconfessional education, which was introduced in 1874 and aimed to integrate both the Roman Catholic Croats and Christian Orthodox Serbs. Both enterprises were burdened with similar concerns about fair representation and the removal of potentially offensive content in textbooks, and which was further complicated in the Bosnian case by the existence of three, rather than just two, major confessional groups. According to Pejić, the portrayal of Bosnian Muslims in provincial textbooks based on the previous Croatian model served the goal of encouraging 'Muslim enrolment in state schools in order to promote their Westernization and integration into Habsburg society'. The introduction of the textbooks analysed by Pejić represents the first systematic attempt towards the formation of a newly interpreted Bosnian Muslim collective identity, and the dissemination of pro-Habsburg patriotism.

'The history of Bosnia's Muslims in a modern bureaucratic state is indeed among the longest in the Muslim world', ascertains Zora Hesová in her chapter devoted to the formation of autonomous Bosnian Islamic institutions under the Austro-Hungarian administration, and its legacy in the twentieth and twenty-first centuries. The practical question of religious authority arose when the Habsburg occupation of Bosnia and Herzegovina severed the previous administrative links with Istanbul. The Austro-Hungarian state de facto replaced the Ottoman Empire as it assumed the role of protector of Bosnian Muslims and their religious rights. In 1909, one year after the annexation of Bosnia and Herzegovina, Emperor Francis Joseph signed the Statute for Autonomous Administration of Islamic Religious Waqf and Educational Affairs in Bosnia and Herzegovina (*Štatut za autonomnu upravu islamskih vjerskih i vakufsko-mearifskih poslova u Bosni i Hercegovini*). The so-called *Štatut* paved the way for the constitution of an autonomous Islamic community of Bosnia and Herzegovina as a hierarchical self-administering structure that managed to survive not only the break-up of the empire and the establishment of the new Yugoslav state in 1918 but also all the subsequent regime changes, formations and collapses of successive state structures, wars, and modernization challenges to the present day (Poulton 1997: 22). The late Habsburg Empire became the first country that recognized and managed to integrate sharia law within a modern European judicial system. The challenges facing the contemporary Islamic Community of Bosnia and Herzegovina (the ICBH, or *Islamska zajednica Bosne i Hercegovine*), Hesová believes, still revolve around the fundamental question of leading a full-fledged Islamic life within a modern secular state. In her opinion, the institutionalization of the Islamic community arguably remains 'the single most formative legacy of the Bosnian encounter with the Austro-Hungarian state'. The ICBH, itself a product of colonization by a modernizing empire, provided a level of religious autonomy and practice of self-administration unique in the Muslim world. The current representatives of the ICBH stress the continuity of the institution with the Habsburg era: the Austro-Hungarian legal acts of 1882, 1909 and 1912 are still hailed as formative documents in public discourse, and are also formally acknowledged as such in the contemporary status of the ICBH from 2014. The unique historical experience of the ICBH with democratic self-administration and coexistence with several successive incarnations of a secular state for over a century has received attention beyond the Balkans and Central Europe in recent years. As Hesová reminds us, 'Bosnian Islam has been intensely debated as a possible model for a future Islam of Europe'. Perhaps the legacy of the Habsburg encounter with Bosnian Muslims from the belle époque of colonialism at the turn of the twentieth century could bear some brave new fruit in the globalized world of the twenty-first century.

The Czech national milieu of the late nineteenth and early twentieth centuries, with its characteristic mix of growing self-confidence in its own cultural and economic successes on the one hand, and dissatisfaction with the political position of the emerging Czech nation within the Habsburg Monarchy on the other, combined with the notions of Slavic solidarity that formed an integral part of the Czech national discourses of the time, produced a number of critical perspectives on Habsburg rule over Bosnia and Herzegovina, frequently stressing the tropes of conquest, colonialism, economic exploitation, and the political subjugation of the local population rather than the official list of successes of the Austro-Hungarian civilizing mission. However, it would be too reductive to categorize the Czech perspective simply as a nationalist counter-discourse to official state propaganda. In Czech sources, representations of Bosnia and Herzegovina from 1878 until 1918 continued to be simultaneously influenced by the mainstream Habsburg discourse and the wider Western Orientalist stereotypes characteristic for the era. Due to linguistic proximity and Slavophile sympathies, sources in the Czech language also typically tried to capture and reflect some native South Slavic perspectives.

In his chapter, František Šístek focuses on the diversification and transformation of the representations of Bosnian Muslims during the Habsburg era in Czech literature, travelogues and memoirs. His contribution emphasizes the relative diversity of Czech images and stereotypes of Bosnian Muslims, and traces their development over several decades. The negative images of Bosnian Muslims as threatening, backward, and fanatical enemies from the initial period of military occupation and establishment of 'civilized order' are similar to those analysed by Martin Garbiel in his chapter on the ambivalent perceptions of the Bosnian Muslims during the occupation campaign through the eyes of the German-language press in the Habsburg Monarchy. In sections devoted to the classical 'golden era' of the Habsburg civilizing mission at the turn of the twentieth century, Šístek pays special attention to conceptualizations of Bosnian Muslim religious and national identity. While admitting that it is impossible to speak of a straightforward evolution towards more realistic (or even positive and emphatic) representations of the Bosnian Muslims (Ljuca 2006), he argues that the images of this Slavic group have been affected in Czech sources by marked secularization and nationalization throughout the observed period.

The relationship between Central European frontier Orientalism, Western Orientalism, and Balkanism, approached through a comparison between the novella *Maca* (1881) by Croatian writer Vjenceslav Novak, which is set in the period of Habsburg expansion into Bosnia and Herzegovina, and the travelogue *Black Lamb, Grey Falcon* (1942) by British author Rebecca West, is explored in the chapter by Charles Sabatos. While Novak no longer conceptualizes the Bosnian Muslims as Turks but rather as Croatian brothers of Islamic faith, West, with her strong pro-Serb sympathies and open support for the centralist regime of royal Yugoslavia of the 1930s, implicitly regards the Bosnian Muslims as misguided Serbs. Sabatos, among other things, makes the important observation that the Muslim identity of Slavic Bosnians has often been perceived as not quite real, and as relatively weak and superficial: 'in the case of literary texts about Bosnia and Herzegovina by South Slavic and Western writers, Bosnian Muslim identity is frequently portrayed not just as an imagined one but as a temporary costume that can be replaced with more suitable garments (Croatian, Serbian, Yugoslav, etc., depending on the author's particular use of historical myths)'. This perceived impermanence and alleged superficiality of Bosnian Muslim identity can in fact be encountered in many other sources dealing with this South Slavic group. Such feelings could, at certain times, manifest themselves in speculations about the return of the Bosnian Muslims to their ancestral faith, and in expressions of disbelief that such exotic and Oriental people continue to live at the threshold of civilized Europe. Curiously enough, many authors provided contrary evidence and represented the Bosnian Muslims as inherently conservative and largely defined by their religious identity: 'The Muslims were indeed confused and opportunistic in a national sense, but they remained steadfast when it came to religious and even wider cultural interests' (Velikonja 2003: 126). A similar notion of the Bosnian Muslim religious identity as weak and fragile, endangered by aggressive immediate neighbours on the one hand and Islamic radicals from afar on the other, appeared in a different context during the Bosnian war of the 1990s and its aftermath.

In the next chapter, Bojan Baskar bridges the late Habsburg, interwar and Cold War decades. In his reconstruction of the life and work of the Croatian anthropologist Vera Stein E(h)rlich (1897–1980), Baskar takes us not only to the expected and already familiar corners of Central Europe and the Balkans but also to North America, Mexico, and even late-medieval Al-Andalus. According to her own self-description, Erlich was a Yugoslav citizen, but a child of the Austro-Hungarian Monarchy. Baskar makes clear that her Austronostalgia developed rather late in life, fuelled by the booming literature celebrating the Habsburg myth at the turn of the 1960s. Nothing seems to suggest that she longed for the good old days during the interwar period while studying in Vienna, living in Zagreb, or conducting anthropological research in Bosnia and Herzegovina and elsewhere around Yugoslavia. Her fieldwork from the late 1930s, however, testified to widespread feelings of nostalgia for old Austria among the peasant population of Bosnia and Herzegovina (by Serbs, Croats and Muslims alike) on the brink of the Second World War. Erlich, who was of Jewish origin, managed to survive the war in occupied Yugoslavia. After the war, she relocated to the United States, where she earned a PhD in cultural anthropology, and continued to work there as an anthropologist until 1960, at which point she moved back to Yugoslavia and taught at Zagreb University until retirement. Her experiences in North America and especially Mexico, Baskar argues, decisively influenced her original and sophisticated, if admittedly somewhat eccentric, conceptualizations of the Bosnian Muslims and their perceived position in wider cultural and civilizational circles – or 'cultural styles', as she called them. In her view, Muslim Bosnia found itself at the crossroads of the Oriental and Central European styles of life in modern times. The traditional Bosnian Muslim cultural style represented a regional variety of a wider Oriental style, whose homeland she somewhat unexpectedly located in Medieval Muslim-dominated Spain. The idea of a historical centrality of Al-Andalus in the development of the Oriental style allowed her to connect the perceived similarities between Muslim Bosnia and Mexico. As an Ashkenazi Jew, she was deeply attracted to the Sephardim culture. Her notion of the Oriental style of life, which allowed her to link Bosnia and Herzegovina with Mexico and Spain, turns out to be implicitly derived from her notions about the Sephardim culture.

The chapter by Marija Mandić focuses on the Serbian proverb *Poturica gori od Turčina* (A Turk-convert is worse than a Turk). Through her reconstruction of the proverb's genesis and her interpretations of its uses, both in the nineteenth century and the present, the author provides an original perspective that allows her to identify and explain the main long-term features of the stereotypical Serbian (and partly also wider South Slavic) discourse on the Slavic Muslims of the Western Balkans, and its instrumentalizations. The central figure of the *poturica* (Turk-convert) refers to local, colingual converts to Islam and their descendants, more precisely the Slavic Muslims of the Western Balkans, historically including not only Bosnian Muslims but also the Muslim inhabitants of modern Serbia, Montenegro and other areas affected by the process of Islamization during the Ottoman era. Analysing the broader historical and sociopolitical context in which the proverb emerged, Mandić links the stigmatization of Balkan Slavic Muslims with the wider process of repudiation and demonization of the Ottoman heritage, which was characteristic for Serbs and Serbia as well as for other Balkan nation states and ethnic groups throughout the nineteenth and twentieth centuries. Unlike in the case of Bulgaria and Macedonia, where an alternative trope of forced conversion achieved prominence in mainstream conceptualizations of local colingual Muslims, the Serbian discourse has instead been characterized by the predominance of the betrayal trope: the Balkan Slavic Muslims are regarded (and condemned) as renegades, traitors, and severed limbs of the national body. The betrayal trope, affirms Mandić, is strongly present in the nineteenth-century classical Serbian literary canon. The results of her research of contemporary discourses, including the increasingly influential e-discourse (electronic discourse available on the internet), testify to the fact that the proverb continues to perform the role of stigmatizer, and nowadays is especially used to belittle the Bosniaks and sometimes also Muslim Albanians. Considering the powerful Western discourse of Orientalism and the influence of the Habsburg Monarchy on the Serbian elites in the eighteenth and nineteenth centuries, Mandić concludes that 'the Serbian case can be seen as leaning on Western and Central European traditions while adjusting them to the oral cultural patterns and the archetypal dichotomy of the "hero-betrayer"'.

The next chapter, by Alenka Bartulović, explores the changing perceptions of Bosnians, particularly Bosnian Muslims, in late Yugoslav and post-Yugoslav Slovenia from the 1980s until the present, with special focus on the transformation of social and cultural cleavages between the Slovene majority and Bosnian migrants (as well as refugees) in the observed period. Her text highlights the continuities and discontinuities in the representations of Bosnian Muslims in Slovenia before and after the break-up of Yugoslavia. Under the socialist regime, Bartulović explains, Yugoslav Muslims were ascribed the same role in popular imagination as the peasants: both groups, linked primarily with their original rural environments, were depicted as obstacles to modernization, and stigmatized as an underdeveloped segment of the Yugoslav population. The urban–rural dichotomy managed to conceal the dormant Islamophobic attitudes already existent in socialist Slovenia. After the break-up of Yugoslavia, affirms Bartulović, 'the interpretative frame in the post-Yugoslav space shifted radically'. After decades of official promotion of brotherhood and unity in the Yugoslav nations, the Bosnian Muslims were increasingly conceptualized as Others, primarily in reference to their Islamic religious identity, sometimes further reduced to a stereotypical vision of Muslims as representing a threat to European identity. The idea of a boundary between the Christian West and the Islamic East, as well as between Europe and the Balkans, played an important role in the wider process of the reconceptualization of Slovene identity and its place in Europe following independence; however, Bartulović makes the additional claim that the urban–rural dichotomy has managed to survive as well, and continues to affect the process of Othering.

The last two chapters take us beyond post-Habsburg Central Europe as they explore the position of Bosnian Muslims in Germany and in the wider context of contemporary European debates on immigration, integration, and the position of Islam in European society. The contribution by Aldina Čemernica is based upon her research on identity constructions and religious views among young people of Bosnian Muslim origin in Berlin. As a result of the war that followed the collapse of the Yugoslav federation, some 350,000 refugees from Bosnia and Herzegovina, most of them Muslim, arrived in Germany in the first half of the 1990s. The public response at the time was overwhelmingly positive, not least due to the fact that the Bosnian Muslims were generally regarded as secular and white Europeans (similar positive stereotypes could be observed in other Central European countries that received Bosnian war refugees at the time). There are currently some 30,000 Bosnian Muslims (Bosniaks) living in the German capital. The results of Čemernica's research indicate that religion continues to serve as an important cohesive factor in the constructions of collective identity of young Bosniaks in Berlin, 'because it functions as a feature through which these people are categorized and seen as a group'. Moreover, the war in Bosnia, accompanied by the genocide against the Bosnian Muslims on both ethnic and confessional grounds, 'reduced them to their religion even more'; however, as Čemernica shows, their own interpretations of Islam, degrees of identification, and religious practice are in fact diverse and very individual. The contacts and friendships of young Bosnian Muslims with Muslims from other mostly non-European countries seem to strengthen their conviction that the Bosnian form of

Islam represents a kind of European Islam – one that is tolerant and able to thrive in a predominantly secular European society. (For a discussion on similar topics relating to the contemporary Islamic community of Bosnia and Herzegovina, see the chapter by Zora Hesová in this volume.)

The closing chapter, by Merima Šehagić, addresses the phenomenon, already discussed from different angles by Aldina Čemernica and Zora Hesová, that the Bosnian Muslims are often lauded as exemplary representatives of a European form of Islam (tolerant and domesticated rather than aggressive and foreign), and, by extension, as successful immigrants who have integrated well into their host societies in countries such as Germany, Austria and the Netherlands. Šehagić, however, problematizes this superficial success story. She confirms that governmental sources in Germany and other European countries do indeed often classify the Muslims from Bosnia and Herzegovina as European and unproblematic. When compared with most non-European migrant groups, Bosnian migrants experience lower levels of discrimination and stigmatization. As Šehagić tells us, the Bosniaks have even been considered as a white refugee elite in some receiving countries. It seems evident that the integration of Bosnian Muslims into Western countries, including in Central Europe, has been greatly facilitated by their European origin and physical appearance. Their inconspicuous presence could in fact be perceived as invisibility in the predominantly white host societies. Open embracement of a European or – even more explicitly – white identity, Šehagić maintains, can be interpreted as a mechanism of advantageous self-identification or self-inclusion. Her findings, based primarily on material from Germany and other European countries, correspond to similar conclusions on the issue of self-identification as whites discussed recently by authors who have conducted research among members of the Bosnian diaspora elsewhere, including the United States (notably Halilovich 2013). The identification with whiteness not only helps to downplay the importance of Islamic confessional identity but, as Šehagić notes, it simultaneously helps to shed the similarly unwelcome Balkan identity with its stereotypical, mostly violent, backward and barbarian connotations. The obvious need of the Bosnian Muslim diaspora in Central and Western European countries to emphasize their European and white identity, she concludes, is rooted in their perceived need to legitimize their place in Europe.

František Šístek is a research fellow at the Institute of History, Czech Academy of Sciences, and an associate professor at the Institute of International Studies, Faculty of Social Sciences, Charles University in Prague. He graduated in history from Central European University in Budapest and earned his PhD in social and cultural anthropology at the Faculty of Humanities, Charles University, Prague. He has focused on former Yugoslavia and representations of the South Slavs and the Balkans in Central Europe, national identities, images and stereotypes of the

Other, and competing interpretations of the past in South Eastern Europe. His monographs include *Narativi o identitetu: izabrane studije o crnogorskoj istoriji* [Narratives of identity: Selected studies in Montenegrin history] (Podgorica: Matica crnogorska, 2015) and *Dějiny Černé Hory* [A history of Montenegro] (Prague: NLN, 2017).

References

Ančić, Mladen. 2015. 'Can Bosnia Do Without Herzegovina?', *Croatian Studies Review* 11: 13–80.
Babuna Aydın. 2018. 'Österreich-Ungarn, die bosnisch-herzegowinischer Muslime und ihr Nationalismus', in Clemens Ruthner and Tamara Scheer (eds), *Bosnien-Herzegowina und Österreich-Ungarn, 1878–1918: Annäherungen an eine Kolonie*. Tübingen: Narr Francke Attempto, pp. 163–92.
Bartulović, Alenka. 2010. '"We Have an Old Debt with the Turk, and It Best Be Settled": Ottoman Incursions through the Discursive Optics of Slovenian Historiography and Literature, and Their Applicability in the Twenty-First Century', in Božidar Jezernik (ed.), *Imaginary Turk*. Newcastle: Cambridge Scholars, pp. 111–36.
Baskar, Bojan. 2008. 'Small Ethnologies and Supranational Empires: The Case of the Habsburg Monarchy', in Máiréad Nic Craith, Ulrich Kockel and Reinhard Johler (eds), *Everyday Culture in Europe: Approaches and Methodologies*. Aldershot, UK: Ashgate, pp. 65–80.
Bieber, Florian. 2006. *Post-War Bosnia: Ethnicity, Inequality and Public Sector Governance*. London: Palgrave Macmillan.
Bjelić, Dušan I., and Obrad Savić (eds). 2002. *Balkan As Metaphor: Between Globalization and Fragmentation*. Cambridge, MA: MIT Press.
Bougarel, Xavier. 2001. 'L'islam bosniaque, entre identité culturelle et idéologie politique', in Xavier Bougarel and Nathalie Clayer (eds), *Le Nouvel Islam balkanique: Les musulmanes, acteurs du post-communisme 1990–2000*. Paris: Maisonneuve et Larosse, pp. 79–132.
———. 2015. *Survivre aux empires: Islam, identité nationale et allégeances politiques en Bosnie-Herzégovine*. Paris: Karthala.
Bringa, Tone. 1995. *Being Muslim the Bosnian Way: Identity and Community in a Central Bosnian Village*. Princeton, NJ: Princeton University Press.
Detrez, Raymond. 2013. 'Pre-National Identities in the Balkans', in Roumen Daskalov and Tchavdar Marinov (eds), *Entangled Histories of the Balkans. Volume One: National Ideologies and Language Policies*. Leiden: Brill, pp. 13–66.
Donia, Robert J. 1981. *Islam under the Double Eagle: The Muslims of Bosnia and Herzegovina, 1878–1914*. Boulder, CO: East European Monographs.
Džihić, Vedran. 2018. 'Ethnonationalismus in der *longue durée*? Vermessungen der historischen und akutellen Widersprüche Bosnien-Herzegowinas', in Clemens Ruthner and Tamara Scheer (eds), *Bosnien-Herzegowina und Österreich-Ungarn, 1878–1918: Annäherungen an eine Kolonie*. Tübingen: Narr Francke Attempto, pp. 495–528.
Feichtinger, Johannes. 2018. 'Nach Said. Der k. und k. Orientalismus, seine Akteure, Praktiken und Diskursen', in Clemens Ruthner and Tamara Scheer (eds), *Bosnien-Herzegowina und Österreich-Ungarn, 1878–1918: Annäherungen an eine Kolonie*. Tübingen: Narr Francke Attempto, pp. 307–24.

Fillafer, Franz Leander. 2016. 'Österreichislam', in Johannes Feichtinger and Heidermarie Uhl (eds), *Habsburg neue denken: Vielfalt und Ambivalenz in Zentraleuropa: 30 kulturwissenschaftlich Stichworte*. Vienna: Böhlau, pp. 163–70.
Gingrich, Andre. 1998. 'Frontier Myths of Orientalism: The Muslim World in Public and Popular Cultures of Central Europe', in Bojan Baskar and Borut Brumen (eds), *Mediterranean Ethnological Summer School*. Piran: Institut za multikulturne raziskave, pp. 99–127.
———. 2016. 'Orientalismus', in Johannes Feichtinger and Heidermarie Uhl (eds), *Habsburg neue denken: Vielfalt und Ambivalenz in Zentraleuropa: 30 kulturwissenschaftlich Stichworte*. Vienna: Böhlau, pp. 153–62.
Goldsworthy, Vesna. 1998. *Inventing Ruritania: The Imperialism of the Imagination*. New Haven, CT: Yale University Press.
Hadžiselimović, Omer. 2001. *At the Gates of the East: British Travel Writers on Bosnia and Herzegovina from the Sixteenth to the Twentieth Centuries*. Boulder, CO: East European Monographs.
Hafez, Farid. 2014. 'Gedenken in "islamischen Gedankenjahr": Zur diskursive Konstruktion des österreichischen Islams in Rahmen der Jubiläumsfeier zu 100 Jahren Islamgesetz', *Wiener Zeitschrift für die Kunde des Morgenlandes* 104: 63–85.
Hajdarpašić, Edin. 2015. *Whose Bosnia? Nationalism and Political Imagination in the Balkans, 1840–1914*. Ithaca, NY: Cornell University Press.
Halilovich, Hariz. 2013. *Places of Pain: Forced Displacement, Popular Memory and Trans-local Identities in Bosnian War-Torn Communities*. New York: Berghahn Books.
Heiss, Johann, and Johannes Feichtinger. 2013. 'Uses of Orientalism in the Late Nineteenth-Century Austro-Hungarian Empire', in James Hodkinson et al., *Deploying Orientalism in Culture and History: From Germany to Central and Eastern Europe*. Rochester, NY: Camden House, pp. 148–65.
Heywood, Colin. 1994. 'Bosnia Under Ottoman Rule, 1463–1800', in Mark Pinson (ed.), *The Muslims of Bosnia-Herzegovina: Their Historic Development from the Middle Ages to the Dissolution of Yugoslavia*. Cambridge, MA: Harvard University Press, pp. 22–53.
Hladký, Ladislav. 2005. *Bosenská otázka v 19. a 20. století*. Brno: Masarykova univerzita.
Jezernik, Božidar. 2004. *Wild Europe: The Balkans in the Gaze of Western Travellers*. London: Saqi.
Kraljačić, Tomislav. 1987. *Kalajev režim u Bosni i Hercegovini (1882–1903)*. Sarajevo: Veselin Masleša.
Kropáček, Luboš. 2017. 'Rakouský Islamgesetz, mezník na cestách mezináboženského dialogu', *Marginalia Historica* 8(2): 81–94.
Ljuca, Adin. 2006. 'Turci a Švábové, nebo slovanští bratři? Český pohled na bosenské muslimy v letech 1878–1918', in Mirjam Moravcová, David Svoboda and František Šístek (eds), *Pravda, láska a ti na 'Východě': Obrazy středoevropského a východoevropského prostoru z pohledu české společnosti*. Prague: Fakulta humanitních studií Univerzity Karlovy, pp. 122–34.
Luketić, Katarina. 2013. *Balkan: od geografije do fantazije*. Zagreb: Algoritam.
Malcolm, Noel. 1996. *Bosnia: A Short History*. London: Papermac.
Malečková, Jitka. 2018. '"Our Turks" or "Real Turks"? Czech Perceptions of the Slavic Muslims of Bosnia-Herzegovina', in *World Literature Studies* 10(1): 15–26.
Mujanović, Mihad. 2018. *Muslimové, a ne mohamedáni! Ke kořenům bosňáckého národního hnutí v letech 1878–1918*. Prague: Filozofická fakulta Karlovy Univerzity.

Okey, Robin. 2007. *Taming Balkan Nationalism: The Habsburg 'Civilizing Mission' in Bosnia, 1878–1918*. Oxford: Oxford University Press.
———. 2011. 'Overlapping National Historiographies in Bosnia-Herzegovina', in Tibor Frank and Frank Hadler (eds), *Disputed Territories and Shared Pasts: Overlapping National Histories in Modern Europe*. London: Palgrave Macmillan, pp. 349–372.
Poulton, Hugh. 1997. 'Islam, Ethnicity and State in Contemporary Balkans', in Hugh Poulton and Suha Taji-Farouki (eds), *Muslim Identity and the Balkan State*. London: Hurst, pp. 13–32.
Promitzer, Christian. 2015. 'Austria and the Balkans: Exploring the Role of Travelogues in the Construction of an Area', in Christian Promitzer, Siegreied Gruber and Harald Heppner (eds), *Southeast European Studies in a Globalizing World*. Berlin: LitVerlag, pp. 189–206.
Rataj, Tomáš. 2002. *České země ve stínu půlměsíce: Obraz Turka v raně novověké literatuře z českých zemí*. Prague: Scriptorium.
Rexhepi, Piro. 2019. 'Imperial Inventories, "Illegal Mosques" and Institutionalized Islam: Coloniality and the Islamic Community of Bosnia and Herzegovina', *History and Anthropology* 30(4): 477–89.
Roksandić, Drago. 1991. *Srbi u Hrvatskoj*. Zagreb: Vjesnik.
Ruthner, Clemens. 2018. *Habsburgs 'Dark Continent': Postkoloniale Lektüren zur österreichischen Literatur und Kultur im langen 19. Jahrhundert*. Tübingen: Narr Francke Attempto.
Ruthner, Clemens, and Tamara Scheer (eds). 2018. *Bosnien-Herzegowina und Österreich-Ungarn, 1878–1918: Annäherungen an eine Kolonie*. Tübingen: Narr Francke Attempto.
Sabatos, Charles D. 2020. *Frontier Orientalism and the Turkish Image in Central European Literature*. Lanham, MD: Lexington.
Said, Edward. 1978. *Orientalism*. New York: Pantheon Books.
———. 1993. *Culture and Imperialism*. New York: Alfred A. Knopf.
Šístek, František. 2016. 'Die nationalen Minderheiten in den internationalen Beziehungen und der Gesetzgebung Jugoslawiens', in Kateřina Králová, Jiří Kocian and Kamil Pikal (eds), *Minderheiten im sozialistischen Jugoslawien: Brüderlichkeit und Eigenheit*. Frankfurt am Main: Peter Lang, pp. 29–71.
Skowron-Nalborczyk, Agata. 2016. 'A Study of the Official Legal Status of Islam in Austria: Between the Law on Islam of 1912 and the Law on Islam of 2015', in Robert Mason (ed.), *Muslim Minority-State Relations: Violence, Integration and Policy*. New York: Palgrave Macmillan.
Sutter Fichtner, Paula. 2008. *Terror and Toleration: The Habsburg Empire Confronts Islam, 1526–1850*. London: Reaktion Books.
Stehlík, Petr. 2013. *Bosna v chorvatských národně-integračních ideologiích 19. století*. Brno: Masarykova univerzita.
———. 2015. *Između hrvatstva i jugoslavenstva: Bosna u hrvatskim nacionalno-integracijskim ideologijama 1832–1878*. Zagreb: Srednja Europa.
Todorova, Maria. 1997. *Imagining the Balkans*. Oxford: Oxford University Press.
Velikonja, Mitja. 2003. *Religious Separation and Intolerance in Bosnia-Herzegovina*. College Station, TX: Texas A&M University.

Chapter 1

THE 'TURKISH THREAT' AND EARLY MODERN CENTRAL EUROPE
Czech Reflections

Ladislav Hladký and Petr Stehlík

The primary motivation behind the formation of the Habsburg Monarchy, a large multinational empire that existed for just under four centuries in Central Europe, was the so-called 'Turkish threat'. As early as the end of the fourteenth century, the Ottoman Turks, driven by their aims of power and religion, began expanding their territory into South East Europe. Initially, they took control of the southern part of the Balkan peninsula, and in 1453 they captured Byzantine Constantinople and made it the capital of their empire. In the beginning of the sixteenth century, Ottoman forces began invading the Great Hungarian Plain. In August 1526 at the Battle of Mohács, the army of Sultan Suleiman I had relatively little difficulty in defeating the troops of the Hungarian and Bohemian king, Louis II Jagiellon, who had attempted to stop them there. The fatal defeat at Mohács led to a decision by the Hungarian, Bohemian and Austrian political elite in 1526–27 to create, in the interest of increasing the military and economic prospects for defending Central Europe against the Ottoman Turks, an Austro-Bohemian-Hungarian confederation with a single ruler – the Austrian archduke Ferdinand I of Habsburg.

At first, representatives of the Bohemian, Hungarian and, to some degree, Croatian estates (representatives of the nobility, clergy and burghers) were not particularly impressed with the persona of Ferdinand I, but the majority of them respected the fact that as the husband of Princess Anna Jagiellon, sister of the deceased Louis II Jagiellon, the Austrian archduke had a legitimate claim to the vacated Hungarian and Bohemian throne. The decisive factor for accepting Ferdinand's candidature, however, was the actuality that, at the time, the Habsburgs represented one of the politically most important dynasties in Europe. As early as the 1520s, thanks to the influence of his brother, Holy Roman Emperor Charles V, Ferdinand had succeeded in securing significant funding from German dukes for the defence of the Austrian lands from the approaching Turkish threat. The Bohemian, Hungarian and Croatian estates believed that the political leverage and money of the Habsburgs would help to safeguard their territories from the Ottomans too (see Vorel 2005: 7–26; Pánek et al. 2011: 191–95). In the interest of a balanced assessment, it must be noted that, in the end, the success of this experiment between Central European aristocracy and the Austrian Habsburgs was in fact determined by multiple factors. The Croatian historian Neven Budak worded it aptly when he wrote that the salvation of the 'remains of the remains of the once great Kingdom of Croatia' (*reliquiae reliquiarum olim inclyti regni Croatiae*), according to the fitting period characterization of the diminishing independent strip of Croatian territory under Habsburg rule, 'must be credited not only to the heroism and sacrifice of the Croatians but to Ferdinand together with Austrian, German and Czech financing' (Budak 2007: 22).

Countless historiographic titles have been written in modern times about the wars with the Ottomans, particularly those waged in lands that became immediate casualties of Ottoman expansion. A lesser known fact is that the Bohemian lands (more precisely the Lands of the Bohemian Crown, i.e. Bohemia, Moravia, Silesia, and Upper and Lower Lusatia) made significant contributions to the defence of Central Europe against the Ottoman Turks between the sixteenth and eighteenth centuries. Even though in the early modern period the Bohemian lands – with the exception of eastern regions of Moravia – were never directly attacked by Ottoman forces, they played an important role in protecting the Habsburg Monarchy, particularly in terms of funding (see Žáček et al. 1975; Veselá 1978; Válka 1995).

The objective of this chapter is to use the example of the Bohemian lands to describe and assess reflections of the phenomenon of the Turkish threat in early modern Central Europe. In the first part, we primarily examine the financial and military contributions of the Bohemian lands to the defence of the Habsburg Monarchy, specifically the area of Upper Hungary (present-day Slovakia), against the Ottoman Turks. Mention is also made of raids by Ottoman militants in Moravia during the seventeenth century and of relations between Bohemian Protestants and the Ottoman Empire. In the second part, we build upon this chronologically structured exposition by characterizing transformations of the image of the Turkish threat that was shaped in the Bohemian lands from the sixteenth to the eighteenth century. In so doing, we endeavour to capture the particularities of the local perception of this phenomenon in the context of the other countries of Central Europe, and also look at it from the perspective of later centuries. Initially, it might seem that the Lands of the Bohemian Crown, in large part spared the military catastrophes brought about by the struggle between the Habsburg Monarchy and the Ottoman Empire, present a somewhat atypical case upon which to base an accurate characterization of Central European reflections of the Turkish threat. In reality, however, it was perceived here much as it was in the territories facing immediate danger or areas directly exposed to Ottoman expansion, but there were certain peculiarities. The changes in the image of the Turk between the sixteenth and eighteenth centuries are helpful in understanding the subsequent (differentiated) development of attitudes among the population of Central Europe towards modern-day Bosnian Muslims.

Bohemian Lands and Defence of the Habsburg Monarchy against the Ottoman Turks

From the sixteenth to the eighteenth century, the Bohemian lands represented the most economically advanced and the wealthiest constituent of the Habsburg Empire. For example, according to Czech historians, of the overall war tax collected within the Habsburg Monarchy in 1541 for defence against the Ottoman Turks, a total of 371,000 guldens was provided by the so-called Austrian Hereditary Lands, 375,000 guldens by Bohemia alone, and 400,000 guldens by the adjacent lands of the Bohemian Crown. Hungary, which by that point had in large part been occupied by the Ottomans, did not pay the tax. Thus, in the middle of the sixteenth century, roughly two-thirds of the total sum of money collected to fight the Ottomans came from the Bohemian lands, while only the remaining one third came from Austrian territories. In the following decades, the tax continued to increase. At the turn of the seventeenth century, during the Long Turkish War (1593–1606), Bohemia provided 590,000 guldens for defence, and immediately prior to the outbreak of the Thirty Year's War (1618–1648) supplied a total of 1,000,000 guldens (Žáček et al. 1975: 118–19).

Military divisions from the Bohemian lands participated in a number of battles against the Ottomans, such as in 1529 during the first Ottoman siege of Vienna when Moravian units defended the left bank of the Danube. In 1532, Bohemian soldiers helped to defend the castle in the town of Kőszeg (German: *Güns*) on the Hungarian–Austrian frontier, as well as at Osijek in Eastern Slavonia in the year 1537 (Žáček et al. 1975: 110–14).

The fall of Buda and the subsequent establishment of the Budin Eyalet by the Ottoman Turks (1541) gave rise to the need for intensive fortification of the towns in the remaining parts of Hungary not yet occupied by the Ottomans. In terms of the duty of the individual Habsburg territories to defend the areas bordering the sultan's empire, the so-called Military Frontier, the Bohemian lands were charged with guarding Upper Hungary, now mostly present-day Slovakia, specifically the western areas around present-day Bratislava (German: Pressburg, Hungarian: Pozsony), the Váh and Nitra river basins, and a number of mining towns in central Slovakia. With financial support from the Bohemian lands, the so-called Old Fortress at the confluence of the Danube and Váh rivers at the town of Komárno (German: Komorn, Hungarian: Komárom) was enlarged between 1546 and 1557, and the fortress Nové Zámky (German: Neuhäufel, Hungarian: Érségújvár) was built on the bank of the River Nitra in western Slovakia between 1573 and 1581. According to historical sources, construction of practically the entire Nové Zámky fortress was financed with money from the Bohemian lands, primarily from Moravia. For several years, the imperial overseer of construction of the fortress was the influential Moravian nobleman Bedřich of Žerotín (German: Friedrich von Žerotin, sometimes spelled Zierotin). The fortress had six massive bastions, two of which were named for Bedřich of Žerotín (one known as 'Žerotin's' and the other as 'Friedrich's', according to the German form of his name). Another of the six bastions was called 'the Bohemian', a clear reference to the fact that most of the financial resources for construction of the fortress had come from the Bohemian estates (see Nové Zámky Fotoalbum 2017).

The ruling Habsburgs also occasionally attempted to engage the estates armies (provincial armies) of the Lands of the Bohemian Crown in wars with the Ottoman Turks. They twice largely succeeded in doing so, specifically during the exceptionally vigorous Ottoman campaigns into Hungary. The first instance was in 1566, when more than ten thousand soldiers from the Bohemian lands were mobilized against the army of Sultan Suleiman I, which had set out to lay siege to the Hungarian fortress of Szigetvár. At the time, the Bohemian provincial armies were commanded by the prominent nobleman William of Rosenberg, whose brother-in-law was Nikola Zrinski, defender of Szigetvár (see Pánek 2015). In the end, however, these forces did not partake in the battles against the Turks. Instead, they waited passively in the north of Hungary near the town of Győr (German: Raab) and then disbanded following word of the fall of Szigetvár. A campaign into Hungary in 1594, involving some eighteen thousand Bohemian soldiers led by Peter Vok of Rosenberg, came to a similar end. This time, too, the Bohemian army advanced only as far as the western part of Upper Hungary without engaging in any significant clashes with their Ottoman adversary (Pánek 1988: 870–71).

An important feature of the Lands of the Bohemian Crown in the sixteenth century and beginning of the seventeenth century was that from the time of the Hussite Wars in the fifteenth century, they were religiously divided. Apart from the Roman Catholics living in Bohemia and Moravia, there was a considerably powerful and politically influential community of Bohemian Utraquists (erstwhile ideological supporters of Jan Hus, later united in the independent Church of the Bohemian Brethren). Relatively soon after the Habsburgs had taken to the Bohemian throne, relations began to deteriorate between the ruling dynasty and the Bohemian estates, which comprised representatives of the nobility, clergy, and burghers of the Bohemian lands. The political attempts by the Habsburgs at centralization at the turn of the seventeenth century, particularly their efforts to continually increase war taxes, to weaken the system of estates in Bohemia and Moravia, and to strengthen the standing of Roman Catholics, came to a head in 1618–20 in an unsuccessful attempt by the Bohemian estates to stage a revolt against the Habsburgs and re-establish the full independence of the Lands of the Bohemian Crown.

In 1620, some of the Bohemian nobility contemplated trying to break free from Habsburg authority by following the example set by certain groups of the Protestant Hungarian and Transylvanian nobility of playing the so-called 'Turkish card'. The Utraquists in particular viewed the Ottomans as a potential ally in the resistance against the Roman Catholic Habsburgs. The rebels first sent their delegation to the capital city of the Ottoman Empire, and then, in 1620, the sultan's envoy, Mehmed Ağa, undertook a brief stay in Prague with the goal of determining how realistic military cooperation between the Ottoman Porte and the Bohemian rebels might be. His guide and interpreter in the Bohemian capital was Václav Budovec of Budov, an influential Utraquist nobleman well versed in the Ottoman Empire and the language of its political centre – Ottoman Turkish. In the 1570s, Budovec spent several years in the Ottoman Empire as a member of an Austrian delegation to Sultan Murad III. At the end of the sixteenth century, he wrote – as a bigoted Christian with unambiguous opinions – an obstinate polemic against Islam entitled *Antialkorán* (Budovec 1989), in which he rejected the Muslim religion as a corrupt Christian heresy, while at the same time warning his co-religionists against certain appealing characteristics of the Muslim religion that could, as he saw it, sway careless Christians in their faith and, when combined with the immense military might of the Ottomans, put an end to Christendom as a whole (Kučera 2010: 286). However damnatory the view Budovec held towards Islam, it did not prevent him as one of the leaders of the anti-Habsburg rebellion from arranging negotiations between Mehmed Ağa and other representatives of the rebels in this politically charged time. According to highly fragmented information, the Ottoman envoy was very cautious in Prague, and made no specific promise of assistance to the rebels (ibid.: 285–86). The revolt of the Bohemian estates came to an abrupt end in November 1620 with the defeat of their army by Habsburg forces at the Battle of White Mountain near Prague. Václav Budovec of Budov and twenty other noblemen and burghers were executed the following year in Prague's Old Town Square.

After the defeat of the anti-Habsburg rebellion, the majority of evangelicals from the Bohemian lands were forced into emigration. Their standing worsened even further with the end of the Thirty Year's War in 1648, which resulted in the strengthening of Habsburg power in Central Europe. The likelihood of the exiles returning to their homeland under such circumstances was minimal. In their political calculations, therefore, some of them, just as they had in the critical year 1620, again placed their hopes in the Ottoman Empire as a potential ally and saviour.

The best-known of the Bohemian exiles of the time, John Amos Comenius, also believed in political (more precisely military) help from the Ottomans (see Lisy-Wagner 2013: 101–17). In the 1650s, he held the opinion that through the efforts of Western intellectuals, the Ottomans could be brought to embrace Christianity, overturn the Habsburgs, and secure the unity of the Christian world. (This utopian school of thought of the period was known as Calvinoturcism.) In 1658, Comenius began work on an international project to translate the Bible into Turkish. The project, however, would never see completion. All that has remained is the book's introductory dedication in Latin (*Bibliorum Turcicorum dedicatio*), which Comenius had addressed to then sultan, Mehmed IV. In it, Comenius describes his humanistic conviction about the unity of all the peoples of the world, who, in his opinion, seek the same God despite taking various paths (Rataj 2002: 232; Kučera 2010: 286–87).

Of the individual Bohemian lands, the Ottoman Turks – or rather their military vassals and allies – only ever posed a direct threat to Moravia, and did so by means of occasional raids conducted from the territory of Hungary. The first raid of Tartars, who were Ottoman vassals, was chronicled in eastern Moravia in 1599. The attack was directed at the areas around the town of Uherský Brod. In the following years, the east and south of Moravia were plundered multiple times by divisions of Hungarian soldiers or Transylvanian anti-Habsburg insurgents who collaborated with the Ottoman Turks: in the year 1605, there were the militants of István Bocskai, and later of Gábor Bethlen (1621–23) and Imre Thököly (1680–82) (Čapka 2001: 82, 93, 107).

The greatest loss of life was inflicted upon Moravia by the Ottomans and their vassals in the year 1663, when Ottoman Grand Vizier Fazil Ahmed Köprülü amassed an army of more than one hundred thousand soldiers, and set out with it to capture the Habsburg fortress of Nové Zámky. In the course of conquering the fortress, approximately ten thousand Ottoman militants – mostly Tartars – crossed the western Slovakian region of Považí to invade Moravia (there were three invasions in total in September–October 1663). The attacks caused substantial material damage in an unbroken swathe of territory from the eastern Moravian towns of Vsetín, Uherský Brod and Uherské Hradiště to the southern Moravian towns of Hodonín, Břeclav and Hustopeče. Dozens of villages and smaller towns were burned down, thousands of people were slain, and some forty thousand – mostly younger people – were taken into slavery by Ottoman militants (Válka 1995: 119–20, Čapka 2001: 104–5).

Moravia was again subjected to smaller destructive invasions in 1683 in connection with the second Ottoman siege of Vienna. Of particular interest is the fact that this was effectively the first time the inhabitants of the western parts of Moravia and even Bohemia had been stricken with panic and fear of the Turks. Records from the period give evidence of an unprecedented increase in the number of suicides among the citizens of the western Moravian town of Jihlava following news of the siege of Vienna by the Ottoman army of Grand Vizier Kara Mustafa Pasha; they also tell that thousands of Bohemian villagers fled in droves to Prague to seek shelter from the Ottoman menace (Žáček et al. 1975: 180).

At the time of the conflicts with the Ottoman armies, Bohemian forces could not boast well-known commanders or heroes of the likes of Charles V the Duke of Lorraine, Ludwig von Baden, Eugene of Savoy, Nikola Jurišić and Nikola Zrinski. Despite this, it is possible to name several noblemen who distinguished themselves honourably in the struggle against the Ottomans. In the sixteenth century, for example, military divisions led by the Moravian nobleman Karel the Elder of Žerotín achieved several victories over the Ottomans in Hungary. In the summer of 1683, remarkable contributions to the heroic defence of Vienna were made by the Bohemian nobleman Kašpar Zdeněk Kaplíř of Sulevic (German: Kaspar Zdenko Kaplir von Sullowitz), a deputy to the commander of the Viennese army garrison Ernst Rüdiger von Starhemberg. Because Rüdiger was seriously injured in the fighting, the majority of the responsibilities relating to defending the city fell to Kaplíř. Czech historiography points out that in recognizing the fact that Vienna, despite the furious months-long siege, did not succumb to the Ottomans in 1683 and was finally liberated by Christian armies, one must not forget to mention the name of Kaplíř of Sulevic (see Macek 1983).

The very bloody, gruelling Austro-Ottoman wars would continue for the whole of the eighteenth century (1716–18, 1737–39, 1788–90); however, it was not the old estates armies that participated in the battles on the side of Austria but, first and foremost, paid mercenaries that the Habsburgs had acquired by recruiting from the territory of the Danubian Monarchy, and occasionally even from more distant territories within the Holy Roman Empire. These wars, too, were often financed by the economically advanced Bohemian lands, and thousands of Bohemian, Moravian and Silesian recruits met their demise in them. Because, however, the struggle between the Habsburgs and the Ottomans was geographically being waged relatively far away from the Lands of the Bohemian Crown (mostly in the Balkans south of the River Sava and the Lower Danube), fear of the Turk among the citizens of these lands gradually faded in the course of the eighteenth and nineteenth centuries.

Image of the Turkish Threat in Early Modern Bohemian Lands

As illustrated by the aforesaid example of John Amos Comenius and his conception of Calvinoturcism, in the early modern Bohemian lands, we encounter utopian ideas positing a certain form of rapprochement between Christians and the Ottoman Turks. Nonetheless, throughout this period the relation is dominated by a discourse that is strongly antagonistic. In the sources from the Bohemian lands, too, the Turkish threat is projected onto the image of the Turk as the archenemy of Christendom (see Rataj 2002; Mendel, Ostřanský and Rataj 2007; Lisy-Wagner 2013), which was constructed and propagated on the pages of numerous texts of anti-Turkish orientation. Newspapers of the time, propaganda printings, songs, sermons, polemics, chronicles, travelogues and memoirs often influenced the reader not only through words but also through vivid visual illustrations. Their purpose was not only to inform and enlighten about recent battles of the Ottoman Empire and its history, and the customs of its people, but also to provide a suggestive warning against the Ottomans and Islam, to appeal for unity among Christians in defending against the Ottoman menace, and to demand deliverance for Christian co-religionists from the 'Turkish yoke'. The second objective of these texts was to fortify awareness among readers of their fellowship with Christendom, with their homeland, and with the sovereign dynasty, whose achievements in the struggle against the Turks were celebrated in propagandistic publications. At times, though, the authors and publishers pursued somewhat more tangible goals. By means of the fear evoked through exaggerated depictions of Turkish cruelty, they reinforced the obedience of subjects to their landlords and the resolve of the nobility to help bear the financial burden of future wartime campaigns.

Initially in this regard, society in the early modern Bohemian lands was predominantly influenced by Ottoman-themed works translated from Latin and German. In the course of time, however, texts written by local authors in Czech or Latin (exceptionally also in German) began to appear. Among the works in this relatively abundant corpus, attention should be called to an extensive and richly illustrated travelogue about a pilgrimage to the Holy Land by Kryštof Harant of Polžice and Bezdružice (1608) brimming with information on the geography, history, and day-to-day reality of the Ottoman Empire (Harant 2017). There is also the aforementioned obstinate polemic against Islam by Václav Budovec of Budov entitled *Antialkorán* (1593, published 1614), as well as the readable and, in their perspective of Ottoman society, unusually balanced memoirs of a Bohemian nobleman held captive by the Turks named Václav Vratislav of Mitrovice (1599, published 1777), which are evidently the most valuable early modern source of insight into Ottoman everydayness by an author from the Bohemian lands (Vratislav 1977; Vratislav 2013).[1] Among later writings worthy of mention is a treatise written in Latin by Tomáš Pešina of Čechorod, who in 1663 – a critical year for the monarchy and Moravia within its borders – took up the long-standing tradition of works of an evocative nature and called for the formation of a coalition of European states, which would, without delay, rush to the aid of a Hungary under attack in the latest of Ottoman military offensives (Pešina 1663).

It is important to point out that all the original texts by authors from the Bohemian lands contain a set repertory of the same stereotypical motives related to the Turks, the Ottoman Empire, and Islam that we encounter in the works of their European predecessors and contemporaries (see Schwoebel 1967; Soykut 2001; Jezernik 2010; Harper 2016; see also Beller and Leerssen 2007: 256–58 for a more detailed bibliography on the topic). Accordingly, the image of the Turkish threat in the local discourse differs in no substantial way from the image constructed in lands directly exposed to Ottoman territorial expansion or in the German-speaking parts of the Holy Roman Empire. This means that in the original works and translations read in the early modern Bohemian lands there prevails the image of the cruel Turk plundering Christian lands and murdering, raping and enslaving Christians in the pursuit of ultimately wiping the Christian faith from the face of the Earth. All the while, the distinction between the terms 'Turk' and 'Muslim' is blurred. Islam is presented as a heresy of Christianity, purposefully contrived by the false prophet Muhammad with the objective of obtaining power and justifying territorial expansion to the detriment of neighbours. The Turk appears as the chief and hereditary enemy of Christendom, who has displaced the older Jews and Arabs (the Saracens) from this position, and his coming is interpreted as divine punishment for the sins of the faithful. In this context, Roman Catholics and Protestants place blame on followers of the opposite confession, and discredit them as spiritual kin or secret allies of the Turks.

This religiously conceived image of the Turkish threat gradually gives way to a civilizationally defined otherness of the Turks (Rataj 2002: 223–24, 277; Mendel, Ostřanský and Rataj 2007: 273–332; see also Sutter Fichtner 2008). One of the consequences of this tendency is that, for many authors in the sixteenth century, demonization of the Turks went hand in hand with admiration for their military prowess, effective governance, and the lavish opulence of their royal court, whereas from the second half of the eighteenth century, the Ottoman Empire was depicted as a militarily and civilizationally inferior adversary, or even a contemptible Oriental tyranny. The stage was set for the long nineteenth century, during which the archenemy became the 'sick man of Europe', and the Turkish threat gave way to the white man's burden, or, more precisely, an Orientalist discourse in the services of colonialism (see Said 1978; Cavaliero 2010; Hodkinson et al. 2013).

In this light, the question that presents itself as locally more relevant is the manner in which early modern texts address the role of the Lands of the Bohemian Crown in the defence against the Turkish threat. On the basis of a thorough examination of period sources, Tomáš Rataj showed that Ottoman territorial expansion was only reflected more substantially in the Bohemian lands after the Battle of Mohács, and was perceived as a matter primarily associated with Hungary; awareness of the early phases of expansion, including incursions into the Balkans, was peripheral at best (see Rataj 2002; Mendel, Ostřanský and Rataj

2007: 273–332). According to Rataj and co-authors of the book *Islám v srdci Evropy* (Islam in the heart of Europe) (Mendel, Ostřanský and Rataj 2007), the image of the Bohemian lands helping the invaded Hungary even appears in sources prior to 1526. However, only afterwards do period texts depict Hungary as a stage upon which Bohemians and Moravians fight alongside the Hungarians in the name of Christendom and, from the 1590s, in the name of their homeland (Mendel, Ostřanský and Rataj 2007: 273–74, 289–90, 299, 330–31). There are also rare mentions in the literature of the notion of the homeland as a bulwark of Christianity (*antemurale christianitatis*), albeit without any claim to the certain exclusivity typical for the Croatian, Hungarian and Polish interpretations of the conception. In these considerably rare texts, the Bohemian lands figure solely as a component of the greater Central European wall of defence formed also by Hungary and Poland (ibid.: 273–74, 311, 331).

As the Ottomans withdrew from Central Europe at the turn of the eighteenth century, the Turkish threat became a thing of the past for the inhabitants of the Bohemian lands. Reminders of the times when scholars and military strategists contemplated the role of the Lands of the Bohemian Crown in defending Central Europe against the Ottomans are now found only in the Turkish motifs of folk songs and legends, Turkish heads in the coats of arms of certain noble families (e.g. the Schwarzenbergs), and in the names of once exotic foods from the East, most notably Turkish coffee (Rataj 2002: 272–74, 287–89). Throughout the long nineteenth century, the image of the cruel Turk likely lingered in the collective memory, as evidenced in Czech perceptions of the efforts by the Serbs, Bulgarians, and other 'Slavic brethren' to break free from Ottoman subjection (see Šístek 2009; Šístek 2011; Žáček et al. 1975). The present-day concerns of a large portion of the Czech populace about Muslim migrants, however, are founded rather on fear of the unknown and the calculated incitement of Islamophobia by certain Czech politicians than on any lingering remnants of early modern reflections of the Turkish threat over Central Europe (see Hesová 2016; Slačálek and Svobodová 2018).

Looking at the Czech experience with the Ottoman presence from the context of the countries that form the core of Central Europe (Austria, Hungary, the Czech Republic, Slovakia and Slovenia), it is possible to identify several instances where local circumstances differ from the rest. Unlike present-day Hungary and parts of Slovakia, the present-day Czech lands never came directly under Ottoman dominance. While Vienna was long seen as the golden apple in the minds of Ottoman conquerors, who unsuccessfully besieged the city in 1529 and again in 1683, the Bohemian lands were never a target of conquest for the regular Ottoman army. Eastern Moravia did indeed experience repeated raids by Ottoman marauders (*akinji*), but their frequency and the response to them in the local folk and elite culture never acquired the same intensity as in the case of Styria, Carniola or Carinthia. The Bohemian lands did play a relatively significant role in defending the Habsburg Monarchy against the Ottoman Turks, and, for most of the period in question, the Bohemian estates identified with the more broadly conceived idea of defending Christian Europe against the spread of Islam. On the other hand, however, the Bohemian/Czech context fails to provide us with a detailed vision of the homeland as a bulwark of Christianity, let alone its later instrumentalization within the framework of a national ideology, which is characteristic for Croatian or Slovenian national discourse (see Žanić 2005; Bartulović 2010; Baskar 2010; Stehlík 2014). For obvious reasons, in the case of the present-day Czech lands, it was also impossible to use the aforesaid early modern idea (antemurale myth) in a sense that would have been analogous to the imperial self-presentation of the Habsburgs as defenders of the Christian faith (see Karner, Ciulisová and García 2014). All of the dissimilarities described herein share the same denominator: the absence of long-term direct interaction between the inhabitants of these lands on the one hand, and the Muslims and the world of Islam on the other, to which the other aforesaid territories in Central Europe were naturally exposed as a result of their geographic location and the evolution of the historical struggles with the Ottoman Empire.

In our opinion, therefore, the Czech Republic cannot be grouped together with the countries that fully developed 'a relatively coherent set of metaphors and myths' (Gingrich 1996: 119), which Andre Gingrich called frontier Orientalism. In the Czech case, it is ever only hinted at, and makes no appearance in the pure form typical for Austria, Hungary, Slovenia and Croatia. By no means does the role of the present-day Czech lands in defending the Habsburg Monarchy hold an important place in the collective consciousness of their inhabitants. This is also why in the present-day Czech Republic it is not a part of the widespread anti-immigration rhetoric or Islamophobic discourse. The image of the Turkish threat constructed on the pages of early modern works and its reflection in local folklore played practically no role in the formation of the Czech national identity. Throughout that process, it was the German who would embody the enemy, while the cruel Turk gradually faded into oblivion. Not even after the Czechs began sharing their greater homeland with the Bosnians and Herzegovinians was the Turk, an evil Muslim Oriental, replaced with the figure of the good Muslim, which would be comparable to the image of Bosnian Muslims as loyal allies (Gingrich 1996: 109) in the imperial discourse of the Habsburg Empire, or the 'noblest members of our nation' in the Croatian national ideology (Stehlík 2013: 183–86; Stehlík 2015: 173–76). The Czech perception of the Bosnian Muslims at the turn of the twentieth century was primarily characterized by a pronounced ambivalence (Malečková 2018: 24; see also Ljuca 2006) stemming from a widely shared belief about the incompatibility of their Slavic ethnic identity and religious affiliation with Islam (see the chapter by František Šístek in this volume).

Ladislav Hladký is a research fellow at the Institute of History of the Czech Academy of Sciences, Brno, and associate professor at the Faculty of Arts, Masaryk University in Brno, the Czech Republic. He has focused on the history of former Yugoslavia (especially Bosnia and Herzegovina, and Slovenia) and Czech relations with the South Slavs in the nineteenth and twentieth centuries. His publications include the monograph *Bosenská otázka v 19. a 20. století* [The Bosnian question in the 19th and 20th century] (Brno: Masarykova univerzita, 2005) and the edited volume *Czech Relations with the Nations and Countries of Southeastern Europe* (Zagreb: Srednja Europa, 2019). Hladký is coeditor-in-chief of *Slovanský přehled* [Slavonic Review], a journal for the history of Central, Eastern and South Eastern Europe, published in Prague since 1898.

Petr Stehlík is a Slavist and historian teaching South Slavic literatures and history of the Balkans at the Department of Slavonic Studies in the Faculty of Arts, Masaryk University in Brno, Czech Republic. His principal areas of academic interest are national ideologies and the formation of national identities in South Eastern Europe. He is the author of the monographs *Bosna v chorvatských národně-integračních ideologiích 19. století* [Bosnia in Croatian ideologies of national integration in the 19th century] (Brno: Masarykova univerzita, 2013), and *Između hrvatstva i jugoslavenstva: Bosna u hrvatskim nacionalno-integracijskim ideologijama 1832–1878* [Between Croathood and Yugoslavdom: Bosnia in Croatian ideologies of national integration, 1832–1878] (Zagreb: Srednja Europa, 2015). His current research project deals with the history of the Yugoslav idea and its representations in South Slavic literatures.

Note

1. Evidence that the inspirational value of Vratislav's *Příhody* (Stories) endures to the present day can be found in the fact that some of the themes connected to the author's recounting of his hardships in Ottoman captivity were borrowed by the renowned Turkish writer Orhan Pamuk for his novel *The White Castle* (1985, Beyaz Kale) (Sabatos 2015: 241–42).

References

Bartulović, Alenka. 2010: '"We Have an Old Debt with the Turk, and It Best Be Settled": Ottoman Incursions through the Discursive Optics of Slovenian Historiography and Literature and Their Applicability in the Twenty-First Century', in Božidar Jezernik (ed.), *Imagining 'The Turk'*. Newcastle upon Tyne: Cambridge Scholars, pp. 111–37.

Baskar, Bojan. 2010. '"The First Slovenian Poet in a Mosque": Orientalism in the Travel Writing of a Poet from the Imperial Periphery', in Božidar Jezernik (ed.), *Imagining 'The Turk'*. Newcastle upon Tyne: Cambridge Scholars, pp. 97–110.

Beller, Manfred, and Joep Leerssen (eds). 2007. *Imagology: The Cultural Construction and Literary Representation of National Characters – A Critical Survey*. Amsterdam: Rodopi.
Budak, Neven. 2007. *Hrvatska povijest u ranome novom vijeku, 1. svezak. Hrvatska i Slavonija u ranome novom vijeku*. Zagreb: Leykam International.
Budovec z Budova, Václav. (1614) 1989. *Antialkorán*. Prague: Odeon.
Čapka, František. 2001. *Dějiny Moravy v datech*. Brno: Akademické nakladatelství.
Cavaliero, Roderick. 2010. *Ottomania: The Romantics and the Myth of the Islamic Orient*. London: I.B. Tauris.
Gingrich, Andre. 1996. 'Frontier Myths of Orientalism: The Muslim World in Public and Popular Cultures of Central Europe', in Bojan Baskar and Borut Brumen (eds), *Mediterranean Ethnological Summer School*. Piran: Institut za multikulturne raziskave, pp. 99–127.
Harant z Polžic a Bezdružic, Kryštof. (1608) 2017. *Putování, aneb, Cesta z království českého do města Benátek, odtud po moři do země Svaté, země jůdské a dále do Egypta a velikého města Kairu, I–II*. Prague: Host.
Harper, James G. (ed.). 2016. *The Turk and Islam in the Western Eye, 1450–1750: Visual Imagery before Orientalism*. New York: Routledge.
Hesová, Zora. 2016. 'Islamofobie, antiislamismus a negativní stereotypy'. Asociace pro mezinárodní otázky. Last accessed 27 January 2019 from http://www.amo.cz/wp-content/uploads/2016/01/amocz_BP_01_2016_web.pdf.
Hodkinson, James, et al. (eds). 2013. *Deploying Orientalism in Culture and History: From Germany to Central and Eastern Europe*. Rochester, NY: Camden House.
Jezernik, Božidar (ed.). 2010. *Imagining 'The Turk'*. Newcastle upon Tyne: Cambridge Scholars.
Karner, Herbert, Ingrid Ciulisová and Bernardo J. García (eds). 2014. *The Habsburgs and Their Courts in Europe, 1400–1700: Between Cosmopolitism and Regionalism*. Last accessed 27 January 2019 from http://www.courtresidences.eu/uploads/general/Habsburgs%20 2014%20contents.pdf.
Kučera, Petr. 2010. 'Česko-turecké vztahy', in Ladislav Hladký et al. (eds), *Vztahy Čechů s národy a zeměmi jihovýchodní Evropy*. Prague: Historický ústav, pp. 281–94.
Lisy-Wagner, Laura. 2013. *Islam, Christianity and the Making of Czech Identity, 1453–1683*. New York: Routledge.
Ljuca, Adin. 2006. 'Turci a Švábové, nebo slovanští bratři? Český pohled na bosenské muslimy v letech 1878–1918', in Mirjam Moravcová, David Svoboda and František Šístek (eds), *Pravda, láska a ti na 'Východě': Obrazy středoevropského a východoevropského prostoru z pohledu české společnosti*. Prague: FHS UK, pp. 122–34.
Macek, Josef. 1983. 'Kaspar Zdenko von Sullowitz und seine Bedeuteng für die Verteidigung der Stadt Wien', *Österreich in Geschichte und Literatur* 27: 203–24.
Malečková, Jitka. 2018. '"Our Turks", or "Real Turks"? Czech Perceptions of Slavic Muslims of Bosnia-Herzegovina', *World Literature Studies* 10(1): 15–26.
Mendel, Miloš, Bronislav Ostřanský and Tomáš Rataj. 2007. *Islám v srdci Evropy: vlivy islámské civilizace na dějiny a současnost českých zemí*. Prague: Academia.
Nové Zámky Fotoalbum. 2017. 'História Mesta Nové Zámky'. Last accessed 27 January 2019 from https://www.novezamkyfotoalbum.sk/historia-mesta-nove-zamky.
Pánek, Jaroslav. 1988. 'Podíl předbělohorského českého státu na obraně střední Evropy proti osmanské expanzi I', *Československý časopis historický* 36: 856–72.
———. 2015. 'Poslední Rožmberkové a Zrinští. Mikuláš Zrinský a Eva z Rožmberka – setkání na pozadí protiosmanských bojů', in Jaroslav Pánek (ed.), *Češi a Jihoslované: Kapitoly z dějin vzájemných vztahů*. Brno: Tribun EU, pp. 35–62.

Pánek, Jaroslav, et al. 2011. *A History of the Czech Lands*. Prague: Karolinum Press, Charles University in Prague.
Pešina z Čechorodu, Tomáš. 1663. *Ucalegon Germaniae, Italiae et Poloniae Hungaria, flama belli Turcici ardens*. Prague: Univerzitní tiskárna.
Rataj, Jan. 2002. *České země ve stínu půlměsíce: Obraz Turka v raně novověké literatuře z českých zemí*. Prague: Scriptorium.
Sabatos, Charles. 2015. 'The Ottoman Captivity Narrative as a Transnational Genre in Central European Literature', *Archív orientální* 83(2): 233–54.
Said, Edward W. 1978. *Orientalism*. New York: Pantheon.
Schwoebel, Robert. 1967. *The Shadow of the Crescent: The Renaissance Image of the Turk (1453–1517)*. Nieuwkoop: B. de Graaf / New York: St. Martin's Press.
Šístek, František. 2009. *Naša braća na jugu: Češke predstave o Crnoj Gori i Crnogorcima, 1830–2006*. Cetinje: Matica crnogorska.
———. 2011. *Junáci, horalé a lenoši: Obraz Černé Hory a Černohorců v české společnosti 1830–2006*. Prague: Historický ústav.
Slačálek, Ondřej, and Eva Svobodová. 2018. 'The Czech Islamophobic Movement: Beyond "Populism"?', *Patterns of Prejudice* 52(5): 479–95. https://www.tandfonline.com/doi/full/10.1080/0031322X.2018.1495377?af=R.
Soykut, Mustafa. 2001. *Image of the 'Turk' in Italy: A History of the 'Other' in Early Modern Europe, 1453–1683*. Berlin: Klaus Schwarz Verlag.
Stehlík, Petr. 2013. *Bosna v chorvatských národně-integračních ideologiích 19. století*. Brno: Masarykova univerzita.
———. 2014. 'Both Bulwark and Bridge: The Symbolic Conceptualization of the Frontier Position of Croatia in the Original Yugoslavism', *Oriens Aliter* 2: 9–21.
———. 2015. *Između hrvatstva i jugoslavenstva: Bosna u hrvatskim nacionalno-integracijskim ideologijama 1832–1878*. Zagreb: Srednja Europa.
Sutter Fichtner, Paula. 2008. *Terror and Toleration: The Habsburg Empire Confronts Islam, 1526–1850*. London: Reaktion Books.
Válka, Josef. 1995. *Dějiny Moravy, díl 2 – Morava reformace, renesance a baroka*. Brno: Muzejní a vlastivědná společnost v Brně.
Veselá, Zdenka (ed.). 1978. *Ottoman Rule in Middle Europe and Balkan in the 16th and 17th Centuries*. Prague: Academia.
Vorel, Petr. 2005. *Velké dějiny zemí Koruny české, svazek VII, 1526–1618*. Prague: Paseka.
Vratislav z Mitrovic, Václav. (1777) 1977. *Příhody Václava Vratislava z Mitrovic, které on v tureckém hlavním městě Konstantinopoli viděl, v zajetí svém zakusil a po šťastném do vlasti navrácení sám léta páně 1599 sepsal*. Prague: Mladá fronta.
———. (1862) 2013. *Adventures of Baron Wenceslas Wratislaw of Mitrowitz*. Cambridge: Cambridge University Press.
Žáček, Václav, et al. 1975. *Češi a Jihoslované v minulosti: Od nejstarších dob do roku 1918*. Prague: Academia.
Žanić, Ivo. 2005. 'The Symbolic Identity of Croatia in the Triangle Crossroads – Bulwark – Bridge', in Pål Kolstø (ed.), *Myths and Boundaries in South-Eastern Europe*. London: Hurst & Company, pp. 35–76.

Chapter 2

THE MUSLIMS OF BOSNIA AND HERZEGOVINA BETWEEN MILLET AND NATION

Božidar Jezernik

After the conquest of Byzantium in 1453, the Ottomans did not attempt to impose their state institutions on their new subjects or to assimilate the Christian populations they had conquered. Sultan Mehmed II, conqueror of Byzantium, conferred upon the monk Gennadios, whom he installed as Patriarch of Constantinople, the title of *milletbaşi* (chief of the nation) and allowed Orthodox citizens to retain some of their churches and free exercise of their religion. He also entrusted the patriarch with the administration of the spiritual and secular needs of his flock. In this way, the clergy formed a body of functionaries invested with broad administrative and judicial powers. All cases involving marriage, divorce and inheritance were tried before an episcopal court, and in matters of a civil nature, Christians did not have to go to Ottoman tribunals. Non-Muslims were also excluded from military service. Every religious community was responsible for collecting taxes from its members and paying them to the state exchequer. As Voltaire put it, the Ottomans suffered and even protected Christians throughout the empire and in their capital. They were allowed to make processions through the streets in the vast quarter that was set apart for them in Istanbul; and four Janissaries marched ahead of the procession to shield them from insults (Voltaire 1761: VI, 114).

When Sultan Mehmed II conquered Bosnia, he followed the same policy. In 1453, for instance, he issued a firman to Bosnian Franciscans, in which he pledged by his sabre that he would cut off the head of anyone who would prevent them from enjoying the rights that he had given them by his grace (Kapetanović Ljubušak 1886: 11).

Religion and Nation

In the Ottoman Empire, there was no visible dividing line between secular and religious law. The Ottoman state divided its subjects according to their religion into *millets*, consisting of both a lay and an ecclesiastical council, which dealt with the internal affairs of the people. These millets, or church nations, as a Turkish professor of Western literature translates the word (Edib 1930: 68), were the only subdivisions recognized by the state. The diverse Muslim elements (Slavs, Albanians and Turks) had no community of ethnicity. They spoke their own languages in their homes, Turkish being an acquired tongue. But they were Muslims, and all were Turks in a political sense: they belonged to the dominant caste.

On one hand, this system provided a degree of religious, cultural and ethnic continuity within these communities, while on the other hand, it permitted their incorporation into the Ottoman administrative, economic and political structures. It essentially consisted of people of the same faith. The leadership of the community in the villages and in the *mahallas* (town quarters) consisted of the representative of the religion and a prominent layman living there. The communal leaders of the town enjoyed greater authority and influence on account of their connection with the higher Ottoman authorities and their own ecclesiastical heads, and also because of their wealth and their responsibility in collecting taxes and supervising the distribution of state lands to cultivators. They represented the community in its dealings with the Ottoman administration and were responsible for order, security, the collection of taxes, and so on (Karpat 1982: I, 142–43).

Religion was the basis for these divisions; language and ethnological theories merely played a secondary role (Jezernik 2004: 180). The divisions were firmly established after the conquest of Bosnia and Herzegovina by the Ottomans in the fifteenth century. As reported by Benedict Curipeschitz, who travelled through Bosnia in 1530 together with Josip de Lamberg and Nikola Jurišić, both of whom had been sent to Istanbul to negotiate with Sultan Suleiman, the Kingdom of Bosnia was populated by people of three nations and three religions: the native Bosnians (*Wossner*), who were Roman Catholic; the Serbs (*Surffen*), whom they called Vlachs (*Wallachen*), who came to Bosnia from the towns of Smederevo (*Schmedraw*) and Belgrade (*Griechisch weyssenburg*) and were of St Paul's (*sant Pauls*) religion; and the third nation, the Turks, mainly soldiers and officials who tyrannically ruled both Christian nations (Curipeschitz 1531: 19).

The rationale for this state of affairs was the system of government. Ottoman law was a religious code that could not be imposed on unbelievers, who were not eligible for recruitment into the army. These purely theocratic principles of state organization formed the basis of the Ottoman Empire; the Qur'an and the law of the empire were so bound together that non-Muslims could not be ruled by it. The non-Muslim millets were subject to their own native regulations, not to sharia (Islamic) law. However, owing to the peculiarity of this policy, the Christians in the Ottoman Empire enjoyed relative independence and were able to preserve their nationality, language and customs. These exceptional historical circumstances also explain why, for these Christians, patriotism was transformed into attachment to their religious communities and national church.

In the Ottoman Empire, the millet system lasted in its entirety until the beginning of the twentieth century, when there were still towns in Albania with no civil court and where the Qur'an was the only source of law. At the beginning of the twentieth century, the system was abolished amid extensive political reforms in the Ottoman Empire, and a code based on the Napoleonic model was introduced instead (Jezernik 2004: 180). In the age of modernity, when societies were more secular, the influence of religion diminished and it began to be replaced by nationalism. According to Serif Mardin, the term 'millet' was used as the equivalent of the French *nation* during the reign of Sultan Mahmud II (Mardin 2000: 174, 189).

In the Ottoman Empire, the Spring of Nations did not come to the Ottoman nation but occurred among the ethnic groups who, for a long time, were under Ottoman rule and adopted its organizational scheme of dividing groups of people as their own. When nationalism won the hearts and minds of the people, the Ottoman policy of separating nationalities according to their religion had much graver consequences, and contributed significantly to the downfall of the Ottoman Empire. As argued by Ernest Renan, in cities such as Thessaloniki and Izmir, there lived together five or six communities, each with its own memories and almost nothing in common. The essence of a nation, however, is that 'all individuals have many things in common, and also that they have forgotten many things' (Renan 1882: 7–8).

Bosnian and Herzegovinian society was not a typical Ottoman possession, though. The Muslims in Bosnia and Herzegovina were taxed less and enjoyed greater autonomy than other Ottoman subjects; Bosnian fiefs became hereditary, and the notables a genuine hereditary nobility. Mass conversion to Islam in Bosnia and Herzegovina, and the notion, encouraged by the local Muslim population, of being the *vaumure* (bulwark) of the Ottoman fortress assured this province a special status within the Ottoman Empire. Unlike the other conquered Balkan lands, it was not pulled asunder, nor were its towns settled by Anatolian migrants. The *eyalet* (province) of Bosnia was in fact expanded to include heartlands on the Adriatic coast, its hinterland, and parts of Slavonia. The central portion of old Raška, later organized into a special *sancak* (banner, district), the Sandžak of Novi Pazar, also belonged to Bosnia, and its population thought of itself as Bosnian (Banac 1984: 41).

Unlike the Muslims in the eastern Balkans who were largely bilingual, in the mid-nineteenth century there were still many agas living in Sarajevo who could not speak Turkish or any other language besides Bosnian (Jedan Domorodac 1842: 54), and they made a careful distinction between themselves and the handful of Ottoman officials in their midst. The Bosnian Muslims often referred to themselves as Turks on account of their Turkish faith, but they called themselves *Turci* in distinction from the Anatolians, whom they used to call the *Turkuše* (Rebac 1930: 9–10; Begović 1938: 30; Salihagić 1940: 19; Banac 1984: 41). Suljaga Salihagić claims that in olden times not a single Bosnian Muslim would call himself a *Turkuša*; they were proud *Bošnjaci* (Bosniaks) instead (Salihagić 1940: 19). Bosnian Muslims clung firmly to Islam and energetically defended it even from the Osmanlis, claiming there were no worse people under the sky than they; some called them unbelievers or even *giaours*[1] (Jedan Domorodac 1842: 53; Gil'ferding 1859: 85, 342; Yriarte 1981: 98). But the Muslims from other parts of the Ottoman Empire, too, thought unfavourably of Bosnian Muslims, calling them Bosnian animals, Bosnian giaours, and so on (Jedan Domorodac 1842: 53–54; Kurtović 1914: 14). This hatred has entered many proverbs and even history (Jedan Domorodac 1842: 53; Salihagić 1940: 19).

According to the French Slavist Louis Léger, in the 1870s the names 'Bosnian', 'Croat' and 'Serb' connotated religious affiliation, not nationality (Léger 1873: 79). He illustrates his statement with a conversation he had with a *momak* (boy) from Bosnia who introduced himself as a Turk.

– Do you speak Turkish?
– No.
– How can you say that you are a Turk if you don't speak Turkish?
– I don't know; they tell me that I am a Turk.
– In which language do you speak to me now?
– I don't know.
– I speak Serbian, and you respond to me in Serbian. So, we are both Serbs.
– Not at all; you speak to me in Serbian, and I answer you in Bosnian. You are Serbian, and I am Turkish. (Léger 1873: 79)

A Kind of Happy Family

Ottoman domination was social as well as political, and it deeply affected not only manners and morals but also social life. Nevertheless, it is a singular fact that no determined attempt was made to assimilate the Balkan peoples into the Ottoman way of life or into Islam during all the centuries of occupation. According to Ivo Banac, the Ottomans did not promote Islam by force; the economic and political advantages to be gained by joining the state religion were sufficiently compelling. For instance, the profession of Islam enabled the feudatory to enter into the new elite, and it was beneficial to the peasant converts, too, as they were exempted from the special poll tax (*cizye*) (Banac 1984: 41).

The Ottomans did not try to assimilate their subject peoples, and in this respect they differed greatly from the contemporary governments of Western Europe. To the great surprise of the contemporary Western Europeans, the Ottomans had not destroyed the churches but had given permission to their Christian subjects to practise their religion freely (Belon 1554: 180; Rycaut 1668: 103; Burbury 1671: 114; Randolph 1687: 15). Whereas the Ottoman Empire had followed a policy of non-interference, the European governments made every effort to extinguish the national spirit and the mother tongue of their subject peoples (Urquhart 1838: II, 236–37). As Captain Sutherland explained to his readers, the Ottomans did not, like the Romans, incorporate the vanquished with the conquerors so as to, in time, become one people, and thereby increase in numbers as they increased in territory (Sutherland 1790: 186–87). As a result, despite its theocratic structure, the Ottoman Empire actually became a home of multiculturalism: the land where 'all the nationalities of the world' carried on their daily lives side by side, as if 'immediately after the fall of the Tower of Babel'. The attitude of the Sublime Porte towards the various creeds professed by its Christian subjects was described by Western travellers as one of quite exceptional tolerance (Garnett 1911: 141). French traveller Jean Du Mont, who visited the island of Scio in December 1690, was much surprised by what he saw there:

> The Greeks, and in general all the Christian inhabitants, enjoy so many privileges and retain so many marks of their ancient liberty that if I did not sometimes see a *turbant*, I shou'd almost forget that I am still in Turkey. The whole compass of the Island does not amount to 100 Miles; yet there are above 200 Churches in it, and at least 30 Monasteries belonging to the Greeks and Latin Christians, who perform their several rites without the least disturbance. (Du Mont 1696: 185–86)

It is well known that about 170,000 Jews were given asylum and granted freedom to practise their religion in Istanbul, Thessaloniki, Sarajevo, and other Ottoman towns after they had been expelled by the Spanish monarchs Ferdinand and Isabella in 1492 (see e.g. Nicolay 1568: 149; Dallaway 1797: 389; Baker 1913: 194). It is less well known that there was once a large Trappist monastery, Marija Zvijezda, near Banja Luka. The monks had been expelled from France during the Revolution; they first took refuge in Germany but were driven out in 1868. As no Christian state was willing to take them in, they asked and received the sultan's permission to purchase land in the neighbourhood of Banja Luka and build their monastery there (see e.g. Ruthner 1877: 20; Asboth 1890: 389; Zavadil 1911: 3, 36).

From the Western point of view, even more surprising was the establishment of the Patriarchate of Peć in 1557, which embraced an enormous territory stretching from present-day Slovakia in the north to the Adriatic littoral in the south. Ottoman-held Serbia, Montenegro, Hungary, Croatia, Slavonia, Dalmatia, and Bosnia and Herzegovina were all under its jurisdiction. It was established in response to urgings of Grand Vezir Mehmet Paşa Sokollu (Sokolović), who was himself an *acemi oğlan* (foreign youth), taken by the Ottomans in his childhood and Islamicized and trained for the Janissary service. The first patriarch was Makarije Sokolović, who was either a brother or a nephew of the grand vezir; Makarije was succeeded by three other relatives of the paşa. As part of their overall policy towards the conquered Christian peoples, the Ottomans transferred almost all civil authority of the former Serbian state to the patriarchs of Peć, whereas all other Orthodox churches in Greece, Bulgaria and Romania came under the jurisdiction of the patriarchate at Constantinople (Savić 1918: 63–64; Salihagić 1940: 15; Banac 1984: 64).

The Patriarchate of Peć was called Serbian, consequently all the Christian Orthodox people living under its jurisdiction were called 'Serbs', which meant the same as 'Orthodox'. All churches were called 'Serbian Orthodox' or the shorter 'Serbian churches', 'Serbian monasteries', 'Serbian schools', and so on. The terms Serb and Serbian had a purely religious denotation, not national. When the Ottoman Empire began losing power and economic pressure on the raya grew, all movements and insurrections were religious in nature or, as was said, were fought for the honourable cross; they were economic in nature, too, in the interest of achieving golden freedom. But later, when the national consciousness developed, earlier religious-economic movements and insurrections took on national colours (Rebac 1930: 7–8).

Despite this, the tolerance and multiculturalism did not mean that those who lived in late Ottoman Bosnia really formed a kind of happy family, as British archaeologist and traveller Arthur Evans put it (Evans 1876: 273). They were indeed allowed to practise their religion, but they were second-class citizens all the same, with higher offices being available only to Muslims. They did not mix but instead lived their lives side by side, each in their own *mahalla* (quarter), and were animated with the strong sentiments of enmity and rancour for one another (Jedan Domorodac 1842: 58; Denton 1876: 162).

Riding the Wave of Imperialism

Historian Kemal Haşim Karpat explains that the millet system was a social-cultural and communal framework based, for the most part, on religion as well as on ethnicity. Religion gave each millet a universal belief system, while ethnic and linguistic differences provided for divisions and subdivisions within each one of the two Christian millets (Karpat 1982: I, 142). When a new spirit of national consciousness awoke among the peoples of the millets, they attempted to create civil laws to replace religious ones. This happened as a result of an ever-growing gap between the Ottoman Empire and the modernizing West. They had to reorganize themselves on national lines if they were to hold their own in modern international politics, because nationality was the contemporary basis of Western states, and owing to the ascendancy of the West in the world, the relations of non-Western peoples to each other and to Western powers had to approximate to the forms that the Western world took for granted. However, according to Arnold Toynbee, this principle of nationality in politics was taken for granted in Western Europe simply because it had grown naturally out of the special conditions, not because it was of universal application (Toynbee 1922: 15–16).

Ottoman administration divided the population of Bosnia and Herzegovina on the basis of religion into two groups: the Turks (Muslims) and the Vlachs (all other religions). The Muslims were the privileged group on account of other religions – rayahs. Croatian author Matija Mažuranić, who visited Bosnia from 1839 to 1840, observed that Christians in Bosnia were not allowed to call themselves *Bošnjaci* (Bosniaks). The name was reserved exclusively for the ruling Muslims, and for them the rest were merely *raja Bošnjačka* (Bosnian rayah) or *vlasi* (Vlachs). The Vlachs, however, differentiated between themselves: some were *Šokci*, and the others *Šiaci* (Jedan Domorodac 1842: 5, 53, 58; Thomson 1897: 170; Radić 1899: 300; Čelebija 1957: I, 113).

During the twentieth century, the inhabitants of Bosnia and Herzegovina learned in elementary school to give their national affiliation when replying to the same question, although for most of them it was hard to conceive the novelty brought about by the concept of nation, and they simply adopted it as a translation of millet. Identification with the millet, or religious community, was replaced with the more secular concept of *narod* (nation). However, by doing so they did not cut the ties between nation and religion. At the beginning of the twentieth century, for the majority of people in Bosnia and Herzegovina, for centuries divided as members of three different religious groups, a national community that would embrace people of diverse religious affiliations was simply inconceivable. For them, it was hard to comprehend how one could have something in common with a neighbour of a different faith (Kurtović 1914: 36–37).

In his memoirs, which he dictated to the stenographer Mohorić in 1901, Fra Grgo Martić remarked that in 1848 there was no Serbdom in Bosnia; it began to flourish only in the 1860s (Martić 1906: 10, 43). Serbian and Croatian consciousness did not develop until the second half of the nineteenth century. The dragoman of the Austrian consulate in Sarajevo, Tomo Herkalović, who served there from 1862 to 1880, mentioned the Serbian Committee that was established there. It developed contacts with Orthodox priests, merchants and teachers in Bosnia and Herzegovina, and advised them to teach the people that they should not call themselves derogatory names such as *Vlach*, *Rišćanin* or *Rkač* but rather 'Serbs'; and the Roman Catholics should not call themselves *Šokci* but 'Croats' (Herkalović 1906: 17). In these nationalistic agitations, a special role was intended for teachers. In 1867, Vasilije Pelagić published a manual for Serbian teachers in which he explained to them that their first goal should be to teach their pupils to properly answer the question 'Who are you?' by replying 'I am a Serb' (Hadžijahić 1974: 48). We can imagine what this form of education looked like from a description by a Serbian journalist and historian, Danilo Medaković (1819–81), who himself attended a Serbian school in Lika (modern-day Croatia). At the beginning of a new school year the catechist (Orthodox priest) asked his pupils 'Who are you?' If someone responded with 'A Vlach', the catechist would react quickly with a knock on his head followed by the remark: 'You are a Serb, you wretch!' In this manner the pupils quickly learned that they were Serbs, not Vlachs (Popović 1882: 594–95).

The Croatian national movement in Bosnia and Herzegovina was younger than the Serbian one, and it also developed at a slower pace. In his travel report from north-eastern Bosnia in 1842, Bosnian Franciscan Ivan Frano Jukić gave a description of a local hat called a *hrvatka* or *rvatka*. Upon his enquiry into the origins of the name, nobody could tell him; and nor did they know about the *Hrvati* (Croats), not even the name (Jukić 1953: 94). In 1867, an association was set up in Sarajevo with the task of abolishing the name *Šokac* and introducing the name *Hrvat* (Croat) instead. Members of the association were young Franciscans as well as the dragoman of the Prussian consulate, Klement Božić. According to Herkalović, when Božić noticed what the Serbs were doing, he became frightened they would capture the whole of Bosnia. He rose against the process of Serbianization, proving that Bosnia was a Croatian land. He paid visits to all Roman Catholic monasteries and churches with the objective of making Bosnia a Croatian land. Herkalović says that Božić did for the Croats what the Serb Committee did for the Serbs: the names *katolik* and *šokac* were replaced with *Hrvat* (Herkalović 1906: 19–20). However, as reported by Antun Radić in 1899, this process was quite slow, as he was able to inadvertently assure himself many times during his travels that 'the Croatian name in Bosnia and Herzegovina was absolutely unknown to the rural people' (Radić 1899: 308–9).

Serbian and Croatian national awakening in Bosnia and Herzegovina had its roots in impulses from abroad, from neighbouring Serbia and Croatia (Hadžijahić 1974: 45). Bosnia and Herzegovina was surrounded by Roman Catholic and Christian Orthodox communities, the Croats and the Serbs, who spoke the same language as their co-confessionals in Bosnia and Herzegovina. These neighbours also enjoyed varying degrees of great-power protection, which made their cooperation with the Bosnian Muslims less attractive (Glenny 2000: 162). What they had in common was the fact that national differentiation was based on confession: Bosnian Orthodox identifying themselves as Serbs, and Bosnian Catholics as Croats. Both the Serbs and the Croats started their national propagandas in Bosnia and Herzegovina as two different political parties interested only in their followers and sympathizers. As they strove to strengthen themselves, they worked on attracting the Muslims to their sides. Such propaganda, however, attracted only a small number of Muslims, who typically always refused to identify themselves nationally as Serbs or Croats (Kurtović 1914: 45; Hadžijahić 1974: 5, 159; Purivatra 1974: 538).

Because the struggle of the Cross and Crescent in Bosnia and Herzegovina lived on until the end of the Ottoman era, and with it the hatred between the Muslims and Christians, modern nationalism could not fully develop there. Although the people of the two provinces had a common ethnic origin and spoke the same language, there was no community between followers of different religions; solidarity went hand in hand with faith, and faith was the basis for differentiation between them. This was the reason the members of all three main religious communities lived side by side, separated from the others by an unsurmountable wall of exclusion and unable to form a single community.

The process of nationalization accelerated after the Austro-Hungarian occupation in 1878. In a series of articles titled 'The Mohammedans and the National Question', which were published in the Croatian periodical *Hrvatska*, a Muslim from Bosnia, who signed his name as Fehim, wrote that until the occupation, people in Bosnia and Herzegovina had not even known about their nationality. Referring to themselves based on their regional origin, they were either *Bošnjaci*, *Hercegovci* or *Krajišnici* (the inhabitants of Krajina), and they called their language *naški* (ours). Nonetheless, after the occupation, when the rattling of swords and the shooting of guns had ceased, everything took a new direction. People started to read and write, and began to take an interest in newspapers and in events in the world around them. Then, they also started to think about the questions: 'Who are we?' and 'Where are we?' (Bogdanov 1895: 21).

If in the West during the process of modernization religion had steadily been losing its influence on public life, in Bosnia and Herzegovina it remained very much alive, 'a real watershed of individual nations' (Dugandžija 1985: 80). It remained an important factor in defining their national identity, as a Croat was still identified as a Catholic, and a Serb as an Orthodox. With Muslims, this was even more obvious: here, a *musliman* (a member of a religious community) became a *Musliman* (a member of a nation) (Salihagić 1940: 21; Hadžijahić 1974: 238; Purivatra 1974: 572; Dugandžija 1986: 18). In other words, the wall that had previously divided the different religious groups was almost intact in the process of nationalization (Rebac 1930: 29). As a result, in that process, the inhabitants of Bosnia and Herzegovina adopted the term *nacija* (nation) simply as a translation of the old term 'millet' (Jelić 1930: 12).

The Bosnian Muslims reacted to the pressure they were exposed to from their Christian fellow citizens by strengthening their unity. Every attack on Muslims provoked the need for self-defence, which they could only achieve by strengthening mutual interconnection and creating a closer unity. The importance of the religious factor was fostered under these conditions (Purivatra 1974: 542). Josip Ljubić, writing under the pen name Ild Bogdanov, explained how an unwanted result of the endeavours of the Serbian and Croatian nationalists in Bosnia and Herzegovina was the rise of the Bosniaks. The Serbs alleged that Bosnia east of the Vrbas River belonged to Serbia and that its inhabitants were Serbs, while the Croats assumed that all inhabitants of Bosnia who wrote using Latin characters were Croats. There were also some Serbs who claimed all inhabitants of Bosnia were Serbs, and some Croats who held them for Croats. A result of this nationalistic exclusivism was the rise of the Bosniak identity – the Muslims – who, according to Ljubić, proclaimed themselves a separate nation and simply copied the Serbs and Croats by applying their logic to themselves (Bogdanov 1895: 23–24).

Since national belonging in centuries past also denoted class divisions within society, in the process of the nationalization of society, some families divided themselves between Christianity and Islam so as to have friends on both sides, no matter what happened. In such cases, the members of the family recognized each other as relatives, but generally used different names for the two branches conveying the same meaning in Slavic and Turkish respectively – for example, Rajković and Dženetić (*raj* and *dženet*, from Turkish *cennet*, both meaning 'paradise'), and Sokolić and Šahinagić (*sokol* and *şahin* both meaning 'falcon') (Eliot 1900: 380).

In Bosnia and Herzegovina, nationalism emphasized similarities and solidarity among brothers by blood and tongue, while at the same time it underlined differences between members of a certain nation and its immediate foreign neighbours, citizens of the same country. In order to successfully conceal essential similarities among nations, nationalists of all nations jointly emphasized small differences between them, both in the present and the past. In nationalist rhetoric, nations were the embodiment of differences among people; therefore, the images of members of different nations were clearly distinctive from one another, especially among neighbouring nations (Kuljić 2006: 191). Everyone's national colours included the narcissism of small differences written in gold lettering. Nonetheless, these small differences gave rise to serious consequences, most notably perhaps in Bosnia and Herzegovina.

Nationalists created national histories in accordance with their views, and used this basis to form the political community of the present and determine the direction of its development in the future. National leaders also had significant help from science in their efforts (see e.g. Bartulović 2013: 140). Historians provided interpretations of the real 'national' history, while ethnologists devoted special attention to uncovering those authentic (i.e. distinguishing) elements of national material culture, national traditions and customs, and national songs and art that clearly distinguished a nation from its neighbours. The press made scientific findings available to the masses, while exhibitions and museum displays presented them as obvious and permanent.

Constructing the Bosnian Nation

At the Berlin Congress, Count Andrássy, commenting on possible problems in executing the occupation of Bosnia and Herzegovina, foretold that Austria–Hungary would carry it out with one music band and one army regiment 'in the most peaceful manner' (Ljubović 1895: 3). However, when the Berlin Congress gave mandate to Austria–Hungary for the occupation, Bosnian Muslims were very disappointed, objecting that Bosnia and Herzegovina was their homeland and that the sultan could have given away Istanbul if he wanted to, but not Bosnia and Herzegovina. They pledged that they would resist the occupation with arms (Kreševljaković 1937: 18). And they did so with great resilience and enthusiasm, as witnessed by Lieutenant Jernej de Andrejka, who served in the Austro-Hungarian occupation forces. The occupation was not a triumphant march but a bloody adventure that lasted more than three months and left many dead and wounded lying scattered across the two provinces (Andrejka 1904; Martić 1906: 96–108; see also chapters by Martin Gabriel and František Šístek in this volume). After the occupation, many Muslims left Bosnia and Herzegovina in fear that they would lose their religion. 'Bosnia flooded Turkey', they used to say in Bosnia (Messner-Sporšić 1937: 241).

Armed resistance was mainly the struggle of the Muslims; only a few Serbs took part, and no Croats. The Muslims who, during the centuries of Ottoman rule, had grown accustomed to enjoying the privileged status of landowners, found it difficult to accept the equal status of their Christian co-citizens. They had taken it for granted that the Ottoman Empire was good for Muslims because it was a Muslim state, and on account of this they were afraid that in a Christian state they would have to assume the status of raya (Kurtović 1914: 9–10). The Bosnian Serbs, on the other hand, were worried that their hopes for unification with Serbia would be thwarted by the Austro-Hungarian occupation. This common enemy was instrumental in creating a platform for common political action on the part of the Bosnian Muslims and Serbs. Together, they resisted the new regime, declaring it provisional and arguing that the sultan was the only legitimate sovereign of Bosnia and Herzegovina. An expression of this common cause were celebrations of the sultan's birthday held from 1900 until annexation in 1908 (Bogičević 1969: 325).

In order to foil rapprochement between the Bosnian Muslims and the Serbs, the new regime abandoned the old feudal system of land ownership, which greatly worsened relations between the Muslims and the Orthodox Christians

(Begović 1938: 33). The administration also pitted the Croats against the Serbs, and encouraged the Bosnian Croats and Muslims to cooperate (Sked 1989: 245). However, the most important and effective means of dividing the population into smaller units antagonistic to one another was the particular way the Austro-Hungarian administration allocated political offices between the three main religious groups. A seed of discord was sown between the Orthodox and Roman Catholic Christians, and it bore plentiful fruit. The Bosnian government took care to ensure that three different schools operated in the two provinces, strictly educating the Muslims as Muslims, the Orthodox as Orthodox Christians, and the Croats as Croats. Within this framework, religious conversions became a political question of the greatest importance. Although conversions were rare, numbering only about twenty-five per year at the turn of the century (Čupić-Amrein 1987: 97), the hierarchy and laity of all three major religions were especially sensitive on the matter, and conversions provoked more demonstrations, petitions, and communal infighting than any other issue in Bosnia and Herzegovina following the occupation (see e.g. Jedan Domorodac 1842: 21; Durham 1920: 161). According to Misha Glenny, this had little to do with piety and everything to do with politics (Glenny 2000: 267–68). Political leaders of the three main religious groups opposed conversions so as to secure their positions. In order to achieve this, no means seemed improper (see e.g. Chaumette 1822: 73–75; Jedan Domorodac 1842: 21; Durham 1905: 161).

In the mid-nineteenth century, almost half of the population of Bosnia and Herzegovina was Christian Orthodox. Next in number were the Muslims, with the Roman Catholics forming the smallest group (Jedan Domorodac 1842: 54; Mužík 1876: 25; Kurtović 1914: 54; Čurkina et al. 1997: 187). Ethnically, they were almost all Southern Slavs, divided by their religions into the Orthodox, also *hrišćani*, *Grci* and *Vlasi* (Serbs), Muslims (Turks) and Catholics, also *kršćani*, *Šokci* and *Latini* (Croats) (Mužík 1876: 25). After the occupation, these divisions offered the Austro-Hungarian administration a good basis for the application of the legendary imperialistic principle *divide et impera* (Wendel 1925: 491). The Bosnian and Herzegovinian political elites, unable to shed their old habit of seeing the world around them exclusively through the lens of religion (Rebac 1930: 20–21), played into their hands.

Particularly in the period of Benjámin von Kállay, who served as Austro-Hungarian minister of finance and administrator of the Condominium of Bosnia and Herzegovina from 1882 to 1903, the Austro-Hungarian administration worked hard to extinguish the consciousness of ethnic proximity of the local population with the Serbs of Serbia. Minister Kállay followed this aim so enthusiastically that he even declared it illegal to read a history of the Serbs (Kalláy 1878) that he himself wrote (Wendel 1925: 491).[2] He proclaimed the Bosnian nation on a scientific basis, negating the existence of the Serbian and Croatian nations in Bosnia and Herzegovina, and abolished the name 'Serbian' and the term 'Serbo-Croatian language' for the vernacular, replacing it with the 'Bosnian language' (Kurtović 1914: 10–11; Rizvić 1973: I, 69). Serbian newspapers and books with any national content were banned, and public speeches were not allowed. Austro-Hungarian authorities supported Bosnian patriotism in the hope of strengthening old separatist tendencies. They introduced a new Bosnian flag and started a new newspaper called the *Bošnjak*, which was intended for Bosnian Muslim readers with the aim of turning them away from Serbian influence (Kurtović 1914: 11; Ćorović 1925: 81).

The political, educational and entertainment newspaper *Bošnjak* first appeared on 2 July 1891, and was intended to support Kállay's efforts. As explained in the editorial on the front page of the first issue, the objective of the publication was to show the civilized world 'what kind of noble attributes our dear Allah has given us' (Anon. 1891a: 1). In Issue no. 4, the author of the editorial further explained that Bosnian Muslims felt uneasy due to the pressure from *rišćani* and *katolici* who, in their view, sought to appropriate not only their ('our') language but also take away the dear heritage left to them by their ancestors (Anon. 1891b: 1).

The Muslim political elite found themselves under pressure from the Serbian and Croatian sides to politically and culturally Serbianize or Croatianize. Concerned for their Muslim identity and for the land they had inherited in Ottoman times, they were not prepared to accept either a land reform or a common Bosnian identity (Džaja 2004: 200; see also M.M. 1892: 1).

Such views, based on a one-sided political ideology that took into consideration exclusively the interests of the Muslims, were unacceptable to their Christian Orthodox and Roman Catholic co-citizens, more so if they worked towards the imposition of the name 'Bošnjak' on all the inhabitants of Bosnia and Herzegovina on the basis of Muslim superiority and aboriginity (Rizvić 1973: I, 116–17). Issue no. 2 presented a poem by Safvet-beg Bašagić dedicated to the Bošnjak, with two short but telling verses:

> *Od Trebinja do brodskijeh vrata*
> *Nije bilo Srba ni Hrvata.*[3] (S.B. 1891: 2)

As a result of religious divisions during Ottoman rule, Bosnian Muslim politicians were not capable of mobilizing the Bosnian Christian masses. Since not a single religious group could claim an absolute majority, and because they were also territorially scattered throughout the two provinces, Bosnian Christians sensed a degree of security in becoming, on the basis of their Orthodox or Catholic religious affiliation, a part of the Serbian or Croat national orientation, and looked for support from Christian Orthodox Serbia or Roman Catholic Croatia. There was no such possibility at hand for the Bosnian Muslims, who turned their attention to the past and learned that in the mid-fifteenth century the name 'Bošnjanin' was used to denote the inhabitants of Bosnia. A number of tombstones of local nobles preserved from the middle ages bore the chiselled inscription 'Here lies a good Bosnian (*dobar Bošnjanin*)'. Writing in 1940, Suljaga Salihagić argued that a country with its own statehood, its own religion, and its own script also had its own national Bosnian name and its own Bosnian name for the language. Ever since the Bosnian Ban Kulin (d. 1204), the inhabitants of Bosnia had called themselves Bošnjani; later this name changed to Bošnjaci (Salihagić 1940: 10–12).

Ousting of the Bosnian Spirit

When the Kingdom of Serbs, Croats and Slovenes was established in 1918, it was inaugurated as a nation state of a single nation with three names. In the new nation state, Muslims were treated as part of the Serbian and Croatian nations (as the Serb-Mohammedans or Croat-Mohammedans), the official explanation being that they were not aware of their 'tribal name', or that they were anational. From this standpoint, the ethnical individuality of the Bosnian Muslims was negated in the service of the question of to whom the two provinces belonged – the Serbs or the Croats. This is why Serbian and Croatian nationalists insisted on the nationalization of Muslims in Bosnia and Herzegovina as Serbs or Croats. In their attempts to nationalize the Muslims, the Serbian and Croatian nationalists engaged their cultural, political, economic, social, educational and scientific capabilities to prove the Serbian or Croatian origins of the Bosnian Muslims and to strengthen their national identity (Purivatra 1974: 551–52). Various Muslim intellectuals and politicians who had been educated in Belgrade or Zagreb also followed this line, together with Muslim cultural associations such as the Serbian Muslim cultural society Gajret and the pro-Croatian Muslim cultural society Narodna uzdanica (ibid.: 546–47). It was not uncommon for individual members of the same family to adopt different national identities. Thus, in Sarajevo, for instance, in the Spaho family, a member of which was Mehmed Spaho, leader of the Yugoslav Muslim Organization, one brother, later Reis-ul-ulema Fehim Spaho, declared himself a Croat, and a second, Mustafa, declared himself a Serb. Mehmed Spaho remained silent (Hadžijahić 1974: 226).

Since the members of all Bosnian communities considered their religion the finest, their history the most beautiful, and their dialect the most right and proper, they all guarded them jealously and sought to impose them on the rest of the community. This resulted in increased antagonism and friction, an unstable foundation upon which to unite the whole population into a single body (Salihagić 1940: 37). After liberation and unification in 1918, political newspapers began to emerge, and the number of political parties mushroomed. Characteristically for Bosnia and Herzegovina, all these political parties and groups were founded on the national (respectively religious) basis. Thus, as conveyed by the newspaper *Glas slobode*, the two provinces soon had a Serbian democracy, a Croatian democracy, and a Muslim democracy: one people with three different democracies divided by religion into Orthodox, Catholic and Muslim factions (cit. by Janković 1959: 108). There was no one to establish an initiative designed to mobilize everyone regardless of their group affiliation. If a course was held, it was organized on the basis of religious affiliation; if cooperation was set up, it was done so on the basis of religion; and if a school was built, it too was built on the basis of religious affiliation. They were divided in every aspect as though they were complete strangers (Rebac 1930: 22–23). Political, cultural, economic and educational groupings on the religious and national basis gave rise in the two provinces to mutual antagonism (Janković 1959: 108–9). Thus, after 1918, Bosnia and Herzegovina continued on the path that was well trodden in the times of Austria–Hungary: 'Everywhere division, belligerency, and almost hatred' (Rebac 1930: 22).

Official favouring of *Bošnjaštvo* (Bosnian nationalism) during the era of Benjámin von Kállay, however, did more to compromise this ideology than support it. Kállay's regime was hugely unpopular, especially with the Serbs, who equated official support for Bošnjaštvo as a common national identity to imposing a foreign national identity on already formed Serbian and (to a lesser extent) Croatian national identities. Serbian and Croatian national movements resolutely resisted any efforts in this direction. An ideologue of the Mlada Bosna (Young Bosnia) nationalist movement, Pero Slijepčević, wrote in 1910:

> Our younger generation should know just two native names: the Serbs and Croats. Bosnia and Herzegovina must no longer be Bosnian but simply Serbian and Croatian, and the language not *zemaljski* nor Bosnian but Serbo-Croatian. (Cit. by Hadžijahić 1974: 45–46)

After the end of the First World War and national unification in 1918, Bošnjaštvo stood as 'an artificial product of Benjámin Kállay, or foreign administration, and as such it was strictly criticized, in particular by the Serbian side, which behaved as the conqueror and the liquidator of *austrijanština*'[4] (Džaja 2004: 200). Serbian and Croatian nationalists insisted that *Bošnjakluk* (Bosnian national identity) never existed at all, and they created the new term *Bosanac* in place of 'Bošnjak', with the intention of replacing the national name with the provincial one (Salihagić 1940: 37). No Bosnian Muslim political leaders, not even those from the Yugoslav Muslim Organization, endorsed Bošnjaštvo as the national identity of Muslims in Bosnia and Herzegovina. They deemed the idea of Bošnjaštvo so rotten that it could bear no healthy fruit. Only Seidalija Filipović, a deputy in the Constitutive Assembly, declared himself a Bošnjak (Purivatra 1974: 570).

The majority of Southern Slav Christian historians claimed that the Ottomans spread Islam with fire and the sword, presenting themselves as the embodiment of toleration and as having exterminated Islam from Lika, Slavonia, and quite recently from Serbia too (Salihagić 1940: 14). After 1918, the tables began to turn in Bosnia and Herzegovina, and the religious toleration of the bygone era gave way to change: many mosques were demolished, as regulation plans typically targeted them and deemed them to be in danger of collapse (ibid.: 15).

As could be expected,[5] the pressure on Bosnian Muslims to nationalize – that is, to opt for a Serbian or Croatian identity – only increased after the establishment of the Kingdom of Serbs, Croats and Slovenes. Soon, the very name Bošnjak became a source of fury (Salihagić 1940: 10). In public meetings organized by the Yugoslav Muslim Organization, the main political party of Bosnian Muslims in the Kingdom of Serbs, Croats and Slovenes, participants were repetitively heckled with hostile calls: 'Go to Asia!' (Purivatra 1974: 102–3). An appropriate ideology was created for action against Muslims, framing it as retribution for crimes committed by Muslims against the Serbs immediately after the assassination in 1914, as well as those carried out by the *Schutzkorps* (Purivatra 1974: 65). Charles Rivet, a correspondent to the Parisian *Temps*, testified that Reis-ul-ulema Džemaludin Čaušević told him in Sarajevo (in the presence of two prominent representatives of the Bosnian Muslims and a high-ranking French general) regarding the situation of the Muslims in the new nation state:

> Thousands of men were killed, six women burned, 270 villages robbed and destroyed. This is the balance for us Muslims during the solemn creation of Yugoslavia, which we were prepared to serve with all our soul. We are still Slavs, but the Serbs refuse to consider us as such. They consider us to be intruders. (Rivet 1919: 170)

In the press, in political meetings, and even in the National Assembly of the Kingdom of Serbs, Croats and Slovenes, time and again the question was raised regarding the status of the Muslims in the new South Slavic nation state. Should they be tolerated after five hundred years of their tyrannical rule over Christians? (Salihagić 1940: 34). Bosnian Muslims were systematically pressured to nationalize or declare themselves Serbs or Croats. Moreover, after King Alexander abolished the constitution in 1929 and proclaimed integral Yugoslavism, the regime insisted that the Muslims should declare themselves Serbs, not Yugoslavs, and that adopting Serbian (or Croatian) identity was a precondition for adopting Yugoslav identity (Hadžijahić 1974: 223, 239). After 1918, the majority of the teachers in the school system in Bosnia and Herzegovina were Serbs (as had been the case with the Croats after 1878), and they taught their students to nationalize in the Serbian sense (ibid.: 186).

Under this pressure, Bosnian Muslims were forced, like it or not, to think about who they were: Serbs or Croats, Yugoslavs, or perhaps just Slavs (Salihagić 1940: 34). There was no instant or clear answer to these questions, and the political rivalries between the Serbs and Croats only contributed to the confusion. Serbian and Croatian nationalism among Bosnian Muslims was largely built on mutual negation. Thus, for the Muslims, accepting Serbian or Croatian identity implied an anti-Croatian or anti-Serbian orientation (Hadžijahić 1974: 216). To make matters worse, religion remained the primary factor of national differentiation (ibid.: 243). The way faith and the nation were interwoven in Bosnia and Herzegovina illustrates the very title of the principal ecclesiastic of the Orthodox Church, the 'Serbian Patriarch'; and several Orthodox clerics publicly claimed that Serbdom was identical to Orthodoxy, even though some Muslims (as well as a few Catholics), who under no circumstances would acknowledge the Patriarch as their religious head, declared themselves Serbs (Salihagić 1940: 39–40).

In the programmes of the political parties in Bosnia and Herzegovina, an important place was given to religious questions, and they played a dominant role in political action. Serbian, Croatian and Muslim politicians used the same routine in their efforts to mobilize their respective masses in the two provinces. Political meetings, for instance, were held at the time of religious ceremonies, religious prayers, and similar occasions in the courtyard of mosques, in *maktabs* (religious schools), and other religious facilities (Purivatra 1974: 541, 544). During parliamentary elections, religious motives were stirred up. Political leaders of the Yugoslav Muslim Organization repeatedly alleged that Islam was endangered (*din je u opasnosti*) and that it should be rescued. According to Čedomil Mitrinović, it meant that Islam was under threat from the Christians – that is to say, the giaours – and he further questioned the real meaning of the Yugoslav name in the official title of the main Muslim political party in Bosnia and Herzegovina (Mitrinović 1926: 70).

Although Muslims in Bosnia and Herzegovina were under intense and unrelenting pressure, as if between a rock and a hard place, the majority of them were not willing to decide for either the Serbian or the Croatian national idea, with the exception of a part of the Muslim intelligentsia who accepted one ideology or the other, albeit more so in political and cultural terms. Bosnian Muslims, above all their intelligentsia, were inclined to favour the overcoming of the division between the Serbs and Croats, and substitute it with the Yugoslav (or Bosnian) identity, with expectations for complete respect of the Muslim component. Hence, Yugoslav (or Bosnian) identity actually endeavoured to avoid disagreeable Serbian and Croatian identifications, since the former would upset the Croats, and the latter would provoke the Serbs. The emphasis on Muslim, Bosnian or Yugoslav identity produced the same result. Regarding their nationality in Bosnia and Herzegovina, the Muslims understood themselves to be a distinct group regardless of the Muslim, Bosnian or Yugoslav name. By creating youth organizations in the 1930s, the national movement in Bosnia and Herzegovina achieved full expression and revolutionary strength. Educated Muslims largely opted for Serbian nationality and gathered around Gajret; one part, however, defined themselves as Croats, stood for Yugoslav nationalism, and gathered around Mlada Bosna (Begović 1938: 34). Thus, by joining forces and taking advantage of mutual exclusivism, the political and/or religious leaders of the three main groups ensured that the divisions between different communities in Bosnia and Herzegovina would perpetuate themselves for many years to come.

Božidar Jezernik is a professor at the Department of Ethnology and Cultural Anthropology, University of Ljubljana, Slovenia. His monograph *Wild Europe: The Balkans in the Gaze of Western Travellers* (London: Saqi Books, 2004) has been translated into Turkish, Polish, Serbian, Italian, Albanian, Slovenian, Bulgarian, German, Russian, and Czech. His book on coffee and coffeehouses, *Kava – čarobni napoj* [Coffee – a magical drink] (Ljubljana: Modrijan Založba, 2012) received the Gourmand Award Best in the World (Beijing, 2014) and the Gourmand Award Best Coffee Book (Yentai, 2015). His recent publications include the monograph *Jugoslavija, zemlja snova* [Yugoslavia, land of dreams] (Beograd: Biblioteka XX vek, 2018). He edited the volume *Imagining 'the Turk'* (Newcastle upon Tyne: Cambridge Scholars, 2010), which was translated into Serbian, Turkish, Slovenian and Albanian. In 2015, Jezernik received the Matija Murko Award for his lifetime achievements.

Notes

1. An offensive term used in the Ottoman Empire for Christians in the Balkans.
2. The Bosnian name for the language spoken in Bosnia and Herzegovina was also supported by the renowned Croatian Slavist Vatroslav Jagić. Jagić argued, firstly, that giving preference to one name – be it Serbian or Croatian – would provoke opposition from the other side. Then, as the name 'Bosnian language' had been in use in the seventeenth and eighteenth centuries, he agreed that the government in Bosnia and Herzegovina, 'as long as we do not agree', might use this name (Jagić 1896: 1).
3. 'From Trebinje to the gates of Brod / There were no Serbs nor Croats.'
4. A relic of the Austrian era.
5. As recollected by Croatian sculptor Ivan Meštrović, a leading Serbian politician, Stojan Protić, said to him: 'When our army crosses the Drina, it will give the Turks 24 hours, maybe even 48, to return to the religion of their ancestors; and those who would not want to do so, we will hew down, as we did in Serbia in former times' (Meštrović 1961: 73).

References

Andrejka, Jernej pl. 1904. *Slovenski fantje v Bosni in Hercegovini 1878*. Celovec: Družba sv. Mohorja.
Anonymous. 1891a. 'Čitaocima "Bošnjaka"', *Bošnjak*, 2 July, p. 1.
Anonymous. 1891b. 'Svačije poštujemo a svojim se dičimo', *Bošnjak*, 23 July, p. 1.
Asboth, Johann de. 1890. *An Official Tour through Bosnia and Herzegovina*. London: Swan Sonnenschein.

Baker, B. Granville. 1913. *The Passing of the Turkish Empire in Europe*. London: Seeley, Service & Co.
Banac, Ivo. 1984. *The National Question in Yugoslavia: Origins, History, Politics*. Ithaca, NY: Cornell University Press.
Bartulović, Alenka. 2013. *'Nismo vaši!' Antinacionalizem v povojnem Sarajevu*. Ljubljana: Znanstvena založba Filozofske fakultete.
Begović, Mehmed. 1938. *Muslimani u Bosni i Hercegovini*. Beograd: A.M. Popović.
Belon du Mans, Pierre. 1554. *Les observations de plvsievrs singvlatitez & chosez memorables, trouuées en Greece, Asie, Iudée, Egypte, Arabie, & autres pays estranges, redigées en trois liures*. Paris: Gilles Corrozer.
Bogdanov, Ild. 1895. *Spor izmegju Srba i Hrvata*. Zadar: Izdanje štamparije S. Artale.
Bogičević, Vojislav. 1969. 'Džulusi-humajun hazreti šerifi'. *Godišnjak Društva istoričara Bosne i Hercegovine*, god. XVII, pp. 315–40.
Burbury, John. 1671. *A Relation of a Journey of the Right Honourable My Lord Henry Howard, From London to Vienna, and thence to Constantinople*. London: T. Collins, I. Ford & Hickman.
Čelebija, Evlija. 1957. *Putopis*. Sarajevo: Svjetlost.
Chaumette des Fossés, Amédée. 1822. *Voyage en Bosnie dans les années 1807 et 1808*. Paris: J. Didot.
Ćorović, Vladimir. 1925. *Bosna i Hercegovina*. Beograd: Srpska književna zadruga.
Čupić-Amrein, Martha M. 1987. *Die Opposition gegen die österreichisch-ungarische Herrschaft in Bosnien-Hercegovina (1878–1914)*. Bern: Peter Lang.
Curipeschitz, Benedict. 1531. *Itinerarivm Wegrayß kön. May. potschaft gen Constantinopel zudem Türkischen keiser Soleyman*. Vienna.
Čurkina, Iskra V., et al. 1997. *Na putah k Jugoslavii: za i protiv*. Moskva: Indrik.
Dallaway, James. 1797. *Constantinople Ancient and Modern, with Excursions to the Shores and Islands of the Archipelago and to the Troad*. London: T. Cadell Jun. & W. Davies.
Denton, William. 1876. *The Christians of Turkey: Their Condition under Musliman Rule*. London: Daldy, Isbister & Co.
Dugandžija, Nikola. 1985. *Jugoslavenstvo*. Beograd: NIRO 'Mladost'.
———. 1986. *Religija i nacija. Istraživanje u zagrebačkoj regiji*. Zagreb: Stvarnost.
Du Mont, Jean. 1696. *A New Voyage to the Levant*. London: M. Gillyflower, T. Goodwin, M. Wotton, J. Walthoe and R. Parker.
Durham, Mary Edith. 1905. *The Burden of the Balkans*. London: Edward Arnold.
———. 1920. *Twenty Years of Balkan Tangle*. London: George Allen & Unwin.
Džaja, Srećko M. 2004. *Politička realnost jugoslavenstva (1918–1991): S posebnim osvrtom na Bosnu i Hercegovinu*. Sarajevo: Svjetlo riječi.
Edib, Halidé. 1930. *Turkey Faces West: A Turkish View on Recent Changes and Their Origin*. New Haven, CT: Yale University Press.
Eliot, Charles Norton Edgeumbe. 1900. *Turkey in Europe*. London: Edward Arnold.
Evans, Arthur John. 1876. *Through Bosnia and Herzegovina on Foot during the Insurrection, August and September 1875; With an Historical Overview of Bosnia; And a Glimpse at the Croats, Slavonians, and the Ancient Republic of Ragusa*. London: Longamns, Green, and Co.
Garnett, Lucy M.J. 1911. *Turkey of the Ottomans*. London: Sir Isaac Pitman.
Gil'ferding, Aleksandr. 1859. *Poezdka po Gercegovine, Bosnii i Staroj Serbii*. S. Peterburg: Zapiski imperatorskago russkago geograficheskago obshchestva XIII.
Glenny, Misha. 2000. *The Balkans: Nationalism, War and the Great Powers, 1904–1999*. New York: Viking.

Hadžijahić, Muhamed. 1974. *Od tradicije do identiteta: Geneza nacionalnog pitanja bosanskih Muslimana*. Sarajevo: Svjetlost.
Herkalović, Thomas. 1906. *Vorgeschichte der Occupation Bosniens und der Herzegovina*. Zagreb: Druck von Milivoj Majcen.
Jagić, Vatroslav. 1896. 'Naziv "bosanski"', *Bošnjak*, 16 July, p. 1.
Janković, Dragoslav. 1959. 'Društveni i politički odnosi u Kraljestvu Srba, Hrvata i Slovenaca uoči stvaranja Socijalističke radničke partije Jugoslavije (komunista)', in Dragoslav Janković et al. (eds), *Istorija XX veka*. Beograd: Kultura, pp. 7–152.
Jedan Domorodac. 1842. *Pogled u Bosnu, ili Kratak put u onu krajinu, učinjan 1839–40, po Jednom Domorodcu*. Zagreb: Tiskom i troškom kr. pr. ilir. Narodne tiskarne Dra. Ljudevita Gaja (= Matija Mažuranić).
Jelić, Milosav. 1930. *Letopis Juga: Listine – zapisi – dnevnik – pomenik*. Beograd: Štamparija 'Privrednik'.
Jezernik, Božidar. 2004. *Wild Europe: The Balkans in the Gaze of Western Travellers*. London: Saqi Books.
Jukić, Ivan Frano. 1953. *Putopisi i istorisko-etnografski radovi*. Sarajevo: Svjetlost.
Kalláy, Béni. 1878. *Geschichte der Serben*. Budapest: Lauffer.
Kapetanović Ljubušak, Mehmed beg. 1886. *Što misle muhamedanci u Bosni*. Sarajevo: Tiskom i nakladom Spindlera i Löschnera.
Karpat, Kemal H. 1982. 'Millets and Nationality: The Roots of the Incongruity of Nation and State in the Post-Ottoman Era', in Braude and Benjamin Braude and Bernard Lewis (eds), *Christians and Jews in the Ottoman Empire: The Functioning of a Plural Society*, Vol. I. New York: Holmes & Meier Publishers, pp. 141–70.
Kreševljaković, Hamdija. 1937. *Sarajevo u doba okupacije Bosne 1878*. Sarajevo: Naklada piščeva.
Kuljić, Todor. 2006. *Kultura sećanja: teorijska objašnjenja upotrebe prošlosti*. Beograd: Čigoja štampa.
Kurtović, Šukrija. 1914. *O nacionalizovanju muslimana*. Sarajevo: Štamparija 'Naroda'.
Léger, Louis. 1873. *Le monde slave: Voyages et littérature*. Paris: Didier et Cie.
Ljubović, M. Derviš Beg. 1895. *O stanju Bosne i Hercegovine*. Beograd: Štamparija Petra Đurića.
Mardin, Serif. 2000. *The Genesis of Young Ottoman Thought: A Study in the Modernization of Turkish Political Ideas*. Princeton, NJ: Syracuse University Press.
Martić, Fra Grga. 1906. *Zapamćenja (1829–1878)*. Zagreb: Nakladom Jure Trpinca.
Messner-Sporšić, Ante. 1937. *Od Bukurešta do Ankare: Crtice iz Rumunjske, Bugarske i Turske*. Zagreb: Tipografija D.D.
Meštrović, Ivan. 1961. *Uspomene na političke ljude i dogadjaje*. Buenos Aires: Knjižnica Hrvatske revije.
Mitrinović, Čedomil. 1926. *Naši muslimani: Studija za orientaciju pitanja bosansko-hercegovačkih muslimana*. Beograd: Izdanje biblioteke 'Društvo'.
M.M. starinom Bošnjak. 1892. 'Nekolike o bosanstvu. Proslejgenje, a odgovor usput uredniku "Glasa Hercegovca"', *Bošnjak*, 18 February, p. 1.
Mužík, Antonín. 1876. *Listy o Bosně, zemi a národu*. Prague: Katolický spolek tiskový.
Nicolay de Dauphinoys, N. 1568. *Les quatre premiers livres des navigations et peregrinations Orientales*. Lyon: Gvillavme Roville.
Popović, Đorđe. 1882. 'Dr. Danilo Medaković (Nekrolog.)', *Otadžbina* 9: 594–614.
Purivatra, Atif. 1974. *Jugoslavenska muslimanska organizacija u političkom životu Kraljevine Srba, Hrvata i Slovenaca*. Sarajevo: Svjetlost.

Radić, Ante. 1899. 'Izvješće urednika akademijskoga o putovańu ńegovu po Bosni i Hercegovini obavĺenu u vrijeme od 20. srpńa do 21. kolovoza 1899', in *Zbornik za narodni život i običaje Južnih Slavena*, vol. 4, pp. 292–324.
Randolph, Bernard. 1687. *The Present State of the Islands in the Archipelago*. Oxford: Theatre.
Rebac, Hasan M. 1930. *Šta je ometalo i ometa bratsku slogu Srba muslimanske i pravoslavne vere: Predavanje održano 12. maja 1930 godine u Mostaru*. Beograd: Štamparija 'Jedinstvo'.
Renan, Ernest. 1882. *Qu-est-ce qu'une nation? Conférence fait en Sorbonne, le 11 Mars 1882*. Paris: Calman Lévy.
Rivet, Charles. 1919. *En Yougoslavie*. Paris: Libraire académique Perrin et Cie.
Rizvić, Muhsin. 1973. *Književno stvaranje muslimanskih pisaca u Bosni i Hercegovini u doba austrougarske vladavine*. Sarajevo: Akademija nauka i umjetnosti Bosne i Hercegovine, Odjeljenje za književnost i umjetnost.
Ruthner, Francesco. 1877. *Un Viaggio a Maria Stella convento dei trappisti nella valle dell'Urbas presso Banjaluka in Bosnia colla descrizione della vita e delle opere dei poveri monaci di San Bernardo*. Venice: L. Merlo.
Rycaut, Paul. 1668. *The Present State of the Ottoman Empire*. London: R. & J. Dodsley.
Salihagić, Suljaga. 1940. *Mi bos. herc. muslimani u krilu jugoslovenske zajednice: Kratak politički pogled na našu prošlost od najstarijih vremena do danas*. Banja Luka: Štamparija Zvonimir Jović i Co.
Savić, Vladislav R. 1918. *South-Eastern Europe: The Main Problem of the Present World Struggle*. New York: Fleming H. Revell Company.
S.B. 1891. 'Bošnjaku', *Bošnjak*, 9 July, p. 2.
Sked, Alan. 1989. *The Decline and Fall of the Habsburg Empire 1815–1918*. London: Longman.
Sutherland, Captain. 1790. *A Tour Up the Straits, from Gibraltar to Constantinople: With the Leading Events in the Present War between the Austrians, Russians, and the Turks, to the Commencement of the Year 1789*. London: Printed for the Author.
Thomson, Harry Craufuird. 1897. *The Outgoing Turk*. London: William Heinemann.
Toynbee, Arnold J. 1922. *The Western Question in Greece and Turkey: A Study in the Contact of Civilisations*. London: Constable and Company.
Urquhart, David. 1838. *The Spirit of the East, Illustrated in a Journal of Travels through Roumeli during an Eventful Period*. London: Henry Colburn.
Voltaire, Francois Marie Arouet de. 1761. *The Works. With Notes, Historical and Critical*. London: J. Newbery, R. Baldwin, W. Johnston, S. Crowder, T. Davies, J. Coote, G. Kearsley and B. Collins.
Wendel, Hermann. 1925. *Der Kampf der Südslawen um Freiheit und Einheit*. Frankfurt am Main: Frankfurter-Sociatäts.
Yriarte, Charles. 1981. *Bosna i Hercegovina: putopis iz vremena ustanka 1875–1876*. Sarajevo: Veselin Masleša.
Zavadil, Antonín. 1911. *Obrázky z Bosny*. Prague: Josef Pelcl.

Chapter 3

AMBIVALENT PERCEPTIONS
Austria–Hungary, Bosnian Muslims and
the Occupation Campaign in Bosnia and Herzegovina (1878)

Martin Gabriel

The Strategic Setting

During the second half of the nineteenth century, political, economic and social stability in South Eastern Europe was increasingly challenged by emerging nation states, as well as by the decay of one of the great powers, the Ottoman Empire. At the end of the bloody Russo-Ottoman War (1877–78), the Tsarist Empire dictated the Peace of San Stefano (now Yeşilköy, Turkey), which, if carried out, would have served as the 'basis for its domination in the Balkans' (Grijak 2009: 64). France and Great Britain, both powers with strong strategic and economic interests in the Ottoman Empire, opposed the expansion of Russian influence; in Vienna, also, neither the emperor nor his foreign minister, Count Andrássy, wanted to accept the treaty, even at the cost of enlarging the Slavic element in the Austro-Hungarian population (which was not very popular among Hungarian political and intellectual elites) (Wertheimer 1921/22: 463; Gottas 1976: 68). An international congress summoned to Berlin (June/July 1878) took aim at one final goal: realizing a new political order in the Balkans and Eastern Europe, while, at the same time, thwarting Russian strategies to push the Ottomans from these regions. In my opinion, the story of Otto von Bismarck as an honest broker trying to create long-term stability in the Balkans (Hildebrand 1989: 10; Roberts 2007: 251), should, at least in part, be seen as a myth. It can be assumed that he attempted to find a (temporary) compromise and prevent a widespread international conflict without really solving the Eastern Question, thus enabling Germany, in the long term, to act as a referee between all the great powers of Europe (Angelow 2000: 28), a position in which German policies could be implemented without provoking other countries.

Even before diplomatic activities in Berlin began, Austro-Hungarian politicians had taken steps towards occupying Bosnia and Herzegovina. In March 1878, Andrássy asked the Reichsrat delegations for a credit of 60 million guilders; he did not clarify whether the money was to be spent on preparations for a war with Russia or the occupation of Bosnia and Herzegovina (Auffenberg-Komarów 1921: 43; Bled 1988: 333). On 14 May 1878, Count Rudolf Auersperg, on behalf of the entire government, announced that any offensive action taken by Austria–Hungary would be aimed at creating a stable and peaceful international order (Kolmer 1972: 435f).

Compared to other great powers, the Habsburg monarchy had an especially strong interest in stabilizing the Balkan region. The years from 1815 to 1845 saw a number of armed confrontations between Habsburg troops and Bosnian bands (*Banden*) in the border areas. The damage caused by illegal and criminal intrusions into Habsburg territory between 1815 and 1830 amounted to approximately 9 million guilders (Sosnosky 1913: 131). In early 1834, a total of four thousand Austrian troops were massed near the border with Bosnia after an attack in the Slunj area to prepare for a punitive expedition into Ottoman territory (Buchmann 1991: 372). Later that year the expedition became reality, and resulted in the Bosnian settlements of Tržac and Velika Kladuša being burned down by Austrian forces (Klaić 1885: 451). As the Habsburg Monarchy, following the decisions of the Congress of Vienna, had taken control of Dalmatia in 1815, the Ottoman provinces were present in the minds of political and military leaders not only because of near-permanent conflict but also because of their role in Austrian strategic planning on a larger scale. 'Bosnia and Herzegovina represented an obvious area for Austrian expansion into South East Europe. Geographically the province formed a wedge that ran deep into the Habsburg lands, making the hinterland of Dalmatia insecure from a military and economic standpoint' (Donia 1981: 8). It was insecure not only because of the possibility of armed intrusions into Austria but also because of conflict within the Ottoman territories between the central government and local interests. In 1831, Husein Kapetan Gradaščević took control of the Bosnian capital of Travnik, and marched his rebel army into Kosovo; he called for an end to reforms in the Ottoman Empire and for political autonomy for Bosnia before the uprising was crushed by army troops (Koller 2004: 71). There is little doubt that events of the nineteenth century were shaped by the specific history of Bosnia and Herzegovina. During the seventeenth and eighteenth centuries, when the Porte lost large areas in Central Europe, tens of thousands of Muslim refugees resettled in regions still under Ottoman control. In frontier areas like Bosnia and Herzegovina, oscillating between war and peace, a warrior mentality emerged, which, quite importantly, was characterized by an existential angst (Okey 2007: 5). We must also consider that it was not only the conservative elites of Bosnia and Herzegovina who were responsible for the internal and international conflicts; from the 1840s onwards, lower strata, especially Christians, had voiced unreasonable demands in their interactions with the Porte, and counted on the fact that the great powers Austria and Russia would support them against their 'Muslim oppressors' (Riedel 2005: 53). Finally, even in remote regions like Bosnia and Herzegovina, global factors came into play. When the worldwide economic crisis of 1873 hit, Ottoman bureaucracy reacted by trying to collect pending taxes to strengthen state finances – a course of action that resulted in even more violent conflict (Geiss 1991: 152). From 1875 onwards, Christian rebellions, not only against specific injustices or brutalities but against Ottoman rule itself, became a widespread phenomenon that threatened the foundations of political stability. In August of that year, around twenty thousand Bosnian Christians fled across the Sava and Una rivers into the territory of the Austro-Hungarian *Militärgrenze* (military frontier) over the course of just a few days, while many other families took refuge in Dalmatia (Mollinary 1905: II, 284f). Within one year, the number of refugees in the lands of the Habsburg Monarchy stood at roughly one hundred thousand, and costs for supplying them had risen to 4.8 million guilders in 1876 and 1877 (Gabriel 2004: 28f). Following the decisions made at the Berlin Congress, Bosnia and Herzegovina was to be 'occupied and administered by Austria–Hungary' (*occupées et administrées par l'Autriche-Hongrie*) (Classen 2004: 35). Thus, the monarchy was to take control of regions that for decades had been controlled by conservative families who saw themselves as a 'stronghold of righteousness, guardians of the old order and holding a special position within the Ottoman Empire' (Heuberger 1997: 96). Many of their values stood in stark contrast to developments in Constantinople, where (pro-Western and/or nationalist) progressives had been trying to modernize the state by ending, for example, traditional Muslim privileges (Riedel 2005: 53).

Military Operations

During his discussions with Emperor Francis Joseph, foreign minister Julius (Gyula) Andrássy argued that the number of troops (as well as the date for the beginning of military operations) depended on whether the Porte would officially agree to the occupation of the provinces. In the event no agreement could be reached, the troops were to begin their campaign even before completing their mobilization; quick action was meant to make up for lower troop strength. Initially, political leaders believed that two *Infanterie-Truppendivisionen* (infantry divisions) with about thirty-five thousand troops would be sufficient; however, in June 1878, high-ranking army officers convinced Francis Joseph to deploy four divisions (Kos 1984: 145). On 2 July, *Feldzeugmeister* (General) Joseph Philippovich von Philippsberg was named Commanding General of the XIII Army Corps, and commander-in-chief of all occupation forces (Gabriel 2004: 36).

The strategic situation was quite favourable to a well-organized resistance movement – if one existed. Observations made by the British on the Afghan frontier during the 1860s (Adye 1867: 34) applied to the situation in the occupation area: the most important positions were controlled by a local population well adapted to the climate and terrain, and trained in the warrior tradition of their homeland. Nonetheless, one must keep in mind that many inhabitants only joined the resistance movement when their immediate home seemed to be threatened; they did not participate in military operations outside their home region, and most of them aligned themselves with the new rulers very quickly.

The majority of the insurgents were recruited from the largest religious group, the Muslims, but many Christian Orthodox Serbs – who hoped for a union with Serbia (Babuna 1996: 44) – also fought against the Austro-Hungarian troops. Regarding the Muslim populace, Richard Plaschka and Clemens Ruthner have defined different levels of motivation for taking part in the resistance: (a) the desire of influential Muslims to keep alive or restore a conservative system; (b) the desire to repel invaders and to protect the *dār al-islām*; (c) the traditional perception of rebels as heroes; (d) the discontent of specific social groups paired with a large number of discharges from the Ottoman army; and (e) a feeling of having been betrayed by the government in Constantinople (Plaschka 2000: I, 89; Ruthner 2008: 3). Obviously, it would be insufficient to explain the resistance only through xenophobia and religious zeal; the fanaticism shown by many Muslim fighters should not be seen as the reason but rather as a symptom of deep-rooted social problems. Moreover, the Muslim population remained divided over the question of whether or not accepting a non-Islamic ruler (without any resistance) was sanctioned by the Qur'an (Doder 1999: 178). The activities of Serb resistance groups were motivated by political ideas rather than by the supposed Slavic 'lust for murder and fight' often mentioned by the Austro-Hungarian press (PT 1878: no. 262, 2). The small Jewish community did join the *Volkskommissionen* (people's commissions) after the Ottoman system had been overthrown in July 1878, but it remained neutral during the campaign (Koetschet 1905: 100). A majority of Catholics were neutral or actively supportive of Austria–Hungary; for example, Ivan Mušić, a Franciscan priest, formed a combat unit in Herzegovina and placed it at the disposal of the 18th Infantry Division's commander, Stephan von Jovanović (Bencze 2005: 103; DV 1878: no. 225, 2).

While the first days of Austro-Hungarian operations did not see any fighting, on 3 August 1878 a hussar squadron was ambushed near Maglaj in the

Bosna Valley, with the loss of forty-two men dead or missing; based on this event, General Philippovich ordered martial law to be implemented in the entire occupation area (Haardt 1878: 36). The operation, publicly characterized as some kind of humanitarian intervention for the good of the Balkan Christians, 'almost turned into a conquest' (Pavlowitch 1999: 116). Most military leaders, such as the influential General Friedrich von Beck-Rzikowsky, had expected a peaceful operation; General Philippovich planned to occupy Sarajevo within two weeks (Diószegi 1999: 420). Only a few officers had been more cautious; one of them was Philippovich's chief of staff, Colonel Leonidas Popp, who was aware of the possibility of irregular Muslim forces waging a protracted guerrilla war against the occupying army (Bencze 2005: 59). Austro-Hungarian forces had no clear picture of what they would encounter after entering Bosnia and Herzegovina, but judging from reports circulating between the different commands in late July and early August of 1878, armed resistance should not have been a total surprise.[1] In the end, it took the heavily reinforced occupation troops more than three months to accomplish their mission. Austro-Hungarian losses numbered 3,300 dead and 6,700 wounded (Deák 1995: 81). How many insurgents, Ottoman soldiers, and civilians perished as a result of the armed conflict is still unknown, but without doubt there were thousands of victims during combat operations; occupation forces also executed many real or suspected enemy fighters (DP 1878: no. 255, 2; NFP 1878: no. 5053, 2; PT 1878: no. 244, 2), and, at least to some extent, the execution of Muslims on the gallows was not only meant to be a form of punishment but also of (religious) humiliation (Holtz 1908: 13f; Gabriel 2011: 4).

Perceptions and Representations of the Muslim Populace

In the Austro-Hungarian public, media and military, there were those who saw Muslims – more specifically the educated and landowning class – as the most culturally developed ethnic stratum of Bosnian society, especially when comparing them to 'primitive' Christian peasants who lived in desolate villages without the possibility of uplifting themselves.[2] These views must also be seen vis-à-vis nineteenth-century European discourses that recognized the impressive tradition of Islamic cultures in general, as well as their past greatness. On the other hand, reporters and soldiers alike seem to have focused on painting a more negative picture of Muslims as soon as it became clear that many members of this ethnoreligious group were resisting the occupation. Cruelties against Austro-Hungarian forces or local civilians, real or alleged, received more space in newspaper reports, letters, diaries and memoirs. The image of Bosnian Muslims (men as well as women) as bloodthirsty, fanatic and gruesome adversaries can be found throughout Austro-Hungarian media and literature. However, it can be argued that these specific images were not necessarily forged by an (absolute) racist attitude towards Muslims but rather by the simple fact that a large number of irregular Muslim fighters dared to resist the occupation of 1878.

In his orders to the XIII Army Corps dated 27 July 1878, the occupation army's commander-in-chief, General Philippovich, reminded his troops of the specific nature of the upcoming operations. He did not primarily motivate them for a fierce fight but instead included quotes seemingly suited for a humanitarian intervention: for example, to treat all inhabitants 'as true friends, to honour the rights of each nationality and religion as well as to respect traditions and customs'. He also spoke of the occupation as 'hard work' carried out 'in the service of humanity and civilization'.[3] In August, the *Tages-Post* (Linz, Upper Austria) would go even further in its civilization rhetoric, stating that '(t)he Austrian sword has made the herd (i.e. the Christian *raya* populace) into humans' (TP 1878: no. 193, 1). However, in contrast to, for example, US expansionist actions ranging from the destruction of Native American cultures to occupying the Philippines, or the countless so-called small wars that British troops fought in the late nineteenth century that can be seen as '*missione civilizzatrice condotta in nome dei valori cristiani*' (Leonhard 2006: 43), the importance of motives attached to the fulfilment of a religious destiny was minimal in the Habsburg discourse.

Although the campaign could only be completed after the loss of thousands of lives, there were strong voices arguing for its nature as an intervention based on the wishes of a constantly terrorized population and designed to end what Theodor von Stefanović-Vilovsky called 'the despotism, robbery and looting' that characterized daily life in all the places where 'the Janissary sabres were the highest and holiest law' (Stefanović-Vilovsky 1884: 105). The ambivalence of the Austro-Hungarian media and military towards the populace was rooted in the complex ethnic and religious realities of Bosnia and Herzegovina as well as in the different strata of society in the occupation area. Soldiers as well as journalists could look at some parts of the populations with sympathy, while demonizing others as part of a racist discourse, thus creating what Michael Hochgeschwender, in his studies on colonial wars, called a 'radicalized dichotomy of the civilized versus the barbarians' (Hochgeschwender 2007: 285).

As soon as the insurgency began, enemy fighters were portrayed as savages waiting to cut off heads and other body parts. The *Linzer Volksblatt* newspaper, on 25 August 1878, argued:

> This much is clear, that a more brute, inhuman people as the local Turks can hardly be imagined. It is true, they know how to fight and to die courageously, without fear; the other Bosniaks, however, are a treacherous rabble. But the horror and the anger that came over all of us, when we got to know with every new day, in which unconceivably wild manner the Turks treated our fallen comrades, and even more so our wounded, unfortunate enough to fall into their hands, may serve as explanation for the sentiments we are currently feeling. (LV 1878: no. 195, 2)

The satirical *Kikeriki* newspaper, on 26 September 1878, printed a depiction of a man whose looks concurred with the typical Austro-Hungarian public images of a Bosnian fighter. He was pictured as a cruel and wild bogeyman standing in a mountainous ravine, his khanjar dripping with blood. On a cord, he was wearing a number of severed ears of soldiers, while half a dozen other ears were strewn on the ground around him. An allegorical representation of the newspaper (a man with a cockerel mask) can be seen hiding behind a tree in the background. The picture's sarcastic caption read: 'These insurgents have a strange way of making themselves *heard* by the Austrians!' (DK 1878: no. 77, 2).

There are several examples of how the expeditionary force dealt with its real or perceived enemies during the fight for Sarajevo in mid-August 1878. The battle for the city was characterized by enormous brutality and not by the Austro-Hungarian troops' benevolence later noted by General Philippovich (NFP 1878: no. 5022, 1). A participant of the campaign, the officer Georg Freiherr vom Holtz, wrote that 'whoever was carrying a weapon was indiscriminately butchered' (Holtz 1907: 182). Fighting was especially severe near a mosque in northwest Sarajevo, where Bosnian women also participated in the defence; details, like armed women taking part in combat, are frequently mentioned (not only in the Austro-Hungarian discourse but also in the global context of imperial and colonial warfare) to illustrate how savage the enemy really was. After the mosque had been taken, 'these shrews' (*diese Megären*) were thrown down from the minaret by Austro-Hungarian soldiers. In another house, a pregnant woman and a young boy shot at soldiers, only to be immediately cut down; because the soldiers were not able to storm the first floor of the house, the entire structure was burnt (Holtz 1908: 2f).

As Swiss doctor Josef Koetschet, who had been living in Bosnia for years, remembered, many of the poor Muslim inhabitants resisted this desperately because of their beliefs of what their material property and (even more so) 'the women and girls had to fear from the victorious giaours' (Koetschet 1905: 108). If we look at the horrendous massacres Christians committed against Muslim civilians in the early phase of the anti-Ottoman uprising in 1875, this fear does seem understandable. It is also notable that on some occasions in mid- and late August, newspapers such as *Die Presse* and *Das Vaterland* argued that many Muslims were in fact ready to accept Austro-Hungarian rule but had been forced to resist by other fanatics (DP 1878: no. 258, 3; DV 1878: no. 218, 1).[4] Although this can be seen as pro-Habsburg propaganda, the problem fits into the context of theological debates within the Muslim populace on whether or not to accept and support Christian rulers.

On the other hand, the soldier Franz Noir, in his memoirs published in 1884, wrote about insurgents in a style that can be seen as symptomatic of how many soldiers despised the enemy, as well as of the cruelty that characterized much of the fighting: 'During the last attack, carried out in darkness, it so happened that 20 to 30 men got lost and were captured by the Turks. We would shortly thereafter hear what this meant, and then see it the next day'. When guards saw campfires during the night, they initially thought these were Austrian, however 'a cry showed the falsity of our assumption: it was the Turks; but even the Hurons in the Northern American woods with their Indian war cries would have to hide, because only a Turk can cry this brutishly, beastly and infernally. . . . a cry of anger and millions of swears rang out when we found our comrades' bodies on the graves, naked but for their shirts and underpants, their heads cut off and thrown around in the grass' (Noir 1884: 96). Under these circumstances, it seemed justified to many observers that Austro-Hungarian troops took hostages[5] or killed suspicious persons, even if they were unarmed.[6]

Sometimes it did not matter if the expeditionary troops had to deal with a Christian or a Muslim populace. A Kaiserjäger soldier wrote to his parents about the fighting near Stolac in Herzegovina: 'Our platoon, which earlier had to set fire to the huts in the closer vicinity not yet burning, moved forward in the course of the morning at the right flank. Also, while pushing further forward, no hut was spared. Neither the cross, put on almost everything and painted on the doors, nor the cries of the begging women – "Christiani!", "Christiani!" – would help' (Vallaster 1978: 99). Generally speaking, however, Christians fared better when it came to their contacts with the occupation forces during the course of the insurgency, even though earlier on the Austro-Hungarian public discourse had depicted them as servile and stupid peasants who had lost much of their culture during the long period of Ottoman dominance in the two provinces, while Muslims from higher social strata were seen as sophisticated and honourable. At the same time, it was quite clear that there were many poor Muslims in Bosnia and Herzegovina as well, and they did not really fare any better in their everyday lives than Christian peasants (Baumann, Gawrych and Kretchik 2004: 6).

For some time, the fighting in 1878 changed perceptions of ethnic realities in the areas that were to be occupied, not least because many Muslims, rich as well as poor, resisted the occupation, while a large percentage of the Christian populace (and Roman Catholics in particular) passively welcomed or even actively supported the arriving Austro-Hungarian troops. Catholic militias operated alongside the 18th Infantry Division in Herzegovina, while others carried out raids in north-western Bosnia that, by and large, must be characterized not as real military operations but rather as terror against the local Muslim population and their property (Bencze 2005: 104). A lesser-known fact, however, is that units of the Second Army (which, from mid-August 1878, was the overall command for the occupation forces) actively cooperated with Muslim militias as part of military actions aimed at destroying criminal bands (*Räuberbanden*).[7]

Conclusion

In many of the modernity discourses in nineteenth-century Europe, the considerable influence of clergymen on a relatively uneducated populace was typically seen as characteristic for an outdated society; however, in Bosnia and Herzegovina in 1878, Austria–Hungary could take advantage of the influence of Christian orders, especially the Franciscans, whom Imre Ress has called 'the constitutive national intelligentsia for the Croats in Bosnia' (Ress 2006: 59). From a religious point of view, replacing the Islamic traditions of the Ottoman Empire with those of the Roman Catholic Habsburg Empire must have seemed attractive – and from a nationalist perspective, the integration into Austria–Hungary would definitely enhance possibilities for a unification of Catholics in Bosnia, Herzegovina, Croatia, Dalmatia and Slavonia. In the worst-case scenario, Catholics in the occupation area were generally seen as rather primitive but harmless; in the best-case scenario, they were viewed as a possible support force ready to take on the enemies of Austro-Hungarian troops. One high-ranking general, Anton Mollinary, mentions Catholic insurgents fighting against the army (Mollinary 1905: II, 308), but their actions did not radically change the larger picture (and might very well have been motivated by reasons other than ethnicity or religion). In regard to Christian Orthodox Serbs, the *Neue Freie Presse* stated in August 1878 that, based on a nationalist agenda, 'not just the Turkish but also the Slavic people's element in Bosnia and Herzegovina is our enemy' (NFP 1878: no. 5009, 3). We must also keep in mind at this point that Islam was not much of an issue when it came to the many Muslim soldiers or zaptiehs who did not take up arms against Austria–Hungary but instead surrendered to the occupation army without firing a shot.

In the end, perceptions of the Muslim populace in general, and those of Muslim insurgents in particular, centred rather heavily on religious identity.[8] Nationalist motives (unsurprisingly) and the higher social strata's need to defend material property (more surprisingly) are essentially absent, although it is clear that profane reasons for resistance existed, for example, among Muslim landowners, who had much to lose but had the power to influence a relevant number of people from lower social groups.

During the occupation campaign, many depictions of Bosnian Muslim insurgents resembled typical images taken from the collective memory of the early modern Ottoman wars in Central and East Central Europe. Combined with the perception of Islamic societies as cultures in stagnation or even decline, and of the Balkans as an area of traditionally unregulated, brutal and irregular warfare, these depictions resulted in the portrayal of large parts of the Bosnian and Herzegovinian Muslim populace as backward, cruel and fanatic.[9] When put into the larger context of Habsburg rule, however, these images, based on both real and fictional experiences from the occupation campaign, cannot be seen as constitutive for too long; indeed, fairly soon after the campaign, Austro-Hungarian policies showed that in dealings with Muslims, especially the traditional landowning elites, a pragmatist approach would prevail.

Martin Gabriel teaches modern history at the University of Klagenfurt, Austria. His PhD thesis focused on the military character and perceptions of warfare during the Austro-Hungarian occupation of Bosnia and Herzegovina in 1878. He co-edited (together with Stefan Rabitsch, Wilfried Elmenreich and John N.A. Brown) the book *Set Phasers to Teach! Star Trek in Research and Teaching* (Cham: Springer International Publishing, 2018). His areas of interest and expertise include the history of imperial powers (Austria–Hungary, Spain, Great Britain, United States), military history, social history, colonial warfare, and racism.

Notes

1. See, for example, Kriegsarchiv Wien (Austrian Military Archives Vienna), Alte Feldakten, 1878 (KA AFA 1878), HR 2393, 18. Infanterie-Truppendivision, Fasc. 1878 VII 7 28, Rodich to Jovanović (22 July 1878); HR 2393, 18. Infanterie-Truppendivision, Fasc. 1878 VII 7 107, 4. Kompanie, Feldjägerbataillon 7, to Headquarters, Feldjägerbataillon 7 (31 July 1878); HR 2394, 18. Infanterie-Truppendivision, Fasc. 1878 VIII 8 11, Militär-/Landwehrkommando Zara to Headquarters, 18. Infanterie-Truppendivision (1 August 1878).
2. See, for example, the views of Croatian writers Eugen Kumičić or Milan Ogrizović (Banac 1984: 364; Kadić 1994).
3. Philippovich's general orders were reprinted, for example, in *Prager Tagblatt* no. 208 (29 July 1878).
4. Spaits notes that before the fighting started, the influential Mufti of Plevlje had told his followers that resistance against the occupation was every Muslim's duty; those who would not take part were to be exiled and their houses destroyed (Spaits 1907: 91f).
5. See, for example, the reports on a disarmament operation in Tešanj in September 1878, during which Austro-Hungarian troops (as reprisal for an insurgent attack at Kosna Pass) took ten hostages; Kriegsarchiv Wien, Alte Feldakten, 1878 (KA AFA 1878), 2. Armee, Fasc. 1878 XIII 48/7.
6. See, for example, the case of two unarmed persons who were shot down from behind while fleeing from approaching Austro-Hungarian soldiers (the report states that they had not been observed carrying any weapons and that no weapons were found on the bodies); Kriegsarchiv Wien, Alte Feldakten, 1878 (KA AFA 1878), 2. Armee, Fasc. 1878 IX 9 57/1.
7. See, for example, Kriegsarchiv Wien, Alte Feldakten, 1878 (KA AFA 1878), 2. Armee, Fasc. 1878 X 28/2.
8. A scientific study published in 2003 stated that the fighters battling the Austro-Hungarian forces were 'led by their high priests' (Velikonja 2003: 118).
9. In my opinion, at least some of the violence that occurred in the Balkans throughout the nineteenth century as well as in the 1878 campaign should be seen as subcultural warfare. Stephen Morillo points out that in conflicts between subcultures of the same larger

culture, ritualization of combat becomes more important; enemies and even civilians are demonized, resulting in lower inhibition levels regarding the use of violence (Morillo 2006: 40).

References

Contemporary Periodicals (1878)

Das Vaterland (abbr. DV)
Der Kikeriki (abbr. DK)
Die Presse (abbr. DP)
Linzer Volksblatt (abbr. LV)
Neue Freie Presse (abbr. NFP)
Prager Tagblatt (abbr. PT)
Tages-Post (abbr. TP)
All periodicals cited in this chapter are available online via the Austrian National Library's digital newspaper collection (URL: http://anno.onb.ac.at/).

Printed Sources

Adye, John. 1867. *Sitana: A Mountain Campaign on the Borders of Afghanistan in 1863*. London: Bentley.
Angelow, Jürgen. 2000. *Kalkül und Prestige: Der Zweibund am Vorabend des Ersten Weltkrieges*. Cologne: Böhlau.
Auffenberg-Komarów, Moritz. 1921. *Aus Österreichs Höhe und Niedergang: Eine Lebensschilderung*. Munich: Drei Masken.
Babuna, Aydın. 1996. *Die nationale Entwicklung der bosnischen Muslime: Mit besonderer Berücksichtigung der österreichisch-ungarischen Periode*. Frankfurt am Main: Peter Lang.
Banac, Ivo. 1984. *The National Question in Yugoslavia: Origins, History, Politics*. Ithaca, NY: Cornell University Press.
Baumann, Robert F., George W. Gawrych and Walter E. Kretchik. 2004. *Armed Peacekeepers in Bosnia*. Fort Leavenworth, KS: Combat Studies Institute Press.
Bencze, László. 2005. *The Occupation of Bosnia and Herzegovina in 1878*. Boulder, CO: Social Science Monographs.
Bled, Jean Paul. 1988. *Franz Joseph: Der letzte Monarch der alten Schule*. Vienna: Böhlau.
Buchmann, Bertrand M. 1991. *Militär, Diplomatie, Politik: Österreich und Europa von 1815 bis 1835*. Frankfurt am Main: Peter Lang.
Classen, Lothar. 2004. *Der völkerrechtliche Status von Bosnien-Herzegowina nach dem Berliner Vertrag vom 13.7.1878*. Frankfurt am Main: Peter Lang.
Deák, István. 1995. *Der k. (u.) k. Offizier 1848–1918*. Vienna: Böhlau.
Diószegi, István. 1999. *Bismarck und Andrássy: Ungarn in der deutschen Machtpolitik in der 2. Hälfte des 19. Jahrhunderts*. Budapest: Teleki László Stiftung.
Doder, Dusko. 1999. 'Reflections on a Schizophrenic Peace', in Robert L. Rothstein (ed.), *After the Peace: Resistance and Reconciliation*. London: Rienner, pp. 167–189.
Donia, Robert J. 1981. *Islam under the Double Eagle: The Muslims of Bosnia and Herzegovina, 1878–1914*. New York: Columbia University Press.

Gabriel, Karl. 2004. *Bosnien-Herzegowina 1878: Der Aufbau der Verwaltung unter FZM Herzog Wilhelm v. Württemberg und dessen Biographie*. Frankfurt am Main: Peter Lang.
Gabriel, Martin. 2011. 'Die Einnahme Sarajevos am 19. August 1878: Eine Militäraktion im Grenzbereich von konventioneller und irregulärer Kriegführung'. *Kakanien Revisited*. http://www.kakanien-revisited.at/beitr/fallstudie/mgabriel3.pdf; last accessed 8 August 2018.
Geiss, Imanuel. (1990) 1991. *Der lange Weg in die Katastrophe: Die Vorgeschichte des Ersten Weltkriegs, 1815–1914*. Munich: Piper.
Gottas, Friedrich. 1976. *Ungarn im Zeitalter des Hochliberalismus: Studien zur Tisza-Ära (1875–1890)*. Vienna: Verlag der Österreichischen Akademie der Wissenschaften.
Grijak, Zoran. 2009. 'Croatian-British Views of the Eastern Question: The Correspondence of William Ewart Gladstone and Josip Juraj Strossmayer (1876–1882)', *Review of Croatian History* 1: 47–84.
Haardt, Vinzenz von. 1878. *Die Occupations Bosniens und der Herzegovina: Nach verlässlichen Quellen geschildert von Vinzenz v. Haardt*. Vienna: Hölzel.
Heuberger, Valeria. 1997. *Unter dem Doppeladler: Die Nationalitäten der Habsburger Monarchie 1848–1918*. Munich: Brandstätter.
Hildebrand, Klaus. 1989. *Deutsche Außenpolitik 1871–1918*. Munich: Oldenbourg.
Hochgeschwender, Michael. 2007. 'Kolonialkriege als Experimentierstätten des Vernichtungskrieges?', in Dietrich Beyrau, Michael Hochgeschwender and Dieter Langewiesche (eds), *Formen des Krieges: Von der Antike bis zur Gegenwart*. Paderborn: Schöningh, pp. 269–290.
Holtz, Georg Freiherr vom. 1907. *Von Brod bis Sarajevo*. Vienna: Stern.
———. 1908. *Die letzten Kämpfe und der Heimmarsch*. Vienna: Stern.
Kadić, Ante. 1994. 'The Occupation of Bosnia (1878) as Depicted in Literature', *East European Quarterly* 28(3): 281–96.
Klaić, Vjekoslav. 1885. *Geschichte Bosniens von den ältesten Zeiten bis zum Verfalle des Königreiches*. Leipzig: Friedrich.
Koetschet, Josef. 1905. *Aus Bosniens letzter Türkenzeit: Hinterlassene Aufzeichnungen von Med. Univ. Dr. Josef Koetschet*. Leipzig: Hartleben.
Koller, Markus. 2004. *Bosnien an der Schwelle zur Neuzeit: Eine Kulturgeschichte der Gewalt (1747–1798)*. Munich: Oldenbourg.
Kolmer, Gustav. (1902) 1972. *Parlament und Verfassung in Österreich. Vol. 2: 1869–1879*. Graz: Akademische Druck- und Verlagsanstalt.
Kos, Franz-Joseph. 1984. *Die Politik Österreich-Ungarns während der Orientkrise 1874/75–1879: Zum Verhältnis von politischer und militärischer Führung*. Cologne: Böhlau.
Leonhard, Jörn. 2006. 'Nati dalla guerra e macchine da guerra? Nazione e stato nazionale nell'età del bellicismo fino al 1871', *Ricerche di Storia politica* N.S. 9(1): 31–52.
Mollinary, Anton. 1905. *Sechsundvierzig Jahre im österreichisch-ungarischen Heere 1833–1879. Vol. 2*. Zurich: Orell Füssli.
Morillo, Stephen. 2006. 'A General Typology of Transcultural Wars: The Middle Ages and Beyond', in Hans-Henning Kortüm (ed.), *Transcultural Wars from the Middle Ages to the 21st Century*. Berlin: Akademie-Verlag, pp. 29–42.
Noir, Franz. 1884. *Die Oesterreicher in Bosnien: Erlebnisse eines österreichischen Infanteristen in Bosnien und in der Hercegowina*. Prague: Reinwart.
Okey, Robin. 2007. *Taming Balkan Nationalism: The Habsburg 'Civilizing Mission' in Bosnia 1878–1914*. London: Oxford University Press.
Pavlowitch, Stevan K. 1999. *A History of the Balkans, 1904–1945*. London: Longman.

Plaschka, Richard G. 2000. *Avantgarde des Widerstands: Modellfälle militärischer Auflehnung im 19. und 20. Jahrhundert. Vol. 1.* Vienna: Böhlau.

Ress, Imre. 2006. 'Versuch einer Nationenbildung um die Jahrhundertwende: Benjámin Kállays Konzeption der bosnischen Nation', in Endre Kiss and Justin Stagl (eds), *Nation und Nationenbildung in Österreich-Ungarn 1848–1938: Prinzipien und Methoden.* Münster: Lit.

Riedel, Sabine. 2005. *Die Erfindung der Balkanvölker: Identitätspolitik zwischen Konflikt und Integration.* Wiesbaden: Verlag für Sozialwissenschaften.

Roberts, Elizabeth. 2007. *Realm of the Black Mountain: A History of Montenegro.* London: Hurst.

Ruthner, Clemens. 2008. 'Habsburg's Little Orient: A Post/Colonial Reading of Austrian and German Cultural Narratives on Bosnia and Herzegovina, 1878–1918'. *Kakanien Revisited.* http://www.kakanien-revisited.at/beitr/fallstudie/CRuthner5.pdf; last accessed 21 April 2020.

Sosnosky, Theodor von. 1913. *Die Balkanpolitik Österreich-Ungarns seit 1866. Vol. 1.* Stuttgart: Deutsche Verlags-Anstalt.

Spaits, Alexander. 1907. *Der Weg zum Berliner Kongress: Historische Entwicklung Bosniens und der Herzegowina bis zur Okkupation 1878.* Leipzig: Stern.

Stefanović-Vilovsky, Theodor von. 1884. *Die Serben im südlichen Ungarn, in Dalmatien, Bosnien und der Herzegovina.* Vienna: Prochaska.

Vallaster, Christoph. 1978. 'Augenzeugenberichte Josef Neuners vom Okkupationsfeldzug 1878', *Montfort* 30(2): 96–99.

Velikonja, Mitja. 2003. *Religious Separation and Political Intolerance in Bosnia-Herzegovina.* College Station: Texas A&M University Press.

Wertheimer, Eduard von. 1921/22. 'Neues zur Orientpolitik des Grafen Andrássy (1876–1877). Teil II', *Historische Blätter* 3: 448–94.

Chapter 4

SLEEPING BEAUTY'S AWAKENING
Habsburg Colonialism in Bosnia and Herzegovina, 1878–1918

Clemens Ruthner

These regions . . . had remained completely unknown to the wide public; the Bosnian Sleeping Beauty still slept her age-old magical slumber and was only reawakened when the imperial troops crossed the border and ushered in the new era. The thicket that had sprawled around Sleeping Beauty's castle was then cleared, and, after less than two decades of restless and arduous work, Bosnia is now known and respected by the world. What has been achieved in this land is practically unparalleled in the colonial history of all peoples and epochs.
—Heinrich Renner, *Durch Bosnien und die Hercegovina kreuz und quer*

In the fairy-tale rhetoric of Heinrich Renner's fin-de-siècle travelogue, the success story of the Austro-Hungarian 'civilizing mission' (see Okey 2007; Telesko 2015; Feichtinger 2016) after the military occupation of Bosnia and Herzegovina in 1878 is told. The occupied territory becomes an Oriental Sleeping Beauty of sorts that was cursed or even poisoned by the Ottoman Empire and later awakened by the kiss of Europe, so to say – or, in particular, Prince Charming of Habsburg, the identity of the colonizer unnamed in the quote.

However, the metaphorical phrase of 'clearing . . . the thicket' contains the whole ambiguity of the undertaking, as Western colonialism in the nineteenth and twentieth centuries had two faces. On the one hand, it stood for military conquest and foreign domination, for economic exploitation, for inequality and patronizing identity politics for the sake of a civilization based, more or less, on racist discourses that evoke a lazy native who needs to be tamed. On the other hand, colonialism triggered modernization as it introduced infrastructure, new goods, unknown lifestyles, and, especially, educational and legal systems that were the first steps towards a civil society – which, ironically, enabled the colonized to overthrow foreign rule eventually. Both faces were shown to Bosnia and Herzegovina by Austria–Hungary from 1878 to 1918. In the following, I will try to provide answers to the question of to what extent the colonial paradigm is applicable to this particular historical case, synthesizing my research work with that of many other scholars in recent decades (e.g. Csáky, Feichtinger and Prutsch 2003; Müller-Funk, Plener and Ruthner 2004; Ruthner 2008; Gammerl 2010; Ruthner et al. 2015; Ruthner 2018; Ruthner and Scheer 2018).

History

Why precisely did Austria–Hungary intend to occupy Bosnia and Herzegovina in 1878, and what agenda did its 'Balkan peace mission' actually conceal? These are questions not easily answered, even more than 140 years later. However, one would do well to accept 'The Age of Empire' (Eric Hobsbawm) as a significant backdrop, as, for example, do Arnold Suppan (1978) and Evelyn Kolm (2001). In the canonized historiography of our present, the sequence of events does not deviate substantially from the narrative advocated by the renowned Balkan historian Barbara Jelavich (1969: 115ff; cf., among others, Dedijer et al. 1974: 393ff; Donia 1981; Bridge 1989; Bérenger 1994: 129ff; Hösch 2002; Imamović 2006: 171–87; Detrez 2015).

In 1875, a revolt broke out in the European territories of the Ottoman Empire, pitting dissatisfied Herzegovinian farmers against their Muslim landlords. It produced a large number of casualties and refugees, for Serbia and Montenegro soon supported the uprising against Ottoman rule, which by 1876 had spread to Bulgaria. While Ottoman troops remained victorious in the ensuing battles, the war was accompanied by a political crisis in the power centre Istanbul, which led to changes in leadership, even in the form of a coup d'état (Jelavich 1969: 115–20).

Faced with both the instability of the 'Sick Man of Europe' and ambitious Russian plans, Austria–Hungary clearly no longer saw itself in the position of adhering to the double maxim of its traditional Balkan policy, which had been in place since Kaunitz and Metternich: '(1) to keep the Russian presence and influence to a minimum; and (2) to maintain the status quo with the Ottoman administration' (Pinson 1994: 86). Furthermore, there is some indication that the new expansionist reorientation of Austria–Hungary's *Orientpolitik* was not only the ambition of Austrian court and military circles but also connected to one of its major actors, Count Gyula (Julius) Andrássy, joint foreign minister (Wertheimer 1913; Haselsteiner 1996: 9–30; Kolm 2001: 105–6).

In 1877, during the Russo-Ottoman War, which followed on the heels of the clashes in 1875 and 1876, the Habsburg Monarchy declared its readiness to adopt a benevolent neutrality towards the Tsarist Empire. The Russians countered this move by offering up Bosnia and Herzegovina to the Austrians as an inducement (Dedijer 1974: 396; Donia 1981: 8ff; Jelavich 1983: 59; Haselsteiner 1996: 15ff; Hösch 2002: 132ff). On 3 March 1878, this arrangement was abandoned when the Treaty of San Stefano was signed, but the resulting territorial reorganization of the Balkans (e.g. the emergence of a large new Bulgarian state) did not satisfy the great European powers either. In response, the Congress of Berlin was convened on 13 June of the same year to discuss the drawing of the borders anew. One important outcome of the negotiations was the ceding of the administration of the old Ottoman *Vilayet Bosna* to Austria–Hungary at the request of the British representative, Lord Salisbury. For the future, article XXV of the Treaty of Berlin formulated that

> [t]he Provinces of Bosnia and Herzegovina shall be occupied and administered by Austria-Hungary. The Government of Austria-Hungary, not desiring to undertake the administration of the Sandjak of Novi-Pazar,[1] which extends between Servia [*sic*] and Montenegro in a southeasterly direction to the other side of Mitrovitza, accepts the Ottoman Administration will continue to exercise its functions there. Nevertheless, in order to assure the maintenance of the new political state of affairs, as well as freedom and security of communications, Austria-Hungary reserves the right to keep garrisons and have military and commercial roads in the whole of this part of the ancient Vilayet of Bosnia. To this end, the governments of Austria-Hungary and Turkey reserve to themselves to come to an understanding on the details. (Qtd. after Israel 1967: II, 985)

Scrutiny shows that this agreement is rather vague, particularly when it comes to the future consequences of the occupation of Bosnia and Herzegovina. The particular motivations for this last (and finally fatal) expansion of the Habsburg Monarchy before the First World War are not very clear either; they fall into three categories of historical argument:

1. *Strategic Grounds.* The assumption here is that Austria–Hungary needed to safeguard its territory against Russian pan-Slavism and suspected Serbian expansion plans through the military and infrastructural occupation of the Dalmatian hinterland (see Sugar 1963: 20ff; Jelavich 1983: 59; Haselsteiner 1996: 16ff; Malcolm 2002: 136). Yet this motivation is weakened by a fact foreseeable already at the time, namely that the further acquisition of a significant South Slavic population (numbering over a million) would, in the process, also potentially exacerbate the existing ethnic tensions in the Habsburg Monarchy (Sugar 1963: 26; Pinson 1994: 119; Malcolm 2002: 136).

2. *Economic Grounds*. Bosnia and Herzegovina harboured large deposits of coal and various ores, a mining potential that was only extensively exploited in Tito's Yugoslavia. These vast natural resources lead some historians like Jean Bérenger (1994: 255) to impute certain economic interests to Austria–Hungary (also see Kolm 2001: 18–19, 105–6, 244–50; Malcolm 2002: 136; Okey 2007: 17). Given the available historical evidence, however, it is difficult to assess to what extent such possible gains, along with the prospect of a new market for Austrian goods, actually played a motivational role in the occupation of Bosnia and Herzegovina.[2] On the other hand, the *Naturschätze* (natural treasures) of the territory are explicitly mentioned in the concluding remarks to the official military report on the occupation campaign (k.k. Kriegsarchiv 1879: 908).
3. *Territorial Expansion*. This line of argument maintains that, after the founding of the German Empire in 1871, the only remaining opportunity for imperial(ist) growth still open to Austria–Hungary lay in the South, in the fallback regions of the declining Ottoman Empire in the Balkans (Sugar 1963: 20; Pinson 1994: 87). Other European powers did the same to the 'Sick Man of Europe', which is commonly seen under the label of colonialism by most historians: for instance, the usurpation of Tunis by France in 1881, and of Egypt by Great Britain in 1882 (cf. Hösch 2002: 137).

However, massive drawbacks were arrayed against the geopolitical assets of occupying Bosnia and Herzegovina. Robert Kann writes:

> In a financial sense, the acquisition was considered not only no gain but a definite loss . . . Occupation was considered the lesser of two evils. It would mean bad business economically, but it might offer some relief against the threat of Balkan nationalism and Russian-inspired Panslavism. (Kann 1977: 68)

Apart from increasing both the empire's expenditures and its Slavic population (out of the latter, plans for both Croatian hegemony and Trialism would arise alongside Serbian nationalism; see Jelavich 1983: 60), it should not be underestimated that with the occupation of Bosnia and Herzegovina, for the first time in history, a significant Muslim community became part of Austro-Hungarian society and culture (Pinson 1994: 91; Hadžijahić 1974). This new population group was by no means comprised of a few historical converts, as it contained the regional elites: landowners, Ottoman dignitaries, clergymen, and quite a few merchants (see Donia 1981; Pinson 1994; Neweklowsky 1996). With this composition, the religious divide in Bosnia and Herzegovina, which would later become increasingly ethnicized, was interwoven with the social hierarchy, especially since the majority of the free peasants and dependent tenant farmers (*kmetovi*) were of the Christian faith, either Orthodox or Roman Catholic (Pinson 1994: 117–18). Thus, all Austro-Hungarian administrative measures that would lead to interference with the existing (and frankly problematic) late-feudal system of cultural, religious and social difference (Imamović 2006: 108–28) were politically sensitive, especially since they would mostly affect those elites on whose benevolence Austro-Hungarian rule rested – even if reforms were implemented with well-meaning intent vis-à-vis the majority of the population.

Moreover, Austria–Hungary's occupation of Bosnia and Herzegovina in the summer of 1878 was not at all the military *Parademarsch* (Wertheimer 1913: 15) the Austro-Hungarian foreign minister Andrássy had envisaged for the imperial army, but rather a gory conquest (Pavlowitch 1999: 116) that was fiercely battled by local militias and the remnants of Ottoman troops in the region. Thus, by the end of the campaign in November 1878, the Austro-Hungarian occupying forces were about as strong in number as the American contingent deployed in the second Iraq War of 2003 – roughly a quarter of a million (for details on this campaign, see Bencze 2005).

In this military context, the colonialist undertones of the whole operation become perceptible for the first time, when, for example, a Czech veteran later recalls the heads of Austrian soldiers being skewered by the *Insurgenten* (the official term for the local resistance already used in 1878). Here, old Balkan clichés of barbaric bandits and cutthroats (cf. Todorova 1997 and Jezernik 2004) re-emerge along with anti-Turkish sentiments from long ago – instrumentalized, it appears, for an almost propagandistic outcry for a new and 'civilized' administration:

> We stood in full battledress against the ignoble cannibal enemy, and it is no exaggeration to say that the Zulus, Bagurus, Niam-Niams, Bechuans, Hottentots, and similar South African bands behaved more chivalrously towards European travellers than the Bosnian Turks did towards us. I always recollect with dismay the peoples of the Balkans, where the foot of the civilized European has not trod for decades, how the Turks, native lords, probably rule down there. (E. Chaura, *Obrázky z okupace bosenské* [Prague, 1893]: 38; qtd. after transl. by Jezernik 2004: 139)

After three months of fighting, some thousands of dead, and many tens of thousands of refugees, the Austro-Hungarian *mission civilisatrice* was to be accomplished next. In 1882, after a new uprising, a civil administration was put in place by the occupiers, and finally, in 1908, Bosnia and Herzegovina was annexed by the Habsburg Monarchy, which almost caused the premature outbreak of the First World War. Ironically, its opening shots would still be fired right here, in Sarajevo, on 28 June 1914; its finale in 1918 also meant the end of Habsburg rule over Bosnia and Herzegovina, which became part of the first Yugoslav state (the Kingdom of Serbs, Croats and Slovenes, SHS). The question still remains, in many respects, of how those forty years should be assessed: in terms of the civilizing mission they were supposed to be, or within the paradigm of European colonialism around 1900?

Assessments

In recent decades, various scholars have discussed the applicability of post/colonial approaches to Habsburg Central Europe as a third way – one that avoids the fallacies of Habsburg nostalgia (*Viribus unitis*) and the nationalist discourse of self-victimization (*Völkerkerker*). As I have stated in earlier lectures and writings (see e.g. Ruthner 2018), Bosnia and Herzegovina might be the only territory among all the parts of the empire that fully qualifies for a case study of k. u. k.[3] colonialism in a non-figurative sense of the term. However, such a claim had already been ardently contested by the historian Robert Kann:

> The thesis put before us, namely that the administration of Bosnia and Herzegovina represented trends of colonialism, is highly problematical. We must first ask whether the concept of colonialism, commonly understood as the rule of European powers over native coloured people on other continents, can be transferred to a master–subject relation within Europe, pointing to a system of colonial administration and exploitation of whites by whites. (Kann 1977: 164)

It was thus in the capacity of an apologist that Kann joined the debate of 'internal' European colonization, which had started in the years following the publication of Michael Hechter's (1975) book on the Celtic fringe of Great Britain (see, also, Verdery 1979; Nolte and Bähre 2001). For Kann, however, colonialism constitutes 'the unholy trinity of imperialism, capitalist exploitation and oppression on racial grounds, all of them imposed by force' (Kann 1977: 164); on this basis, he rejects the application of the concept to Bosnia and Herzegovina, albeit with arguments that are hardly convincing.

In a more recent formulation by key postcolonial theorist Gayatri Spivak, based on the protean nature of colonialism, the term becomes plausible again, particularly in Russian, Slavonic and Soviet studies:

> The terms 'colonizer' and 'colonized' can be fairly elastic if you define them scrupulously. When an alien nation-state establishes itself as a ruler, impressing its own laws and system of education and rearranging the mode of production for its own economic benefit, one can use these terms, I think'. (*Ulbandus* 2003: 15; also see Müller-Funk and Wagner 2005)

Unfortunately, due to space constraints, other important definitions of colonialism in historiography and the social sciences, such as Jürgen Osterhammel's (2001), for instance, cannot be discussed in as much depth here as in an earlier publication (Ruthner 2018: ch. A1). Also, it should be noted that the propagandistic undertones of how the term 'colonialism' was used in communist Yugoslavia[4] for the country's past seem to have left a bad taste in many scholars' mouths.

On the other hand, Austro-Hungarian sources from the k. u. k. period itself love to repeat the mantra of Habsburg mythology, i.e. the selfless cultural and/or peace mission that must inevitably follow the decline of the Ottoman Empire and the bloody chaos of war.[5] A statement made by the Austro-Hungarian joint finance minister, Benjámin von Kállay, who from 1882 to 1903 was responsible for the civil administration of the *Okkupationsgebiete* (occupied territories) is one of many symptomatic examples. In an interview with the *Daily Chronicle* in London, he commented: 'Austria is a great Occidental Empire ... charged with the mission of carrying civilization to Oriental peoples'; in this respect, 'rational bureaucracy' would be 'the key to Bosnia's future ... to retain the ancient traditions of the land vilified and purified by modern ideas' (qtd. in Donia 1981: 14).

It is precisely this talk of Austria–Hungary's civilizing mission that has led not only Yugoslav but also several Western historians (such as Detrez 2002, Donia 2007 and Judson 2016: 378 *et passim*) to extend the critical paradigm of colonialism to the Habsburg Monarchy. This was already the case with A.J.P. Taylor, who eighty years ago handed down the following polemical verdict on Habsburg rule:

> The two provinces were the 'white man's burden' (!) of Austria–Hungary. While other European Powers sought colonies in Africa for the purpose, the Habsburg Monarchy exported to Bosnia and Herzegovina its surplus intellectual production – administrators, road builders, archaeologists, ethnographers, and even remittance-men. The two provinces received all benefits of imperial rule: ponderous public buildings; model barracks for the army of occupation; banks, hotels, and cafés; a good water supply for the centres of administration and for the country resorts where the administrators and army officers recovered from the burden of empire. The real achievement of Austria–Hungary was not on show: when the empire fell in 1918, eighty-eight per cent of the population was still illiterate. (Taylor 1990: 166)

Many more examples could be given of how the semantics of colonialism was used for Bosnia and Herzegovina in contemporary sources as well, critically or affirmatively (for details, see Kolm 2001: 237ff). A striking case of the latter is Ferdinand Schmid, former head of the official statistics department in Sarajevo, who would later, as a university professor in Leipzig, write an academic monograph on Bosnia, in which he also discusses the applicability of the colony concept:

> The concept of 'colonies' has been widely debated in German and Western literature on the topic; often, it only meant overseas territories that were ruled by the motherland, economically and legally. In this sense, Austria–Hungary does not have colonies and it has never done colonial politics, at least not recently. However, if you define the notion of 'colonies' in a broader sense, then there can be no doubt that Bosnia and Herzegovina were obtained as colonial territories by Austria–Hungary, and that they have remained so until today. (Schmid 1914: 1)

Coloniality

If the case is to be made for an Austro-Hungarian colonialism of sorts as a critical term beyond contemporary rhetoric, the following points should be taken into consideration (along the theoretical and historical lines laid out by Balandier 1966, Fieldhouse 1981, Stoler and Cooper 1997, Osterhammel 2001, Cooper 2005, Young 2015, and many others):

1. *Military Conquest*. A military conquest after a mandate provided by an international summit is exactly the mode by which many colonies were taken over by the great powers of Europe – for example, as a consequence of the so-called Congo Conference in Berlin, 1884–85 (cf. Fieldhouse 1981: 16ff).
2. *Legal Status of the Territory*. Throughout its forty Austro-Hungarian years, Bosnia and Herzegovina never became a *Kronland* (crownland, i.e. an imperial province) but remained a sort of appendix to the empire, a *Reichsland* (comparable to the status of Alsace-Lorraine in imperial Germany), which in essence did not belong exclusively to either of the two constitutive entities of the empire – Austria (*Cisleithanien*) or Hungary (*Transleithanien*) – but to both (Sugar 1963: 26). As a consequence of this special status, the territory was the only one under Habsburg rule to have no legal representation in the parliament in either Vienna or Budapest;[6] it 'existed in a kind of unacknowledged legal limbo' (Judson 2016: 379). A regional assembly, the so-called *Sabor / Landtag* (Diet), was finally introduced in 1910, but it soon became dysfunctional and was closed down by emergency laws in the First World War soon thereafter (cf. Juzbašić 2002; Imamović 2006: 244–50).
3. *Indirect Rule*. Similar to British reign in India (Gammerl 2010: 73–216), the Austro-Hungarian occupiers established their rule over a majority of the native population through the participation and gradual 'reformation' of existing elites in Bosnia and Herzegovina, particularly the Muslim landowners (cf. Fieldhouse 1981: 29–40).[7] This, for example, prevented a major land reform from happening, which added to the frustrations among the mostly Christian tenant farmers who, hoping for change, had at first been partly welcoming of the Austro-Hungarian takeover of the territory (see Katus 1961: 210–11; Sugar 1963: 33ff; Imamović 2006: 210–11).
4. *Patronizing Civil Administration*. An ever-growing[8] bureaucracy was put in place shortly after the occupation, which rested to a large extent in the hands of foreigners, even in its lower ranks. It discriminated against local applicants, particularly Bosnian Muslims and Serbs.[9] On the other hand, the eager administrators would try to micromanage almost every aspect of civic life (Donia 2007: 4). However, their achievements are also diminished by corruption allegations in foreign diplomatic reports, which paint a very different picture to the alleged civilizing mission (Sugar 1963: 26, 30–31).

5. *Establishment of an Epistemic Regime.* As was typical for colonial powers all over the world during the nineteenth century (cf. Stoler and Cooper 1997: 15ff), the k. u. k. regime in Bosnia and Herzegovina also relied on the generation of hegemonic knowledge, especially through the new Austrian discipline of *Volkskunde* [ethnology] (Johler 2018). For this purpose, the Kállay administration built the *Landesmuseum / Zemaljski muzej* as a central institution for research, documentation and publication. With the help of his friend Lajos von Thallóczy, Governor Kállay also tried to (re)write a specific Bosnian version of regional history, based on the medieval kingdom, to oppose the national historiographies of Serbia and Croatia and to legitimize Austro-Hungarian rule (Donia 2007: 5–6).
6. *Identity Politics.*
    (a) In the two decades during which joint finance minister Kalláy headed the occupied territories, he tried to create a unifying Bosnian identity (*Bošnjaštvo*) top-down in order to combat the particularist movements of the three major population groups: the Muslims, the Orthodox and the Catholics – a modern tool of government also known from colonial contexts outside of Europe. Paradoxically, however, this paternalistic policy played into the hands of the nationalists, and further deepened and ethnicized the religious divide between the three groups (see Donia 1981: 12ff; Kraljačić 1987; Pinson 1994: 113; Vrankić 1998; Sethre 2004; Ress 2006; Imamović 2006: 213–31; Babuna 2015; Ruthner et al. 2015; Ruthner and Scheer 2018).
    (b) *The Othering of the Other.* Austria–Hungary's 'civilizing mission' was used as a discursive tool to justify structures of governance that were less democratic than in the motherland, as well as the status of Bosnians and Herzegovinians as second-rate k. u. k. citizens. In order to legitimize this inequality, they were (re)presented and formatted as the Other through popular Orientalist discourses (Heiss and Feichtinger 2013) in the hegemonic culture, and as such they even became a commodity[10] instead of simply being seen as an extension of the existing South Slavic populace of the empire (cf. Stachel 2003; Sirbubalo 2012; Ruthner 2018: ch. C). Thus, othering also became an important pretext for the necessary 'education' of the Other, a project which, not surprisingly, failed.
7. *Economic Aspects.* The self-imposed official restriction through Austro-Hungarian legislation that Bosnia and Herzegovina was, on the one hand, controlled by an almost almighty bureaucracy but, on the other hand, had to finance itself from its own provincial incomes, to a large extent prevented the development and exploitation of the territories through private capital until the late days of Habsburg rule, when increasing numbers of primarily Hungarian banks moved in. Habsburg nostalgists try to use this point as a counterargument against the colonialism hypothesis, together with the fact

that the Austrians had built hundreds of kilometres of roads and railway tracks, school buildings, and so on. However, this phenomenon of creating modern infrastructure is characteristic of most Western colonial regimes overseas as well (cf. Fischer-Tiné and Mann 2004: 17), as is, more or less, the economic situation of Bosnia-Herzegovina in general (see Sugar 1963; Lampe and Jackson 1982: 264–322; Wessely 1989): 'a mercantilist concept of trade, through which the metropole assures privileged access to markets and raw materials by restricting the colony's ability to trade freely with all partners, and a conception of the colony as a domain in which a state can act in particular ways' (Stoler and Cooper 1997: 19; see also the introduction of Alatas 1977).

8. *Lab of Modernity vs Administrative Conservatism.* On the one hand, Bosnia and Herzegovina, like other imperial peripheries and also the colonies of the great powers,[11] served as a testing ground for social and technological experimentation – for example, for the first electrical tramway system of the monarchy. On the other hand, however, the inherent traditionalism of the Austro-Hungarian administration is striking, as it tries to conserve and improve existing structures rather than radically replace them. According to Donia (2007), the resulting contradictions and aporias would become most central and damaging for the occupied territories (also see Judson 2016: 330).

9. *Military Exploitation.* Similar to the Gurkha units within the British army, in 1881 the k. u. k. military began drafting the male population of Bosnia and Herzegovina into special infantry regiments; these were never fully incorporated into the Austro-Hungarian army but run by its officers (see Neumayer and Schmidl 2008). These *Bosniaken* were designed as elite units of sorts that terrified their enemies with their cruelty and combat efficiency, particularly on the Italian front during the First World War. Thus, the alien Other from the periphery, whose barbarism was to be tamed by the *mission civilisatrice*, was also put on hold as a natural military resource, as it were, to be unleashed whenever the imperial centre wanted it.

10. *Settlers.* Like in many colonies, the provincial government and other organizations encouraged farmers from other regions of the empire and abroad (e.g. from Germany) to move in and create role-model villages, but this initiative was fiercely opposed by local activists and the newly established regional assembly in Sarajevo (see Bethke 2018; Ruthner 2018: 276).

In Lieu of a Conclusion

If one tries to put this data puzzle together in order to see the greater picture, a comparative perspective might prove helpful (see e.g. Gammerl 2010). Then, there would be a whole range of phenomena available to illustrate what colonialism can be(come). At the top of the blacklist there should be, for instance, the Congo colony as described by Adam Hochschild (1998), particularly when the territory was the private property of the Belgian king and run as a hybrid of capitalist corporation and violent labour camp that cost the lives of millions of native Africans. In comparison, Austria–Hungary's intervention in Bosnia and Herzegovina was fairly soft(-spoken?) and perhaps, in ways, even well intended.

Still, the arguments listed in the outline above show that the k. u. k. intermezzo from 1878 to 1918 can be considered a kind of Austrian quasi-colonialism (Detrez 2002; cf. Okey 2007: 220), a substitute for the 'scramble for Africa' (and Asia) that the Habsburg Monarchy had been too late for (cf. Sauer 2002). The only reason others hesitate to call Bosnia and Herzegovina a colony is that it is not separated from its motherland by a large body of saltwater,[12] but lies at the peripheries of Europe. Here one can argue that it is the rather imaginary concept of what Europe is (and thus Eurocentrism) that paradoxically prevents us from recognizing colonialism on its very soil.

Clemens Ruthner is an assistant professor in German and European studies at Trinity College Dublin, Ireland. His research focuses on Austrian literature and culture, Central European history (nineteenth and twentieth centuries), Bosnia and Herzegovina under Habsburg rule, Otherness (e.g. gender, ethnicity, monstrosity), and cultural theory in general. His latest publications include the monograph *Habsburg's Dark Continent: Postkoloniale Lektüren zur österreichischen Literatur und Kultur im langen 19. Jahrhundert* (Tübingen: Narr Francke Attempto, 2018) and the edited volume *Bosnien-Herzegowina und Österreich-Ungarn: Annäherungen an eine Kolonie* (Tübingen: Narr Francke Attempto, 2018, co-editor Tamara Scheer) on Bosnia-Herzegovina under Habsburg rule.

Notes

1. Cf. Scheer 2013.
2. The central authorities of Austria–Hungary decreed that the new province had to finance itself with its own income; in this way there were no substantial subsidies from Vienna except for railway building (and even then, only circuitously). Moreover, both the newly established Imperial and Royal Mining Authority and the Bosna mining corporation proved inefficient at developing new mineral resources; the flow of information to private investors either failed or was omitted completely; further planning errors also occurred. For details, see Sugar 1963: 105ff, 159ff; Malcolm, 2002: 141; also, Lampe and Jackson 1982; Wessely 1989).
3. 'k. u. k' (*kaiserlich und königlich*) is a term frequently used for the Dual (imperial and royal) Habsburg Monarchy whose ruler was emperor of Austria and at the same time king of Hungary and other territories, such as Bohemia and Croatia.

4. E.g. in Dedijer et al. 1974: 448; also see the discussion in Vervaet 2004.
5. This discourse has been uncritically adapted and repeated, even by some modern-day historians (e.g. Suppan 1978: 128).
6. This is why an American historian, borrowing from the example of the Soviet Union, speaks of a Bosnian *satrapy* (McCagg 1992: 50–51).
7. Okey sees even more analogies: 'Applied to territories taken over by European powers, it [the regime of Austro-Hungarian administrator Kállay, CR] presupposed a slow but steady advance in security and prosperity, accompanied by the contraction of militant resistance and a growing understanding of the occupiers' goals and values. Such processes can be seen at work in British India and French Algeria between the end of physical resistance and the emergence of modern nationalist movements' (Okey 2007: 123).
8. Compared with the Ottoman era, the total number of civil servants hired for the administration of Bosnia and Herzegovina had risen from 120 to around 9,500 by 1908 (Sugar 1963: 29; Pinson 1994: 119–20).
9. In 1904, only 26.5% of all officials with placements in Bosnia and Herzegovina were natives; the majority were Catholic, a further 3% Serbs and 5% Muslims (Dedijer et al. 1974: 449; Jelavich 1983: 60; Pavlowitch 1999: 117).
10. 'Just as imperialists "administer" the resources of the conquered country, colonialist discourse "commodifies" the native into a stereotyped object, and uses him as a "resource" for colonialist fiction' (JanMohamed 1985: 83).
11. See Stoler and Cooper 1997: 5; Fischer-Tiné and Mann 2004: 8.
12. See the discussion in Ruthner 2018: ch. A1.

References

Alatas, Syed Hussein. 1977. *The Myth of the Lazy Native: A Study of the Malays, Filipinos and Javanese from the 16th to the 20th Century and its Function in the Ideology of Colonial Capitalism*. London: F. Cass.

Babuna, Aydin. 2015. 'The Story of Bošnjastvo', in Clemens Ruthner et al., *WechselWirkungen. Austria-Hungary, Bosnia and Herzegovina, and the Western Balkans, 1878–1918*. New York: P. Lang, pp. 123–38.

Balandier, Georges. (1951) 1966. 'The Colonial Situation: A Theoretical Approach', in Immanuel Wallerstein (ed.), *Social Change: The Colonial Situation*. New York: Wiley, pp. 34–81.

Bencze, László. 2005. *The Occupation of Bosnia and Herzegovina in 1878*, ed. Frank N. Schubert. Boulder, CO: Social Science Monographs.

Bérenger, Jean. 1994. *L'Autriche-Hongrie 1815–1918*. Paris: A. Colin.

Bethke, Carl. 2018. 'Einwanderung und Kolonisten im k. u. k. Bosnien-Herzegowina: Überblick mit bosniakischen Perspektiven', in Ruthner and Scheer (eds), *Bosnien-Herzegowina und Österreich-Ungarn: Annäherungen an eine Kolonie*. Tübingen: Francke, pp. 237–50.

Bridge, Francis Roy. 1989. 'Österreich(-Ungarn) unter den Großmächten', in Adam Wandruszka and Peter Urbanitsch (eds), *Die Habsburgermonarchie 1848–1918*, vol. VI/1. Vienna: ÖAW, pp. 196–373.

Cooper, Frederick. 2005. *Colonialism in Question: Theory, Knowledge, History*. Berkeley: University of California Press.

Csáky, Moritz, Johannes Feichtinger and Ursula Prutsch (eds). 2003. *Habsburg postcolonial: Machtstrukturen und kollektives Gedächtnis*. Innsbruck: Studien-Verlag.

Dedijer, Vladimir, et al. 1974. *History of Yugoslavia*, ed. Marie Longyear, trans. Kordija Kveder. New York: McGraw-Hill.
Detrez, Raymond. 2002. 'Colonialism in the Balkans: Historic Realities and Contemporary Perceptions'. *Kakanien Revisited*, www.kakanien.ac.at/beitr/theorie/RDetrez1.pdf; last accessed 20 April 2020.
———. 2015. 'Reluctance and Determination: The Prelude to the Austro-Hungarian Occupation of Bosnia and Herzegovina in 1878', in Ruthner et al., *WechselWirkungen: Austria–Hungary, Bosnia and Herzegovina, and the Western Balkans, 1878–1918*. New York: P. Lang, pp. 21–40.
Donia, Robert J. 1981. *Islam under the Double Eagle: The Muslims of Bosnia and Herzegovina, 1878–1918*. New York: Columbia University Press.
———. 2007. 'The Proximate Colony: Bosnia and Herzegovina under Austro-Hungarian Rule'. *Kakanien Revisited*. http://www.kakanien-revisited.at/beitr/fallstudie/RDonia1.pdf; last accessed 20 April 2020.
Feichtinger, Johannes. 2016. 'Modernisierung, Zivilisierung, Kolonisierung als Argument: Konkurrierende Selbstermächtigungsdiskurse in der späten Habsburgermonarchie', in Christof Dejung and Martin Lengwiler (eds), *Ränder der Moderne: Neue Perspektiven auf die europäische Geschichte (1800–1930)*. Cologne: Böhlau, pp. 147–81.
Fieldhouse, D.K. 1981. *Colonialism 1870–1945: An Introduction*. London: Weidenfeld & Nicolson.
Fischer-Tiné, Harald, and Michael Mann (eds). 2004. *Colonialism as Civilizing Mission: Cultural Ideology in British India*. London: Anthem.
Gammerl, Benno. 2010. *Untertanen, Staatsbürger und Andere: Der Umgang mit ethnischer Heterogenität im Britischen Weltreich und im Habsburgerreich 1867–1918*. Göttingen: Vandenhoeck & Ruprecht.
Hadžijahić, Muhamed. 1974. *Od tradicije do identiteta*. Sarajevo: Svjetlost.
Haselsteiner, Horst. 1996. *Bosnien-Herzegowina: Orientkrise und die südslawische Frage*. Vienna: Böhlau.
Hechter, Michael. 1975. *Internal Colonialism: The Celtic Fringe in British National Development, 1536–1966*. London: Routledge & Kegan Paul.
Heiss, Johann, and Johannes Feichtinger. 2013. 'Uses of Orientalism in the Late 19th-Century Austro-Hungarian Empire', in James Hodkinson et al. (eds), *Deploying Orientalism in Culture and History: From Germany to Central and Eastern Europe*. Rochester, NY: Camden House, pp. 148–65.
Hochschild, Adam. 1998. *King Leopold's Ghost: A Story of Greed, Terror, and Heroism in Colonial Africa*. New York: Pan Macmillan.
Hösch, Edgar. 2002. *Geschichte der Balkanländer von der Frühzeit bis zur Gegenwart*. Munich: C.H. Beck.
Imamović, Mustafa. 2006. *Bosnia and Herzegovina: The Evolution of its Political and Legal Institutions*. Sarajevo: Magistrat.
Israel, Fred L. (ed.). 1967. *Major Peace Treaties of Modern History, 1648–1967*. New York: Chelsea House.
JanMohamed, Abdul R. 1985. 'The Economy of Manichean Allegory: The Function of Racial Difference in Colonialist Literature', in Henry Louis Gates Jr (ed.), *'Race', Writing, and Difference*. Chicago: Chicago University Press, pp. 78–106.
Jelavich, Barbara. 1969. *The Habsburg Empire in European Affairs, 1814–1918*. Chicago: McNally.

———. 1983. *History of the Balkans*. Cambridge: Cambridge University Press.
Jezernik, Božidar. 2004. *Wild Europe: The Balkans in the Gaze of Western Travellers*. London: Saqi.
Johler, Reinhold. 2018. 'Die Okkupation Bosnien-Herzegowinas und die Institutionalisierung der österreichischen Volkskunde als Wissenschaft', in Clemens Ruthner and Tamara Scheer, *Bosnien-Herzegowina und Österreich-Ungarn: Annäherungen an eine Kolonie*. Tübingen: Francke, pp. 325–58.
Judson, Pieter M. 2016. *The Habsburg Empire: A New History*. Cambridge, MA: Belknap, Harvard University Press.
Juzbašić, Dževad. 2002. *Politika i privreda u Bosni i Hercegovini pod austrougarskom upravom*. Sarajevo: Akademija nauka i umjetnosti Bosne i Hercegovine.
Kann, Robert A. 1977. 'Trends towards Colonialism in the Habsburg Empire, 1878–1918: The Case of Bosnia and Herzegovina, 1878–1914', in D.K. Rowney and G.E. Orchard (eds), *Russian and Slavonic History*. Columbus, OH: Slavica Publications, pp. 164–80.
Katus, László. 1961. 'Hauptzüge der kapitalistischen Entwicklung der Landwirtschaft in den südslawischen Gebieten der Österreichisch-Ungarischen Monarchie', in Pál Sándor and Péter Hanák (eds), *Studien zur Geschichte der Österreichisch-Ungarischen Monarchie*. Budapest: Akadémiai Kiadó, pp. 113–63.
k. k. Kriegsarchiv. 1879. *Die Occupation Bosniens und der Hercegovina durch k.k. Truppen im Jahre 1878: Nach authentischen Quellen dargestellt*. Vienna: Verlag des k.k. Generalstabes / W. Seidel.
Kolm, Evelyn. 2001. *Die Ambitionen Österreich-Ungarns im Zeitalter des Hochimperialismus*. Frankfurt/M.: P. Lang.
Kraljačić, Tomislav. 1987. *Kalajev režim u Bosni i Hercegovini, 1882–1903*. Sarajevo: Veselin Masleša.
Lampe, John, and Marvin Jackson. 1982. *Balkan Economic History, 1550–1950: From Imperial Borderlands to Developing Nations*. Bloomington: Indiana University Press.
Malcolm, Noel. 2002. *Bosnia: A Short History*. New York: Pan Macmillan.
McCagg, William O. 1992. 'The Soviet Union and the Habsburg Empire: Problems of Comparison', in Richard L. Rudolph and David F. Good (eds), *The Habsburg Empire and the Soviet Union: Nationalism and Empire*. New York: St. Martin's Press, pp. 45–63.
Müller-Funk, Wolfgang, Peter Plener, and Clemens Ruthner (eds). 2004. *Kakanien Revisited: Das Eigene und das Fremde (in) der österreichisch-ungarischen Monarchie*. Tübingen: Francke.
Müller-Funk, Wolfgang, and Birgit Wagner (eds). 2005. *Eigene und andere Fremde: 'Postkoloniale' Konflikte im europäischen Kontext*. Vienna: Turia + Kant.
Neumayer, Christoph, and Erwin A. Schmidl (eds). 2008. *Des Kaisers Bosniaken: Die bosnisch-herzegowinischen Truppen in der k.u.k. Armee*. Vienna: Militaria/Ed. Rest.
Neweklowsky, Gerhard. 1996. *Die bosnisch-herzegowinischen Muslime: Geschichte, Bräuche, Alltagskultur*, with Besim Ibišević and Žarko Bebić. Klagenfurt: Wieser.
Nolte, Hans-Heinrich, and Klaas Bähre (eds). 2001. *Innere Peripherien in Ost und West*. Stuttgart: Steiner.
Okey, Robin. 2007. *Taming Balkan Nationalism: The Habsburg 'Civilizing Mission' in Bosnia, 1878–1914*. Oxford: Oxford University Press.
Osterhammel, Jürgen. 2001. *Kolonialismus: Geschichte – Formen – Folgen*. 3rd edn. Munich: C.H. Beck.
Pavlowitch, Stevan K. 1999. *A History of the Balkans, 1904–1945*. London: Longman.

Pinson, Mark. 1994. *The Muslims of Bosnia and Herzegovina: Their Historic Development from the Middle Ages to the Dissolution of Yugoslavia*. Cambridge, MA: Harvard University Press.
Renner, Heinrich. 1896. *Durch Bosnien und die Hercegovina kreuz und quer: Wanderungen*. Berlin: Reimer.
Ress, Imre. 2006. 'Versuch einer Nationenbildung um die Jahrhundertwende: Benjámin Kállays Konzeption der bosnischen Nation', in Ende Kiss and Justin Stagl (eds), *Nation und Nationenbildung in Österreich-Ungarn 1848–1938: Prinzipien und Methoden*. Münster: LIT, pp. 59–72.
Ruthner, Clemens. 2008. 'Habsburg's Little Orient: A Post/Colonial Reading of Austrian and German Cultural Narratives on Bosnia and Herzegovina, 1878–1918', in *Kakanien Revisited*, http://www.kakanien.ac.at/beitr/fallstudie/CRuthner5.pdf; last accessed 20 April 2020.
———. 2018. *Habsburgs 'Dark Continent': Postkoloniale Lektüren zur österreichischen Literatur und Kultur im langen 19. Jahrhundert*. Tübingen: Francke.
Ruthner, Clemens, Diana Reynolds Cordileone, Ursula Reber and Raymond Detrez (eds). 2015. *WechselWirkungen: Austria–Hungary, Bosnia and Herzegovina, and the Western Balkans, 1878–1918*. New York: P. Lang.
Ruthner, Clemens, and Tamara Scheer (eds). 2018. *Bosnien-Herzegowina und Österreich-Ungarn: Annäherungen an eine Kolonie*. Tübingen: Francke.
Sauer, Walter. 2002. *K. u. k. kolonial: Habsburgermonarchie und europäische Herrschaft in Afrika*. Vienna: Böhlau.
Scheer, Tamara. 2013. *'Minimale Kosten, absolut kein Blut': Österreich-Ungarns Präsenz im Sandschak von Novi Pazar (1879–1908)*. Frankfurt/M.: P. Lang.
Schmid, Ferdinand. 1914. *Bosnien und die Herzegovina unter der Verwaltung Österreich-Ungarns*. Leipzig: von Veit.
Sethre, Ian. 2004. 'The Emergence and Influence of National Identities in the Era of Modernization: Nation-Building in Bosnia and Herzegovina, 1878–1914'. *Kakanien Revisited*. www.kakanien.ac.at/beitr/fallstudie/ISethre1.pdf; last accessed 20 April 2020.
Sirbubalo, Lejla. 2012. *'Wie wir im 78er Jahr unten waren (. . .)!' Bosnien-Bilder in der deutschsprachigen Literatur*. Würzburg: Königshausen & Neumann.
Stachel, Peter. 2003. 'Der koloniale Blick auf Bosnien-Herzegowina in der ethnographischen Populärliteratur der Habsburger Monarchie', in Moritz Csáky, Johannes Feichtinger and Ursula Prutsch (eds), *Habsburg postcolonial: Machtstrukturen und kollektives Gedächtnis*. Innsbruck: Studien-Verlag, pp. 259–88.
Stoler, Ann Laura, and Frederick Cooper (eds). 1997. *Tensions of Empire: Colonial Cultures in a Bourgeois World*. Berkeley: University of California Press.
Sugar, Peter F. 1963. *Industrialization of Bosnia and Herzegovina: 1878–1918*. Seattle: Washington University Press.
Suppan, Arnold. 1978. 'Zur Frage eines österreichisch-ungarischen Imperialismus in Südosteuropa: Regierungspolitik und öffentliche Meinung um die Annexion Bosniens und der Herzegowina', in Adam Wandruszka et al. (eds), *Die Donaumonarchie und die südslawische Frage von 1848 bis 1918: Texte des ersten österreichisch-jugoslawischen Historikertreffens Gösing 1976*. Vienna: ÖAW, pp. 103–31.
Taylor, A.J.P. (1948) 1990. *The Habsburg Monarchy 1809–1918: A History of the Austrian Empire and Austria–Hungary*. Harmondsworth: Penguin.
Telesko, Werner. 2015. 'Colonialism without Colonies: The Civilizing Missions in the Habsburg Empire', in Michael Falser (ed.), *Cultural Heritage as Civilizing Mission: From Decay to Recovery*. New York: Springer, pp. 35–48.

Todorova, Maria. 1997. *Imagining the Balkans*. New York: Oxford University Press.
Ulbandus 7. 2003. *Empire, Union, Center, Satellite: The Place of Post-Colonial Theory in Slavic/Central and Eastern European/(Post-)Soviet Studies*. New York: Columbia University Press.
Verdery, Katherine. 1979. 'Internal Colonialism in Austria-Hungary', *Ethnic and Racial Studies* 2: 378–99.
Vervaet, Stijn. 2004. 'Some Historians from Former Yugoslavia on the Austro-Hungarian Period in Bosnia and Herzegovina (1878–1918)'. *Kakanien Revisited*. www.kakanien.ac.at/beitr/fallstudie/SVervaet1.pdf; last accessed 20 April 2020.
Vrankić, Petar. 1998. *Religion und Politik in Bosnien und der Herzegowina, 1878–1918*. Paderborn: Schöningh.
Wertheimer, Eduard v. 1913. *Graf Julius Andrássy: Sein Leben und seine Zeit*, vol. 3. Stuttgart: DVA.
Wessely, Kurt. 1989. 'Die wirtschaftliche Entwicklung von Bosnien-Herzegowina', in Adam Wandruszka and Peter Urbanitsch (eds), *Die Habsburgermonarchie 1848–1918*, vol. 1. Vienna: ÖAW, pp. 528–66.
Young, Robert J.C. 2015. *Empire, Colony, Postcolony*. Chichester: Wiley Blackwell.

Chapter 5

THE PORTRAYAL OF MUSLIMS IN AUSTRO-HUNGARIAN STATE PRIMARY SCHOOL TEXTBOOKS FOR BOSNIA AND HERZEGOVINA

Oliver Pejić

The Challenges of Interconfessional Education in Habsburg Bosnia and Herzegovina

The question of adequate educational reform undoubtedly ranked high among the issues troubling the Habsburg authorities after the 1878 occupation of Bosnia and Herzegovina. In order to shed light on how they tackled the problem of preparing textbooks that would not offend Bosnian and Herzegovinian Muslims and could integrate them into the state's interconfessional school system, this chapter aims to analyse and assess the portrayal of Muslims in the Austro-Hungarian state primary school textbooks for Bosnia and Herzegovina.[1] It considers both contemporary and historical depictions of Muslims, their relations with other confessional groups and the manner in which the textbooks addressed topics that a Muslim readership may have found offensive. It finally attempts to situate the results of the analysis into the wider context of Austria–Hungary's policy towards Bosnia and Herzegovina's Muslims, with special consideration to their roles as a support base for the Austro-Hungarian regime and as a state-forming element inside a future Bosnian nation.

On 12 September 1878, less than two months after the Austro-Hungarian invasion of Bosnia and Herzegovina, the military authorities had already announced they would establish a public education system in accordance with the norms of 'advanced European countries' (Bogićević 1965: 146). Indeed, the Habsburg occupation of Bosnia and Herzegovina had largely been framed as an imperial civilizing or cultural mission, and '[b]y 1878 a cultural mission had to show some aspiration towards popular primary education' (Okey 2007: 49). By 17 August 1880, the Bosnian-Herzegovinian provincial government had reached an agreement with the Austro-Hungarian Joint Ministry of Finance regarding the character of the regime's newly established state schools: they were to be non-compulsory but strictly interconfessional and open to children of all religious groups. This stood in stark contrast with the province's established tradition of confessional education (Bogićević 1965: 147–60).[2]

Muslim parents who had enrolled their children into the new state schools could hardly, however, have been pleased with the textbooks their children were using. The primer, for example, contained descriptions of churches, Christmas, and other festivities that 'we Christians' observe (*Početnica* 1877: 123–27). According to a text from the third-grade reader, the Turks are 'the greatest enemy of our people' as their religion teaches them to persecute Christians (*Čitanka za treći razred* 1890: 94). The children would also learn in the fourth-grade reader that the reason Europeans are the most spiritually and morally developed people in the world is their Christian religion (*Čitanka za četvrti razred* 1890: 87–88).

The fact that textbooks containing such passages had ended up in primary schools attended by Muslim pupils reflects the cumbersome manner in which the organization of Bosnia and Herzegovina's education system had been handled during the first few years of Habsburg rule. When the provincial government had to decide which textbooks should be used in the new schools, it initially opted for Croatian textbooks, the official reasoning being that they, unlike contemporary Serbian textbooks, contained texts in both the Latin and the Cyrillic alphabets (Dlustuš 1894: 100–01). The decision to use Croatian textbooks should, however, also be understood in the context of the initial pro-Croat phase of Habsburg rule, during which the administration employed the Croatian standard language for official use, and Croatian patriotic sentiments were even expressed in the province's official newspapers (Grčević 2015: 388–90). Croatian political aspirations in Bosnia and Herzegovina, viewed by Magyars as a threat to the monarchy's dualist system, were, however, largely incapacitated by the growth of Magyar influence in the province's affairs. This process culminated in Benjámin von Kállay's appointment as joint finance minister and governor of Bosnia and Herzegovina on 4 June 1882, after which a purge stripped the provincial bureaucracy of its hitherto pronounced Croatian character (Okey 2007: 29, 32; Grčević 2015: 390–93).

While interconfessional education was not unknown in the Habsburg Monarchy – it was also introduced in the nearby Kingdom of Croatia–Slavonia in 1874

(Jelavich 1990: 41–46) – its implementation in a Muslim-populated province still amounted to an undertaking without precedent. As the authors of the Croatian textbooks could not have expected that their works would one day be read by Muslim pupils, it is not surprising that complaints soon surfaced regarding their alleged anti-Islamic content (Šator 2004: 103–05; Okey 2007: 50). After an enquiry into the content of history and geography textbooks in February 1883, the Joint Finance Ministry finally decided that the Croatian textbooks should be replaced with a set of new textbooks that would be especially adapted to Bosnian-Herzegovinian circumstances (Okey 2007: 67).

Thus, between 1883 and 1893, the provincial government produced a history textbook, two geography textbooks and four new readers and mathematics textbooks for use in the province's state primary schools (Dlustuš 1894: 158). The textbooks were then reviewed by a special committee composed of government officials and native Muslim and Orthodox notables, whose primary task was to inspect the textbooks for linguistic 'purity' (Dlustuš 1910: 220–21). Although the available sources do not allow a detailed reconstruction of the committee's activities, they evidently went beyond the scope of mere linguistics. The native members would also comment on and sometimes make direct suggestions regarding the content of the textbooks (Kraljačić 1987: 256), which means they possessed a certain degree of agency in the creation of the textbooks and likely played an important role in identifying and removing potentially offensive content from them.[3]

The Issue of Fair Confessional Representation in Textbooks

One of the first shortcomings we notice when looking at the Croatian readers initially used in the province's new state schools is their evident lack of fictional characters with Muslim personal names. While this is not surprising considering the fact that they were written for a Christian audience, it can be assumed that this lack of Muslim personal names not only made Muslim children feel alienated and underrepresented but also provided grounds for Muslim allegations of confessional partiality on the part of the new state schools. The potential for such allegations was, however, decisively dealt with in the new state readers, in which the share of Muslim names represented roughly 24 per cent of all names of fictional characters and 19 per cent of total occurrences of such names in the textbooks.[4] While these figures may appear low compared to the overall share of Muslims in the province's population (38 per cent, according to the 1879 census – Okey 2007: 8), they still by far surpassed the share of Muslims among children enrolled in the state schools (10 per cent) in the school year of 1882/83 (Dlustuš 1894: 102).

It is interesting to note that this strategy for achieving adequate confessional representation on an onomastic level was most likely inspired by the interconfessional textbooks written after the adoption of the secular Croatian education law of 1874. It too had made necessary the creation of textbooks that would neither alienate Christian Orthodox children nor provide any grounds for criticism of the Christian Orthodox community, whose spokesmen attacked the secularization of education in Croatia, employing both traditional religious and Serbian nationalist arguments (Jelavich 1990: 44–47). While this phenomenon would warrant a separate study, a cursory glance at the Croatian textbooks reveals that they too contained typical Orthodox personal names such as 'Milorad' and 'Radovan' (*Početnica* 1877: 38). Prior Croatian experiences with interconfessional education thus seemed to have provided an example for overcoming related albeit more complex problems in Bosnia and Herzegovina.

The need for confessional parity did not, of course, reflect itself merely on the onomastic level but also in the depiction of interconfessional relations themselves. In accordance with the recurring proverb *Brat je mio, ma koje vjere bio*, translatable as 'Cherish your brother, his faith be yours or other' (Hajdarpasic 2015: 117), the readers implied to the students that they should be warm, friendly and helpful towards their compatriots of other faiths. Typical in this sense are three texts that represent friendly exchanges of letters between Muslim and non-Muslim children, one of which, for example, takes place between Mustafa Vukčić of Mostar and his friend Ivan Boljarević of Slavonski Brod in neighbouring Croatia (*Druga čitanka* 1887: 53–54, 60–61). The boys, who even refer to each other as blood brothers (*pobratimi*), supposedly met when Ivan visited Mostar with his father. Along with his letter, Mustafa sent a basket of figs from his native Herzegovina, knowing that such fruit was not available in his friend's region, while Ivan invited his friend and his father to visit him in Slavonski Brod and partake in the local grape harvest.

Not all of the interconfessional relations portrayed in the textbooks, however, took place between individuals of the same wealth or class, as is demonstrated in a text intended to show children how to write a certificate (*svjedočanstvo*). The text in question is essentially a letter of recommendation, and was written for Marija Vulović, a Christian housemaid, by her former employer and Muslim nobleman (*vlastelin*) Avdaga Nović. He describes her with attributes such as 'obedient, careful and dexterous', and says that her conduct is 'in every sense worthy of praise' (*Četvrta čitanka* 1912: 296–97). This text may be considered a surprising example of interconfessional realism, reflecting the fact that the confessional divide between Muslims and Christians in Bosnia and Herzegovina was often also a class divide.

Contemporary and Historical Portrayals of Bosnian-Herzegovinian Muslims

Although Muslim characters in the textbooks tend not to stand out by any specific characteristics and in most cases could easily be replaced by characters of other confessions, there are certain contexts in which we may presume that the decision to make a certain character Muslim had deeper political motivations. For example, the fourth-grade reader contained a letter that Ahmed Pozderac, an Austro-Hungarian military officer, had written to his brother, in which he describes a leisurely steamboat journey he undertook on the Danube, reaching Orşova in modern-day Romania on what was once the eastern fringe of the Monarchy (*Četvrta čitanka* 1912: 44–46). We may presume that the confessional identity of the officer in question was not coincidental, and was most likely chosen to show Muslim children that they too could someday achieve an illustrious career in the Habsburg military. A second example of model Muslim behaviour can be found in a text titled *Prijatelji zavičaja svoga* (Friends to their homeland), which describes a group of non-fictional villages near Bijeljina, whose inhabitants supposedly wanted to erect schools but lacked the funds and land to do so (*Druga čitanka* 1887: 132). To remedy this, the so-called lords of these villages, all of them Muslim *begs*,[5] each decided to donate a plot of their land. This text was not only a positive portrayal of the landed Muslim elites, depicting them in an altruistic and humanitarian light, but it was also an example of philanthropic activism and agency for wealthy Muslims to partake in, and thus contribute to, Austria–Hungary's civilizing mission.

The extraordinarily positive portrayal Muslim begs enjoyed in the textbooks went beyond their purported philanthropy, and reflected their prestigious social status in a more general sense. This can be seen in the short story 'Kesica' (The small pouch) (*Druga čitanka* 1887: 79–80), which was adapted from an earlier Croatian textbook (*Čitanka za treći razred* 1890 [1879]: 19–20), and describes an encounter between a poor boy who had lost his pouch and an 'excellent, rich gentleman' who had found it while hunting. The gentleman would first show the boy a separate pouch filled with gold ducats in order to check if he would claim it as his own and, seeing that he was honest, would then give him both pouches as a reward. While the Croatian version only mentions the man's wealth, the Bosnian-Herzegovinian one explicitly describes him as a 'beg from a nearby town' (*Druga čitanka* 1887: 79).

Of course, the textbooks did not include only contemporary portrayals of Bosnian-Herzegovinian Muslims but also spoke about their history. The history book thus traces their origin to a purported mass conversion of Bogomil heretics after the Ottoman conquest,[6] placing special emphasis on the supposed continuity between the medieval Bogomil gentry and later Muslim elites:

> When the Sultan became the ruler of the land, these nobles converted by and large to the Mohammedan faith, and the Sultan confirmed them the rights and privileges they had always possessed ... Our homeland had fared better than other lands taken over by the Turks, to the extent that the land largely remained in the same hands as before – only that now the finer and richer nobles called themselves *begs* and the less fine and rich agas ... Since the land mostly did not change masters, neither did the position of the peasantry become much different under the Turks. (*Povijest* 1893: 42)[7]

The history book also made sure to point out the esteemed role that Bosnian-Herzegovinian Muslims played in the Ottoman state. It claimed that Sultan Suleiman the Magnificent 'grew fond of Bosniaks very quickly', and that he considered them his best janissaries; however, he proved his love for the Bosniaks most clearly by appointing Sokollu Mehmed Pasha (Mehmed-paša Sokolović) as teacher to his son and heir (*Povijest* 1893: 43). When describing the provincial rebellions of the nineteenth century, the history book again drew parallels between medieval and Muslim elites when describing their defiant character: 'The begs and agas thus completely preserved the old Bosnian virtue of chivalry and heroism! But, on the other hand, they remained just as unruly and forceful as they used to be' (ibid.: 49–50).[8]

Both the flattering portrayal the landed Muslim elites enjoyed in the textbooks and the persistent emphasis on their supposed medieval Bogomil roots reflect the Habsburg administration's amenable policy towards them. Not only was the Muslim community judged to be the most reliable support base for Austro-Hungarian rule – the Roman Catholic and Christian Orthodox communities were considered prone to destructive Croat and Serbian nationalism – its elites were also expected to play the role of a state-building element in a Bosnian political nation (Kraljačić 1987: 82–83; Grčević 2015: 391–93; Hajdarpasic 2015: 177). While Habsburg support for the Muslim landowners manifested itself in the stalling of agrarian reform and in their persistent ascendancy in society, the regime's attitude towards the viability of Muslim survival in a modern environment was ambiguous and largely informed by contemporary Orientalist beliefs in Western civilizational superiority. Indeed, in confidential papers and memoranda, Kállay had even entertained the idea of a Muslim apostasy in the distant future, in which case Catholicism should be enhanced in order to ensure they would not join the Orthodox confession (Okey 2007: 59–61; see also chapter by František Šístek in this volume on the possible conversion of Muslims to Christianity found in Czech language sources). As argued by Robin Okey, '[n]ot Islam so much as the independent spirit of a Bogumil aristocratic elite was what Kállay wished to support, believing as he did that the Bosnian begs were direct descendants of medieval leaders who accepted Islam to retain their predominance in the land' (Okey 2007: 60). The quotes cited from the analysed textbooks leave no doubt that this tendency was also pursued in the Bosnian-Herzegovinian state school system, and offered the Muslims an attractive narrative of their community's roots and historical glory.

Avoiding Offence to Muslims and Addressing Sensitive Topics

Although the content of the new Bosnian-Herzegovinian readers differed significantly from that of their Croatian predecessors, at times they still replicated the general layout of the Croatian readers (cf. *Početnica* 1877 and *Prva čitanka* 1894), and inherited from them numerous texts that were then adapted to suit local circumstances. While the majority of offensive texts appear to have been simply left out of the Bosnian-Herzegovinian textbooks, the ones that were not offer us an interesting glimpse into how such texts were censored and adapted in order to function in the Bosnian-Herzegovinian context. If we look at a text in which a child describes an average school day, we can see that its Croatian version contained references to Christian religious practices that could have been problematized by Muslim readers: 'We begin [class] with a short prayer. When we pray, we join our hands together. . . . When class is over, we pray and calmly go home' (*Početnica* 1877: 47–48). The Bosnian-Herzegovinian version, however, lacked any references to prayer and included only a verbal expression of gratitude: 'When class is over, I say: Thank you, God! [A]nd calmly go home' (*Prva čitanka* 1894: 43).[9]

Another feature of the Croatian textbooks that Muslim readers most likely did not receive well was their typically antagonistic portrayal of the Ottoman Empire, since the Croatian contribution to the defence of Christendom from the 'infidel Turks' was, after all, a very important source of national pride and patriotism (Jelavich 1990: 112–14). Since loyalty to and identification with the Ottoman Empire was still very strong among Bosnian-Herzegovinian Muslims (Kraljačić 1987: 85–86), it was necessary to address both the Ottoman Empire and its military conflicts with the Habsburgs in a considerate and non-offensive manner. The history book, which otherwise described Ottoman history more or less in accordance with the Ottoman decline thesis, then made sure to emphasize the empire's historical high points. It claimed that the janissaries were once the greatest army in the world (*Povijest* 1893: 43) and praised the virtues of sultans such as Mehmed II and Suleiman the Magnificent (ibid.: 46). It also addressed the violent character of Ottoman conquest by placing it in its appropriate historical context:

> In the olden days, when two nations would fight, the stronger would take away from the weaker all the property it had not burnt or destroyed, and the people it had not killed it would capture into slavery. In the age when the Ottomans conquered Bosnia, the conqueror would still often inflict all sorts of violence upon the conquered, especially when religion also separated them. Still, if we compare the Ottomans to other victorious nations, we must admit that they were no worse than many others. (*Povijest* 1893: 41)[10]

Particularly interesting is the manner in which the history book described the debated character of Ottoman religious tolerance, which it again historicized and framed into a wider European context of religious strife during the early modern period:

Once you get to know history better, you will see that during Sultan Suleiman's reign, and long after it, there was an age when Christian nations themselves would lead long and bloody wars because of religion, and that even Christian rulers did not tolerate any other religion in their state beside their own. The Turkish sultans – even if they did not allow their subjects (Christians) to raise bell towers or build churches – still did not deny them the right to praise the Lord and to practise their rituals in their own custom. (*Povijest* 1893: 44)[11]

We may also notice an obvious difference in how the Croatian and Bosnian-Herzegovinian textbooks approached the Ottoman–Habsburg wars. The passionate references to the battles 'our' ancestors fought to liberate Christians from the 'shameful Turkish yoke' in the Croatian description of the 1683 Ottoman Siege of Vienna were thus completely absent from the more unbiased description of the same event in the Bosnian-Herzegovinian textbooks (*Čitanka za četvrti razred* 1890: 117–19; *Četvrta čitanka* 1912: 79–81). The history book also claimed that the best evidence of the former military might of the Ottoman Empire was the fact that the Habsburgs, despite their great power, could not ward it off for several centuries. Indeed, even after the death of Suleiman II, the battles between the emperor and the sultan supposedly seemed like a horrible fight between a tiger and a lion in which there was no clear victor in sight (*Povijest* 1893: 46–47).

Conclusion

We may conclude that the portrayal of Muslims in the textbooks reflects two of the major political goals that the Habsburg government strived to accomplish in its policy towards Bosnia and Herzegovina's Muslim population. The first goal was to encourage Muslim enrolment in state schools in order to promote their Westernization and integration into Habsburg society – the provincial government had already argued at the beginning of the occupation that only an interconfessional school system could provide Muslim pupils the Western education they could not attain in their traditional religious schools (Okey 2007: 50). With primary education remaining non-compulsory until as late as 1911 (Bogićević 1965: 142–44), it was, without a doubt, of utmost importance that the new textbooks conformed to a high standard of political sensitivity so as not to provide grounds for potential Muslim critiques. This chapter has shown the diverse strategies that were employed to uphold this standard, some of which seem to have been inspired by solutions to similar problems already faced during the implementation of interconfessional education in the neighbouring Kingdom of Croatia–Slavonia.

The second goal pursued by the government was to gain the favour of the landed Muslim elites and to impart in them a historical consciousness and patriotism stemming from their alleged medieval Bogomil ancestry. We see throughout the chapter that the textbooks portrayed this community in a particularly flattering light, and would repeatedly stress the putative continuity between Bosnia and Herzegovina's medieval Bogomil aristocracy and the province's later Muslim elites. While this undertaking appears to have had mixed results – a noteworthy number of begs did ally themselves with the Habsburg government, but the majority would remain in opposition until the Ottoman Empire's defeats in the Balkan Wars (Kamberović 2005: 74) – the influence that the Habsburg Bosnian nation-building project had exerted on the development of Bosnian Muslim national thought should not be underestimated. The aforementioned Bogomil historical narrative was also spread through state-sponsored folklore collections and patriotic Muslim journals such as *Bošnjak*, all of which were part of a wider Habsburg enterprise of cultivating Bosnian Muslim national identity. According to Hajdarpasic, this project 'provided a critical boost for an emerging sense of Muslim national distinction, and enabled the creation of a new repertoire of Muslim patriotism that would endure well into the twentieth century' (Hajdarpasic 2015: 182). Despite their limited outreach, there is no doubt that the textbooks analysed in this chapter also played an important role in spreading this patriotism; after all, they represent the first attempt at its institutionalized mass dissemination.

Oliver Pejić earned his first master's degree in late modern and contemporary history at the University of Ljubljana, Slovenia, and his second master's degree in comparative history at the Central European University in Budapest and Vienna. His research has primarily focused on the ideological aspects of the late Habsburg Empire's linguistically heterogeneous school system, with particular emphasis on identity formation and representations of the Other. His wider research interests encompass Central and South East European cultural and political history in the long nineteenth century, as well as postimperial transitions in the Habsburg and Ottoman successor states of the interwar period.

Notes

1. The four new primary school readers (*Prva čitanka* vol. 1, 1894; *Prva čitanka* vol. 2, 1892; *Druga čitanka* 1887; *Treća čitanka* 1893; *Četvrta čitanka* 1912) and the history book (*Povijest* 1893), served as the primary corpus for this research.
2. Separate Muslim, Christian Orthodox, Roman Catholic, and Jewish confessional school systems existed in Bosnia and Herzegovina during Ottoman rule. While the Catholic schools all eventually became state schools (Papić 1982: 112–14), the other confessional school systems remained in operation after the occupation. The two fundamental monographic works on education in Bosnia and Herzegovina during the Ottoman and Habsburg periods are Bogićević (1965) and Papić (1972). For Muslim schools in particular, see Ćurić (1983), for Catholic schools Papić (1982) and for Orthodox schools Papić (1978).

3. The committee's Muslim members were *qadi* Nezir Škaljić and Mehmed-beg Kapetanović Ljubušak, both of whom would later become mayors of Sarajevo. The Orthodox members were Miloš Mandić, Bosnia and Herzegovina's first professional journalist, confessional schoolteacher Nikola Kašiković, archimandrite Đorđe Nikolajević and notable Antonije Jeftanović. The school officials Ljuboje Dlustuš and Đuro Bujher figured as representatives of the government (Dlustuš 1910: 221).
4. To gauge the ratio of Muslim and non-Muslim names in the readers, I noted and added together all the occurrences of names pertaining to fictional characters. The term 'occurrence' presumes that a specific name appears at least once in a given text. The calculation does not take into account the names of characters the children would have identified as foreign, or names the authors could not change at will, such as those of historical figures or mythological characters. It must be stressed that the calculation itself cannot be considered empirical, since it is impossible to determine the exact number of texts in the readers (a formally single text may in practice contain multiple discrete texts that cannot be treated as one). The simultaneous use of neutral and hypocoristic versions of names in the same text also makes determining the exact number of names problematic – in this calculation I have opted to count the neutral, hypocoristic, male and female versions of a given name as one (e.g. Jovan, Jovo, Jovanka). Despite these shortcomings, I believe the results of this enquiry remain relevant, at least as an approximate illustration of the share of Muslim names within the textbooks.
5. The title 'beg' was used in Bosnia and Herzegovina during Austro-Hungarian rule to refer to large Muslim landholders, who used the title based on their family's alleged historical origins. Large non-Muslim landholders were referred to by the title 'gazda' (Kamberović 2005: 13).
6. The Bogomil theory was developed by the Croatian historian Franjo Rački, and at the time was one of two circulating interpretations of the character of the medieval Bosnian Church. While Rački considered the Church dualistic and heretical in character, the Serb historian Božidar Petranović saw it as essentially Eastern Orthodox. Petranović's theory has largely been discredited by modern historiography, as has the use of the term 'Bogomil' for describing the Church. A later third conformist (*pravovjeran*) historiographical interpretative frame sees the church as schismatic rather than heretical in character (Dautović 2015: 129–31).
7. 'Kad je dakle sultan postao gospodarem zemlje, prijegju ta vlastela listom na muhamedovsku vjeru, a sultan im potvrdi njihova dobra i prava, koja su od starine imala . . . U toliko je u našoj domovini bilo bolje, nego u drugim zemljama, koje su Turci zauzeli, što je zemljište najvećim dijelom ostalo u istim rukama, u kojim je i prije njih bilo – samo što su se sad otmenija i bogatija gospoda nazvala 'begovi', a manje otmena i bogata 'age' . . . pa kako zemljište većim dijelom nije promijenilo gospodara, tako nije ni težačko stanje u glavnom drukčije postalo za Turaka' (Povijest 1893: 42).
8. 'Begovi su i age daklen potpuno sačuvali staru bosansku vrlinu viteštva i junaštva! No s druge su strane i isto tako samovoljni i siloviti ostali kao nekada' (*Povijest* 1893: 49–50).
9. 'Počimljemo malom molitvom. Kad se molimo, sklopimo ruke . . . Kad se nauk svrši, opet se pomolimo, te idemo mirno kući' (*Početnica* 1877: 47–48). 'Kada se učenje svrši, onda reknem: Hvala ti Bože! pa mirno idem kući' (*Prva čitanka* 1894: 43).
10. 'U staro doba, kad su se dva naroda zavadila, jači bi slabijem oteo sve imanje, što nije popalio i uništio, a ljude, koje nije pobio, u roblje bi odveo. Pa i onda još, kad su Osmanlije ovladale Bosnom, činio je često pobjeditelj pobijegjenome svakojaka zuluma; osobito

onda, kad ih je vjera dijelila. – No kad Osmanlije isporedimo s drugim narodima pobjediteljima, moramo priznati, da nijesu ni oni gori bili od mnogih drugih' (*Povijest* 1893: 41).

11. 'Dok se bolje upoznate sa istorijom, vidjećete, kako je za sultana Sulejmana i još dugo poslije njega takvo doba bilo, da su i sâmi kršćanski narodi megju sobom duge i krvave ratove vodili zbog vjere, pa da i sami kršćanski vladari nijesu trpjeli druge vjere u svojoj državi nego svoje. Turski sultani – i ako nijesu dopuštali svojim podanicima (kršćanima), da zvonove dižu i crkve grade – ipak im nijesu branili, da služe Boga i da vrše svoje vjerske obrede na svoj način' (*Povijest* 1893: 44).

References

Primary Sources

Četvrta čitanka za osnovne škole u Bosni i Hercegovini. (1887) 1912. Sarajevo: Zemaljska štamparija.
Čitanka za četvrti razred obćih pučkih škola. (1880) 1890. Zagreb: Nakladom kr. hrv.-slav.-dalm. zemaljske vlade.
Čitanka za treći razred obćih pučkih škola. (1879) 1890. Zagreb: Nakladom kr. hrv.-slav.-dalm. zemaljske vlade.
Druga čitanka za osnovne škole u Bosni i Hercegovini. (1884) 1887. Sarajevo: Zemaljska štamparija.
Početnica za obće pučke škole. 1877. Zagreb: Nakladom kr. hrv.-slav.-dalm. zemaljske vlade.
Povijest Bosne i Hercegovine za osnovne škole. 1893. Sarajevo: Zemaljska štamparija.
Prva čitanka za osnovne škole u Bosni i Hercegovini, vol. 1. (1883) 1894. Sarajevo: Zemaljska štamparija.
Prva čitanka za osnovne škole u Bosni i Hercegovini, vol. 2. (1883) 1892. Sarajevo: Zemaljska štamparija.
Treća čitanka za osnovne škole u Bosni i Hercegovini. (1887) 1893. Sarajevo: Zemaljska štamparija.

Secondary Sources

Bogićević, Vojislav. 1965. *Istorija razvitka osnovnih škola u Bosni i Hercegovini: u doba turske i austrougarske uprave (1463–1918)*. Sarajevo: Zavod za izdavanje udžbenika BiH.
Ćurić, Hajrudin. 1983. *Muslimansko školstvo u Bosni i Hercegovini do 1918. godine*. Sarajevo: Veselin Masleša.
Dautović, Dženan. 2015. 'Crkva bosanska: moderni historiografski tokovi, rasprave i kontroverze (2005–2015)', *Historijska traganja* 15: 127–60.
Dlustuš, Ljuboje. 1894. 'Školske prilike u Bosni i Hercegovini od okupacije do danas', *Školski vjesnik* 1(1–10): 1–4, 50–54, 100–06, 155–61, 223–27, 289–93, 341–43, 401–04, 455–58, 531–38.
———. 1910. 'Za narodno jedinstvo', *Bosanska vila* 25(12–15): 221–22.
Grčević, Mario. 2015. 'Vanjskopolitički utjecaji na hrvatski književnojezični razvoj u drugoj polovici XIX. stoljeća', in Ivan Šestak (ed.), *Od Mure do mora, od Save do Seine: Spomen-*

zbornik patru Vladimiru Horvatu SJ za njegov 80. rodendan. Zagreb: Filozofsko-teološki institut Družbe Isusove, pp. 94–106.

Hajdarpasic, Edin. 2015. *Whose Bosnia?: Nationalism and Political Imagination in the Balkans, 1840–1914*. New York: Cornell University Press.

Jelavich, Charles. 1990. *South Slav Nationalisms: Textbooks and Yugoslav Union before 1914*. Columbus: Ohio State University Press.

Kamberović, Husnija. 2005. *Begovski zemljišni posjedi u Bosni i Hercegovini od 1878 do 1918. Godine*. Sarajevo: Ibn Sina.

Kraljačić, Tomislav. 1987. *Kalajev režim u Bosni i Hercegovini: 1882–1903*. Sarajevo: Veselin Masleša.

Okey, Robin. 2007. *Taming Balkan Nationalism: The Habsburg 'Civilizing Mission' in Bosnia, 1878–1914*. New York: Oxford University Press.

Papić, Mitar. 1972. *Školstvo u Bosni i Hercegovini za vrijeme austro-ugarske okupacije (1878–1918)*. Sarajevo: Veselin Masleša.

———. 1978. *Istorija srpskih škola u Bosni i Hercegovini*. Sarajevo: Veselin Masleša.

———. 1982. *Hrvatsko školstvo u Bosni i Hercegovini do 1918. godine*. Sarajevo: Veselin Masleša.

Šator, Muhamed. 2004. *Bosanski, hrvatski, srpski jezik u BiH do 1914. godine*. Mostar: Univerzitet 'Džemal Bijedić' / Fakultet humanističkih nauka.

Chapter 6

TOWARDS SECULARITY
Autonomy and Modernization of Bosnian Islamic Institutions under Austro-Hungarian Administration

Zora Hesová

Bosnian Islam has been intensely debated as a possible model for a future Islam of Europe. The idea arises from the fact that Bosnian Muslims belong to the communities with the longest history in Europe, but even more so, it is rooted in the Bosnian Muslim tradition, which is seen by some – Bosniaks and other Europeans alike – as a source of inspiration for nascent Muslim communities in Europe (Bougarel 2007, van Dijk Bartels 2012, Alibašić 2010). The peculiarity of Bosnian Islam lies not only in Bosniaks' status as the only autonomous Slavic Muslim community on European soil but, above all, it can be found in the Bosnian version of religious modernity: Bosnian Islamic representatives consistently claim the possibility of (and even the desirability of) leading Islamic religious life within a modern secular state. One of the sources of such a claim is the historical legacy of Bosnia and Hercegovina's first encounter with European modernity within the Austro-Hungarian Empire. Between 1878 and 1918, the Habsburg Monarchy not only brought about the rapid modernization of the administration, infrastructure and economy of the province, but it also sought to regulate its relations with the Bosnian Muslims by institutionalizing the Islamic community as well as its economic, legal and educational systems. Moreover, the Austro-Hungarian occupation led to a two-way process in which the nascent Bosnian

Muslim community sought recognition and wrought its religious, financial and educational autonomy from the Habsburg state.

When attempting to define the legacy of the forty-year rule of the Austro-Hungarian state in Bosnia and Herzegovina, it is best to look at the perception Bosnian Muslim scholars and leaders of the Bosnian Islamic community have of their Austrian past, and at the way they define the Austrian legacy in modern-day Bosnian Islam. In so doing, three aspects emerge: the relevance of the historical experience within Austria–Hungary to contemporary debates about Bosnian Islamic identity; the direct institutional legacy of Austrian administration; and the indirect intellectual legacy of Austrian administration. All three of these may well be behind the secularity of contemporary Bosnian Islamic practice.

Bosnian Islamic Tradition and the Austrian Legacy

In his influential definition of the Islamic tradition of the Bosniaks from 2006, Fikret Karčić, a prominent Bosnian Islamic scholar, professor of law, and law historian, defines the six constitutive elements of the so-called Bosnian Islamic tradition: (1) *hanafi-maturidi* doctrinal belonging; (2) Ottoman-Islamic cultural heritage; (3) the Islamization of pre-Ottoman practices; (4) the tradition of Islamic reformism in the interpretation of Islam; (5) the institutionalization of Islam in the form of the Islamic Community; and (6) the practice of expression of Islam in a secular state (Karčić 2006). He does not give a definition of a Bosnian Islam because, like other Bosniak scholars, he understands Islam as a unique normative system with the Qur'an as its foundation, and as such it does not bear adjectives. But the local modalities of interpreting, practising and developing this normative tradition can be defined, defended and developed as a basis of a historically constituted community. Such a local tradition gives the community its identity, and can be defined through its historically constituted features. In this definition, two of the six points listed above – (4) and (5) – refer directly to the Austrian experience.

Karčić has articulated the Islamic tradition of the Bosniaks at the height of a lively debate in the first decade of the twenty-first century, when foreign ways of practising Islam and other *madhab*s (law schools) have made their way to Bosnia and Herzegovina, and openly challenged local practices. The Salafi challengers have criticized, among other things, certain prayer habits (collective open-air prayers, prayers for the deceased recited by women, and prayers recited for certain events, etc.), some of which are Islamized pagan practices and others merely local habits. Bosnian scholars had argued in support of the Islamic character of these peculiarities earlier, but now, under concentrated suspicion from proponents of other *madhab*s, the community has been led to deliberate about what constitutes Bosnian Islamic practice. There seems to be no doubt that Bosnia and Herzegovina has its own way of practising Islam: the Islamic Community of Bosnia and Herzegovina (ICBH) uses this term in its constitution of 2006. Article IV stipulates that 'the foundations of the organs and institutions of the Islamic Community in Bosnia and Herzegovina are the honourable Qur'an, the Prophet's *sunna ali-hi-s-selam*, the Islamic tradition of Bosniaks, and the demands of the time'.[1] More importantly, the ICBH has a constitution, a parliament-like assembly, and its own public and self-reflexive executive leadership that can effectively broach such issues and create a consensus around them.

The notion of a Bosnian Islamic tradition remained largely unarticulated until the debates in the mid-2000s. The definition provided by Karčić proved to be the most succinct and least controversial answer to this question. The text has been published on the Islamic community's website, in its official periodical *Preporod* and in books on the Islamic tradition.[2] It can be safely said that it represents the quasi-official stance of the ICBH, and it is one that the ICBH further develops through research, periodic public debates, and a dedicated institution, the Institute for the Islamic Traditions of the Bosniaks (*Institut za islamsku tradiciju Bošnjaka*, IITB). Tellingly, the first director of the IITB is Dževada Šuško, whose doctoral dissertation bore the title 'The Issue of Loyalty: Reaction of the Bosniaks to the Austro-Hungarian Empire (1878–1918)'.[3]

Karčić's definition goes beyond normative sources of Islam: it includes the historical and institutional experiences – Ottoman, Habsburg and Yugoslav – as constitutive features of Bosnian practice. More specifically, the normative sources of Islam are interpreted in Bosnia and Herzegovina through schools and institutions historically moulded not only by the Ottoman legacy but also by the legacy of the Austro-Hungarian and socialist periods. Two features out of six – the tradition of Islamic reformism and the institutionalization of the Islamic community – emerged during the forty years of Habsburg administration between 1878 and 1918, and a third one – the practice of expression of Islam in a secular state – came about during the four decades of socialist Yugoslavia from 1945 to 1991.

The single most formative legacy of the Bosnian encounter with the Austro-Hungarian state is arguably the fifth feature: the institutionalization of Bosnia's Muslim community. After the occupation of Bosnia and Herzegovina by Austria–Hungary, all its religious infrastructure (teachers, imams, judges, muftis) was severed from the Ottoman state. Under Austro-Hungarian sovereignty, the Bosnian Muslims established a self-administered Islamic community with their own religious authority (the elected *reis-ul-ulema*), which was independent of the authorities of the wider Islamic world and rooted in a locally developed religious justification. It is precisely this early religious autonomy from the state, and the practice of self-administration, which came a bit later, that to this day distinguishes Bosnian Islamic institutions from Islamic traditions elsewhere (Alibašić 2007), because in most of the Muslim world, Muslims do not belong to any institutionalized Islamic community.

Thus, the ICBH is a legacy of colonization by a modernizing empire, defined by at least three distinctive features. During the years 1878 to 1918, the Austro-Hungarian administration (a) allowed and even encouraged a religious autonomy for Bosnian Muslims vis-à-vis the former religious authority of the Ottoman caliph, and (b) urged the Bosnian Muslims to organize themselves in centralized bureaucratic institutions, the autonomy of which it would have to recognize. A parallel indirect legacy (c) was a dynamic intellectual scene in which reformism was linked, in the long run, with the revival and survival of Islam in Bosnia and Herzegovina in changing political contexts.

The Bosnian Religious Authority

The main Habsburg legacy is institutional. The first Islamic institution in Europe to be recognized by a modern European state emerged in the Austro-Hungarian province of Bosnia and Herzegovina in 1909: the Islamic Community in Bosnia and Herzegovina (*Islamska zajednica*). It was based on the example of the Protestant Church: a religiously autonomous and administratively and financially self-governing body to represent the Bosnian Muslim population in its relations with the sovereign state. It emerged in this form as a result of the non-Muslim occupation of a Muslim province with an active elite, and also because of a benevolent modernist administration.

Austria–Hungary occupied Bosnia and Herzegovina in 1878 following the Treaty of Berlin, which obliged the monarchy to safeguard the property rights and religious autonomy of Bosnian Muslims, while details concerning Muslim rights were negotiated bilaterally with the High Porte, and anchored in the Novi Pazar Agreement of 1879 (Karčić 2015). Austria–Hungary was to occupy a land that formally remained under the authority of the Ottoman sultan and to respect the Muslims' continuing religious links to the Ottoman caliph (e.g. their right to hold Friday sermons in the sultan's name, to fly the Ottoman flag on minarets during religious holidays, and to petition the sultan). During the first thirty years of the occupation, which ended in 1908 in official annexation, the Austro-Hungarian administration maintained some illusion of Ottoman sovereignty, while at the same time creating local religious institutions that were largely autonomous from Istanbul but fell under the direct influence of Vienna.

After 1878, the position of Islam in the province of Bosnia and Herzegovina changed entirely. Under Ottoman rule, Islam was the religion of the state, even though the Muslims were not a majority in Bosnia and Herzegovina itself, as was established in the first Austrian census: 38.7 per cent Muslims, 42.9 per cent Orthodox and 18.1 per cent Catholics (Velikonja 2003: 126). The legal, ritual and administrative affairs of the Muslims were handled by the centralized state administration in Istanbul, which combined religious, administrative and military affairs. Religious teachers at state schools, imams, muftis and judges were employees of the state, organized in a strict Ottoman hierarchy of the clerical class – the *ilmiye*. At the top was the Ottoman sultan himself, who since the fifteenth century had claimed the title of caliph. The sultan delegated the administration of religious affairs to the mufti of Istanbul, who bore the honorific title of Sheikh of Islam – the head of Islam, *Şeyhülislam*. With his office (*Meşihat-i Islamiye*) and executive power, he was in fact the highest religious authority over the religious hierarchy in the Ottoman Empire. He then delegated his judicial power to all regional muftis in the empire. The ilmiye, being Ottoman, was not defined ethnically. Between 1866 and 1868, shortly before the Ottoman loss of Bosnia and Herzegovina, this high office was held by a Bosnian Muslim scholar, Mehmed Refik Hadžiabdić, from Rogatica near Sarajevo (Dobrača, 1978: 109).

The retreat of the Ottoman state led to a major transition: the Bosnian Muslims suddenly became a minority in the former Muslim-majority empire in which Islam had been the state religion. The other religious communities, the Christian and Jewish minorities, used to administer their educational, ritual and civil legal affairs through their own institutions within the so-called millet system. There was no Muslim structure separate from the state. In reaction, tens of thousands of Muslims left for the Sandjak of Novi Pazar to remain on the Muslim side of the new imperial border. Nevertheless, unlike earlier Ottoman retreats from Serbia and Hungary, the majority of the Bosnian Muslims stayed in Bosnia and Herzegovina. It was not until 1878 and the reversal of the Muslims' legal situation that the need arose for a special Muslim organization. Being no longer subjects of an Islamic empire nor part of the Muslim ummah, the Bosnian Muslims now had to develop something that had previously been missing – a local Islamic Community (Imamović 1990: 90).

The first question to be decided was which religious authority would lead the community of Muslims now that Bosnian Muslims could not be directly administered from Istanbul. From the outset, the struggle between Istanbul and Vienna over the influence on the Bosnian Muslims focused on the question of who would nominate their new head. In 1880, the Şeyhülislam logically appointed former *rumeli kadiasker* (a chief military judge and his highest Balkan representative) Ahmed Şükrü Efendi as a new authority in Bosnia – a Bosnian grand mufti. But the Austrian government opposed the decision and did not allow him to go to Bosnia. The argument was that the appointment authority should lay with local powers, as it did in Tunisia, where the Tunisian bey appointed the chief mufti. After a long diplomatic exchange, Istanbul conceded, and in March 1882 the Şeyhülislam appointed the then mufti of Sarajevo, Mustafa Hilmi ef. Omerović, to the new office of mufti of Bosnia (Nakičević 1996: 9). In his nomination document the *menšura*, the Şeyhülislam empowered the mufti to 'supervise and carry out all religious tasks and all the sharia necessities, and to name and appoint capable judges' (Lavić 2017). This official delegation of religious powers to the

Bosnian mufti, allowing him to appoint all local judges and muftis, made it easier to create a new Bosnian Islamic hierarchy (Okey 2007: 48). Six months later, the Kaiser gave the mufti the special title of *reis-ul-ulema*, thus creating an original head of the religious hierarchy. To mark the occasion, the Austro-Hungarian administration had him inaugurated with unusual pomp in the hall of ceremonies in the Konak, the headquarters of the government in Sarajevo.

In 1878, a total of fifty-eight Muslim notables petitioned the Kaiser to allow them to appoint a leader of their own to govern Muslim affairs (appointing the ulema hierarchy, organizing religious education, and administering religious endowments – the *awqaf*), and in 1881, another group of twenty-seven, led by Mustafa Hilmi Omerović, repeated the petition (Šuško 2018: 172). Following the aforesaid dispute with Istanbul, the Austrian government accepted these requests, which, according to Fikret Karčić, it would have initiated in the first place (Karčić 2015: 154). In 1882, the *majlis al-ulama* and the *ra'is al-ulama* (a council of scholars and the head of scholars respectively), known in Bosnian as the *madžlis* and the reis-ul-ulema, were appointed.

The new reis, Mustafa Hilmi Omerović, was in fact a pro-Austrian notable. As the Bosnian mufti, he issued a fatwa, a legal opinion stating that serving under a non-Muslim ruler was acceptable in Hanafi law, and that Bosnian Muslims could be drafted to the k. u. k. army. During an uprising provoked by a new conscription law in 1882, he encouraged them to serve under the kaiser. The second reis, Mehmed Teufik Azapagić, was also pro-Austrian. In 1884, when he was the mufti of Tuzla, he published a famous fatwa on migration, the *Risala fi al-hijra*, in which he encouraged Muslims to stay in their homeland instead of emigrating to Turkey, as long as they could freely perform their religious duties (Šuško 2014: 551).

At first, the legitimacy of Islamic offices under Austria–Hungary was to continue being derived from the caliphate. To safeguard the illusion of Ottoman sovereignty over Muslim affairs, the Kaiser sent the nomination of the reis to the sheikh ul-islam in Istanbul, who neither confirmed nor protested the nomination of the first reis. In the subsequent nomination of 1893, the kaiser would no longer ask for confirmation through the menšura, even though the High Porte insisted he should (Durmišević 2008: 219). After mufti Omerović became reis, he replaced five of eight local muftis on his authority. Hence, an autonomous Bosnian Islamic authority came into being, independent from Islamic authority in Istanbul and under the sole sovereignty of the agreeable Austrian kaiser. Only later did the Bosnians struggle for autonomy from the Kaiser.

The office of a nationally elected reis is unique in the Muslim world. According to Fikret Karčić, an office of the same name existed for a while in Palestine under similar circumstances (i.e. during the British Mandate between 1920 and 1948), when the mufti of Jerusalem became the Palestinian reis (Karčić 2015: 163). Elsewhere, after the Ottoman retreat, existing grand muftis would govern

Muslim affairs. The name 'reis-ul-ulema' was a borrowed form of an honorific Ottoman title for Istanbul muftis or for an educated military judge in the Balkans. It was lower than the sheikh-ul islam, and it was associated with the Balkans (Karčić 2015: 156). The meaning of reis-ul-ulema is the 'head' or 'president' of the ulemas. He is a president, a representative, a head of an administration and the highest religious authority for the Bosnian Muslims.

The office of the Bosnian reis was new and original, thus its legitimacy had to be justified by the Bosnian Muslim elite who had suggested its creation. Like an Islamic ruler, the reis has several substantial functions: namely, leadership (*imamah*), interpretation of Islamic regulations (*futya*), and dispensation of justice (*qada*). Bosnian Muslims had to resolve the question of whether the office of a Bosnian reis, as well as the sharia judges and the muftis appointed by him, had a religious basis once they were no longer representatives of the imam or the caliph. The justification offered by Bosnian scholars, summarized by the renowned lawyer Mehmed ef. Handžić (1906–44), derived from precedents in the Hanafi school of law, where officials appointed by non-Muslim rulers had been accepted as part of a historical response to the loss of Muslim territories in the twelfth century (Karčić 2015: 156).

The prominent Bosnian scholar and educator Mustafa Spahić points to the second dimension of legitimacy: that of the legal continuity of the office of the reis with the office of the caliph, who ultimately represents the Prophet. In his book *Od hilafeta do rijaseta* [From the caliphate to the rijaset], he argues that the continuity between caliphate and rijaset (from the office of the Islamic caliph to the *sui generis* office of the Bosnian reis) essentially rests on the delegation of sovereignty by the Ottoman sultan-caliph realized through the Berlin Treaty, the Novi Pazar Convention Agreement, and the assignment of powers to the Bosnian mufti. In particular, Article II of the Novi Pazar Agreement represents a guarantee to Bosnian Muslims of their 'freedom and realization of all religious rituals', the use of revenues of the waqfs for religious purposes, and the 'honour, habits, freedom of religion, safety, person, and property of the Muslim' (Spahić 2015: 276). And indeed, as was demonstrated later, the accords functioned as a legal foundation on which the Muslim elite based their claim to full religious autonomy in the subsequent struggle for autonomy and institutional self-determination.

The Self-Administered Community

The second kind of autonomy, freedom from the direct administration by the Austro-Hungarian state, was gained some twenty-five years after the establishment of the rijaset, and was fought for mostly because of financial and educational autonomy. The question of property, specifically the administration of the many religious endowments (*vakuf*, plural *vakufi*, a South Slavic version of the

Arab term 'waqf') and of their revenues, which constituted the material basis of the nascent Islamic institution, quickly moved to the centre of the autonomy question.

After the creation of the rijaset, the Bosnian provincial Austro-Hungarian administration appointed all other Muslim officials, including judges, teachers, and economic administrators. It created a provincial commission for the management of the waqfs, the Islamic endowments, to inventory, centralize, modernize, and better exploit them under state supervision. The Austrian state compiled the first comprehensive list of the thousands of endowments (land, buildings, enterprises, etc. – a hybrid form of property that was neither entirely private nor entirely public) that had been donated at some point in history to secure the perpetual maintenance of institutions such as mosques, *madrasa*s, and Sufi lodges, often by means of a hereditary administrator.

The provincial government also created a structure for the local administration of waqfs, determined the financing of the functions of the Islamic religious administration, and defined a hierarchy of organs that would eventually become the basis for a central Islamic institution in Bosnia and Herzegovina. Although Muslim notables were represented on every level and even put in executive positions locally, the higher executive powers over the endowments were concentrated in the hands of the provincial government: 'all the power concerning the waqfs was in the hand of the state' (Spahić 2015, 279).

A second phase of institutionalization of the ICBH followed between 1900 and 1909 during the so-called movement for religious and educational autonomy (*Pokret za vakufsko-mearifsku autonomiju*). The demand that animated Bosnian Muslims for a whole decade was sustained around questions of who appointed key officials and who governed religious endowments, as well as around the question of educational reforms. Spurred by alleged Muslim conversions to Christianity and by suspicions of pro-Catholic partiality of the regional administration, Bosnian Muslims organized and sustained a veritable campaign. Led by activist Mostar mufti Ali Fehmi ef. Džabić, Bosnian Muslims sought the right to manage their religious affairs: to appoint the reis through an election, to govern the waqf property through the *medžlis* (council), and to continue with Islamic education despite state efforts to introduce a secular school system. The most contentious issue was the demand for a renewed link between Bosnian Islamic institutions and the office of Şeyhülislam in Istanbul, as it went against Habsburg plans for annexation.

Under mufti Džabić, activists signed repeated petitions to both the kaiser and the sultan, organized public gatherings in Bosnia and Herzegovina and delegations to the Budapest parliament to complain about finance minister Benjámin Kállay, engaged in newspaper debates, and so on. Repressive measures, such as permanently exiling mufti Džabić to Turkey and persecuting other figures, were later abandoned. Negotiations came after two of the figures in the conflict –

Džabić and Kállay – were replaced. The movement coalesced into a political organization, the Muslim National Organization (*Muslimanska narodna organizacija*, MNO), and the new minister of finance responsible for Bosnian administration, István Burián, began negotiating with it.

After the Young Turk revolution and the annexation of Bosnia and Herzegovina in 1908, the Austrian state gave Bosnian Muslims the autonomy they asked for. In 1909, the Kaiser signed the so-called Statute for Autonomous Administration of Islamic Religious Waqf and Educational Affairs (*Štatut za autonomnu upravu islamskih vjerskih i vakufsko-mearifskih poslova u Bosni i Hercegovini*). It made the office of the reis and other ICBH offices elective. Austria accepted a compromise about the election of the reis that the sultan had suggested on its behalf: three candidates for reis were selected by a committee of ulema, the kaiser appointed one of them, and the reis was confirmed by a menšura from the sultan-caliph (Nakičević 1996). Thus, the elected reis would have both popular and religious legitimacy. The first elected reis-ul-ulema, hafiz Sulejman ef. Šarac, was appointed in 1910, but he resigned under pressure from Vienna. The second elected reis, the towering figure of Bosnian modernism Mehmed Džemaludin Čaušević, was elected twice against the will of the local Austrian administration, but was eventually confirmed by the Kaiser in 1913.

The reality of financial and educational autonomy (*vakufsko-mearifska autonomija*) was defined in a four-page statute introducing a self-administering hierarchy. The statute defined the composition, powers and obligations, controls, and the election procedure for government organs from the local community (*džemat*), from the elected local council (*džematski medžlis*) and the regional commission (*kotarska povjerenstva*) to the assembly (*sabor*) and the assembly direction. Every Bosnian-Herzegovinian Muslim male (*musliman*) aged twenty-four or over, who was a permanent resident of the community, paid the ICBH tax, had no criminal record, and was not serving in the military could vote in the elections to the džemat council; all other functions (regional councils, assembly – the sabor) were elected though additional indirect electoral procedures.[4]

The statute served as a constitution of an autonomous and thoroughly self-administered religious community. The Muslims of Bosnia and Herzegovina achieved this self-administrative institution through negotiations with Austria–Hungary, after the provincial administration had laid out centralized organs during the preceding twenty-five years. The statute remained valid until the abolition of the autonomy in 1930 during the centralist dictatorship of the Yugoslav king Alexander Karadjordjević, and was replaced by the constitution of the Islamic religious community in the Kingdom of Yugoslavia in 1936. Autonomy was formally reintroduced in the postwar constitution of 1947, but it was then obviously limited by the character of the communist regime. Not taking into consideration the constitutions adopted in the context of institutional flux in 1990 and 1993, only in 1997 could the assembly of the Bosnian Islamic Community autonomously adopt a new constitution and reaffirm full religious and administrative autonomy for the institutions of the ICBH.

Nonetheless, the 1909 Austro-Hungarian *Štatut* laid out a permanent basic structure for subsequent constitutions of the ICBH, the provisions of which have been retained to this day. The institutional design of the most recent constitution from 2014 is still based on the hierarchical self-administering structure established in 1909. Today, the Muslims of Bosnia and Herzegovina pride themselves on the democratic structure of the ICBH: passive voting rights and many candidature rights have since been extended to all members of the džemat, including women. It is not widely known that the self-administrative innovation is now more than one hundred years old and, as such, is without precedent among other Muslim communities in Europe.

Legal Reforms and Religious Reformism

The current constitution adopted by the assembly of the ICBH not only retains the self-administering structure of the 1909 Štatut but also refers to other legal documents from the Austro-Hungarian period in the itinerary of the Bosnian Muslim community's quest for religious legitimacy. In the preamble to the constitution, the community expresses its will to maintain 'uninterrupted sharia and a spiritual connection with Muhammad' and to safeguard its autonomy and rights as confirmed by international agreements, which bestow a 'unique position' on the ICBH. The constitution lists a large number of legal documents in its chain of legitimacy: the Berlin and Novi Pazar agreements; the appointment of a reis-ul-ulema in 1882 and his menšura from the caliph's šejhu-l-islam; the results of the movement for autonomy; the statute of 1909; the *Islamgesetz* of 1912; the caliph's menšura given to reis Čaušević in 1914; and three other later agreements and constitutions.[5] Hence, to this day the Austro-Hungarian legal acts of 1882, 1909 and 1912 are components of the ICBH's legality and legitimacy. The Habsburg state replaced the Ottoman state, and assumed the role of provider of rights and protector of the religious interests of the Bosnian Muslims, even if they had to assert some of their rights within its legal system.

Apart from this recognition by the constitution of an Islamic community as a link in the chain of Bosnian Islamic legitimacy, the Austro-Hungarian state also left its mark on the Islamic judicial system itself. It recognized, organized and updated the Muslim judicial system and legal thought with respect to modern legality.

After the establishment of the autonomous rijaset, the Austro-Hungarian authorities proceeded to incorporate the existing sharia court system into the imperial judicial order. The Austrian administration first sought to ensure legal security. It recognized the continuity of Ottoman law in sharia courts from 1859 and their jurisdiction over the personal status of Muslims (*al-ahwal al-shakhsiyyah*) and waqfs. In 1883, it adopted a new law to govern the function of sharia courts.[6] sharia, which was the basis of a mixed (sharia and Ottoman) legal system, was relegated to matters of personal status and inheritance. The Austrian provincial government thus assumed sovereignty over the judiciary (i.e. over the appointment of sharia judges, *qadis*), as well as responsibility for organizing sharia judges and financially maintaining the sharia courts (Karčić 2015: 131–32). Accordingly, the power of imparting sharia judgment (*qada*) was taken from the caliph and transferred to the Austrian state, despite the fact that the process of religious legitimation was maintained. The reis was to confirm state appointments with a *murasalah* (letter of authorization) and by supervising the education of judges. Moreover, as Fikret Karčić explains, the monarchy 'modernized sharia courts by encouraging the unification of their substantial and procedural laws, introducing an appellate body within the sharia judiciary – the High Sharia Court in Sarajevo – and providing qadis with a modern legal education' (Karčić 2015: 132).

Besides the first recognition of sharia within the European imperial judicial system, it was the education of the judges that would have a lasting influence on Bosnian Islam. The provincial government decided to educate sharia judges in a modernized local law school rather than to continue employing lawyers educated in Istanbul, as it had done before. As early as 1881, the Kaiser signed a statute for a future school of sharia judges in Sarajevo. In 1887, the Higher Sharia College in Sarajevo (*Šerijatska sudačka škola*) opened in a building designed in an Orientalizing style by the Czech–Austrian architect Karel Pařík, and commissioned especially for the school. The school would not only produce locally educated ulema, but it would have a modernized curriculum. Apart from sharia-related subjects, students also read Islamic theology and philosophy as well as explicitly modern subjects, including religious studies, foreign languages, and Austrian law. The reform of sharia education produced several modernizing effects. In addition to the introduction of traditionally non-existent appellate sharia courts, the new judicial system encouraged legal studies and judicature in the Bosnian language as opposed to Ottoman or Arabic, and it also advanced some codification of sharia. In 1883, a selection of shariatic principles was published in Vienna in German under the title *Eherecht, Familienrecht und Erbrecht der Mohammedaner nach hanefitischen Ritus*, with the aim of familiarizing the mixed courts with sharia justice (Durmišević 2008: 221).

The school existed between 1887 and 1937, and produced 370 graduates, most of whom worked as judges, ICBH officials, and intellectuals in Bosnia and Herzegovina (Durmišević 2008: 235). Apart from adapting sharia to a modern secular legal system, the school paved the way for a subsequent openness towards adaptation to the demands of the times and the necessities of modernity – namely, the reform of the sharia courts and of sharia law, and, later, the formulation of positions on the changing institutional, legal and theological conditions for the practice of Islam. The reformed sharia education system remained in place until 1945. Communist Yugoslavia abolished the sharia courts and the judicial implementation of sharia principles in family law as well as the high sharia school. Since 1945, the separation of the secular state and religious principles has endured.

The Reformist Tradition

Another legacy of the institutions founded during the Austro-Hungary era lived on. Sarajevo's Islamic middle and higher education has produced and employed a class of elites educated in modern ways, which continued both the demand for autonomy from any state as well as the ambition of religious self-determination. Bosnia and Herzegovina's lively intellectual milieu has intensely debated questions of social modernization and religious traditionalism, Islamic reformism from Egypt, and Kemalist modernization from Turkey. The Bosnian intellectual religious scene was often divided and prone to prolonged controversies over political and religious topics, such as the place of women, the question of traditional head coverings (veils and fezes), the question of education, and of foreign intellectual influences. Despite this – or perhaps because neither the reformists not the traditionalists had succeeded in achieving a hegemony – Bosnian Islamic reformism became the fifth element to which Fikret Karčić refers in his definition of the Islamic tradition of the Bosniaks. For Dino Abazović, Bosnian Islamic reformism led the way to a transition 'from Oriental-Islamic to European-Western culture, i.e. the traditionalistic response to the ideas of reformism in the period beginning with the arrival of the Austro-Hungarian rule and ending late in the Second World War'. The answer does not mean that revolutionary change is sought but rather an 'intention of preserving Islamic faith in accordance with the demands of time and modernity' (Abazović 2011: 7).

Islamic reformism had its centres in the Arab world but found a strong echo in Bosnia and Herzegovina during the years of Habsburg rule. In the Islamic community, a public debate developed between the ulema, journalists, and public figures of both the modernist camp and the traditionalist one. People educated in Egypt, such as the first elected reis Džemaludin ef. Čaušević (1870–1938), the wartime religious leader Mehmed ef. Handžić (1906–44), and Husein ef. Đozo (1912–82) are references to this today. Especially the last, Husein ef. Đozo, can be credited with assuring continuity with prewar and interwar reformist school through his role in restoring the sharia school in 1977. Since there are no longer any sharia courts, the school was reopened as an Islamic theological faculty and moved back to the original building in 1993. Since 2004, the Islamic faculty has been a part of the University of Sarajevo.

Husein Đozo was born under the Kaiser but worked long after the end of Austro-Hungarian rule. He was a student at the Sarajevo Sharia School (and later at Al-Azhar in Cairo), a prominent activist imam (he also served as imam to the SS Division Hanjar during the Second World War), and finally a renewer of both the school as the Islamic theological faculty and of prewar reformist thought during communist times. His approach to Islamic thought was explicitly reformist and modernist. He considered it important for Islamic law to adapt to the circumstances of modern life, rejecting traditionalist conformism (*taqlid*) and engaging in critical thinking through ijtihad (Mekić 2017: 3). Apart from his academic influence and his activism in interreligious communication, he gained notoriety through his long-term practical work – he issued hundreds of fatwas, or answers, as they are called now, concerning practical problems of everyday life. Moreover, he produced a generation of Islamic scholars who would further his reformist approach.

The professors at the Faculty of Islamic studies today are Husein Đozo's students. Under his direction, the faculty revived the study of Bosnian reformists and it now fosters academic study of theology under the circumstances of modernity. Today's questions are different from those in the early twentieth century, but they still echo the same fundamental task: contemplation of legitimate Islamic life within a modern secular state. The question of the role of sharia is prominent. It is precisely in legal theory and the role of sharia that contemporary Bosnian scholars reflect on what may be called Islamic secularity: the possibility of an Islamic normative system to find its autonomy in the context of a secularized society and a secular state. This Islamic secularity need not in any way be liberal or permissive, but it may offer a theological reflection of the circumstances of religious life in modern pluralistic societies. Two distinguished contemporary voices, the heirs of Husein Đozo and of Bosnian reformism, formulate an elsewhere uneasy topic: the so-called 'ethicization' of sharia.

Fikret Karčić explains in legal terms the shift in understanding Islam from a basis for a societal and political order, as was the case in the Ottoman Empire, towards another understanding of religious obligations expressed through sharia in secular states. In a secular state, the obligations are no less demanding, but are restricted to the realm of ethical and not legal norms. In modern societies too, Islam remains the normative framework for Muslims, only its norms are no longer sanctioned by the juridical and repressive system of the state. Fikret Karčić maintains that the restriction of a modern and secular state does not belittle the relevance of Islamic norms for Muslims:

> The religious aspect of the norm (diyanetan) is [still] legitimate, but the judicial aspect (qada'an) is not implemented. . . . The first denotes the spiritual and moral aspect of life, and the latter the regulation of interpersonal relations through the institutions and sanctions of the Secular State. When it is stated, therefore, that the religious aspect of the norm is valid but that the judicial aspect is not implemented, this means that such a norm has been converted from a legal code of behaviour into a religious and moral

code. For example, extramarital sexual relations (zina) are still forbidden for Muslims, but the sanctions intended to be implemented, should this act be committed, are not implemented. (Karčić 2015: 91)

Enes Karić, a professor of *tefsir* (Qur'anic theology) at the Faculty of Islamic Studies and one of Đozo's students, understands the secular state as one that is not antireligious but religiously neutral. According to him, European secular states have become an open and positive framework for traditional religious communities. Even more than that, 'Islam in secular, liberal democracies gets a chance as a faith, and Islam gets to be much more religious. It is no longer a state ideology but is interpreted more as a faith, as a morality, and as a basis for ethical norms' (Karić 2009). In a token of secularity, Karčić expresses a case for a partial 'ethicization of sharia', a tendency among liberal European Muslims that still awaits full exploration (Karčić 2007). Such 'reducing Islamic norms to the moral dimension and justifying recourse to . . . legal institutions' of the secular state, in the words of Alexandro Caeiro referring to the *sharia de minorité* of the French imam Tareq Oubrou (Caeiro 2005), is an audacious proposition of a mutual recognition of secular law and a religious normative system yet to gain wider acceptance in Europe.

In the Bosnian context, though, Karić and Karčić merely give an articulated expression to a normalcy of a Bosnian secularity. It certainly reflects the position consistently articulated by the ICBH. The current president of the ICBH, the reis-ul-ulema Husein ef. Kavazović, declares openly that Bosnia and Herzegovina should be a secular state and that religious communities should keep away from state affairs.[7]

All three are indicative of what I will call secularity: a capacity to exist qua religion within a secular context. The point of the concept of secularity is to highlight a capacity of a religious subject to function, with neither subjection nor conflict, within a secular context.

It could be argued that Bosnia and Herzegovina's Muslims are open to secular modernity for a simpler reason – because of a high degree of secularization. The religious history of Muslim Bosnia and Herzegovina may simply be that of a country subjected to a long history of secularization, starting with occupation by a Catholic monarchy in 1878 and continuing with forty years of Yugoslav communist secularism, which left religious institutions subdued, societies religiously lukewarm, and Muslim officials resigned to share a secular state with two other religious communities. But secularization is a process that can be reversed. The sociologist Dino Abazović has attracted attention to the fact that after the 1980s, and particularly in the 1990s, a process of desecularization was taking place, reversing some of the effects of secularization. Religions have again assumed more prominent public functions as markers of identity, and religious institutions have become involved in political crises. Still, those reversed processes have little effect on the 'institutional differentiation of religion within social order' (Abazović 2012: 9) that has remained a feature of Bosnian Islamic practice for more than a hundred years.

Conclusion

It is, after all, the long-established tradition of institutional autonomy that secures a place for Islam in a secular state, free from state interference and free to administer its affairs (including issues related to identity and normative claims) through its own institutions, such as universities, media, and research institutes. We usually speak of a secular state – that is, a state to which the personal religious convictions of its citizens are irrelevant and that guarantees a mutual autonomy between state and church (Ferrari 2005: 11). We should also speak about the secularity of religious institutions – that is, about their cognitive and institutional capacities to participate in a Habermasian secular public sphere, in which no single religious, secularist or ideological actor has a hegemony, and in which societal actors engage in rational deliberation about mutually recognized freedoms and obligations (Habermas 2006). Naser Ghobadzadeh gives a more hands-on definition of secularity as 'the vision for the emancipation of religion from the state' (Ghobadzadeh 2015: 2). In this respect, Bosnian Muslims refer to their Austrian legacy precisely for this reason: 'the institutionalization of Islam in the form of the Islamic Community' in 1909 empowered the Bosnian community to demand, keep and regain several times its self-administrative and religious autonomy.

The history of the Muslims of Bosnia and Herzegovina with a modern bureaucratic state is indeed among the longest in the Muslim world. Unlike many other Muslim countries ruled by a small colonial elite from around the same time (e.g. Algeria, Tunisia, Egypt), the Bosnian Muslims were incorporated into the Austro-Hungarian state not as a population of a whole country but as a relatively small religious community of around one million people. The Austro-Hungarian state has had a direct and, in many aspects, also a formative and a lasting influence on the character of the Bosnian Islamic institutions and practice, to the point that contemporary Bosnian Muslims make explicit references to various aspects of the Austro-Hungarian legacy when defining their Islamic tradition and when developing an original view of Islamic secularity.

Zora Hesová is a fellow at the Institute of Philosophy, Czech Academy of Sciences, and assistant professor at the Institute of Political Science, Faculty of Arts, Charles University in Prague. She studied political science at the University of Toulouse, earned her MA degree in philosophy, Islamology and sociology at Freie

Universität Berlin, and defended her PhD thesis in Islamic philosophy at the University of Sarajevo. She has focused on classical Islamic philosophy (al-Ghazali), contemporary formations of Islamic tradition and its encounter with modernity, secularism, migration and integration. Previously, she headed democratization assistance programmes for Prague's Association for International Affairs (AMO) in Egypt.

Notes

1. 'Ustav Islamske zajednice u Bosni i Hercegovini' (2006), available online: http://www.islamskazajednica.ba/component/content/article?id=43:ustav-islamske; last accessed 1 February 2018.
2. F. Karčić, 'Šta je to "islamska tradicija Bošnjaka"?', *Preporod* 23/841, 1 December 2006, Sarajevo, available on the website of the Bosnian Islamic Community, http://www.islamskazajednica.ba/dini-islam/tekstovi/90-promicljanja/1646-cta-je-to-qislamska-tradicija-bocnjaka; last accessed 1 February 2018.
3. Cf. IITB website: http://iitb.ba/preuzimanja/biografije/Dzevada%20Susko%20-%20Biography.pdf; last accessed 20 April 2020.
4. The historical statute and other constitutions are available online: http://islamskazajednica.ba/images/stories/Ustavi/Statut_IZ-e_iz_1909.pdf; last accessed 1 February 2018.
5. 'Ustav Islamske zajednice u Bosni i Hercegovini': official text, available online, http://islamskazajednica.ba/images/stories/Ustavi/Ustav_IZ-e_precisceni_tekst_2014.pdf; last accessed 1 February 2018.
6. Naredba o ustrojstvu i djelokrugu šerijatskih sudova [Order on the Organization and Scope of Sharia Courts] (Durmišević 2008: 222).
7. Interview in *Der Standard*, 'EU hat die Pflicht Bosnien zu schuetzen', in: derStandard.at, 28 May 2013.

References

Abazović, Dino. 2011. 'Bosnian Muslims at the Beginning of the New Millenia', *Bruckenschlage II*, Akademie der Diozese Rottenburg–Stuttgart.
———. 2012. *Bosanskohercegovački muslimani između sekularizacije i desekularizacije*. Zagreb: Synopsis.
Alibašić, Ahmet. 2007. 'Pravci i elementi razvoja islamske tradicije Bošnjaka u bosanskom kontekstu'. Prilog za simpozij Rijaseta IZ u BiH, '*Islamska tradicija Bošnjaka: izvori, razvoji i institucije, perspektive*', Sarajevo, 14–16 November 2007, available online: https://www.medzlis-konjic.com/index.php/knjige-i-tekstovi/odabrani-tekstovi/1083-pravci-i-elementi-razvoja-islamske-tradicije-bosnjaka-u-bosanskom-kontekstu; last accessed 1 February 2018.
———. 2010. 'The Profile of Bosnian Islam and How West European Muslims Could Benefit from It', in *Islam in Southeast Forum*, 29 June 2010, available online: http://cns.ba/wp-content/uploads/2014/03/The-Profile-of-Bosnian-Islam-And-How-West-European-Muslims-Could-Benefit-from-It.pdf; last accessed 1 February 2018.

Bougarel, Xavier. 2007. 'Bosnian Islam as "European Islam": Limits and Shifts of a Concept', in Aziz AlAzmeh and Effie Fokas (eds), *Islam in Europe: Diversity, Identity and Influence*. Cambridge: Cambridge University Press, pp. 96–124.
Caeiro, Alexandre. 2005. 'An Imam in France Tareq Oubrou', *ISIM Review* 15: 48–49.
Dijk, Mieke van, and Bartels, Edien. 2012. '"European Islam" in Practice in the Bosnian City of Sarajevo', *Journal of Muslim Minority Affairs* 32(4): 467–82.
Dobrača, Kasim. 1978. 'Mehmed Refik-efendi Hadžiabdić šejhul-islam', *Anali Gazi Husrev-begove biblioteke* V–VI (1978): 109.
Durmišević, Enes. 2008. 'Institucionalizacija islama u postosmanskom periodu', in Mehmedalija Handžić (ed.), *Zbornik radova naučnog skupa 'Islamska tradicija Bošnjaka: izvori, razvoj, perspektive'*. Sarajevo: Rijaset islamske zajednice u Bosni i Hercegovini.
Ferrari, Silvio. 2005. 'The Secularity of the State and the Shaping of Muslim Representative Organizations in Western Europe', in J.J. Cesari and S. McLoughlin (eds), *European Muslims and the Secular State*. New York: Ashgate.
Ghobadzadeh, Naser. 2015. *Religious Secularity: A Theological Challenge to the Islamic State*. New York: Oxford University Press.
Habermas, Jurgen. 2006. 'Religion in the Public Sphere', *European Journal of Philosophy* 14(1): 1–25.
Imamović, Mustafa. 1990. 'Islamska zajednica u Bosni i Hercegovini i u bivšoj Jugoslaviji', *Glasnik Rijaseta IZ BiH* 1–2, Sarajevo.
Karčić, Fikret. 2006. 'What Is the Islamic Tradition of the Bosniaks'. *Preporod*, 7 December. English translation by D. Šuško. Available at: https://cns.ba/wp-content/uploads/2014/03/what_is_islamic_tradition_of_bosniaks.pdf; last accessed 1 February 2018.
———. 2007. From Law to Ethics: The Process of Modernisation and Reinterpreting the Shari'a in Bosnia, in: Bosnischer Islam für Europa, Akademie der Diözese Stuttgart-Hohenheim, available online: https://www.akademie-rs.de/fileadmin/user_upload/download_archive/interreligioeser-dialog/071116_karcic_lawethics.pdf; last accessed 20 April 2020.
———. 2015. *The Other European Muslims: A Bosnian Experience*. Sarajevo: Centre for Advanced Studies.
Karić, Enes. 2009. 'Islam i sekularizam', *Gračanički Glasnik* 29(15).
Lavić, Osman. 2017. 'Mustafa Hilmi-ef. Hadžiomerović, prvi reisu-l-ulema'. *Preporod*, 26 December.
Mekić, Sejad. 2017. *A Muslim Reformist in Communist Yugoslavia: The Life and Thought of Husein Đozo*. London: Routledge.
Nakičević, Omer. 1996. *Istorijski razvoj institucije Rijaseta*. Sarajevo: Rijaset Islamske zajednice.
Okey, Robin. 2007. *Taming Balkan Nationalism: The Habsburg 'Civilizing Mission' in Bosnia, 1878–1914*. Oxford: Oxford University Press.
Spahić, Mustafa. 2015. *Od hilafeta do Rijaseta*. Sarajevo: El-Kalem.
Šuško, Dževada. 2014. 'Bosniaks and Loyalty: Responses to the Conscription Law', *Hungarian Historical Review* 3(3): 529–59.
———. 2018. 'Sjećanje na prvog reisu-l-ulemu mustafu hilmi-ef. Hadžiomerovića', *Takvim za 2018*: 171–78.
Velikonja, Mitja. 2003. *Religious Separation and Political Intolerance in Bosnia-Herzegovina*. College Station, TX: Texas A&M University.

Chapter 7

UNDER THE SLAVIC CRESCENT
Representations of Bosnian Muslims in Czech Literature, Travelogues and Memoirs, 1878–1918

František Šístek

Of the three major ethnoreligious communities, the Muslims initially seemed most distant, unknown, hostile and exotic to Czech observers after the Austro-Hungarian occupation of Bosnia and Herzegovina in 1878. At the same time, the physical presence of the adherents of Islam, their lifestyle, religious life, and cultural heritage often represented the most attractive and characteristic feature of the newly acquired provinces of the empire. The following chapter will primarily focus on the diversification and transformation of the representations of Bosnian Muslims during the Habsburg era in Czech literature, travelogues and memoirs. After an initial overview of the images and stereotypes of the Balkan Muslims in Czech society before the occupation, the chapter will focus on Czech language testimonies from the dark and bloody period of conquest and pacification. In the subsequent section dedicated to the golden era of the Habsburg 'civilizing mission' at the turn of the twentieth century, special attention will be given to conceptualizations of Bosnian Muslim religious and national identity. The last section is devoted to images of Muslims in the texts of the artist and scholar Ludvík Kuba and the gendarme František Valoušek, two outstanding but widely different personalities who provide rich yet divergent perspectives on the Bosnian Muslims during Habsburg rule. In conclusion, we will critically reconsider the assumption that the development of mutual relations between the Czechs and the Bosnian Muslims, who suddenly found themselves living under the same roof of the dual monarchy, could be regarded as a positive transformation of 'the Turks and Schwabos into Slavic brothers' as a result of their increased contacts (Ljuca 2006).

Representations of Balkan Muslims before the Occupation of Bosnia and Herzegovina

Czech readers were aware of the existence of the Balkan Muslims long before the Habsburg occupation of Bosnia and Herzegovina in 1878. Their representations in the period immediately preceding the occupation could be divided into several groups. The deepest layer was linked with the collective memory of the Habsburg–Ottoman conflicts of the early modern period. In south-eastern Moravia, not far away from the Hungarian areas controlled by the Ottomans before the Siege of Vienna in 1683, the memories of Ottoman military incursions into the region at the height of the Ottoman territorial expansion left behind rich traces in the folklore. The figure of the Turk (indistinguishable from that of a Muslim) still represented a frightening personalization of a barbarous and murderous alien invader in local legends and folk songs. These images and narratives can best be summed up as classical examples of frontier Orientalism, which was first defined by the Austrian anthropologist Andre Gingrich (Gingrich 1998: 117–24). Lying further to the north-west, the Kingdom of Bohemia never directly experienced Ottoman raids. In this comparably more urbanized, industrialized, and nationally awakened province, images of the Turks inherited from the early modern era were subjected to historical decontextualization and reinterpretation in the nineteenth century. The Turk still appeared in Bohemian fairy tales and visual depictions; however, this imaginary Turk was more likely to be portrayed as a humorous and grotesque figure, or simply as an exotic Other rather than the proverbial horrible Turk from south-east Moravian tales and classical Turkish literature (*turcica*) dating from the early modern era (Rataj 2002: 289–92).

The more recent layer of representations was linked with notions of Slavic kinship and solidarity that constituted an integral part of Czech nationalist discourses in the nineteenth century. The collective self-conceptualization of the Czech nation as a branch of a wider Slavic linguistic, cultural and racial community stimulated long-term interest in the South Slavs of the Balkans, frequently labelled by Czech authors as 'our brothers from the South'. The anti-Ottoman struggles of the Christian Slavic populations were interpreted as being closely linked to the Czech national interest (*národní zájem*) (Žáček et al. 1975: 376). Especially during periods of unrest, uprisings and conflicts, Balkan Muslims tended to be depicted in starkly negative colours as descendants of Asiatic occupiers and Orientals who did not share the norms and values associated with Europe and modernity (Sobotková 2007: 342). At the same time, many were aware of the fact that most Balkan Muslims were descendants of local converts to Islam and usually spoke the same or similar language as their Christian neighbours. Some nineteenth-century Czech authors liked to compare these alleged renegades and traitors to those bad and weak Czechs who had succumbed to the pressures of Germanization. Religious conversion to Islam was, in fact, usually interpreted as a change of national identity (see chapter by Marija Mandić for similar ideas in the Serbian context).

Czech attitudes towards Balkan Muslims also displayed elements characteristic of the wider Western Orientalist discourse of the time (Sobotková 2007: 349). Many texts and visual representations of Balkan Muslims with unmistakable Orientalist tendencies were based on acquired knowledge of the Orient rather than direct encounters and personal experiences (Šístek 2009: 74–75; Šístek 2011a: 77–78). Some authors managed to combine first-hand accounts with the spirit of Orientalism that the age demanded. As regards Bosnia and Herzegovina shortly before the Austro-Hungarian occupation, the poet, writer and journalist Jan Neruda (1834–91) provided a textbook example of a black-and-white Orientalist perspective in his feuillton 'Na Uně' (On the Una), later included in his collection of travelogues entitled *Obrazy z ciziny* (Pictures from abroad). Travelling through the Habsburg–Ottoman borderlands along the Una River in 1868, Neruda highlighted the contrast between the two riverbanks, which also represented a civilizational frontier from his point of view. Despite his conviction that people in both Ottoman Bosnia and Habsburg Croatia were members of the same ethnic group (*národ*) ('The same nation, same language, same memories, and same poetry...') and the fact that the names of frontier towns on opposite sides of the river were identical (the Austrian Kostajnica opposite the Turkish Kostajnica; the Christian Dubica opposite the Mohammedan Dubica), in Neruda's eyes, the differences were immense. On the Habsburg and Christian side, everything was neat, orderly, and well organized. The Ottoman and Muslim bank, on the other hand, was already an outpost of the Orient, a place of anarchy, violence, misrule, disorder and dirt (Neruda 1950: 281).

Czech visual images of the Balkans (especially Bosnia and Herzegovina, Montenegro and Dalmatia) were also strongly influenced by the painter Jaroslav Čermák (1830–78). The artist, who lived in Belgium and France for most of his adult life, spent several years in the Slavic South, making the village of Mandaljena near Dubrovnik his permanent base. Apart from expeditions to neighbouring Balkan regions, the painter took an active part in the Montenegrin–Ottoman military conflict of 1862 and was decorated for bravery in battle by Montenegrin

Prince Nikola. Čermák was influenced by French Orientalism, as is especially evident from his oil paintings, which include Muslim characters and Oriental scenes, such as female slaves in harems and the kidnapping of a Christian woman by Turkish bashibozuks (see Černý, Mokrý and Náprstek 1930; Soukupová 1981; Borozan 2006). Other painters, including Čermák's student Josef Huttary (1841–90), who spent a period of time in the Balkans with his master, presented South Slavic topics in a similarly romantic and Orientalist manner well into the last years of the nineteenth century. In the final years of direct Ottoman control of the provinces, the painter and illustrator František Bohumír Zvěřina (1835–1908) frequently depicted attractive landscapes and dramatic scenes set in Bosnia and Herzegovina, and other regions of the Western Balkans, in both the Czech and German language press, blending realistic motives based upon his own travels and observations with wild fantasy and imagination (Dlábková and Chrobák 2008).

In the period immediately preceding the Austro-Hungarian occupation of Bosnia and Herzegovina, the Czech public closely and enthusiastically followed the Herzegovina uprising of 1875 and 1876, and the anti-Ottoman military conflicts from 1876 to 1878, which took place in different areas of the Balkans and always included the Turks (Muslims) as one of the warring sides. Several Czech volunteers joined the ranks of the Christian Slavic rebels in Herzegovina, while correspondents covered the events for Czech newspapers. The most notable among the latter were the young writers and journalists Bohumil Havlasa (1852–1877) and Josef Holeček (1854–1929). Holeček became the only foreign correspondent to cover the Montenegrin military campaign in Herzegovina in the summer of 1876 (Šístek 2011b: 336). In subsequent decades, he was to publish a number of travelogues and works of fiction devoted to the South Slavs, dedicating great attention to the Slavic Muslims, their coexistence with the Christian neighbours, and the issue of Islamization (Šístek 2009: 81–112; Šístek 2011a: 84–110). Holeček's initial experiences in Herzegovina contributed to his subsequent stubborn opposition of the Habsburg occupation of the provinces (Holeček 1901).

In the late 1870s, Czech representations of Balkan Slavic Muslims were not uniform. They ranged from undifferentiated images of the cruel, non-European Turks, who should be 'chased back to Asia where they belong', and images of Islamicized Slavs as national traitors and renegades who were, as the popular saying went, 'worse than the Turks themselves' (*poturčenec horší Turka*), to neutral or even positive depictions of a curious group of fellow Slavs who just happened to profess a somewhat exotic faith. However, as a consequence of the wars and other dramatic events of the second half of the 1870s, which Czech society followed closely, the negative images of the Balkan Muslims temporarily prevailed in the period immediately preceding the Austro-Hungarian occupation of Bosnia and Herzegovina in 1878.

Reflections of the Occupation and Establishment of the New Order

The Austro-Hungarian occupation of Bosnia and Herzegovina in the summer of 1878 evoked mixed feelings in Czech society. A number of soldiers from the Lands of the Bohemian Crown actively participated in the military campaign and the ensuing pacification of the Ottoman provinces. Members of staunchly Slavophile circles of nationalist intellectuals, who tended to regard the Habsburg imperial policies with suspicion and criticism as essentially anti-Slavic and anti-Czech, did not hide their disagreement or disappointment. In the name of the higher interests of Slavdom, they believed, the provinces should have been divided between the two Christian South Slavic states of Serbia and Montenegro. Some Czech politicians and entrepreneurs of an Austro-Slavic mindset, however, welcomed and supported the occupation. They believed that the increase in the total number of Slavs in the Habsburg Monarchy after the acquisition of the new, overwhelmingly Slavic territories would eventually boost the Czech political demands and fortunes within the Habsburg Monarchy. In the eyes of some Czech industrialists, entrepreneurs, and members of the bourgeoisie, the occupation was also seen as a chance for future Czech economic expansion in South East Europe (Nečas 1972).

The images of Bosnia and Herzegovina and its Muslim population in Czech travelogues, literature and memoirs dealing with the occupation campaign of 1878 present a darker, bloodier, and more disturbing picture than later accounts and testimonies from the golden era of the Habsburg 'civilizing mission' at the turn of the twentieth century. We can distinguish a specific group of sources that deal not only with the occupation of 1878 itself but also with the subsequent and often rough and violent establishment of the new order, which lasted well into the first half of the 1880s. Texts from this period were mostly written by direct observers who had actively participated in the occupation and pacification as members of the imperial army. Topics such as active armed resistance against the occupation, harassment and repression of the locals by the occupying forces, revolts and uprisings (especially the uprising in Herzegovina in 1881), and banditry are among the most characteristic traits, setting sources from the first phase of the occupation apart from later texts, which dealt more with the classical and, outwardly, mostly peaceful and orderly period of Habsburg rule.

The Muslims in many parts of Bosnia and Herzegovina resisted the occupation and regarded the Habsburg army with suspicion and contempt. Not surprisingly, they were primarily conceptualized as a hostile enemy population by many Czech observers. A collection of autobiographic stories from the occupation of 1878 and the uprising of 1881, published by entrepreneur and future member of the Bohemian Provincial Diet Jindřich Lemminger (1857–1906) as *Episody z bosenského povstání* (Episodes from the Bosnian Uprising), is a rather telling case in this respect. It is primarily written from the point of view of a Habsburg soldier. The daily lives and problems of his fellow comrades in arms receive more attention than the fate of the local population. Writing about the bloody battle of Maglaj in August 1878, Lemminger does not describe the Muslim enemy in negative terms as might be expected. He instead writes almost admiringly about the clever strategy of the Turks, who managed to lure the mightier Habsburg units into a well-prepared ambush (Lemminger 1884: 53–57). For the most part, however, these Turks are represented through stereotypes and simplified images immediately familiar to anyone acquainted with the wider transnational Orientalist discourses of the time. At the very centre of Lemminger's representations of Bosnian Muslims lies the familiar image of the cruel Turk (Muršič 2010). Apart from torturing and killing prisoners, Lemminger claims, the Muslim insurgents also desecrated their bodies (usually by cutting off their heads) in order to intimidate their comrades in arms (Lemminger 1884: 160). At one point, he refuses to dwell on the details of their psychological warfare, considering them to be too gruesome. The unspeakable cruelties, he laments, had been committed by 'the people who still have their place in civilized Europe' (ibid.: 161). The conclusion seems clear, although it is not openly stated: the people that resist a European army with such cruelty and barbarity do not belong in Europe. This reasoning resonates well with the more radical anti-Ottoman and anti-Islamic discourses that conceptualized the Muslims as essentially foreign and non-European barbarians who should be driven out of Europe. From this perspective, de-Ottomanization and de-Islamization appeared as inevitable steps on the road to the establishment of a higher civilized European order.

In his autobiographical stories, published in a single volume posthumously in 1909 entitled *Smutné i veselé z Bosny a Hercegoviny* (Sad and humorous stories from Bosnia and Herzegovina), Ignát Hořica (1859–1902) gives more attention and empathy to local inhabitants. Hořica served in Bosnia and Herzegovina as an officer for several years during the initial phase of the occupation, and mastered the local language. After leaving the army in 1884, he worked as a journalist and writer. As a representative of the Young Czech Party (*Mladočeši*), he was elected as deputy to the Austrian parliament (*Reichsrat*) in Vienna in 1897 and the Bohemian Provincial Diet in 1901.

Hořica attempted to provide an honest account of the initial pacification and establishment of civilized order based on his personal experiences. In most stories, he tried to understand the feelings, reasoning and actions of the enemy as well as of local civilians dissatisfied with the occupation. The book is written from an openly ambiguous position. As a member of the Imperial Army, the narrator is bound by solidarity and friendship to his fellow soldiers from Central Europe. As a convinced Slavophile, Hořica also engages in efforts to establish and cultivate friendly relations with the locals. His texts are marked by the painful realization that no matter how much he believes in the ideals of Slavic solidarity, a Czech, Croat, or other Slav serving in the occupation army is primarily perceived as a foreign soldier by the Slavs of Bosnia and Herzegovina. To the displeasure of many Czechs, the Muslims and Christian Orthodox Serbs tended to label all members of the occupation forces and administration coming from the Habsburg lands simply as Švabo (Schwabo in German transcription, literally 'Swabian', a colloquial South Slavic term for a German that progressively acquired pejorative connotations). Hořica repeatedly acknowledges that the high ideals of Slavic kinship and solidarity do not resonate very well with the mindset and practical everyday experiences of the Bosnians, with their particular religious, local and social identities, antagonisms and divisions.

The Bosnians, including Muslims, are generally represented as people of high moral dignity by Hořica. In the story entitled 'Bosňácká morálka' (Bosniak morality), which is set in the town of Zenica in February 1879, the Bosnians appear not only as people who do not steal but who are even reluctant to take a significant amount of money found by the side of the road (Hořica 1909: 15). They are depicted as morally superior to the foreign occupiers, and as more honest and dignified than members of the Imperial Army (especially the Jews). Hořica leaves no doubt that the occupation was often a cruel endeavour and a traumatic experience for the locals and the Habsburg soldiers alike; however, he refrains from essentializing the Muslims of Bosnia and Herzegovina as crueller and less civilized than the conquerors. Instead, he describes the violence and brutality on both sides, making clear that the primary force that produces violence is the war itself rather than differences in mentality, culture or religion.

In the story 'Něco o fanatismu' (Something about fanaticism), Hořica tackles the issue of alleged Muslim fanaticism, one of the recurrent traits inscribed to the Muslims in countless stereotypical representations. The story takes place in Sarajevo in the summer of 1878. It opens with a rough, naturalistic account of a murder. A Bosnian Muslim, standing calmly in front of his house, suddenly attacks a young soldier of the occupation army, who is peacefully passing by, and stabs him to death with a knife. The Muslim does not try to run away and is immediately arrested by other Habsburg soldiers and soon executed by a firing squad. The author then explains that the murderer lost several family members and friends during the Austro-Hungarian siege of Sarajevo, and was likely unable to restrain himself when he accidently encountered a member of the occupation army face to face, walking down his street. Nonetheless, the same story also recounts the cruelty of the occupation troops. The Habsburg soldiers, tired and hungry as they were, frequently overreacted. When a wounded elderly Muslim man unexpectedly shot one of them, the Habsburg soldiers in turn lynched him together with his innocent grandson. Without the speedy intervention of their officers, they would also have massacred a group of defenceless prisoners in their blind rage (Hořica 1909: 45). According to Hořica, Muslim prisoners were mistreated, denied food and water, tortured, and forced to undertake long marches: 'The war of unequal enemies is more horrible and crueller than a war among those on the same cultural level. There was fanaticism and cruelty on one side and furious revenge and cruelty on the other' (ibid.: 47).

The impossibility of overcoming the cultural divides and hostility among the occupiers and local inhabitants lies at the heart of a tragic love story set in the town of Maglaj during the first months of the occupation. Guřík, a Czech officer of the Habsburg army charged with maintaining contacts with local Muslim representatives, falls in love with a married Muslim woman, Fatica, and sneaks into her house whenever her husband is not present. After her relatives find out, they do not make any effort to punish Guřík, who represents the mighty alien army of a victorious infidel empire. Fatica is held responsible for breaking the taboo and disappears. A week later, the mutilated body of the young woman is found floating in the River Bosna, under a bridge, by a military patrol, 'with her tongue cut out, her breasts cut off, and her arms cut at the elbows'. Fatica obviously died as a victim of a crime that today would be referred to as an 'honour killing'. Her heartbroken Czech lover passes away in Maglaj several months later, falling ill after spending a cold night by her grave on the shore of the river. The perpetrators are not found or punished: the identity of the victim is not even officially established (her body being identified only unofficially by her lover) due to a lack of cooperation on the part of the Muslim *muktar* (mayor) of Maglaj (Hořica 1909: 113).

Interestingly, at least two well-known traces of the occupation of Bosnia and Herzegovina in 1878 and the initial pacification of the provinces still remain in the Czech collective memory and language – two traces, or more precisely, one word and one song. As has already been mentioned, some of the fiercest resistance experienced by the Austro-Hungarian units during the occupation campaign occurred in the vicinity of the town of Maglaj (see the chapter by Martin Gabriel for representations of this event in German language sources). After several days of marching into the interior of Bosnia without meeting significant opposition, the Seventh Hussar Regiment, which also included many soldiers from the Lands of the Bohemian Crown, entered Maglaj on 2 August 1878 without firing a single shot. From there, the regiment continued towards Žepče, where it encountered resistance and was forced to retreat. Upon their return to Maglaj, the unsuspecting Austro-Hungarian troops were encircled and attacked by local Muslim militias on 3 August. As a result of the ensuing bloody and chaotic battle around Maglaj, dozens of Habsburg soldiers lost their lives or were wounded. In the words of the Prague journal *Světozor* of 23 August 1878: 'At Maglaj, the blood of Austrian soldiers was spilled for the first time. It is here that it became clear that the peaceful occupation, which was everybody's firm wish, must give way to bloody conquest' (Ljuca 2006: 125). Details of the surprisingly fierce battle against local Muslim forces resisting the occupation were spread by the newspapers as well as by direct participants. Soon, the name of the Bosnian town of Maglaj even entered the Czech language. The term 'maglajz', derived from Maglaj, is still quite frequent in colloquial Czech (as well as in Slovak). It has come to signify something messy, chaotic or disorderly, sometimes even sleazy or disgusting (Ljuca 1999: 347). The word 'maglajz' emerged from the twentieth century almost completely devoid of its historical context: everybody knows the word and most even use it, but few are aware of the fact that it originally referred to a bloody encounter in Maglaj between the Habsburg soldiers, with many Czech among them, and the Bosnian Muslims in the summer of 1878.

The song 'Hercegovina' refers to the uprising in Herzegovina in 1881 (rather than the occupation of 1878, as is sometimes assumed), which had to be put down by Habsburg troops. Several variations of the lyrics exist along with two variations of the title. The song is also known as 'Za císaře pána' (For the emperor) in reference to the opening line: 'Za císaře pána a jeho rodinu / museli jsme vybojovat Hercegovinu' (For the emperor and his family / we had to conquer Herzegovina). The lyrics by an unknown author paint a mocking and grotesque image of the Muslim enemy: 'Támhle na stráni šnelcuk uhání, / tam na stráni jsou schováni mohamedáni. / Mohamedáni, to jsou pohani / kalhoty maj roztrhaný, smrkaj do dlaní. / Tyhle Turkyně, to jsou vám svině, / císař pán je nerad vidí ve svý rodině.' [On that hillside over there a fast train is rushing / on that hillside over there the Mohammedans are hiding. / The Mohammedans, they are pagans / they wear ripped up trousers, blow their noses into their palms. / And those Turkish women, oh what swine they are / the good emperor is not happy to see them in his family.] (Mücke 2004: 232). An alternative version mentions 'Tyhle Turkyně / tlustý jak dýně' (These Turkish women / fat as pumpkins).

'Hercegovina' was originally composed as a military song. According to historian Pavel Mücke, it became notorious among Czech soldiers in the Habsburg army during the First World War, and remained popular even after the dissolution of Austria–Hungary. As Mücke's research showed, 'Hercegovina / For the emperor' was a favourite song of Czechoslovak pilots serving in the British Royal Air Force during the Second World War, and was also sung by British military personnel and pilots of other allied armies who spent their free time with the Czechs (Mücke 2004: 233–34). In Communist Czechoslovakia, singing the allegedly pro-Habsburg and reactionary tune during military service could result in severe punishments. Nevertheless, 'Hercegovina' survived the turbulent twentieth century as a popular pub song, and can quite frequently be heard even today in pubs and at various festivities.

Until recently, the song was primarily considered a funny and nostalgic relict from the golden times of the late Habsburg Monarchy. The images of the Mohammedans were more or less decontextualized in collective memory, turning into so-called floating signifiers (signifiers without a signified) for all practical purposes due to limited contacts between the Czech milieu and Bosnia and Herzegovina, and the Muslims in general, for much of the twentieth century. Judging from some recent internet discussions and comments, the old song has been attracting attention again precisely for its anti-Muslim tone. At the time of writing, it seems possible that 'Hercegovina' might get a new lease on life as a result of a contemporary Islamophobic reinterpretation. One version of the song was already labelled a 'Czech Remove Kebab Song' on YouTube. Much like in some other countries, kebab has become a symbol of the perceived threat of Islamization, widespread in the predominantly anti-immigrant and anti-Muslim setting of the present-day Czech Republic, an ethnically homogeneous country almost free of Muslim immigrants. The fact that there is absolutely no mention of kebab in the lyrics, and that kebab does not represent the cuisine of Bosnia and Herzegovina, is obviously of secondary importance today.

Bosnian Muslims into Catholics and Slavic Brothers?

Apart from soldiers, a growing number of Czech administrators, engineers, teachers, doctors, musicians, entrepreneurs, artisans and workers settled in Bosnia and Herzegovina in the 1880s and 1890s. The census of 1910 recorded 7,095 Czechs living in the province, which was roughly 13 per cent of the total number of newcomers from the Habsburg Monarchy. Personnel from the Lands of the Bohemian Crown, typically fluent in both German and Serbo-Croatian, comprised approximately a quarter of the total number of employees of the Habsburg administration in Bosnia and Herzegovina (Hladký et al. 2010: 79; see also Uherek 2000). The number of Czech tourists and other visitors was steadily growing, as was the number of travelogues and other texts dedicated to the provinces and their inhabitants. The Austro-Hungarian policies in Bosnia and Herzegovina were frequently criticized by Czech liberal and nationalist politicians and journalists as colonialist, anti-Slavic and autocratic. However, even the critics usually praised the technical, economic and cultural progress achieved over a relatively short period of time by the dual monarchy (ibid.: 83).

The critical texts, speeches and polemics discussing the nature and results of the absolutist rule of the finance minister and chief administrator of the provinces, Benjámin Kállay (1839–1903), usually only glossed over the existence of the Muslims; however, there were some interesting exceptions to this. In 1899, three Czech deputies of the Austrian parliament – Emanuel Dyk (1852–1907), Max Hájek (1835–1913) and František König (1853–?) – published a report from their journey through the occupied provinces with the telling title 'Dvacet let práce kulturní' (Twenty years of cultural work). Unlike those Czech authors who tended to be highly critical of Habsburg policies in the Balkans, the three deputies provided a more positive assessment of the overall progress achieved under Habsburg rule in the previous two decades. Dyk, Hájek and König also paid special attention to the Muslims (*mohamedáni*):

The Slavic press commits a big error by practically ignoring the Mohammedans. They are usually imagined as an insignificant mass, despite the fact that they are almost as numerous as the Orthodox and despite the fact that they are Slavs, who will quite certainly, and perhaps even in a relatively short time, shed the yoke of Islam and join their Christian brothers. We have become accustomed to the belief in the approaching disappearance of the Turk from Europe, throwing the Bosnian Mohammedans (*bosenské mohamedány*) into the same basket as the Turks, forgetting that they are in fact Slavic Moslems (*slovanští moslimové*) and not Ottomans. (Dyk, Hájek and König 1899: 17)

In the last years of the nineteenth century, the national consciousness of the Mohammedans was still in its initial stages. The multiple effects of modernization under Habsburg rule, however, increased the intensity of contacts between the Muslims and other Bosnian communities. Their alleged conservative habits had been changing, Muslim children started to attend public schools and even the Mohammedan women were making attempts to break out of their social isolation. 'The Slavic spirit and blood cannot be denied. Despite the fact that they have been true followers of the Turkish religion for several centuries, they have been awakening as if from a magical sleep, and starting to identify with their tribe. These are just humble beginnings. However, the attempts of the Bosnian Mohammedans to rid themselves of their national colourlessness (*národní bezbarvost*) are more evident every year' (Dyk, Hájek and König 1899: 15–16).

Like other Czech authors, Dyk, Hájek and König perceived a close link between religious conversion and the change of national identity. 'The contacts between Christians and Mohammedans have become unlimited, mostly even friendly. The time when the question arises of whether it would not be better if Mohammedans returned to the embrace of the Christian church is perhaps not that far away' (Dyk, Hájek and König 1899: 17). While failing to provide convincing evidence that would support their vision of an approaching (re-)Christianization of the Bosnian Muslims, they focused on the question of which church and ethnic group the Muslims would identify with in the future. They argued that the Bosnian Muslims felt a greater affinity to Roman Catholic Croats than to Orthodox Serbs:

> Recently, the Orthodox were the greatest enemies of the Turks, whether they were fighting man against man on the Drina or in the wild mountain valleys of Montenegro. There was, of course, much blood spilled during the occupation as well; however, that was done by foreigners, by the Švabos, not by the Croats. The family memory preserving the recent tribal hostilities is biased against the Orthodox and not against the Croats. (Ibid.)

Catholicism also enjoyed greater prestige as the dominant confession of the Habsburg Empire and its political elites. The Muslims 'used to be the ruling class and will therefore prefer to join the confession that represents the greatest majority in our empire'. The fact that Muslims switched to the Latin script after the occupation was cited as additional proof of their pro-Catholic leanings. Dyk, Hájek and König admitted that it was still too early to predict whether the Bosnian Muslims would become Serbs or Croats in the end: 'However, regardless of the outcome, the Slavs can only gain. Whether the Mohammedans become Serbs or Croats, in either case this will mean the resurrection of a dead branch of the Slavic tree. ... We welcome the fact that the Mohammedans have been approaching the Croats, which also opens the way for their conversion to Catholicism, the faith that we profess as well' (Dyk, Hájek and König 1899: 18). Ideas similar to those expressed by the three Czech deputies were not entirely unique in the earlier phases of the Austro-Hungarian occupation: 'To most Europeans, the Bosnian Muslims appeared doomed, like a lagoon cut off from the receding tide of a shrivelling Ottoman sea' (Okey 2007: 92). According to the historian Robin Okey, even the longest-serving chief administrator of the province, Benjámin Kállay, accused of favouring the Muslims over other communities by some of his critics, was not immune to similar considerations: 'Kállay himself had reservations about Islam's viability in the modern world' and in private did not completely exclude the possibility of Muslim conversion to Christianity in the future (ibid.: 59–61, 98).

Ten years later, the geographer, naturalist, and future Czechoslovak diplomat Jiří V. Daneš (1880–1928) published another short synthetic volume on Bosnia and Herzegovina in an attempt to provide Czech readers with a fresh overview of the main problems of the recently annexed provinces. His book is predominantly a scholarly work focusing on geography, demographic changes, population density, migration, the economy, and other topics. Daneš underlined the multiple and far-reaching transformation of Bosnia and Herzegovina under Habsburg rule. In its attempts to introduce reforms and stimulate modernization, Daneš admitted, the government proved to be ruthlessly effective. Nevertheless, Bosnia and Herzegovina was, for all practical purposes, treated as a mere colony. Under closer scrutiny, many positive changes and signs of progress did in fact appear as secondary results of other government-sponsored projects whose primary aim was to exploit the conquered land (Daneš 1909: 3). According to Daneš, the main Czech national interest in Bosnia and Herzegovina was the preservation and strengthening of its Slavic identity, perceived as being threatened by the influx of foreign capital (particularly Austrian and Hungarian), settlement of ethnic German colonists, and the predominance of the German language in provincial administration.

The particular religious identities and national identifications of the local Slavs seemed to be of secondary importance to Daneš, who was writing three decades after the occupation of 1878 and several months after the annexation of 1908. From a scholarly point of view, the inhabitants of Bosnia and Herzegovina were conceptualized as a single group – they were all Slavs of 'Serbo-Croatian nationality':

Thanks to their physical strength, uncorrupted morals, purity of language, and devotion to old national customs, these Slavs represent the true core of the Serbo-Croat nation, and will as such certainly play an important role in the field of national regeneration in the future. Their misfortune, at least for the time being, lies in the fact that they are divided into three elements, sharply differing in their historical and cultural tradition and political aims. (Daneš 1909: 89)

Unlike Dyk, Hájek and König ten years earlier, Daneš did not engage in fantasies or speculations about a possible mass conversion of the Muslims. The geographer even reinterpreted the old notion of Muslim fanaticism in a positive way: 'The Mohammedans (*muhammedáni*) are famous for the purity and honesty of their character. Their religious fanaticism provides a firm moral anchor against the corruption that has been emanating from cultural Europe (*z kulturní Evropy*)' (Daneš 1909: 92). Another evergreen from the repertoire of Orientalist clichés – the notion of Turkish/Muslim decadence and degeneration – is not missing either, but it is in fact reserved exclusively for portrayal of the Bosnian Muslim upper classes, especially the old aristocracy 'which often likes to enjoy the delights forbidden by the Qur'an and sinks into moral as well as financial ruin' (ibid.). Apart from the relatively thin upper strata most closely associated with the old Ottoman regime, the far more numerous Bosnian Muslim masses were conceptualized in the same manner as their Christian Orthodox and Roman Catholic neighbours – as representatives of the healthy, vital and morally uncorrupted core of the Serbo-Croat nation. What set them apart, at least for the time being, was their lower level of national consciousness in comparison with the Serbs and Croats: 'They still call themselves Turks, but they speak Serbian and do not know Turkish at *all*. Their religion is also their nationality' (ibid.). The identification of religious affiliation with nationality as a characteristic tendency of Bosnian Muslim self-understanding was also mentioned in other Central European sources from the period, including the influential volume on Bosnia and Herzegovina that was published as part of the representative series *Die österreichisch-ungarische Monarchie in Wort und Bild* (1901: 4; popularly referred to as *Kronprinzenwerk*) dedicated to particular lands of the Habsburg Empire. Despite considerable efforts by the Habsburg administration to secure the loyalty and cooperation of the Muslim ruling classes, Daneš claimed that the Muslims in general did not become accustomed to or reconciled with the realities of the new Habsburg system. However, he blamed the government rather than the allegedly stubborn, conservative and ungrateful Muslims, as did some of his Czech contemporaries (e.g. see Zavadil 1911). Daneš believed that the insufficient integration and adaptation of the Muslim population was a result of the government's long-term tendency to ignore the will of the local inhabitants.

At the turn of the twentieth century, Czech accounts of Bosnia and Herzegovina often varied in their attitudes towards the Austro-Hungarian presence and policies in the province. The Mohammedans were also depicted from diverse angles, yet their Slavic identity (despite the fact that in practical life it usually did not extend beyond the confines of linguistic affinity) was the most important element in almost all Czech representations from the late Habsburg era, since it was understood as a bond of kinship that tied the Muslims to both their fellow South Slavs and the Czechs. It stimulated Czech interest in this group of Bosnia and Herzegovina's inhabitants, which otherwise seemed more alien and distant than the two other ethnoreligious groups dominating the land. The fantasy of a possible conversion of the Muslims to Christianity gradually faded away after the turn of the century. Czech authors were now usually openly supporting the rise of national consciousness in the modern sense among the Muslims. They anticipated that the envisioned rise of national self-identification would eventually lead to reconciliation and rapprochement among the Muslims, Christian Orthodox Serbs and Roman Catholic Croats. The Muslims could then finally join forces with the Christian Orthodox and Catholics in their struggle against capitalist exploitation and foreign colonial rule. The thought that the formation of a modern national consciousness, nationalist discourse, and political agenda could in fact strengthen rather than weaken the particular collective identities of Bosnia and Herzegovina's Muslims, Serbs and Croats is surprisingly absent in Czech sources from the late Habsburg period.

The Artist and the Gendarme: Bosnian Muslims in the Eyes of Ludvík Kuba and František Valoušek

According to the inscription on his gravestone, Ludvík Kuba (1865–1956) was a Czech painter and Slavic musicologist. On the memorial plaque marking his birthplace in the Central Bohemian town of Poděbrady, 'national artist Ph.Dr. h. c. Ludvík Kuba' is characterized as a painter, musician, writer and researcher in the field of Slavic ethnography. In any case, this truly renaissance personality blessed with a long and productive life was undoubtedly one of the most important and interesting figures to contribute to the development of Czech representations of the South Slavs, the Balkans, and the entire Slavic world in his artistic and scholarly oeuvre. After expanding his original focus on music and musicology, Kuba studied painting in Prague, Paris and Munich. Between the 1880s and the Second World War, he undertook a series of research journeys through the Balkans and Central and Eastern Europe. He first visited Bosnia and Herzegovina in the early 1890s, primarily with the aim of collecting folk songs. Besides compiling and publishing a representative collection of folk songs in the original version accompanied by a Czech translation, Kuba also contributed to the influential volume on Bosnia and Herzegovina, published as part of the respected series of regional studies *Die österreichisch-ungarische Monarchie in Wort und Bild* in 1901, with a chapter on traditional music (Kuba 1901).

Kuba mostly refers to the Muslims of Bosnia and Herzegovina as Turks. He was well aware that this was not an ethnic term but justified its usage by pointing out that this was indeed the term that was common among the land's autochthonous populations, including the Muslims themselves (Kuba 1937: 103). Unlike most Czech authors, Ludvík Kuba emphasized the Bogomil theory in his conceptualizations of the Bosnian Muslims. The Bogomil-influenced Bosnian church, considered heretical by the Roman Catholic Church at the time, had a strong presence in the late-medieval Bosnian kingdom. According to Kuba, the Bogomils and their descendants, who mostly converted to Islam after the Ottoman conquest, had a crucial formative influence on the development of a specific identity (*vyhraněná osobitost*) of the country and its inhabitants. Kuba did not view the Muslim culture and religion of Bosnia and Herzegovina primarily as a foreign implant. For him, the existence of a specific Bosnian Muslim society and culture was a natural result of long-term development that could be traced all the way back to the Middle Ages. Because of the conversions, the Bosnian aristocracy managed to safeguard a great degree of independence. Despite its noted loyalty to the sultan and Islam, the Bosnian Muslim aristocracy cultivated a strong sense of regional patriotism and attachment to its narrow homeland within the large empire. Especially in his texts devoted to the origin and history of Sarajevo, Kuba provides a highly positive image of the Muslims. Islam was associated with equality and toleration of other religions. It represented civilizational progress symbolized by new bridges, roads, waterpipes, public baths, *bezistans* and *hans*. Kuba depicted Ottoman Sarajevo not as a dark and barbarian place but as a city with a highly developed sense of aesthetics and beauty, ethical values, and philanthropy.

In order to attract less attention during his research and travels, Kuba had a habit of wearing local headgear in most Slavic lands. In Bosnia, he chose the fez.

> I opted for a fez, which in Bosnia covers the head of the Catholic, Orthodox and Muslim alike. It gave me the resemblance of a Turk, and sometimes, since I wore glasses, I was even mistaken for a Turkish doctor. . . . In the local conditions, I considered the choice of fez to represent the middle road, since only the Orthodox and Catholics mutually hated each other, but both maintained good relations with the Turks. (Kuba 1937: 102)

However, wearing the fez also brought problems and caused unpleasant experiences, 'first and foremost from our West European element' (*u našeho západoevropského živlu*). His decision to wear local headgear had accidently provided him with a first-hand experience of what it feels like to be a local in an occupied land. Members of the intelligentsia from other parts of the Habsburg Monarchy, the same class to which Kuba himself belonged, dealt with him with particular harshness. Almost any newcomer in any position in Bosnia and Herzegovina, regardless of their origin or social standing – from doormen and servants in new

European-style hotels to officials of the provincial administration – treated him like a second-class citizen, or worse, as Kuba recalled:

> As long as I was riding a horse, it was relatively bearable. I could be taken for a retired pasha, and occasionally I was even greeted with some respect. But whenever I walked, I was completely doomed. And it was walking that I liked best! Generally speaking, a pedestrian does not get much respect in the Balkans anyway, but a pedestrian wearing a Schwabo suit combined with a fez confused everyone, both the locals and the foreigners. (Kuba 1937: 103)

Travelling around Bosnia and Herzegovina with a fez, Kuba realized that most newcomers who settled in the occupied lands automatically (but firmly) believed in the superiority of their own culture and way of life. Contrary to them, Kuba was a convinced cultural relativist who refused the idea of a hierarchy of cultures and civilizations. He believed that habits and attitudes that might at first appear strange and even ridiculous were usually functional and meaningful in the culture from which they sprang, and he used the example of Muslim shopkeepers in the town of Travnik to illustrate his point. At first glance, the immobile and silent shopkeepers may have appeared lethargic and lazy. Travel literature from the period is indeed replete with images of 'Mohammedan shopkeepers, sitting like Buddhas, surrounded by their goods'. Their immobility and self-containment, Kuba claimed, was not a product of Oriental laziness. The Turkish culture, with its high esteem for restraint and calm, naturally discouraged the use of excessive or unnecessary words and gestures. Instead of laziness and degeneration, Kuba discovered an impressive dignity in their calm and silent ways (Kuba 1937: 114).

In the mid-1890s, Kuba decided to settle in Mostar for a longer period. He had previously dedicated most of his energy to systematic travels through the Slavic world, primarily to collect folk songs accompanied by illustrations and travel notes. He lived in Mostar in 1895 and 1896 together with his wife, this time with the aim of developing his skills and reputation as a painter. Their landlord and most of their neighbours were Muslims. Kuba considered Bosnia and Herzegovina 'the most picturesque land of the Balkans', and Mostar and its surroundings were, in turn, one of the most picturesque areas of this most picturesque land. As he later recalled, he initially felt as if the Herzegovinian landscape and its inhabitants had stepped straight out of Čermák's oil paintings of Montenegro from the 1860s and 1870s (Kuba 1955: 176). In Mostar, everybody looked monumental, whether they were Serbs, Turks or Catholics (Croats) (Kuba 1937: 197).

Despite the fact that Kuba found dignity in all inhabitants of this corner of Herzegovina, he particularly linked the noble values and qualities he admired with the Muslims. The high level of dignity and morality he perceived in them was, as he believed, a direct result of the simple but wise teachings of Islam. Kuba wrote with attention and empathy about members of the higher classes – 'the dignified effendis: begs, agas, hojas and hajiyas' – but also about the average and poor Muslims, such as a self-conscious and calm beggar in Mostar 'standing at the street corner, resembling a Roman statue' (Kuba 1937: 196–97). In a chapter entitled 'Vznešený pohřeb' (A sublime funeral) from his collection of travelogues and other writings on Bosnia and Herzegovina, the painter recounts the funeral of the mufti of Sarajevo, who passed away during his visit to Mostar. Descriptions of Muslim attitudes toward death and fate, as well as customs surrounding the last rites, seemed to poignantly demonstrate the main ideas and virtues characteristic of Muslim religion and culture. Kuba found Muslim funerals and graveyards beautiful, soothing and dignified, and felt they cemented the community together and facilitated the return of the bereaved to everyday life (Kuba 1937: 217).

The majority of Czech authors writing about Bosnia and Herzegovina in the late Habsburg era expressed their Slavophile sympathies. This was usually accompanied by critical remarks towards Habsburg policies in the provinces. Ludvík Kuba dedicated a great part of his long life to researching Slavic folk cultures and searching for proper representations of the Slavic world through music, the visual arts and texts. Few Czechs of his generation could compete with his firsthand knowledge of the Slavic peoples and the lands they inhabited. Despite these credentials and his critique of the negative aspects of the occupation, his representations of Bosnia and Herzegovina and its Muslim inhabitants also sometimes closely echo the mainstream Habsburg discourse on the historical identity of the provinces and the inhabitants as embodied, for example, in the representative *Kronprinzenwerk* volume on Bosnia and Herzegovina (to which he also contributed). The images of the Muslims of Bosnia and Herzegovina in his texts (as well as visual depictions) are among the most penetrating, detailed and sympathetic portrayals of this population to be found in the entire body of Czech literature on Bosnia and Herzegovina under Habsburg rule.

Born one year after the occupation in the vicinity of the Moravian provincial capital of Brno, the gendarme František Valoušek (1879–1961) served in eastern Bosnia for the last sixteen years of Habsburg rule. Valoušek served in a remote and relatively underdeveloped corner of Bosnia, mostly as commander of different police stations on the mountainous frontier with Serbia, the Ottoman Empire (Sandžak of Novi Pazar) and Montenegro – Kamenica, Mioče, Metaljka, and others. At the time of the dissolution of the dual monarchy in 1918, he was police commander of the town of Goražde. In remote rural areas, he found fewer opportunities to observe the technological and cultural progress typically associated with the Habsburg civilizing mission. From Valoušek's perspective, even the small provincial east Bosnian towns like Višegrad, Foča and Goražde provided a superior quality of life and comfort to the isolated places where he spent most of his service. In his later years, the diligent former gendarme compiled detailed memoirs of his life, with special focus on his service in Bosnia and Herzegovina (3,600 pages out of 9,000 written in 1933 and from 1946 to 1949). An edited digest from the manuscript first appeared in Czech (Valoušek 1999) and later also in a Bosnian translation (Valoušek 2015). Unfortunately, the original manuscript, owned by Valoušek's descendants, has been inaccessible to scholars since the publication of the selection (Ljuca 2011: 350–51).

Unlike most Czech authors writing about Bosnia and Herzegovina, Valoušek was not a Slavophile intellectual. His manner of writing is matter-of-fact and free of nationalist or poetic exaltation, but rich in detail and replete with his observations, stories and anecdotes. For years, Valoušek spent most of his time serving outside regardless of the weather, and the nature of his work meant he was in daily contact with both the local Muslims (Turks) and Orthodox (Serbs). Valoušek's view of Islam was mostly positive. He refers to Islam as the Turkish religion, and calls the local Muslims 'Turks', as was still common during his service. However, he always made a clear distinction between the Bosnian Muslims and the real, Asiatic Turks. Valoušek learned the Turkish language from imam Nurudin Hajdarbašić of Čelebići in order to communicate with the Ottoman soldiers and officers from the other side of the border. While he usually depicted the Bosnian Muslims with sympathy without repeatedly highlighting the importance of their Slavic identity, as most Czech authors of the time felt obliged to do, the Asiatic Turkish-speaking soldiers serving on the periphery of the Ottoman Empire were mostly portrayed as cruel and wild, with a tendency to plunder. This did not seem to affect his overall positive attitude towards Islam: 'The Turks are incorrectly called pagans, but they do not have any statues or pictures of saints, angels, etc. in their prayer rooms. They believe in one invisible God, and in Muhammad they respect only a prophet of God. Prophet Muhammad, the founder of the Turkish religion, who lived in Asia some 1,400 years ago, must have been a very wise, reasonable, practical, and smart man for his times' (Valoušek 1999: 13).

Despite his praise for the teachings of Islam, Valoušek remained deeply critical of the unequal position of Bosnian Muslim women in everyday life:

> It would always hurt me whenever I met a Turk while on duty, even a very young one, riding on a horse in the saddle with his wife hopping behind him on foot. The Turks had no regard for their wives, and treated them as slaves and abused them. The Orthodox were not very gallant to their wives either; and their wives had to do everything, even the heaviest work, together with them. However, when an Orthodox travelled somewhere and had only one horse, it was always the woman who was riding while the man walked behind her. (Valoušek 1999: 85)

Echoing the words found in letters, articles and memoirs written by female Czech doctors who worked in Bosnia and Herzegovina primarily with Muslim women (see Nečas 1992), Valoušek concluded that Muslim women spent most of their adult years imprisoned in their family houses, living in dark rooms without much sunlight, subjugated first to their parents and then to their husbands: 'Before they turn twenty, they are good looking, even beautiful, but then they start to age very quickly. At the age of thirty or forty, they already look like old ladies. They die at a relatively young age. Many parents marry them off as early as twelve years of age' (Valoušek 1999: 210).

In the beginning of the twentieth century, the comparably more conservative attitudes of the Muslims towards women, including the sensitive issue of seclusion and hiding female family members from the gaze of foreign visitors, became a standard feature that distinguished the Muslims from other ethnoreligious communities of the land with whom they otherwise shared much of their lifestyle, everyday habits, and values. Ferdinand Velc (1864–1920), author of the first Czech guidebook on Bosnia and Herzegovina, advised tourists to 'respect the old local customs and refrain from various jokes and sneers'. Upon entering a 'Turkish' house, one should first knock on the door, wait for the male head of the household to open it, explain the reason of the visit, and then provide enough time for the women to hide (Velc 1907: 2). Bosnian Muslim women were not depicted by František Valoušek merely as passive victims of religious oppression and patriarchal mentality who were enslaved by their husbands; he also showed them to be intelligent human beings who were well aware of their own situation and who longed for change, even actively struggling for greater equality. This tendency is most evident in Valoušek's recollection of the case of a woman who killed her oppressive husband and his favourite new wife in their sleep before walking for miles in deep snow to the nearest police station to turn herself in and confess. Despite the gruesome details, the Czech gendarme openly sympathizes in his memoirs with the woman, who had taken justice into her own hands (Valoušek 1999: 83–84).

Valoušek's perception of everyday Muslim life in the rough eastern borderland of Habsburg Bosnia is largely free of the usual exoticization, poetic exaltation, and Orientalist associations frequently encountered in the texts of authors who focused on the larger, more developed towns known for their attractive Ottoman architectural heritage. One striking example of these different perspectives is the attitudes towards death and Muslim funeral practices. In the travelogues of Ludvík Kuba as well as other authors, Muslim funerals are usually described as dignified rites of passage. From the gendarme's point of view, the Muslim funeral customs as practised in the rural areas of Eastern Bosnia were more problematic than romantic. Owing to traditional customs, the Muslim graves were simply too shallow in comparison with those of the Christians. In the countryside, as he recounts, foxes and other wild animals were easily able to dig up the recently buried corpses from the graves. It was a horrible sight and not a very pleasant experience for the nose when one came across the half-rotten, half-eaten corpses sticking out from the earth at rural Muslim cemeteries. Last but not least, the continuation of these traditional practices also meant additional work for the overstretched police officer, who each time had to make sure that local villagers took care of the delicate hygiene problem as soon as possible (Valoušek 1999: 30).

Valoušek remained sensitive to the particular differences between the Muslims and Orthodox Christians in everyday life, always primarily from the point of view of a gendarme. Murders and other serious crimes were 'a daily occurrence in Bosnia', Valoušek writes. 'The local people were easily excited, fearless, and mostly illiterate. Especially among the Turks, blood revenge based on the "eye for an eye" principle was widespread' (Valoušek 1999: 32). Muslim men were also more likely to commit crimes motivated by their heightened sense of honour, especially when the sensitive issue of the seclusion of women happened to be in question. The Muslims of Eastern Bosnia sometimes appear extremely conservative. During the census of June 1904, jealousy was aroused when a local Habsburg official accidently glimpsed a man's unveiled wife, which resulted in the immediate murder of the unsuspecting official by the woman's husband (ibid.: 33). Other Muslim men displayed more liberal attitudes, and in the years that followed, Valoušek had the opportunity to speak freely to many Muslim women. Inside the houses of his friends, they were not even covered by a veil during his visits. However, due to the wild and unpredictable nature of the locals, Habsburg gendarmes still maintained the habit of walking around in pairs, never alone: 'In Bosnia, a lonely gendarme was in great danger at all times and in all places. The locals in Bosnia are easily aroused, revengeful, and ready to fight' (ibid.: 33). Nevertheless, Valoušek's overall picture of Bosnia's population remains largely sympathetic and positive. In many passages, he conceptualizes the entire population of the land as sharing the same basic characteristics, mentality and lifestyle. 'The whole of Bosnia and its people represent one big mystery. There is probably no other people in Europe that has lived so primitively and with such low expectations when it comes to living standards; yet despite that, the people of Bosnia are happy, satisfied, merry, healthy, and they live very long lives' (ibid.: 41).

Valoušek's memoirs represent a unique testimony, one markedly less influenced by the Czech Slavophile ideology of the time, romanticism, and Orientalism in the classical sense of the term. We can suppose that other Czechs living in Bosnia and Herzegovina under Habsburg rule might have held similar views based on their own experiences, but failed to leave written testimonies. Valoušek's images of the Bosnian Muslims are also quite particular due to the fact that he served in a specific part of the country seldom visited by his compatriots. His colourful, at times harsh but at others highly sympathetic, representations of the Bosnian Muslims and indeed the entire population of Bosnia and Herzegovina defy simplistic categorizations.

Conclusion

Representations of the Muslims of Bosnia and Herzegovina in Czech sources during the four decades of Habsburg rule were relatively rich and diverse. In recent scholarly literature, it is generally assumed that the formation and transformation of the images of the Bosnian Muslims mirrored the overall intensification of contacts, the gradual improvement of mutual relations, and a growing trust between the Czechs and the Bosnian Muslims. From this perspective, the Austro-Hungarian occupation and later annexation enabled the two Slavic peoples, who previously had almost no contact or knowledge of each other, to finally become acquainted. When they suddenly found themselves living in the same state after 1878, the story goes, the Czechs and the Bosnian Muslims gradually overcame their mutual prejudices. When it comes to the topic of representations, the 'Turks' and 'Schwabos' from the first phase of the occupation were discursively transformed into Slavic brothers thanks to their shared experience of living under the one roof of the dual monarchy (see Ljuca 2006; Hladký 2010). This thesis can be meaningfully applied to the Czechs living in Bosnia and Herzegovina on a more or less permanent basis during the period. However, many Czechs who wrote about the Bosnian Muslims lacked the experience of living side by side with them. Indeed, it seems that the contacts between most Czech visitors and the local Muslims remained relatively limited until the First World War. The simple act of living together in one state and sharing similar experiences could not fully explain the transformation of the overall discourse on the Muslims of Bosnia and Herzegovina from predominantly negative to predominantly neutral or even positive.

On closer examination, it is not always possible to speak of the straightforward evolution of the original image of a threatening (culturally and religiously) non-European Other into a Slavic brother and potential ally in the common struggle of the Slavic peoples against foreign domination. Old stereotypes never completely disappeared, and sometimes surfaced even after the turn of the twentieth century (Ljuca 2006: 134). The concept of a '(br)other', an ambivalent figure who is neither an enemy nor an ally but could potentially become either, as postulated by Edin Hajdarpašić primarily in connection with the Croat and Serb discourses on the Bosnian Muslims before the First World War, also deserves mention here for its close resemblance to analogical Czech conceptualizations of this Slavic population (see Hajdarpašić 2015: 16–17). Nevertheless, if we step back and look from a greater distance at the big picture, it is indeed possible to observe a general trend towards positive representations and an overall humanization of the Muslims in Czech texts between the 1870s and 1918. Apart from direct contacts, the transformation of the discourse was primarily motivated by the dynamics of Czech cultural, social and political life throughout the observed period. It is obvious that the importance of religious identity, and the role of religion in daily life in general, decreased in Czech society from the late 1870s until the end of the First World War and the break-up of Austria–Hungary. The importance of national identity, on the other hand, had been steadily on the rise in the same period, and had witnessed great progress in Czech national life across a number of fields. The simultaneous processes of secularization, increasing nationalization, and multifaceted modernization of Czech society at the turn of the twentieth century had profound effects on the rethinking and renegotiation of the place of the Czech nation within both the Habsburg Monarchy and the world. This was probably the main underlying factor enabling the transformation of the representations of the Balkans, the South Slavs, and the Bosnian Muslims in particular. The image of the South Slavs, including Muslims, became secularized and ethnicized during the period in question, and special emphasis was put on the shared Slavic identity.

Czech attitudes towards the Muslims of Bosnia and Herzegovina represent a specific national variation and diversification of attitudes towards Muslims in general. The observation of the anthropologist Andre Gingrich, who distinguishes between the good and the bad Orientals (Gingrich 1998: 117), can usefully be applied to our case as well. While the images of the 'real' (Asian or Anatolian) Turks remained mostly negative during the last four decades of the Habsburg Monarchy (Heiss and Feichtinger 2013: 148–65), the Muslims of Bosnia and Herzegovina were elevated to the status of good Orientals. From the perspective of Czech authors living in an increasingly nationalizing environment afflicted with a growing Czech–German antagonism, the fact that 'our' Muslims happened to be fellow Slavs tended to be highlighted far more frequently than the fact that both the Czechs and the Bosnians of all creeds found themselves under the spectre of the same emperor and were subjected to the laws of the same state. The lively interest in other Slavs, including the Muslims of Bosnia and Herzegovina, was also closely linked to the Czech nation's search for potential political, cultural and 'racial' allies within the Habsburg Monarchy, as well as beyond its borders.

František Šístek is a research fellow at the Institute of History, Czech Academy of Sciences, and an associate professor at the Institute of International Studies, Faculty of Social Sciences, Charles University in Prague. He graduated in history from Central European University in Budapest, and earned his PhD in social and cultural anthropology at the Faculty of Humanities, Charles University, Prague. He has focused on former Yugoslavia and representations of the South Slavs and the Balkans in Central Europe, national identities, images and stereotypes of the Other, and competing interpretations of the past in South Eastern Europe. His monographs include *Narativi o identitetu: izabrane studije o crnogorskoj istoriji* [Narratives of identity: Selected studies in Montenegrin history] (Podgorica: Matica crnogorska, 2015) and *Dějiny Černé Hory* [A history of Montenegro] (Prague: NLN, 2017).

References

Borozan, Vjera. 2006. 'Černá Hora a Černohorci optikou obrazů Jaroslava Čermáka', in Mirjam Moravcová, David Svoboda and František Šístek (eds), *Pravda, láska a ti na 'Východě': Obrazy středoevropského a východoevropského prostoru z pohledu české společnosti*. Prague: FHS UK, pp. 162–83.

Černý, Vratislav, František V. Mokrý and Váša Náprstek. 1930. *Život a dílo Jaroslava Čermáka*. Prague: Výtvarný odbor Umělecké besedy.

'Czech Remove Kebab Song – Za císaře pána', 22 December 2016, from https://www.youtube.com/watch?v=AszJCpNmxOo; last accessed 27 April 2020.

Daneš, Jiří V. 1909. *Bosna a Hercegovina*. Prague: Eduard Grégr a syn.

Die österreichisch-ungarische Monarchie in Wort und Bild: Bosnien und Hercegovina. 1901. Vienna: Verlag der kaiserlich-königlich Hof- und Staatsduckerei.

Dlábková, Markéta, and Ondřej Chrobák (eds). 2008. *František Bohumír Zvěřina, 1835–1908*. Jihlava: Oblastní galerie Vysočiny.

Dyk, Emanuel, Max Háje and František König. 1899. *Dvacet let práce kulturní: Cesta Bosnou a Hercegovinou*. Plzeň: J. Císař.

Gingrich, Andre. 1998. 'Frontier Myths of Orientalism: The Muslim World in Public and Popular Cultures of Central Europe', in Bojan Baskar and Boris Brumen (eds), *Mediteranean Ethnological Summer School*. Piran: Institut za multikulturne raziskave, pp. 99–127.

Hajdarpašić, Edin. 2015. *Whose Bosnia? Nationalism and Political Imagination in the Balkans, 1840–1914*. Ithaca, NY: Cornell University Press.

Heiss, Johann, and Johannes Feichtinger. 2013. 'Uses of Orientalism in the Late Nineteenth-Century Austro-Hungarian Empire', in James Hodkinson et al. (eds), *Deploying Orientalism in Culture and History: From Germany to Central and Eastern Europe*. Rochester, NY: Camden, pp. 148–65.

Hladký, Ladislav, et al. 2010. *Vztahy Čechů s národy a zeměmi jihovýchodní Evropy*. Prague: Historický ústav.

Holeček, Josef. 1901. *Bosna a Hercegovina za okupace*. Prague: vlastním nákladem.

Hořica, Ignát. 1909. *Smutné i veselé z Bosny a Hercegoviny*. Prague: J. Otto.

Jezernik, Božidar (ed.). 2010. *Imaginary Turk*. Newcastle upon Tyne: Cambridge Scholars.

Kuba, Ludwig (Ludvík). 1901. 'Gesang und Musik', in *Die österreichisch-ungarische Monarchie in Wort und Bild: Bosnien und Hercegovina*. Vienna: Verlag der kaiserlich-königlich Hof- und Staatsduckerei, pp. 376–90.

Kuba, Ludvík. 1937. *Čtení o Bosně a Hercegovině: Cesty a studie z roků 1893–1896*. Prague: Družstevní práce.

———. 1955. *Zaschlá paleta: Paměti*. Prague: SNKLHU.

Lemminger, Jindřich. 1884. *Episody z bosenského povstání*. Kutná Hora: Karel Šolc.

Ljuca, Adin. 1999. *Maglaj: na tragovima prošlosti*. Prague: Općina grada Maglaja.

———. 2006. 'Turci a Švábové, nebo slovanští bratři? Český pohled na bosenské muslimy v letech 1878–1918', in Mirjam Moravcová, David Svoboda and František Šístek (eds), *Pravda, láska a ti na 'Východě': Obrazy středoevropského a východoevropského prostoru z pohledu české společnosti*. Prague: FHS UK, pp. 122–34.

———. 2011. 'František Valoušek: sudionik i svjedok zbivanja u istočnoj Bosni u vrijeme aneksione krise', in Zijad Šehić et al. (eds), *Bosna i Hercegovina u okviru Austro-Ugarske*. Sarajevo: Sarajevski univerzitet, pp. 349–55.

Mücke, Pavel. 2004. 'Hercegovina: Musela ji vybojovat infantéria?', in Radmila Slabáková (ed.), *O exilu, šlechtě, Jihoslovanech a jiných otázkách moderní doby: Sborník k narozeninám Arnošta Skoupého*. Olomouc: Univerzita Palackého.

Muršič, Rajko. 2010. 'On Symbolic Othering: "The Turk" as a Threatening Other', in Božidar Jezernik (ed.), *Imaginary Turk*. Newcastle upon Tyne: Cambridge Scholars.

Nečas, Ctibor. 1972. *Balkán a česká politika: pronikání rakousko-uherského imperialismu na Balkán a česká buržoazní politika*. Brno: Univerzita J. E. Purkyně.

———. 1992. *Mezi muslimkami: Působení úředních lékařek v Bosně a Hercegovině v letech 1892–1918*. Brno: Masarykova univerzita.

Neruda, Jan. (1868) 1950. *Obrazy z ciziny*. Prague: Československý spisovatel.

Okey, Robin. 2007. *Taming Balkan Nationalism: The Habsburg 'Civilizing Mission' in Bosnia, 1878–1918*. Oxford: Oxford University Press.

Rataj, Tomáš. 2002. *České země ve stínu půlměsíce: Obraz Turka v raně novověké literatuře z českých zemí*. Prague: Scriptorium.

Šístek, František. 2009. *Naša braća na jugu: Češke predstave o Crnoj Gori i Crnogorcima, 1830–2006*. Cetinje – Podgorica: Matica crnogorska.

———. 2011a. *Junáci, horalé a lenoši: Obraz Černé Hory a Černohorců v české společnosti 1830–2006*. Prague: Historický ústav.

———. 2011b. 'Češki pisac i novinar Josef Holeček: kritički pogled na austro-ugarsku okupaciju Bosne i Hercegovine', in Zijad Šehić et al. (eds), *Bosna i Hercegovina u okviru Austro-Ugarske*. Sarajevo: Sarajevski univerzitet 2011, pp. 333–48.

Sobotková, Hana. 2007. 'The Image of Balkan Muslims in Czech and French Journals around 1900', in Steven G. Ellis and Luďa Klusáková (eds), *Imagining Frontiers, Contesting Identities*. Pisa: Edisioni Plus – Pisa University Press, pp. 339–51.

Soukupová, Věra. 1981. *Jaroslav Čermák*. Prague: Odeon.

Uherek, Zdeněk. 2000. *Češi v Bosně a Hercegovině: Úvod do problematiky s výběrovou bibliografií*. Prague: Etnologický ústav AVČR.

Valoušek, František. 1999. *Vzpomínky na Bosnu*. Brno: Albert.

———. 2015. *Sjećanja na Bosnu*. Sarajevo: Bosanska riječ.

Velc, Ferdinand. 1907. *Průvodce Bosnou a Hercegovinou*. Prague: Klub českých turistů.

Žáček, Václav, et al. 1975. *Češi a Jihoslované v minulosti: Od nejstarších dob do roku 1918*. Prague: Academia.

Zavadil, Antonín. 1911. *Obrázky z Bosny: Trappisti, Turci, Židé, Cikáni*. Prague: J. Pelcl.

Chapter 8

DIVIDED IDENTITIES IN THE BOSNIAN NARRATIVES OF VJENCESLAV NOVAK AND REBECCA WEST

Charles Sabatos

While the threat of Ottoman conquest was shared by the nations of the Balkans, it also served to strengthen national identities. The historical experience of Central Europe has been shaped by the Ottomans, but more indirectly, in the sense of a cultural frontier between imperial powers that shifted over time (Sabatos 2020). As a region deeply marked by centuries of Ottoman rule yet abruptly modernized under Habsburg occupation, Bosnia and Herzegovina represents a quintessential case of national identity divided by East and West, best known through the works of Ivo Andrić and his epic narrative *Na Drini ćuprija* [The bridge on the Drina] (1945). Among the societies of the Balkans, Bosnia and Herzegovina is divided by competing loyalties among its Croatian, Serbian and Muslim populations; the multiculturalism that made it a microcosm of Yugoslavia subsequently left it vulnerable to the atrocities of civil war. As Srećko Džaja has suggested in his work on the 'mythological complexes, metaphors for spiritual, cultural and political delimitation among Balkan peoples', the purpose of these historical myths is 'to validate a cultural and political infrastructure for the domination of only one people' while allowing other ethnicities of Bosnia and Herzegovina 'to lose their identity and disappear from the stage of history' (Džaja 2005: 109). While all national identities are arguably imagined, as analysed in Benedict Anderson's *Imagined Communities* (1983) and Maria Todorova's *Imagining the Balkans* (1997), in the case of literary texts about Bosnia and Herzegovina by South Slavic and Western writers, Bosnian Muslim identity is frequently portrayed not just as an imagined one but as a temporary costume that can be replaced with more suitable garments (Croatian, Serbian, Yugoslav, etc., depending on the author's particular use of historical myths).

Adapting Edward Said's Orientalism to the Central European (more specifically Austrian) context, Andre Gingrich has proposed the concept of frontier Orientalism as 'a relatively coherent set of metaphors and myths that reside in folk and public culture', which 'places the home country and its population along an adjacent territorial and military borderline imbued with a timeless mission'. He identifies contrasting images of the Turk as the bad Muslim who attacked the homeland, while the Bosnian is the good Muslim who helped to defend it: 'Frontier orientalism is the folkloristic glorification of decisive local military victories in past times, either against Muslims or together with Muslims, but serving present nationalist purposes' (Gingrich 1996: 119, 123). The relationship between Central European frontier Orientalism and the Balkan variant of Western Orientalism (which Todorova has termed 'Balkanism') can be seen in a comparison between the Croatian writer Vjenceslav Novak's novella *Maca* (1881), set during the Habsburg Empire's period of expansion into Bosnia and Herzegovina, and Rebecca West's *Black Lamb and Grey Falcon* (1942), the most influential representation of the Balkans in British literature. Novak claims that Bosnian Muslims are not Turks but rather Croatian brothers of the Muslim faith, while West explicitly identifies with Serbia as the true defender of Yugoslav tradition, and implicitly sees the Bosnian Muslims as misguided Serbs. Despite their chronological and ideological separation, both Novak and West come themselves from ethnically mixed backgrounds, which arguably shapes their perception of Bosnia and Herzegovina's imperial and national divisions. Novak's father was from Bohemia, one of the most active centres of anti-Habsburg sentiment in the nineteenth century, while West's father was Anglo-Irish. West's occasional comparison of Yugoslavia to the Irish case shows her own perception of the Balkans as divided between that of nations colonized by neighbouring powers (as was the case with Ireland) and that of monarchy as a civilizing force.

Croatia's historical relationship with the Bosnian Muslims was influenced not just by its position as a bulwark on the imperial frontier but also because of the perception of Bosnia and Herzegovina as a captive yet integral part of the Croatian homeland. In his study of the discourse of captivity in Bosnian national rhetoric, Edin Hajdarpašić has stated:

> The emerging Illyrian patriots of the 1820s and 1830s – stimulated not only by romanticism but also more directly by the Serbian and Greek uprisings – repurposed the early modern tropes of captivity and revival for their projects of national awakening.

As in the earlier Christian Slavic literatures, the divide between the captive and the free, the sad and the happy, often carried religious connotations, with Islam mostly associated with captivity, darkness and ruin, and Christianity with liberty, light and morality. (Hajdarpašić 2015: 57)

Vjenceslav Novak, often known as the Croatian Balzac for his use of literary realism, uses both captivity and darkness as key metaphors in his first published work, *Maca*.[1] He begins with a direct address to his young readers:

Come with me to Bosnia, my dear child! You have heard stories about it, that it is a wild country, one of slit throats and killings, where the Turks impale. Don't be afraid! Bosnia and her beautiful sister Herzegovina have long been two gorgeous daughters of the Croatian Kingdom. There is not even one Turk there – they are all Croats, your own brothers. (Novak 1944: 93)

As Berislav Majhut points out, the story is expressive of the duality among the Muslims: the Muslim Turks, who are blamed for the troubles in the country, and the Croatian Muslims, the fallen ethnic brothers (Majhut 2010: 31).

While Novak's introduction draws on the barbaric tropes of frontier Orientalism familiar from folk songs and legends, his novella for children, *Maca*, is not, as John Cox has suggested, 'a romantic historical work about the fate of a Bosnian girl at the hands of the Turks during the Ottoman occupation of the Balkans in the Middle Ages' (Novak 2014: xii). In reality, the story is set during the final decline of Ottoman rule in the 1870s, not during its expansion in previous centuries. Since the narrative was intended for young readers, the implicit sexual threat remains beneath the surface, but it does allude to the sexual exploitation that became a metaphor for imperial oppression. As Irvin Cemil Schick has explained, 'the stories of sexual violation told and retold in myriad poems, novels, plays, paintings, prints and sculpture elicited political support for national independence movements by establishing victim status, and thus demonstrating entitlement' (Schick 2007: 195–96).

While Novak genders the Ottoman oppressor as male and the symbol of the Christian homeland as female, the eponymous Maca's role in the narrative is largely passive until the end of the story, surviving traumatic events without resisting them. The central character is actually the aga, or wealthy Muslim landlord, whose greed initially destroys Maca's family, but who ultimately loses his wealth and is redeemed for the Croatian nation by being converted to Christianity. In the beginning, the dying peasant Rade Žigić tells his son Milan (Maca's father) that he has saved and buried gold coins for him to start a new life. However, the greedy aga learns of this treasure and comes to claim it for himself, asking the recently bereaved Milan: 'So, that pagan dog is dead?' (Novak 1944: 99). Angry at being unable to find the gold, he throws Maca out into the snow and burns down the house. Milan and his wife escape, thinking their daughter is dead, but she is saved by a neighbour named Joco, who vows revenge. Some years later, in a chapter entitled 'We Have Found the Lost Sheep', Joco leads the people of the town in a rebellion. The aga's own house is burned down and he emerges, phoenix-like, from its ruins:

> The Bosnians looked in surprise at the ugly, hideous person, on whom the fire illuminated his black face. His Turkish clothing was hanging from him in burned rags, and his face was wounded, bloody, and blackened with coal. Only his eyes looked out of the black face calmly, shining with a serene contentment, as if in that hideous body was a pure, angelic soul. (Ibid.: 118)

Novak's translator, John Cox, has commented on 'the frequency of Novak's use of birth imagery and the notion of ideas or emotions finding form or being clothed in certain conventions' (Novak 2014: ix). The former aga is not only washed clean and baptized with the name Ivan, but is also dressed in traditional Croatian costume, suggesting a rebirth, both spiritual and national.

However, another Muslim landlord takes Maca into his house and imprisons Joco as well as Ivan, who has joined the rebels. In her moment of triumph, Maca frees not only herself but also Joco and Ivan from captivity, and the rebels set the house aflame. There is no redemption for the second aga, presumably a native Turk rather than a convert: 'The house ... burns with the body of the sleeping sinner, and was the last candle for the Mohammedan who had set off for heaven [*cennet*]'[2] (Novak 1944: 137). The salvation of the homeland is complete with the return of Maca's parents, just as Croatia and Bosnia have been reunited with the coming of Austro-Hungarian rule. While Gingrich's outline of frontier Orientalism, in which overcoming a bad Muslim is made possible by relying on a good Muslim, holds true for Maca as well, Novak suggests an inner division among the Bosnian Muslims between those lost sheep who can be reclaimed for the nation and the unredeemable ones who must be sacrificed.

Three years after publishing *Maca*, Novak received a scholarship to study in Prague. His experience in his father's homeland was personified in the Czech musician Jan Jahoda, the mentor of the Croatian protagonist Amadej in Novak's novel *Dva svijeta* [Two worlds] (1901). The atmosphere of pan-Slavic idealism is reflected at its peak through Jahoda's participation in the Prague Slavic Congress presided over by František Palacký in the revolutionary year of 1848:

> After its literary renaissance, the Czech nation was coming back to life politically as well. The idea of the indomitable strength of united Slavdom filled the young Jahoda, just as it did his co-nationals, with fervid inspiration ... It was his goal for this flowering of his soul, this hymn from his heart, to ignite a holy struggle equally in everyone's heart, right down to the last Slav. He believed he was simply the one chosen by Providence to play the feverish chords that would resound all throughout the Slavic world and gather millions of people under the glorious flag of concord and unity. (Novak 2014: 42)

Following Jahoda's death, the young Amadej himself goes to study in Prague. While his life there is one of deprivation and partial disillusionment, the Czech metropolis gives him a broader Central European perspective on Slavic identity. As Jitka Malečková has explained, Czech views of Bosnian Muslims underwent a 'continual fluctuation . . . as Slavs they were seen as relatives, yet as Muslims they traditionally belonged to the (Turkish) enemies of the Slavs' (Malečková 2018: 15, 20). While Novak's own Czech experience took place after he published *Maca*, it changed his perception of Austro-Hungarian imperialism from that of a liberating force (towards the Bosnian Christians) to one of oppression (towards its own national minorities).

A much better-known and more influential text, Rebecca West's *Black Lamb and Grey Falcon* (based on West's travels through the region shortly before the Second World War), portrayed the situation in the Balkans over fifty years later. With the fall of the Austro-Hungarian Empire in 1918, Bosnia and Herzegovina had become part of the Kingdom of Serbs, Croats and Slovenes (after 1929, the Kingdom of Yugoslavia). Despite the political changes, Western travel writing on the region followed familiar Orientalist patterns, as Omer Hadžiselimović has seen in the works of early twentieth-century American writers: 'In Austro-Hungarian Bosnia, they still see Turkish Bosnia; in Yugoslav Bosnia, they still see an Austrian province superimposed on Ottoman Bosnia' (Hadžiselimović 2002: 29). In general, Rebecca West portrays the Ottoman influence as an oppressive legacy, particularly in Bosnia and Herzegovina. Yet Laura Cowan has suggested that West's work is anti-imperialist rather than Orientalist in the classic sense:

> West argues that cultural traditions are essential to healthy individuals and healthy countries . . . She condemned imperialism because it denies countries their own traditions . . . Critics rightly disparage West's treatment of the Turks – as more clichéd and more biased than her treatment of especially the Serbs. Nevertheless, even her descriptions of the Turks demonstrate her reluctance to oversimplify. She deplores them as 'barbarous' . . . and yet praises their art and opulence. (Cowan 2015: 136)

West's ambivalence towards the Ottoman role in Bosnia and Herzegovina is arguably influenced by her own ambiguous relationship attitude towards British imperial power. Through her Anglo-Irish father, she identified with Ireland, an oppressed former territory, at a time when the independence of both Ireland and Yugoslavia was within recent memory, and England's role in the world was threatened by the rise of the Third Reich.

West's description of Bosnia and Herzegovina, one of the most fascinating sections of her travelogue, is thus marked by a typically British Orientalism given a more ambiguous form by the parallels between the Irish and Balkan experience. Her frequent references to gender add an additional perspective. Bernard Schweizer suggests that the disruptive, radical edge of her work is due not so much [to] the gendered nature of her writing as the actual politics that motivate it . . . West's discourse displays . . . an Orientalist bias that could pass as a symptom of masculine cultural arrogance . . . At the same time, however, West is one of the most outspoken critics of empire among all travel writers of her time, a fact that squares well with her feminist critique of patriarchal power structures. (Schweizer 2001: 81–82)

The gendered aspect of West's critique of imperialism can be seen after her visit to Trebinje in southern Herzegovina, her first entrance into former Ottoman territory. She begins with a relatively positive impression of the landscape, describing the minarets as 'among the most pleasing architectural gestures ever made by urbanity' (West 1942: 277). However, she laments Bosnia and Herzegovina's backwardness, which she attributes to Ottoman oppression:

> All such Slavs who had never known the misery of Turkish rule harbour an extremely unhappy feeling about the fellow-Slavs of Bosnia and Herzegovina and Macedonia, who have so often suffered a real degradation under their Turkish masters. It is as if the North and East of England and the South Coast were as they are now, and the rest of our country was inhabited by people who had been ground down for centuries by a foreign oppressor to the level of the poor white trash of the Southern States or South Africa. (Ibid.: 280)

In Trebinje, West is given a tour of a historic Ottoman mansion with the owner's former servant as tour guide. Pandering to Western stereotypes, the guide reveals a supposedly traditional Turkish harem, which West realizes is a group of women pretending to weave traditional carpets while gossiping about her in Bosnian.

Leaving this crude imitation of Ottoman life in disgust, West finds the scene pitiful because of the 'decent Moslem men and women . . . [who] knew themselves dead and buried in their lifetime, coffined in the shell of a perished empire, whose ways these poor wretches were aping and defiling' (West 1942: 285). As she tells her husband:

> I hate the corpses of empires, they stink as nothing else. They stink so badly that I cannot believe that even in life they were healthy. '"I do not think you can convince mankind,'" said my husband, '"that there is not a certain magnificence about a great empire in being."' Of course there is, I admitted, but the hideousness outweighs the beauty. . . . Here the Herzegovinians had found that one empire is very like another, that Austria was no better than Turkey. (Ibid.: 287)

The underlying object of West's critique is not merely the Habsburg or Ottoman empires, which have been gone for decades, but her native Britain, which views itself as a civilizing force yet is unable to stand effectively against the menace of fascism. According to Andrew Hammond, in 'West's thousand-page aggregation of apocalyptic musing, dramatized historical vignettes, and sustained rhetorical flourishes . . . [t]he decline of British democracy into indolence and frailty is no longer viewed as the lassitude of an empire in its autumn years but as an actual urge toward death. With the nature of the Western malaise clarified, the apocalyptic tone of her writing gains powerful validity' (Hammond 2007: 149–50).

West's description of Sarajevo contains a number of these historical vignettes and rhetorical flourishes that illustrate the city's unique historical role. She admires the city for its dedication to the pleasures of life, but sees a contrast between the traditional Ottoman clothing of its Muslim inhabitants and their European (almost Nordic) appearance:

> The costumes, which we regard as the distinguishing badge of an Oriental race, are worn by people far less Oriental in aspect than, say, the Latins; and this makes Sarajevo look like a fancy-dress ball. There is also an air of immense luxury about the town, of unwavering dedication to pleasure, which makes it credible that it would hold a festivity on so extensive and costly a scale. (West 1942: 302)

West creates an extended metaphor to explain the way Bosnia and Herzegovina resisted Ottoman domination even as it seemed to yield to it, in which the Slavs are symbolized by a woman and the Turks as a man: 'He marvels at the way she allows him to take possession of her and perhaps despises her for it. Then suddenly he finds that his whole life has been conditioned to her . . . It is at this point that he suddenly realizes he has not conquered her mind and that he is not sure if she loves him . . . or even considers him of great moment' (West 1942: 307). The Bosnian nobles had relinquished their religion, the heretic Bogomil sect, in exchange for Ottoman protection,

> but they were aware that these people were their enemies. There could be no two races more antipathetic than the Slavs, with their infinite capacity for enquiry and speculation, and the Turks, who had no word in their language to express the idea of being interested in anything, and were therefore content in abandonment to the tropism of a militarist system. (Ibid.)

The divided nature of Bosnian identity, for West, can be compared to the differences of gender:

> This beautiful city speaks always of their preoccupation with one another: of what the Slav, not to be won by any gift, took from the Turk, and still was never won, [and] of the unappeasable hunger with which the Turk longed throughout the centuries to make the Slav subject to him, although the Slav is never subject, not even to himself. (West 1942: 311)

West sees true Bosnian culture as Slavic (and, by implication, Serbian), and sees Yugoslav rule over the region as the rectification of a historical injustice. Yet this Slavic nature is also represented by two men: the Serbian-Jewish poet Stanislav

Vinaver (who served as West's guide through much of her journey, and is referred to in the book as Constantine); and, indirectly, West's own father, Charles Fairfield, who had left her family when she was young. Twenty years after writing *Black Lamb and Grey Falcon*, Rebecca West wrote an essay in which she compares her father physically to the Bosnians: 'He was not at all like the inhabitants of these [British] isles, and the only place where I have ever seen large numbers of people cast in his mould was in the Bosnian part of Yugoslavia. The men who came down to the markets from the upland villages all looked at me out of my father's face' (Fleischer 2000: 33). This almost Freudian identification helps to explain how West links her own divided sense of self to Bosnia's contested heritage. In Belgrade, West tries to explain her background to her Slovenian chambermaid, who understands that 'to be Anglo-Irish was to be like an Austrian or Hungarian landowner among the Slovenes or Croats, or to be a Turkish landowner among the conquered Slavs' (West 1942: 472). By comparing her own background to the Bosnian context, West illustrates the ambivalent position of Bosnian Muslims as simultaneously empowered and marginalized: dominated by the Turks but privileged in relation to the Christian peasants in the surrounding countryside.

West and her husband have the opportunity to witness a remarkable event, the visit to Sarajevo by İsmet İnönü (the then prime minister of Turkey, soon to become the country's second president) and the war minister, Kâzım Özalp. These two leaders of the secular Turkish Republic are uncomfortable with the crowd of veiled women and fez-wearing men representing the Ottoman past that their state had repudiated: 'So, might Englishmen look if, in some corner of the Empire, they had to meet as brothers the inhabitants of a colony that had been miraculously preserved from the action of time . . . They had said not one word of the ancient tie that linked the Bosnian Moslems to the Turks, nor had they made any reference to Islam'. West sees this episode as a historic turning point: 'We had seen the end of a story that had taken five hundred years to tell. We had seen the final collapse of the old Ottoman Empire . . . But that tragedy was already accomplished. The Ottoman Empire had ceased to suffer long ago' (West 1942: 322–23). West analyses the significance that this Turkish state visit had for Bosnian Muslims:

> I suppose an Irish-American politician would suffer deep pain if time should bring to power in Eire a president who wanted to break with the past and sent an emissary to the States to beg that the old Catholic nationalism should be forgotten . . . just as in an Irish ward in an American town one was aware that the actions and reactions of history had produced a formidable amount of politics. One could feel them operating below the surface, like a still in a basement. (Ibid.: 331–32)

The Bosnian Muslims' deep identification with the Ottoman legacy (with which the Turkish Republic no longer identified) caused a trauma that was arguably only resolved many years later when Bosnia and Herzegovina's multicultural identity was shattered by the Yugoslav civil war, and its Muslims were supported by the Turkish state as it rediscovered its own long-repressed Islamic identity.

Whether from a nineteenth-century Central European perspective, as in Novak's *Maca*, or from a twentieth-century West European perspective, as in West's *Black Lamb and Grey Falcon*, Bosnia and Herzegovina's divided identity challenges the cultural essentialism that underlies modern European society. In Novak's frontier Orientalism, the resistance of determined Croats can redeem Bosnian Muslims, while in West's Balkanist perspective, the Yugoslav peoples need to look to their Slavic folk traditions to discover their true history. While Novak and his contemporaries hoped to inspire the holy struggle of freedom 'right down to the last Slav', the twentieth century showed that the legacies of empire are not as easily changed (to use West's ironic comparison) as the costumes at a fancy-dress ball.

Charles Sabatos is a professor at Yeditepe University in Istanbul, Turkey. He has been a Global Europe Fellow at the Woodrow Wilson Center in Washington, DC, a Fulbright scholar at Comenius University in Bratislava, and a visiting researcher at the Slovak Academy of Sciences (Institute of World Literature) in Bratislava. His research interests include comparative and world literatures, with a focus on the Central and Eastern European novel as well as ethnic and immigrant American writers. He is the author of the monograph *Frontier Orientalism and the Turkish Image in Central European Literature* (Lanham, MD: Lexington 2020). He has also translated contemporary Slovak literature into English.

Notes

1. My thanks to Andjelko Vlašić for obtaining the text in Zagreb, and to Ana Sekulić for translations from the Croatian.
2. Either Novak meant this reference to heaven ironically, or as Ana Sekulić has proposed, he meant to use the word *džehenem* (hell) in place of *dženet* (heaven).

References

Cowan, Laura. 2015. *Rebecca West's Subversive Use of Hybrid Genres, 1911–41*. London: Bloomsbury.
Džaja, Srečko. 2005. 'Bosnian Historical Reality and its Reflection in Myth', in Pål Kolstø (ed.), *Myths and Boundaries in South-Eastern Europe*. London: C. Hurst & Company.
Fleischer, Georgette. 2000. 'Her Own Lambs and Falcons', *The Nation* 270(6): 31–36.
Gingrich, Andre. 1996. 'Frontier Myths of Orientalism: The Muslim World in Public and Popular Cultures of Central Europe', in Bojan Baskar and Borut Brumen (eds), *Mediterranean Ethnological Summer School*. Piran: Institut za multikulturne raziskave.

Hadžiselimović, Omer. 2002. 'Snowy Domes and Gay Turbans: American Writers on Bosnia', *East European Quarterly* 36(1): 27–38.

Hajdarpašić, Edin. 2015. *Whose Bosnia: Nationalism and Political Imagination in the Balkans, 1840–1914*. Ithaca, NY: Cornell University Press.

Hammond, Andrew. 2007. *The Debated Lands: British and American Representations of the Balkans*. Cardiff: University of Wales Press.

Majhut, Berislav. 2010. 'Muslimanska tema i njezin razvoj u hrvatskom povijesnom romanu za djecu i mladež do 1945', *Nova Croatica* 4(4): 25–47.

Malečková, Jitka. 2018. '"Our Turks" or "Real Turks"? Czech Perceptions of the Slavic Muslims of Bosnia-Herzegovina', *World Literature Studies* 10(1): 15–26.

Novak, Vjenceslav. 1944. *Baba Marta*. Zagreb: Galebovi.

———. 2014. *Two Worlds*, trans. John K. Cox. Budapest: Central European University Press.

Sabatos, Charles D. 2020. *Frontier Orientalism and the Turkish Image in Central European Literature*. Lanham, MD: Lexington.

Schick, Irvin Cemil. 2007. 'Christian Maidens, Turkish Ravishers: The Sexualization of National Conflict in the Late Ottoman Period', in Amila Buturović and Irvin Cemil Schick (eds), *Women in the Ottoman Balkans: Gender, Culture, and History*. London: I.B. Tauris.

Schweizer, Bernard. 2001. *Radicals on the Road: British Travel Writing in the 1930s*. Charlottesville: University of Virginia Press.

West, Rebecca. 1942. *Black Lamb and Grey Falcon*. London: Macmillan.

Chapter 9

AUSTRONOSTALGIA AND BOSNIAN MUSLIMS IN THE WORK OF CROATIAN ANTHROPOLOGIST VERA STEIN ERLICH

Bojan Baskar

Vera Stein Erlich (1897–1980) was building a successful career in the field of psychology and education science when, in 1937, she embarked on an exploratory project that deeply redefined her professional and private life, and resulted in her becoming an anthropologist. The initiative for this project came from the young primary school teachers who attended her teacher seminar at a mountain resort somewhere in the Slovenian Alps. Earlier that same year, in her native Zagreb, a group of Bosnian student friends suggested to her – as an already recognized feminist publicist – that she should write a series of articles for the Yugoslav press on the position of Muslim women (Stein Erlich 1966: v). She was, as she recalled in the preface to her book titled *Family in Transition: A Study of 300 Yugoslav Villages*, 'not very enthusiastic about attacking the women's veil or the lattice window, but I was willing to study and report on Bosnian family life' (ibid.).[1] When teachers from other places attending the seminar learned about this, they enthusiastically pressed her to widen the geographical scope of her research to other Yugoslav regions as well, declaring their readiness to help her with her research.

The research was envisaged as a survey based on a questionnaire, which they immediately began discussing. The final version of it consisted of 134 questions. The teachers provided her with a list of suitable respondents, mostly rural teachers and doctors from all Yugoslav regions except, as she often mentioned with regret, from Slovenia (Stein Erlich 1971b).[2] The questionnaire was sent to roughly one thousand addresses, and one-third of them were returned to her, of which 305 were usable (Stein Erlich 1966: v). The survey triggered a wave of enthusiasm throughout the country. New teachers, students, and rural doctors contacted her and asked for the questionnaires to be sent to them. Stein Erlich was now also receiving other kinds of material such as testimonies and life histories. She was also sent numerous invitations from the teachers and doctors to visit them. In her retrospect, she mentions, for instance, one Ilija Grbić, a teacher from the Romanija Mountain (above Sarajevo) and his wife Vukica, who 'had helped her discover Bosnia' (Stein Erlich 1971b: 161). Traces of their shared experience can be discerned in several places in her book. She also received invitations from academics and academic institutions.[3] The impression that medical doctors played a significant role as Stein Erlich's interlocutors and guides is strongly corroborated by two influential and popular local doctors of the time, Isak Samokovlija from Sarajevo and Lovro Dojmi di Delupis from Mostar. They were both noted intellectuals and prolific writers in the field of medical literature (especially social medicine), and both scholarly popularisers. Dojmi in particular had a strong influence on Stein Erlich's notion of the 'nervous disposition' characterizing the cultural tradition of Herzegovina. He was a descendant of a rich latifundist family from the island of Vis that was famous for several remarkable personalities (in particular his uncle Lorenzo, also a very successful and popular doctor, among other things).[4] While as a rule they defined themselves politically as Dalmatian autonomists, he was the only one to choose the Croatian national identity. He adhered to the teaching of Andrija Štampar, another pioneer in the field of social medicine, prevention, hygiene, and the general health of the population. Štampar demanded that rural doctors should go among the people, live in their midst, and proactively work on healthcare. They should take care of the material and social progress of the countryside instead of waiting for patients to visit them in their community health centres. Such a doctor was also supposed to be an expert in folk culture and the life of the rural people. And Lovro certainly was such an expert (Jamnicki Dojmi 2015: 150–51). As the director of the community health centre in Mostar, he built an effective rural healthcare network, but he was also a poet and writer experimenting with various genres of short prose, writing both in Italian and Croatian.

Isak Samokovlija, on the other hand, was a notable member of the Sarajevan Sephardic community. He also studied medicine in Vienna and was active in his profession until the Nazi occupation of Sarajevo, but it was the prose writer that eventually prevailed in him and made him famous. Regardless of his postwar abandonment of the medical profession, his interwar style of practising medicine in Goražde and Sarajevo had much in common with Dojmi's: a profound familiarity with – and accessibility to – the humble people; an intimate knowledge of life in the countryside and of folk customs and traditions; and, lastly, literary expression. Samokovlija mostly wrote short stories and dramas typically set in the relatively closed and marginal Sephardic community of Sarajevo or Goražde with humble people as their protagonists. Most of these stories take place towards the end of the nineteenth century (the time of Samokovlija's birth), and hence have a bit of a nostalgic feel that is aptly captured in the title of the only collection of his short stories translated into English: *Tales of Old Sarajevo*. Samokovlija's short stories and dramas clearly have ethnographic value, and they apparently depict an exotic, closed, and locally coloured ethnoreligious community (some claim that they depict the 'mentality' of Bosnian Sephardim). But their protagonists are also capable of transcending the cultural enclosure by crossing the boundaries of ethnicity, culture, and social class. Samokovlija, however, makes them transcend their fate, as Predrag Palavestra (2000: 67) has convincingly argued, not as a 'universal' writer but in the unique style of the Jews in the diaspora. Although mostly unknown outside former Yugoslavia, Samokovlija has been recognized as one of the greatest Bosnian writers.

Vera Stein Erlich was born into a well-off Zagrebian Jewish family.[5] Her father, Adolf Ehrlich, was a rich and influential entrepreneur in the construction business. Her husband, Benno Stein, whom she married when she was twenty-three years old but then divorced prior to 1937, was another popular and respected doctor and psychologist 'known throughout the city and involved in Zionist circles' (Vulesica 2018: 58). Embedded in the Zionist milieu (her father was also a sympathizer, while her husband was one of the leading Zionist intellectuals in Croatia), Stein Erlich published articles tackling questions regarding the situation of modern Jewish women, the proper articulation of the women's question in the Zionist movement, the Jewish identity, antisemitism, and especially German Jewish immigrants who escaped from Germany when Hitler came to power (Sklevicky 1984; Vulesica 2018). Once divorced from her husband and having embarked on her big research project, however, no trace of Zionism or interest in Israel can be detected in her scholarly work. Her study choice and her earlier social engagement, on the other hand, fitted nicely with the ideal role of a Zionist woman as envisaged in the Zionist movement of the time: daughters of the notable families were expected to limit their outside activities to social welfare, education, and cultural activities. When they studied, they typically studied art, education, psychology or medicine (Kovač 2016), as well as philosophy and law (Freidenreich 2001: 66; Freidenreich 2002: xv). Stein Erlich first studied art in Zagreb and went on to study psychology in Vienna and pedagogy (between 1929 and 1933) in Berlin (Vulesica 2018: 58).

Faced with a huge mass of material but lacking proper quantitative skills, Stein Erlich realized that she needed a statistician and turned for help to the renowned social psychologist Marie Jahoda. In her preface, she claims that 'a few days before the *Anschluss* of 1938 and her own emigration', Professor Jahoda gave her 'precious advice, and recommended a statistician' to work with her (Stein Erlich 1966: xiii). (Ten years younger than Stein Erlich, Jahoda was originally a Viennese scholar, but I was unable to establish whether or not the two had met during Stein Erlich's study years in Vienna.[6]) Stein Erlich also claimed that Marie Jahoda sent a friend from Vienna, Theo Neumann, who went to Zagreb and worked with her on the survey material for many months. 'Without Dr Neumann, I would not have been able to complete the tables in the shadow of the threatening German attack, and I could never have made this up, since the original questionnaires were lost during the German occupation' (ibid.).[7] Several Yugoslav scholars, especially Rudolf Bićanić, an economic historian and rural sociologist, also helped her analyse the data and provided her with additional statistics. The tables, graphs, figures and maps, as well as extensive excerpts from the questionnaires and other sources, feverishly produced during the final few years before the Nazi occupation of Yugoslavia, were sufficiently voluminous to fill a heavy suitcase, which indeed accompanied Vera Stein Erlich during her decade of war-related adversities. The original questionnaires, deposited at a secret location in Zagreb, were irretrievably lost. Only in 1951, arriving at the Department of Anthropology of the University of California at Berkeley and backed by a Wenner-Gren grant, was Stein Erlich at last in a position to start preparing the book.

Longing for Old Austria

Stein Erlich's nostalgia for the Habsburg Empire can easily be discerned in virtually everything she published after her return to Zagreb in 1960 as well as in her correspondence and various manuscripts held by the National and University Library (Nacionalna i sveučilišna knjižnica, HSK) in Zagreb. Its manuscripts division, where Stein Erlich's collection of manuscripts and correspondence is archived, is also in possession of nineteen stenographic notebooks filled with the titles of the books and articles she was reading (or had intended to read) from 1951 onwards. This evidence of her reading interests during the last quarter century of her scholarly career is an amazingly rich resource for studying the evolution of her intellectual interests. In addition to books and articles, there are a few separate notebooks with the titles of novels, short stories, and other literary genres. It is not always clear which bibliographical units she studied, which ones she briefly inspected, and which ones remained only reading desiderata. Many titles are accompanied by her commentaries, while others contain meticulously transcribed tables of contents. Some are marked with a small red cross, the purpose of which was to indicate the titles she deemed particularly important or interesting.

Perhaps the most explicit statement of her nostalgia for the Old Austrian rule can be found in her book on Yugoslav families in the chapter on cultural contacts. There, the section discussing contact with the Habsburg Empire ends on a more personal note:

> A note from my diary of 1940 from Bosnia shows how the peasants remembered Austria twenty-two years after its death: 'From all conversations with the peasants, a nostalgia for old times can be heard. It is remarkable that the Muslims, the Catholics, and the Orthodox all speak in the same way, constantly pointing out how things used to be in the Austrian times. I now heard the same words repeated in tiny houses on the Romanija Mountain as well as in the surroundings of Jajce, at the market, in the courtrooms of Visoko, in the health centres of Herzegovina and in the *avlije* (courtyards) of Banja Luka. They constantly repeat how it was easier to live before, how life [had been] well ordered . . . But my companions are silent. How could they argue against such reasoning when it was they who had strived to undermine Austria? The same applies to me'. (Stein Erlich 1971a: 438)[8]

I know of no evidence of Stein Erlich's early political or intellectual activities aimed towards the overthrow of the Dual Monarchy. In any case, she was only seventeen when the First World War started. When, in the aftermath of the war, she left for Vienna to study psychology, she was apparently confronted with the standard array of options available to Austrian, and in particular Viennese, Jews. Forced to renegotiate their previous identities, they could largely convert (or assimilate), rediscover their ethnic identity (Zionism), or make a 'nostalgic turn to the past and a longing for the Habsburg Empire' (Holmes and Silverman 2009: 11; see also Rozenblit 1983). Zionism and Austronostalgia were not simply irreconcilable, at least not in Stein Erlich's view. Thus, soon after finishing her studies, she could present herself as a 'Yugoslav citizen, but a child of the Austro-Hungarian Monarchy' (Feldman 2014: 145).[9] This does not imply, of course, that during her Vienna years (she graduated in 1924) Stein Erlich frequently visited monarchists or similar right-wing political nostalgics. On the contrary, she seems to have frequented the leftist (and Zionist?) circles of 'red' Vienna with their socialist ideals of the proletarian revolution, equality, collective action, and community cohesion. She was particularly inspired by the work and the personality of the charismatic Viennese social psychologist Alfred Adler, whose lectures she attended in Vienna. After breaking from Freud and psychoanalysis, Adler renamed his doctrine and called it Individual Psychology (IP). The name was misleading to some, since IP was a full-fledged 'social' psychology envisaging the individual as inextricably embedded in her social group. In addition to her husband, Benno, and Dojmi and Samokovlija, Adler was another instance of a medical doctor whose psychological and psychiatric knowledge stemmed from his dealings with the common people (he provided his counselling in his native lower-middle-class neighbourhood on the outskirts of Vienna). As founded by Adler, IP was not only plebeian, down to earth, and 'immensely practical' (Ansbacher and Ansbacher 1937: 259), it also focused on social and, especially, educational reform. As David Freis has argued, 'Adlerian psychotherapists and pedagogues were no strangers to direct, educating approaches, and many of them put the rights of the individual behind the demands of society. They firmly believed that the aim of pedagogy and psychotherapy was to integrate individuals into society and to instil in them a "sense of community"' (Freis 2017: 44). It is thus impossible to overlook the very Adlerian inspiration permeating Stein Erlich's psychological and pedagogical activism of the 1930s, her enthusiasm for social reform and progress in rural areas, her struggle for the improvement of the position of women and gender equality, her efforts to introduce the educational and teaching methods of the New Pedagogy, etc. (see, especially, Grubački 2017 and Sklevicky 1984). One of her booklets published in the education and psychology series in the mid-1930s is titled *Individual Psychology in School Practice* (Stein Erlich 1934). Her husband, Benno, seems to have been an Adlerian as well; in 1930s Zagreb, the couple had an IP counselling service, and Stein Erlich wrote an obituary for Adler when he died in 1937.

While it is probable that life in the interwar Yugoslav kingdom brought many disappointments, frustrations and anxieties to the Croatian and Bosnian Jewry who, like the Jews in the rest of the Habsburg Empire, had been particularly in favour of the supranational monarchy, for Stein Erlich the interwar period likely represented a period of forward-looking activity animated with the intellectual and cultural excitement of the interwar red Vienna and Berlin rather than a period of backward-looking pessimism and longing for the good old times. There is very scarce evidence of her nostalgic mood for the interwar period. When then did her Austronostalgia begin to express itself? When did her interest in things Habsburg increase?

If Stein Erlich had begun filling her notebooks before the war with information on her reading habits, we would have stronger evidence. Her notebooks suggest, however, that she did not start reading 'nostalgic' Austrian literature more systematically until the 1960s after she had returned to Zagreb. Throughout her decade in America, she extensively studied anthropological literature. When in 1951, supported by a Wenner Gren grant, she came to the Department of Anthropology at Berkeley, she was expected to write up her previous research. In the following years, she was also busy searching for a publisher for the yet to be finished book. But the field of anthropology, and specifically American cultural anthropology, was largely unknown to her, even though she possessed some unsystematic knowledge of German-type ethnology and a pronounced ethnographic sensibility. One can only admire her intellectual breadth and curiosity in approaching such an immense field. In notebooks no. 5 and no. 6 (years 1952–53), for example, there is a sudden massive irruption of book titles on Mexico, especially around September 1953. Croatian anthropologist Olga Supek, who followed Stein Erlich's Introduction to Social Anthropology course when she started studying ethnology in 1967 and who, after Stein Erlich's death, unexpectedly received her nineteen notebooks in the post, told me that Stein Erlich first went to Mexico when she accompanied Robert Redfield's graduate students on a field excursion there (Olga Supek, personal communication).[10] May we dare to guess that September 1953 was the month that Stein Erlich found out she was definitely going with them? Her trip across the southern border resulted in a passionate interest in Mexico, which persisted until the end of her life. Close examination of her writings reveals that this interest was closely linked with her older passion for Muslim of Bosnia and Herzegovina. I want to argue that it was also linked with her later interest in Old Austria, which needed time to emerge but would eventually develop into a peculiar kind of Austronostalgia. Her Mexican experience might have been its early trigger.

In the late 1950s, specifically in 1958 when Stein Erlich had just turned sixty, a major shift occurs in her reading. After eight years of very focused and intense reading of anthropological literature, it seems she took a break, with more time now available for reading literature as well as some sociological literature. It was here that the first titles of the so-called literature of the Habsburg myth began to appear in the notebooks, still rare in the beginning – a few works by Heimito von Doderer and Peter Rosegger – and becoming increasingly frequent as the 1960s progressed. In 1960, Stein Erlich returned to Zagreb and, after some time, began teaching social anthropology at the sociology department at the University of Zagreb. This was now her first stable academic position.

In the notebooks spanning from 1963 to 1965, Joseph Roth appears for the first time (*Radetzky March*), followed by Rosegger, Egon Erwin Kisch, Croatian historian and art conservator Gjuro Szabo, author of the book *Old Zagreb* (Stari Zagreb, 1941), and others. At that time, Stein Erlich also began reading historians of the Habsburg Empire, starting with Emil Franzel's book on Franz Ferdinand, and continuing, largely between 1967 and 1979, with historians as diverse as the leftist A.J.P. Taylor, the liberal Oszkár Jászi and the far-right 'Austro-Fascist' Karl Tschuppik. Other authors she listed in the 1960s were Franz Werfel (several books), Paula von Preradović (several books), Elias Canetti, Stefan Zweig, and once again Joseph Roth and Peter Rosegger. These were precisely the years when Stein Erlich was giving her book on Yugoslav families (both Croatian and English versions) its definite shape. It seems a fairly safe assumption that her portrait of the 'Austrian style of life', which first appeared in this book, could only have resulted from her immersion in the Habsburg myth literature. Working on this portrait demanded some further theoretical reflection on the Kroeberian notion of the 'style of culture' as well as the notion of acculturation. The notebooks from these years suggest that Stein Erlich was rereading and rethinking certain chapters of Kroeber's early synthetic book on anthropology (Kroeber 1948; see also Supek-Zupan 1984), which she first picked up immediately after arriving at Berkeley. She most likely achieved a deeper comprehension of the subject only later, when she was back in Zagreb. Her original contribution to the concept of cultural style – which can be condensed in the following formula: *cultural style takes a long time to form; it travels fast; but it persists for a very long time* – appears for the first time in 1964 in her Croatian version of the book. While she had her portrait of the Dinaric and the Oriental style of life largely completed by the end of the prior decade at the latest, it was only further reflection on the persistence of the Habsburg legacy that allowed her to add the finishing touches to her depiction of regional Yugoslav styles.

At the Crossroads of the Oriental and Austrian Style of Life: Muslim Bosnia

While keeping a certain distance from Kroeber's formalist and culturally elitist conceptual developments, Stein Erlich fully accepted the prevailing view in the acculturation studies that cultural contact can result in two diverse acculturations: one that develops as a consequence of the embrace of the conqueror's civilization, and the other that is the result of its rejection. Accordingly, in Stein Erlich's view, the Ottoman conquest of Yugoslav regions resulted in the development of the Oriental style as the embracement of the Ottoman civilization and the Dinaric (also Tribal Dinaric, Heroic Dinaric) style as its rejection. To be sure, she did not oppose these two styles in the sense of a crude dichotomy but rather paid considerable attention to different intermediate degrees as expressed in regional varieties, colourings and hybridizations of these styles. Her favourite metaphor for such cultural mixes was a 'chemical compound', which she characterized as the perfect blend of heterogeneous components (Stein Erlich 1971a; 1974). Accordingly, there is a variety of regional oriental styles to be found wherever we can discern the Moorish influences that penetrated regions as diverse and as far apart as the Balkans, Southern Italy (Sicily in particular), Spain, the Middle East, and even Latin America (in particular Mexico). The Oriental style was brought to Latin America by the conquistadors, who were steeped in Moorish influences, although the Caliphate of Cordoba had already been reconquered by the Spanish Christian kings at the time of their birth.

In Stein Erlich's view, the Bosnian Muslim style of culture (or life) is, therefore, merely a regional variety of a larger oriental style whose homeland she curiously located in medieval Muslim Spain. Of all the Yugoslav varieties of the Oriental style, however, she was especially fascinated by the Bosnian Muslim one. Despite conceiving styles as cultural mixtures, she sometimes referred to the Bosnian Muslim style as the 'purest' of them all, because the medieval Bosnian nobility wholeheartedly embraced the Oriental Islamic civilization and its style of life (or such, at least, was her belief).

When we examine her notion of the Bosnian Muslim variety, we are confronted with a very interesting bundle of ideas and images. Compared to the prevailing notions of the Yugoslav orientalism of her time, this bundle looks rather unusual. There are at least two components that make it so peculiar. The first component is Stein Erlich's feminist and progressivist perspective on gender and intrafamilial relations within a given society. The second component is her aesthetic sense and her appreciation of 'the simple beauty of folk artefacts' of considerable artistic value as well as of the art of enjoying life. As a psychologist with a Viennese intellectual formation, she was singularly disposed to recognize the sociocultural significance of emotions and the importance of the associated relations of power and (in)equality. As we have already indicated, the initiative for the survey came from her Bosnian students and colleagues, and Muslim Bosnia with its veiled women was widely perceived as having a special problem with gender relations. (Muslim Macedonia was too little known and too far away in her view to represent the least developed case.) And we have also seen that Stein Erlich was unwilling to join the campaign for the unveiling of Muslim women's faces. What at first glance might seem like an orientalist exoticism thus deserves a subtler interpretation. This has also recently been noticed by the feminist historian Chiara Bonfiglioli, who has, unlike earlier feminist sociologists and ethnologists commenting on the work of Stein Erlich, fully considered the significance of diverse imperial legacies and resulting regional diversity to her work (Bonfiglioli 2012). Stein Erlich's idiosyncratic focus on the regional diversity of emotional regimes was a prerequisite to her lucid (and certainly surprising) observations about the propensity for (romantic) love as an important element of the Oriental style. In the early 1960s, recognizing the existence of (romantic) love among the common folks was anything but usual among the historians of love and the family; anthropologists, on the other hand, have yet to fully recognize it as a legitimate object of study. Stein Erlich was not only precocious in recognizing this, she also tried to show how to study the phenomenon in its regional variability.

Stein Erlich's aesthetic sense and her high appreciation of the *art de vivre* can also be related to her cultural positioning as a Central European, Viennese-educated Ashkenazi Jew. Habsburg imperial ethnology from the turn of the century, for example, shows an easily discernible tendency to study the artefacts of material culture in terms of their ascribed aesthetic value. But contrary to the elitist standpoint of this ethnology, which privileged material culture and the aesthetics of the bourgeois and aristocratic classes and accordingly evaluated folk material culture as a 'trickled-down' form of their elite culture (eventually to be baptized the *gesunkenes Kulturgut*), Stein Erlich's attitude was far more democratic. In her view, even the humble peasants from the regions characterized by the Oriental style, either from Bosnia and Herzegovina or from Southern Italy or Mexico, had developed a full aesthetic sense and elevated beauty, in the same vein as love, to one of the central values of their culture. In her view, they were creators of genuine artistic – visual, musical, poetic – works: they were anything but belated imitators of higher culture.

Vera Stein Erlich offered several depictions of the Oriental style in the Muslim regions of Yugoslavia, and especially in Bosnia and Herzegovina. The one in her book on Yugoslav families in transition remains fundamental, but her further analysis of diverse forms of love in various cultural traditions in her textbook of anthropology (Stein Erlich 1968) is equally unavoidable. She returned to the same topic in several articles published in various sociological journals in Croatia and Serbia. (Ethnological journals seemingly did not show any interest in her work.) And finally, there remain a number of unpublished manuscripts in the National Library; the most prominent among them is the manuscript of a voluminous book she never managed to publish, titled *Amerika izbliza* (America in close-up).[11] In this book, which contains a detailed ethnographic description and analysis of the US style of life (or 'American way of life') as observed over the 1950s, the Oriental style obviously appears only marginally, but it holds a strategic position because it allows for the critique of the American way of life as being bereft of the two aforesaid central values of the Oriental style.

Of the writings she published in Yugoslavia after her return from Berkeley, one of the most noteworthy is an article that is likely to have been her last (Stein Erlich 1974). This paper, while largely repeating and reaffirming what had already been stated several times before, introduces the image of emotional climates, and makes a distinction between extreme and temperate climates. Four climates correspond to four cultural traditions or styles of culture (Central European, Mediterranean, Oriental, and Tribal Dinaric), and special attention is again paid to different mixtures or 'chemical compounds' between the types. Basic ideas, such as the formative role of fatalism in the genesis of the Oriental style, or the notion that the soil in Oriental regions was favourable to the development of love, remain unchanged; but the tight connectedness and the high valuation of the sense of the beautiful (enjoyment of a relaxed life; i.e. *merak* and *ćejf*) and the deep preoccupation with love is now more explicit than ever. The Oriental tradition is put in direct opposition to the heroic tribal tradition: its fatalism, more or less indifferent to the warrior and ascetic values of the tribal zone, leads to the focus on the private sphere and its enjoyments that have a strong artistic note. The importance of beauty, *merak*, and enjoyment (including carnal enjoyment) favour the development of intimacy and love sentiments. Love is considered the most important thing in the world; consequently, there is nothing as mortifying as sad love – *od sevdaha goreg jada nema*, as Stein Erlich enjoyed quoting the popular saying. The everyday idiom is saturated with expressions and sayings from the emotional sphere, and the very same style of life is capable of high artistic achievements: prior to the Second World War, 'these songs could have such an overwhelming power that women and girls were not allowed to sing in the presence of men, as their singing could arouse a passion in them that was too strong. The collections of Bosnian lyrical folk songs are among the most profound and beautiful love songs in the world' (ibid.: 65).

Naturally, in making such bold claims, which many would find somewhat extravagant, Vera Stein Erlich did not intend to patriotically extol a part of her wider *Heimat* in the sense of a *Bosnien über alles*, but rather was indulging in her enthusiasm for the style of life she described as Oriental. While being clearly fascinated by the affective economy of the Oriental way of thinking about love, passion and sex, she was not naive to its implications for gender relations. In the same vein, she did not consider the Oriental style superior to other regional cultural styles (with the possible exception of the Dinaric style) but compared its practices and understanding of love with those of the Western style (both in its Central European and Mediterranean varieties – i.e. its Habsburg and Venetian imperial legacy). Considering her implicit evolutionism (which sometimes becomes explicit), it is more likely that in many regards she found Western style to be superior to the Oriental, but her yearning for the simple joys in life, for the beautiful and gratifying things and experiences that money cannot buy, was irresistible. Even more so when it was heightened by her stressful decade-long and ultimately unsuccessful endeavour to establish herself as an American academic.

Critique of Stein Erlich's nowadays largely outdated anthropological approach is beyond the scope of this chapter; nevertheless, her obviously Eurocentric conviction that the Oriental style originated in medieval Al-Andalus calls for a critical elucidation. Given that, in addressing the Oriental style of Yugoslav regions, she basically had to consider the Ottoman legacy, her insistence on its Iberian origins is certainly paradoxical. It implies that the Ottoman civilization was the legacy of the Islamic Al-Andalus, if not outrightly originating in Spain. Stein Erlich thus ignored the other, non-European foci of medieval Islamic civilization, such as Damascus, Baghdad and Cairo, that preceded the rise of the Ottomans. To my mind, this 'Andalusianization' of the Ottoman Empire was not a simple error, as it does not seem to have been supported by any historical work she might have read. On the contrary, it appears to have something to do with her fascination with the myth of Al-Andalus, and even more so with her desire to link Oriental Bosnia as tightly as possible with her second favourite region, Mexico. If Oriental style penetrated Latin America through the Spanish conquistadors, and if Mexico represented 'another Bosnia', Bosnia was assumed to somehow share a common source with Mexico. There are many places in her work where she claims to recognize patterns in the Mexican style of singing, folk costumes, and drawing that are identical to Balkan Oriental patterns, and deems them to be from the same Iberian source. In her German manuscript titled *Mexico and Yugoslavia* (Mexico–Jugoslawien), she tells an anecdote that took place in Mexico City while she was attending an 'inter-American' conference of psychiatrists. One day, the group was listening to a solo concert by a singer guitarist. When he began singing 'Guadalajara', a certain Juan (a local colleague attending the conference? their guide?) started to dance and rejoice (*jauchzen*), eventually reaching into his pocket and throwing his 'daily wage' at the singer, which caused Stein Erlich to have a strong sense of déjà vu. This sort of sensory hallucination transferred her for a few moments to Bosnia.[12]

What is puzzling here is that Stein Erlich did not refer to 'Guadalajara' as a mariachi song – the song being one of the best-known specimens of the genre – but preferred to relate it to cante jondo (although she did not claim straightforwardly that 'Guadalajara' was a cante jondo). This is not the only place in her work where she referred to cante jondo, and she seems to have been very aware of its continuing presence in Sarajevo. It was brought there (and to other Bosnian and Balkan towns) from Andalusia by the exiled Sephardic Jews who found their haven in the Ottoman Empire. It thus seems that in her work the term 'cante jondo' might be a code word for the Sephardic presence. At the beginning of this chapter, we mentioned the significant influence on her perception of Bosnia and Herzegovina exerted by the Sarajevan Sephardic writer Isak Samokovlija. There was another Sephardic writer (once again, a doctor who studied medicine in Vienna) whose humorous tales set in rural Serbia Stein Erlich loved to read. His name was Jacques Confino, the post-Second World War chairman of the Jewish community in Belgrade. Is it too daring to hypothesize that in Vera Stein Erlich's perception of Muslim Bosnia and Herzegovina the Muslims and the Sephardim were somehow blended together?

Bojan Baskar is a professor of social anthropology and Mediterranean studies at the Department of Ethnology and Cultural Anthropology of the University of Ljubljana, Slovenia. His current research interests include Mediterranean anthropology, empires and imperial legacies, anthropology of landscape, anthropology of food, and travel writing. His recent research has focused on the cult of national poets, in particular the nineteenth-century Montenegrin poet Njegoš. Among his recent publications is the book *Nacionalna identiteta kot imperialna zapuščina* [National identity as imperial legacy] (Ljubljana: Znanstvena založba FF, 2016).

Notes

The chapter has benefited greatly from discussions with Croatian anthropologists and historians, in particular Olga Supek and Andrea Feldman, as well as from the comments of Sabine Rutar.

1. A few years later, she wrote in one Yugoslav sociological journal that her Bosnian friends had asked her to 'start the action for the emancipation of women from the *zar* and *feredža*, and from secluded Muslim life' (Stein Erlich 1971b: 160).
2. In reality, several other regions were, essentially, left out of the survey, in particular Istria (then annexed by Italy), Vojvodina, Montenegro and Kosovo.
3. 'The University of Belgrade sent for me, and I had to accompany their ethnologists and sociologists on their expeditions. This resulted in an engagement for a series of lectures

at Belgrade University, where I reported on the preliminary results of my inquiry' (Stein Erlich 1966: vi).
4. Another descendant of the Dojmi di Delupis family recently compared him to the 'Leopard', the literary protagonist Prince of Salina of the famous Tomasi di Lampedusa's novel *Il gattopardo* (Jamnicki Dojmi 2011).
5. She changed her name from Ehrlich to Erlich intentionally, likely during her stay in the USA. Everything she published after her return to Croatia in 1960 was also signed Stein Erlich (or St. Erlich). Referring to her as E*h*rlich is characteristic for the Zagrebian milieu. In the inscription on her grave, shared by her sister and some other relatives, she again appears as Ehrlich.
6. Jahoda emigrated in 1937 after release from prison. For more information on Jahoda, see Rutherford, Unger and Cherry 2011; also Sandner 2002.
7. Information on Theo Neumann is rather scarce. He collaborated scientifically with Marie Jahoda and her husband, Paul Lazarsfeld, at the Institute of Psychology in Vienna, but it seems that he hardly published anything.
8. Whenever I find it necessary, I prefer to cite and translate from the original Croatian edition from 1964 (using the second edition from 1971) instead of the English version. The English version of the book (Stein Erlich 1966) was substantially reorganized and heavily edited. While it may be more 'user friendly' for an American reader, it is clearly less rewarding for scholarly usage. The last sentence in the cited passage – i.e. 'The same applies to me' – for example, is omitted in the English version.
9. The integral sentence is: '[a] Yugoslav citizen, but a child of the Austro-Hungarian Monarchy; descendant of an architect's family; married to an internist and psychiatrist; her interests mostly oriented towards the arts and psychology'. Feldman refers to Stein Erlich's manuscript collection in NSK as a source.
10. I was allowed, with Dr Supek's permission, to inspect the notebooks just before she handed them over to the manuscript department of the NSK. I am very grateful to Dr Supek for this privilege. The notebooks are being processed but are not yet available at the time of writing.
11. Vera Stein Erlich, *Amerika izbliza*, 1973, 535 folios (Manuscript. Zagreb, Nacionalna i sveučilišna knjižnica, Manuscripts Division, R-7974 - A-134).
12. Vera Stein Erlich, 'Mexico–Jugoslawien' (Manuscript, 13 folios. Zagreb, Nacionalna i sveučilišna knjižnica, Manuscripts Division, R-7974 - A-252). The manuscript is not dated. From what can be inferred from the document itself, it could not have been written before 1957, and was most likely written between 1960 and 1963. The document reads like a lecture note or perhaps a conference paper. It is not clear when or where it was delivered, if it was delivered at all. The fact that it is written in German should not be confusing. German was Stein Erlich's mother tongue, as it were, the only language she really mastered. Most of the chapters she produced in America were allegedly first written in German and then translated into English. Nevertheless, the paper conveys an impression that it was intended for a European audience.

I could not substantiate the existence of any 'Interamerican Psychiatric Conference' or of a correspondingly named society. But there is an Interamerican Society of Psychology (SIP) which has organized several of its conferences in Mexico City and was even founded there in 1951. Of the two conferences held in Mexico City during the 1950s – those that Stein Erlich could have attended – one took place in 1954 and the other in 1957 (Gallegos 2013: 1313, 1316). If that is indeed the case, psychiatrists might have had their own section, but Stein Erlich curiously refers to the participants as 'doctors' (she was stunned to find the style of reasoning and debating of Latin American doctors to be so familiar, and so similar to the style of Yugoslav doctors).

References

Ansbacher, Heinz, and Rowena Ripin Ansbacher. 1937. 'In Memoriam: Alfred Adler 1870–1937', *Sociometry* 1(1/2): 259–61.

Bonfiglioli, Chiara. 2012. 'An Age Fated to Vanish: Vera Stein Erlich's Anthropological Records of Interwar Yugoslavia'. *Themenportal Europäische Gechichte.* http://www.europa.clio-online.de/2012/Article=547; last accessed 27 April 2020.

Feldman, Andrea. 2014. 'Vera Stein Erlich: skica za jedan podijeljen život', in Matea Jalžečić and Petra Marinčić (eds), *Žene kroz povijest: Zbornik radova sa znanstvenog skupa*, Dies historiae *2012*. Zagreb: Društvo studenata povijesti 'Ivan Lučić-Lucius', pp. 141–62.

Freidenreich, Harriet Pass. 2001. *The Jews of Yugoslavia: A Quest for Community.* Skokie, IL: Varda Books.

———. 2002. *Female, Jewish, and Educated: The Lives of European University Women.* Bloomington: Indiana University Press.

Freis, David. 2017. 'Subordination, Authority, Psychotherapy: Psychotherapy and Politics in Inter-War Vienna', *History of the Human Sciences* 30(2): 34–53.

Gallegos, Miguel. 2013. 'Sixty Years of the Interamerican Society of Psychology (SIP): Origins and Development', *International Journal of Psychology* 48(6): 1313–20.

Grubački, Isidora. 2017. 'Emancipating Rural Women in Interwar Yugoslavia: Analysis of Discourses on Rural Women in Two 1930s Women's Periodicals'. (Unpublished MA thesis, Department of History, Central European University, Budapest.)

Holmes, Deborah, and Lisa Silverman. 2009. 'Introduction: Beyond the Coffeehouse. Vienna as a Cultural Center between the World Wars', in Deborah Holmes and Lisa Silverman (eds), *Interwar Vienna: Culture between Tradition and Modernity.* Rochester, NY: Camden House, pp. 1–18.

Jamnicki Dojmi, Mirko. 2011. 'Dr. Lorenzo Dojmi di Delupis: viški Gepard', *Acta medico-historica adriatica* 9(2): 189–206.

———. 2015. 'Štamparovac i poeta. (Nekoliko biografskih podataka iz života i rada dr. Lovre Dojmija)', *Zadarska smotra* 2: 149–53.

Kovač, Vlasta. 2016. 'Jake žene: Židovke koje su ušle u hrvatsku leksikografiju', *Novi Omanut* 22(1)(130): 1–3.

Kroeber, Alfred. 1948. *Anthropology: Race, Language, Culture, Psychology, Prehistory* (New, Revised Edition). New York: Harcourt Brace & Co.

Palavestra, Predrag. 2000. 'Jewish Writers in Serbian Literature: Isak Samokovlija', *Journal of the North American Society for Serbian Studies* 14(1): 65–68.

Rozenblit, Marsha L. 1983. *The Jews of Vienna, 1867–1914: Assimilation and Identity.* Albany: State University of New York Press.

Rutherford, Alexandra, Rhoda Unger and Frances Cherry. 2011. 'Reclaiming *SPSSI*'s Sociological Past: Marie Jahoda and the Immersion Tradition in Social Psychology', *Journal of Social Issues* 67(1): 42–58.

Sandner, Günther. 2002. 'From the Cradle to the Grave: Austro-Marxism and Cultural Studies', *Cultural Studies* 16(6): 908–18.

Sklevicky, Lydia. 1984. 'Ispred mogućnosti recepcije: neki uvidi Vere Stein Erlich', *Revija za sociologiju* 14(3–4): 309–17.
Stein Erlich, Vera. 1934. *Individualna psihologija u školskoj praksi*. Zagreb: Minerva.
———. 1966. *Family in Transition: A Study of 300 Yugoslav Villages*. Princeton, NJ: Princeton University Press.
———. 1968. *U društvu s čovjekom: Tragom njegovih kulturnih i socijalnih tekovina*. Zagreb: Naprijed.
———. 1971a. *Jugoslavenska porodica u transformaciji: Studija u tri stotine sela*. Zagreb: Liber.
———. 1971b. 'Trideset i tri godine transformiranja porodice (Istraživanja, odjeci, perspektive)', *Sociologija i prostor: Časopis za istraživanje prostornog i sociokulturnog razvoja* 31/32: 159–68.
———. 1974. 'Regionalne razlike u emocionalnoj klimi', *Sociologija* 16(1): 61–72.
Supek-Zupan, Olga. 1984. 'Utjecaj američke antropologije na rad Vere Stein Erlich', *Revija za sociologiju* 14(3–4): 319–26.
Vulesica, Marija. 2018. 'What Will Become of the German Jews? National Socialism, Flight and Resistance in the Intellectual Debate of Yugoslav Zionists in the 1930s', in Ferenc Laczo and Joachim von Puttkamer, *Catastrophe and Utopia: Jewish Intellectuals in Central and Eastern Europe in the 1930s and 1940s*. Berlin: Walter de Gruyter, pp. 45–70.

Chapter 10

THE SERBIAN PROVERB *POTURICA GORI OD TURČINA* (A TURK-CONVERT IS WORSE THAN A TURK)
Stigmatizer and Figure of Speech

Marija Mandić

> Human beings do not live in the objective world alone, nor alone in the world of social activity as ordinarily understood, but are very much at the mercy of the particular language [that] has become the medium for their society.
> —Edward Sapir, 'The Status of Linguistics as a Science'

This chapter focuses on the proverb *Poturica gori od Turčina* (A Turk-convert is worse than a Turk), which for purposes of brevity I refer to simply as 'A Turk-convert is worse . . .'. Despite feeling archaic, it is commonly used and negatively connoted in the Serbian conversational discourse. Since the Ottoman conquest of the Balkans, the ethnonym *Turčin* (Turk) has not been reserved only for people of Turkish ethnicity – primarily viewed as representatives of the Ottoman enslavers of Serbia from the fifteenth to the nineteenth century – but it also functioned as a confessionym for all Ottoman Muslims. Moreover, a particular label, *poturica*, was coined for Christian converts to Islam, and literally means 'Turk-convert' (or Turkified). The term had either a neutral or a slightly pejorative meaning, depending on the context; but as the empire was declining, and especially after its dissolution, it progressively acquired a derogatory meaning and an emotive charge. This contribution thus attempts to show how the linguistic means under discussion have come, via stigmatization, a long way from sociopolitical categorization to figurative speech. It is argued that stigmatization is part of the broader strategic erasure of the Ottoman heritage in the Serbian public discourse. Firstly, the theoretical framework to be applied in the chapter is presented. Then, the Balkan Christians' views on the Ottoman heritage and the Slavic Muslims are discussed. The chapter reflects on the stigmatization of the Slavic Muslims in some of the most representative works of the modern Serbian canon. Finally, usage of the proverb 'A Turk-convert is worse . . .' in contemporary conversational discourse is analysed.

Methodological Framework: Discourse-Historical Approach and Stigmatization Theory

In order to understand the use of the linguistic means under discussion, I turn to the discourse-historical approach (DHA), which is part of the broadly defined field of critical discourse analysis (Wodak and Reisigl 2009). The analytic method of DHA includes the identification of: (a) specific content or topics of a discourse; (b) discursive strategies; and (c) linguistic means (ibid.: 93). The DHA method considers four levels of context: (1) the immediate or text-internal; (2) intertextual and interdiscursive relationships; (3) extralinguistic social variables and institutional frames; and (4) broader sociopolitical and historical context, which discursive practices are embedded in and related to (ibid.). The analysis of the historical context 'permits the reconstruction of how recontextualization functions as an important process linking texts and discourses intertextually and interdiscursively over time' (ibid.: 95).

Concerning the Serbian public discourse, I argue that one of the main strategies employed with regard to Slavic Muslims has been stigmatization, which I try to demonstrate by analysing a broader historical and sociopolitical context and different discourse genres. I draw upon Goffman (1991: 2), who defined stigmatization as an attribution of physical, character, biological, or cultural deficiency to an individual or group that results in perceiving them as tainted or failing. Hence, it has a discrediting effect, and constitutes a discrepancy between virtual and actual social identity, which spoils one's social identity and can result in cutting an individual or a group off from society (ibid.: 19–20). It is important to emphasize that the normal and the stigmatized are not persons but perspectives, whereby the stigmatization is a matter of the relationship we establish, because stigmatizing attributes are only those 'incongruous with our stereotype of what a given individual should be' (ibid.: 3). Thus, that which is discrediting in one social setting may be seen as an advantage in another. The processes that accompany stigma are dehumanization and discrimination. As a final point, once established, stigma terms may be used without giving thought to the original meaning (ibid.: 5).

By analysing the broader historical and sociopolitical context in which the nomination of the Slavic Muslims and the proverb 'A Turk-convert is worse . . .' emerged, I point at interdiscursive relationships, extra linguistic social variables, and institutional frames to which these discursive practices are related. In the following section, I discuss the main discursive strategies employed in the Balkan societies with regard to the Ottoman heritage.

Coping with the Ottoman Heritage in Serbia: Erasure and Internalization

After their liberation from Ottoman rule, all Balkan countries tried to erase and 'purge' themselves of any visible influences of the Ottomans on the one hand, while on the other, many widespread continuances of the Ottoman era merged with local cultures and persisted using mimicry mechanisms. Todorova (1997: 170) argues that 'the creation of autonomous and independent Balkan states was not only a break with but a rejection of the political past', which was enacted in almost all spheres and completed by the end of the First World War. The Balkan elites took a negative approach to Ottoman rule and its legacy by representing it as alien to the native cultures and as a source of serious trauma involving atrocities, injustice, (forceful) conversion, and the loss of any form of autonomy (cf. Sakellariou 2017: 513–14). This memory gives shape to the dominant national narratives, in which Turks have occupied the position of the (historical) Other (ibid.). The Ottoman period is thus (re)presented as a crucial juncture in the history of the Balkan communities: on the one hand, it is believed to have caused a break with previous traditions, but on the other, it initiated (re)invention of the imagined collective identities. However, the Balkan discourses of de-Ottomanization – alongside typologically similar Balkanism and nesting Orientalism (Bakic-Hayden 1995; Todorova 1997) – are influenced and shaped by the socially more powerful Western Orientalism (Said 1994), the underlying logic and rhetoric of which they share.

As regards Serbia, the strategic erasure of the Ottoman heritage has been actuated since the Great Serb Migration from the Ottoman to the Habsburg Monarchy in 1690.[1] This has been manifested in the tendency to represent the many centuries of life under the Ottomans as pure slavery and suffering, when nothing significant in terms of culture or social development occurred. The equivalent expressions in Serbian *ropstvo pod Turcima* (slavery under the Turks) and *pet vekova pod Turcima* (five centuries under the Turks) serve as proverbial mnemonic devices crystalizing what is considered as crucial for understanding this period;

they are also used as explanatory devices for social and cultural backwardness in the country. The strategic erasure can be also seen in the institutional set-up, with only one mosque left in the capital, no scientific Orientalist institute, no (re)presentation of the Ottoman heritage in the Serbian museum institutions, and simplistic and stereotypical interpretations in the historical school textbooks (Vukomanović 2008; Sollie 2012; Mandić 2016: 282–83).[2]

The other macro strategy is internalization of the Ottoman heritage, which left its mark on the modern Balkan cultures, thus creating 'the complex symbiosis of Turkish, Islamic, and Byzantine/Balkan traditions' (Todorova 1997: 164). By merging with local features, the Ottoman heritage was internalized and (re)used as being authentic of Balkan and/or Serbian cultures, which is most obvious in some music, culinary, social and linguistic practices (Buchanan 2007; Jovanović 2009; Archer 2012; Đinđić 2013). In the following section, I discuss the sociohistorical context in which the nomination of the Slavic Muslims originates.

From Millet to National Identity

The origin of the nomination of the Slavic Muslims and the proverb 'A Turk-convert is worse . . .' can be traced back to the sociopolitical system of millets within the Ottoman Empire, which originated in early Islam but was not fully effective until the nineteenth century (cf. Masters 2009; Aviv 2016). As is known, people were bound to their millets by religious affiliations, not by ethnic origin. The Muslim and Christian Orthodox millets were particularly ethnically diverse but dominated in religious and social hierarchy by Turks and Greeks respectively. The Ottoman population was also counted based on religion, whereas accurate registering only began in the nineteenth century (McCarthy 2000: 30–31; see also chapter by Božidar Jezernik in this volume). The term 'Turk' was still used as the heading for classifying the Slavic-speaking Muslims in the Ottoman censuses of the late nineteenth century (Todorova 2004: 138).

Hence, based on the millet system and administrative procedures of the Ottoman Empire, the primary self- and out-group identification of the Balkan Muslims was confessional, designated by either 'Muslim' or 'Turk', regardless of their ethnolinguistic background. This later caused a delay in the development of their national identity in comparison to the Balkan Christians (Mentzel 2000: 8; McCarthy 2000: 31; Bieber 2000: 13). As Todorova (1997: 178) points out, after the liberation wars and the creation of the new nation states, the Orthodox population broke free of the millet terms and began to use national terms when referring to themselves, but kept the millet terms when designating the Slavic-speaking Muslims. In that way, a large number of Balkan Muslims were marginalized and practically excluded from the nation-building processes.

Discourse on the Conversion to Islam

It is evident that the Balkan states adopted strong antagonistic policies in relation to the Ottoman heritage and 'inherited' Muslims, who 'were treated as foreigners to be expelled, were stigmatized by the dominant ethnoreligious group, became the target of forced homogenization, or at best [were] tolerated as a separate but difficult-to-absorb ethnoreligious group' (Elbasani and Tošić 2017: 502). Although Islamophobia is typical for Christian societies (Sakellariou 2017; Olson 2017; Zadrożna 2017), the downplaying of the Ottoman heritage can also be observed in Albania, a predominantly Muslim country (see Elbasani and Tošić 2017: 502).

Since the conversion to Islam considerably changed the demographic picture in the Balkans and its power balance, it was used as a source of plentiful misconceptions and simplifications (Bieber 2000: 21).[3] The indigenous Islamized population was principally viewed as connected to their Christian compatriots by bond of blood and a detached part of the national body. Therefore, in mainly Christian societies, it was under pressure to assimilate into the majority (Olson 2017: 567; Zadrożna 2017: 525), or as Mentzel (2000: 9) puts it, they were 'regarded as renegade members of the dominant national group who needed to be brought back into the fold'. Michael Sells proposed that one of the ideological cores of the Serbian national discourse could be called 'Christoslavism' (a version of Judas syndrome), which (re)presents Slavs as Christians by nature, so any conversion 'then is not only a betrayal of the Slavic people or race but an actual ethnic or racial transformation. To convert to Islam is to become a Turk' (Sells 2001: 183). Although Sells was referring to the Serbs, the same can be applied, with some variation, to other Balkan Christians.

The other ideological core pertains to the nature of Islamization, which all Balkan national historiographies view as the process of splitting the national body, but the causes are subject to different interpretations. By the end of the nineteenth century and first half of the twentieth century, the elites of the Slavic Muslims and some of their grass-roots movements tried to overcome the existing confessional divisions by promoting linguistic unity and common ethnonational consciousness with their co-ethnic Christian fellows (Todorova 2004: 138–40; Bazdulj 2017). Some of the Muslim intellectuals, however, underline their authenticity and view the acceptance of Islam as the process of acculturation (Filipović 1990 cit. in Bakic-Hayden 1995: 927). Dominant in Bulgaria and Macedonia is a historiographical trope of forced conversion (Todorova 2004; Olson 2017; Zadrożna 2017). The Serbian discourse, however, has developed a betrayal trope.

Muhamed Filipović, a Bosnian writer and national ideologist, argues that the Croats exhibit nationalism of tutorial character, whereas the 'Serbs treat Muslims as that part of themselves [that] betrayed the faith of their forefathers' (Filipović

1990 cited in Bakic-Hayden 1995: 927), which Bakic-Hayden calls a 'betrayal syndrome'. Filipović further maintains that 'the same may be retrospectively projected on those who make such allegations, for they too betrayed the ancient Slavic faith of their forefathers with their acceptance of Christianity' (ibid.: 928). In the following section, I reflect on the betrayal trope and associated linguistic means used through different literary genres in the Serbian nation-building literature.

Nation-Building Literature and Stigmatizing Strategy

The cornerstones of the modern Serbian canon were created in the time of the Serbian uprisings against the Ottomans, entailing the bloody struggles for liberation against the Turks and the Balkan Muslims siding with them. Hence, they are strongly ideologically biased. The works I will briefly comment on are the oral epic poetry, *Srpski rječnik* (*The Serbian Dictionary*, 1818) by Vuk Stefanović Karadžić, a Romantic poem 'Gorski vijenac' (*Mountain Wreath*, 1847) by Petar II Petrović Njegoš, and some humanistic scholarship of the nineteenth and twentieth centuries. By exploring the historical dimensions of discourse formation with respect to its epistemological foundation and uses in particular contexts, I aim to grasp some of the aspects of identity construction and stigmatization.

As an overtly ideological genre, the epic, by definition, sings in praise of heroic ancestors. Collected fairly late, mostly in the nineteenth and early twentieth centuries, South Slavic epics embody the paradox of being 'both very old and very up to date' (Detelić 2005; Detelić 2008: 5). In her study on ethnic terms in the South Slavic epics collected in the Shtokavian dialect zone,[4] Delić (2016) found that in both Christian and Muslim epic songs referring to the sixteenth and seventeenth centuries, the basic semiotic opposition of 'ours vs theirs' is established as a confessional one: *Turci* vs *kauri* (Turks vs Giaurs) and *turski* vs *kaurski* (Turkish vs Giaour).[5] When translated into non-figurative language, it should be read as 'Muslims vs Christians'.[6] In the Serbian epic songs created in the midst of the nineteenth-century struggles against the Ottomans, the nationally based opposition of *turski* vs *srpski* (Turkish vs Serbian) also became relevant (ibid.). These findings show that the South Slavic epic antagonism of the Ottoman period was established along confessional (millet) and not ethnic lines. Moreover, it is clear that the epic Turk generally denotes a Muslim character regardless of origin or ethnicity.

In the epic songs, individual heroes typically acquire geographic, title, or patronymic attribution: *od Prilepa Marko* (Marko from Prilep), *od Kladuše Mujo* (Mujo from Kladuša), *car Lazar* (Tsar Lazar), *paša Ali-paša* (Pasha Ali-Pasha) and *Stojan Janković*. When referring to Slavs who converted to Islam, the Christian songs also use 'Turk' and 'poturica' (Turk-convert) interchangeably, even within the same song. The appellative *poturica* is preceded by the fixed epithets *silna* (mighty) or *jedna* (one). The syntagm *silna poturica* (mighty Turk-convert) indexes the social status of Muslim heroes in the Ottoman Empire, which Christians perceived as being linked to the dominant, privileged confession and ruling class.[7] Some examples of the term in epic verses include the following: *Pa ga pita silna poturica* (And the mighty Turk-convert asks him); *A veli mu silna poturica* (And the mighty Turk-convert says to him); and *Istače se silna poturica* (And the mighty Turk-convert has risen up among others).[8] The term *poturica*, however, is almost never used in Muslim epic poetry. Instead, they employ the confessionym 'Turk' for Muslim heroes and Giaour (*kaur*) or 'Vlach' (*vlah*) for Christians, which have either neutral or pejorative connotations depending on the context, much like *poturica* in the Christian songs.[9] These findings suggest that the epic nomination referring to the period of the sixteenth and seventeenth centuries used the millet terms of that time, which were more classificatory and less evaluative. The use of nationally loaded terms and ethnic pejoratives started to gain significance in songs referring to the nineteenth-century fights for liberation from the Ottomans.

In the first dictionary of the modern Serbian language (1818), in which Serbian lexemes were translated into German and Latin, *poturica* was defined as 'unechter Türke' and 'pseudoturca' (fake Turk). In the same dictionary, *poturčenjak* is interpreted as 'Ein Renegat' (a renegade) and 'apostate' (apostate). In order to illustrate the use of this appellative, Karadžić added a proverb: *Nema (zla) Turčina bez poturčenjaka* (There is no [evil] Turk without a Turk-convert). In the same dictionary, *poturčiti* is defined as 'zum Türken Machen' (to make somebody a Turk), while the reflexive form *poturčiti se* is described as 'ein Türke werden' (to become a Turk) (Karadžić [1818] 1987, s.v. *poturica, poturčenjak, poturčiti se*). In this case, *poturica* and *poturčenjak* have moved away from the epic semantics and acquired more negative connotations.

The other canonical literary work relevant for this topic is *Gorski Vijenac* (The mountain wreath) written in 1846 by Prince-Bishop of Montenegro and Serbian poet Petar Petrović Njegoš, and first published in Vienna in the following year. The poem is constructed as a tragic conflict between Christian and Muslim Montenegrins known as *Istraga Poturica* (the eradication of the Turkicized). The moral dilemmas and negotiations call for reconversion to Christianity (the faith of grandfathers) and occupy a central place in the plot, which ends in the mass execution of Muslim Montenegrins. Drawing upon the South Slavic epics, the poem actually follows the logic of the Romantic tragedy and the Romantic ideology of national awakening and revival and national liberation struggle. As Milutinović (2008: 34) points out, Njegoš eventually praised the values of nationalism, but in the eradication of converts he surely saw 'nothing heroic, nothing epic, and nothing to celebrate ... only bitterness and despair' (ibid.: 31).

Considered a masterpiece of South Slavic literature, and required reading in all schools in former Yugoslavia, it was interpreted as a work that promotes ideas of pan-Slavism and the Illyrian Movement, liberation from a foreign ruler, and brotherhood and unity (Milutinović 2008: 27). However, controversial readings of *The Mountain Wreath* have emerged since it was published. From the mid-1980s, its reception has increasingly begun to mirror the rising ethnic tensions in the region and the ideological standpoints of various interpreters. Many of them assign a literal meaning to it: either a canonical justification of the essential enmity between Christians and Muslims, and subsequently of the ethnically motivated crimes, which is embraced by nationalists; or its interpretation as an apotheosis of genocidal ideology rooted in religion, a deeply Islamophobic work and a manual for ethnic cleansing, a view held by some prominent scholars (Sells 2001; Anzulović 1999; Greenawalt 2001). The latter approach, which underlines an implicit genocidal subtext in the poem, is particularly addressed in a series of works arguing that the poem cannot be aptly understood out of its epoch, genre, and specific historical context (cf. Pavlovic 2001; Milutinović 2008; Pavlović 2016).

The scope of this chapter does not allow a detailed analysis of the poem, so I can only point to its two main poetic lines. On the one hand there is the stigmatization of Islamization used to justify the political call for national unity and homogenization at all costs; on the other hand, the human horror caused by religious conflict and bloodshed is depicted. Nevertheless, I focus only on the stigmatization, which is useful to my analysis. The basic opposition in the poem is rendered as *Turčin* vs. *Crnogorac / Srbin* (Turk *vs.* Montenegrin/Serb). The Montenegrin Muslims are called *Turci* (Turks), *domaći Turci* (domestic Turks), *naši Turci* (our Turks), *braća isturčena* (Turkified brothers), and *turska pridvorica* (Turkish vassal). The Muslim faith is designated as *turska vjera* (the Turk's faith), and the conversion to Islam as *isturčiti se, poturčiti se* (Turkification).

There are multiple illustrative examples for the poetic line that stigmatizes Islam and Muslims.[10] In accordance with popular views, Islamization is represented as an act of greed, while the Montenegrin Muslims are dehumanized and demonized, mostly by using adjectives, comparisons, and expressive verbs – for example, *krmska poturica* (swinish renegade), *vražji kot* (brood of the devil), *pogani izrodi* (loathsome degenerates), *izdajica* (traitor), *obrljao obraz pred svijetom/ pohulio vjeru pradedovsku* (You've dishonoured yourself before the world/blasphemed the faith of your own ancestors), *domaće zlo* (evil in our home), *poturice* (Turkish turncoats), *sve je pošlo davoljijem tragom* (everything has gone the devil's way), *živuju ka ostala stoka* (live just like animals), *nevjerna domaćega vraga* (faithless domestic enemy). Uncritically reproduced and with no attempt to grasp its deeper, nuanced and complex meaning, the poem thus offers ample opportunity for mimetic interpretation and abuse.[11]

Variations of the aforementioned popular beliefs have been uncritically used in Serbian scholarship and can serve as an example of how the proverb 'A Turk-convert is worse . . .' is being translated into scientific and educational texts. The first written interpretations, however, came from Serbs educated in the Habsburg Monarchy, who actually (re)produced the Western Orientalist discourse with local variations (Aleksov 2005: 116; Aleksov 2003). Hence, conversion was seen as a temporary state brought on by external forces and, in its essence, a betrayal of ancestry and origin; the domestic Muslims were attributed intrinsic hatred of the former co-ethnics, and fanatic behaviour worse than Turks (Magarašević 1983 cited. in Alksov 2005: 116). There was also a series of influential characterological studies based on ethnogenetic clues – among others by Cvijić, Dvorniković, Mitrinović and Hadži Vasiljević – that attributed Oriental stereotypical attributes to the local Muslims, such as cowardliness, hatred, vanity, wastefulness, lasciviousness, sensuality, rooted mysticism and fatalism, perversions, and the psychology of accommodation (Aleksov 2005: 118–21). The same stereotypical beliefs were reproduced in some of the prominent works of the recent Serbian historiography (Samardžić 1982: 14 cited in Aleksov 2005: 122–23; Ljušić 2013 cited in Miletić 2017a).[12] Miletić (2017b) underlines that this (re)presentation in the format of historiographical text actually stigmatizes a whole nation as a people of converts and national renegades, whereas their allegedly national betrayal is explained exclusively as an act based on pure material interests.

This brief overview shows how the nomination and the proverb 'A Turk-convert is worse . . .' were used in different literary genres, transiting from classificatory terms (like ethno-confessionyms) to apparent pejoratives. The stigmatization of the colingual Muslims served to underpin the nineteenth-century ideology of de-Ottomanization and national homogenization, as well as to justify the suppression and marginalization of the Muslim population. The following section analyses the use of these linguistic means in contemporary discourse.

The Proverb 'A Turk-Convert Is Worse . . .' in Conversational Discourse

As Neal Norrick (Norrick 1985: 1) points out, proverbs are discrete texts rather than part of a larger text of interaction. Proverbs can include phrasal idioms, collocations, and lexical items proper with specific assigned meanings. Norrick differentiates between two usages: 'As an inventorized unit belonging to a particular language, a proverb has its own customary meaning, its standard proverbial interpretation (SPI). This SPI may coincide with the literal meaning of the proverb, in which case the proverbs are said to be literal. But the SPI may also differ from the literal meaning, in which case the proverb is said to be figurative' (ibid.).

The whole set of Serbian proverbs is based on the aforesaid rejection of the Ottoman heritage and the condemnation of the conversion to Islam. The proverb inventory, among others, consists of: *Ljudi smo nismo Turci* (We are people, not Turks), *U Turčina nema vjere* (You cannot trust a Turk), *Prolazim ko pored turskog groblja* (I pass by it as beside a Turkish graveyard [meaning I try not to notice it at all]), *Kadija te tuži, kadija ti sudi* (Qadi is accusing you, qadi is judging you),[13] *Poturica gori od Turčina* (a Turk-convert is worse than a Turk), *Ako je Turčin krvav do lakata, poturica mora biti do ramena* (If a Turk has blood up to his elbows, the Turk-convert must have it up to his shoulders), *Prodali su veru za večeru* (They sold their faith for dinner), and *Izdali su veru pradedovsku* (They betrayed the faith of their grandfathers). Here, too, belongs the collective narrative on the Serbian origin of the Shtokavian Muslims based on the betrayal trope, which can be (re)constructed as follows: 'They were the Serbs who converted to Islam out of pure interest, and since then they have hated the Serbs who stayed true to their genuine religion, as they remind them of who they once were. So, they fight the Serbs more harshly than others would do' (Mandić 2017). All these linguistic devices have been used in conversational and, particularly, nationalistic discourse as a means of explicit or implicit stigmatization, although they are gradually becoming obsolete.

The proverb 'A Turk-convert is worse . . .' is used in the Shtokavian speaking zone in its literal and figurative meaning. It is curious that this expression is also used in Czech, a West Slavic language: *Poturčenec horší Turka* (Endrődy 2004). The Pontic Greeks have the proverb *Ας σον Ορωμαίον π 'ίνεται Τούρκος κι άλλο αφορισμένος ίνεται* (A Turkified Greek is cursed).[14] To the best of my knowledge, such proverbs do not exist in contemporary Bulgarian, Macedonian, Romanian or Hungarian, but there are many other negative stereotypes regarding the Ottoman Turks that today are more or less regarded as anachronisms.[15]

Using the Proverb in Its Literal Meaning

The analysis of contemporary language is based on discourse available on the internet, which I call electronic discourse, or e-discourse.[16] Spontaneity and swiftness make e-discourse close to conversational, and an adequate source of contemporary language use.[17] The literal meaning of the proverb denotes a person who was, by origin, an Orthodox Serb but who converted to Islam and joined the community of the Serb oppressors. It is mainly used to belittle Bosniak social actors as well as, occasionally, Albanian ones. In its literal meaning, it is chiefly employed in nationalistic, offensive conversational exchanges and as an ethnic slur in chats and forums commenting on politically controversial content. This usage can also be described as hate speech, since it attacks and insults a person or group on the basis of race and/or religion (cf. Whillock and Slayden 1995; Waltman and Haas 2011).

The first example comes from the Croatian forum 'Herceg Bosna', in which the topic 'Happenings in the Republic of Srpska', posted in 2015, attracted many anonymous participants, whose ethnic allegiance could be presumed based on their nicknames, identity symbols, and comments. The topic was opened by *seherzada Begovica*, who set a politically provocative tone by generally addressing the Serbs pejoratively (*Srbeki, Srbistan*), which in turn provoked *Grey Wolf* to call Slavic Muslims 'Turks' and 'Serb killers'. The rejection of identification with Turks by *seherzada Begovica* triggered the proverb 'A Turk-convert is worse . . .'. Here is an excerpt from the conversational exchange in the forum:

> *Grey Wolf:* 'Hey Turks, back off! Our time has come! You will never kill Serbs anymore! You cannibal scum! You're junk of the human race.' *seherzada Begovica*: 'There have been no Turks here in our region for 100 years. During these 100 years, someone has destroyed you, that one must admit when looking at the maps of "Serbian lands" – and who it was, I couldn't tell you!' *Vladimir Rus*: 'That's why there are Turk-converts, and Turk-converts are worse than Turks. You should know it very well Miss or Misses Seherzada.'[18]

On the eve of a football match between the Serbian club Partizan and the Turkish club Fenerbahce in March 2012, an administrator of the Partizan Facebook page posted: 'A Turk-convert is worse than a Turk. The Serbs will f. . . you in the end!!!!!!!!!'[19] The function of this post was to downplay and discourage Bosniak footballers playing for Fenerbahce. This post provoked many comments, some of them offering support by mentioning the names of Ratko Mladić and Radovan Karadžić, the ethnic Serb military and political leaders in the war in Bosnia and Herzegovina (1992–95) convicted of war crimes; others were very critical, and reminded readers that some Muslims also play for Partizan or support the football club. Here is an excerpt of the conversational exchange showing how two participants negotiate the use of the proverb in the ideological grid of national identity, football club loyalty, fascism and communism:

> – 'Hello, monkeys. If someone is Muslim, it doesn't matter! If he is not anti-Serb, if he loves Partizan, he is welcome to the South among us! Death to fascism, long live Partizan!'– 'Are you a commie or what?'– 'No, I am a man, I am a Serb. I love Partizan and hate fascism. Is there something you don't understand here?!'– 'Then say that you also hate communism.'[20]

There is, however, a tendency to assign polysemantic or figurative meaning to this proverb. In 2015, the right-wing political party Dveri called for protests against the planned British resolution in the UN intended to mark the twentieth anniversary of the war crimes against humanity committed by the Bosnian Serb Army over the Muslims in Srebrenica. The protest was called 'A Turk-convert is worse than a Turk'. In their invocation, Dveri issued a text, which, among other things, stated:

> These days we also witness, as so many times before, that 'a Turk-convert is worse than a Turk', and that in Serbia we also have Serb-haters and creators of a sick attempt to

proclaim the nation, which suffered triple genocide in the twentieth century, a genocidal people only because in the wars in the former Yugoslavia they were defending themselves on their hallowed hearths and doorsteps from the new criminals and renewed genocidal intentions.[21]

On the one hand, the proverb conveys the cultural memory, which recalls the purported historical 'guilt' of the Slavic Muslims in Ottoman times, and juxtaposes it with their present victimhood in the Bosnian War. On the other hand, it also refers to all the Serbs who are seen as internal enemies ('Serb haters') and who support the policy condemning Serbian atrocities committed on the Bosniaks in the Bosnian War, and are allegedly even louder than the foreign policy actors.

In the Serbian yellow press, a series of articles was published about a supposedly Serbian ethnic ancestry of Hashim Thaçi, the ethnic Albanian prime minister of Kosovo and the chief commander in the Kosovo War (1997–99).[22] The Facebook page Zicer posted one of these articles in December 2015 with the comment: '*Poturica gori od Turčina, vazda bilo i ostalo*' (A Turk-convert is worse than a Turk; so it used to be and so it still is).[23] The proverb thus preserves its literal meaning denoting an Orthodox Serb who took Islam (the great-grandfather of Hashim Thaçi) and whose great-grandson (Hashim Thaçi) is now the main Serbian political opponent, but it also illustrates a transition to figurative speech denoting any man who shifted his allegiances and became more zealous in his new community than its 'authentic' members.

Using the Proverb in Its Figurative Meaning

Meanwhile, the proverb 'A Turk-convert is worse . . .' has also become an idiomatic expression for all manner of social actors who shift their loyalties and become more eager in enacting the new social role than the original social actors. Its figurative meaning is similar to the English 'more Catholic than the Pope' and 'eager beaver', or the German '*Päpstlicher sein als der Papst*'. Nonetheless, even when used in a figurative meaning, in most cases the Serbian proverb establishes an explicit interdiscursive link with the proverb's literal meaning, drawing parallelisms between its different connotations.

In the local Serbian publication *Kolubarske novine* (Kolubara Newspaper), the article headline 'Poturica gori od Turčina' serves as an explanatory framework for people with shifting political loyalties. The entire article is conceptualized on the parallelism between the assumed psychology of Turk-converts and the behaviour of political converts. This claim is reinforced by the authority of science and folk wisdom:

> Science long ago addressed the psychology of converts, and folk wisdom expresses it as 'a Turk-convert is worse than a Turk'. They want success in the party and through the

party, but they are, with good reason and no impingement by the party's ruling people, uncertain about their status in the party . . . Because of that, they constantly have to prove themselves as being 'more Catholic than the Pope' and more faithful than the old members, even than the founders. They are even bigger opponents of all those who do not belong to 'their party'!²⁴

A Croatian blog with an article entitled 'A Turk-convert is worse than a Turk' speaks critically about the Croatian right-wing politicians Andrija Hebrang and Anto Đapić, who condemned the then Croatian president Stjepan Mesić for his nationalist talk. The title actually provides an ironic comment on the hard nationalists criticizing the nationalism of other political actors.²⁵ In another Croatian blog entitled 'Kad je Poturica gori od Turčina – odgovor Zarepčanki koja brani seksizam Matea Kovačića' (When a Turk-convert is worse than a Turk – the answer to the Zagreb girl who defended the sexism of Matea Kovačić), the proverb is used to evaluate a woman who defended a man accused of sexism – that is to say, a woman turning against her own gender and criticizing the emancipation of women more than any man would do:

> A much bigger problem is people like this anonymous girl from Zagreb who astonishingly shows no empathy towards women who think differently . . . and who, with her own attitudes, brings her own gender to the level of obedient servants ready to take orders and bear everything. It reminds me of 'A Turk-convert is worse than a Turk'.²⁶

The proverb can be varied, depersonalized, amalgamated with other constructions, abbreviated, or used in elliptic forms. An article in 2015 in the popular Serbian newspaper *Večernje novosti* (Evening Post) bore the title 'Berlin gori od Turčina' (Berlin Worse than a Turk). In this case, 'Berlin' signifies metonymically the official German policy. It is then put in the proverb syntactic pattern to imply that Berlin is behaving worse than the real Serbian enemy symbolized by the Turk. The following lead, however, unravels this figurative language. Berlin is a political convert obeying a policy hostile to Serbia, which is signified metaphorically by 'Turk' but in actuality denotes the current official American policy. The statement is reinforced by calling upon the authority of proverbial wisdom (i.e. 'as people would say'):

> It is a key for understanding the constant German pressures upon us, with intention to make us also geopolitical converts. As people would say: "A Turk-convert is worse than a Turk". Germany for us now is worse than America, which made this mess in Ukraine!'²⁷

Finally, the proverb is, surprisingly or not, used in Czech, despite the Czechs having never been under Ottoman rule or subjected to the Islamization of their population. It might have originated in solidarity with Christian Slavs in the Balkans, which caused the appropriation of Christian Slavic popular beliefs. In

2016, the newspaper *Parlamentní Listy* (Parliamentary News) ran an article by Josef Ježek under the title of 'Poturčenec horší Turka?' (A Turk-convert worse than a Turk?). The article criticizes the current regime of Turkish president Recep Tayyip Erdogan and Europe's migratory policy. The proverb is elaborated in the story's lead, as follows:

> This Balkan proverb originated at a time when the Ottoman Empire threatened Europe as such. It took place also in our country, in the Czech basin. Translated into our conversation, it meant that the agent of a regime was worse than his representative. Looking, for example, at the period of the Protectorate, the proverb's meaning is more than true. Unfortunately![28]

Using a Synonymous Proverb

Proverbs are synonymous if they express the same idea, or the same abstract logical content (Kuusi 1966 cited in Norrick 1985: 156). The proverb *Ako je Turčin krvav do lakata, poturica mora biti do ramena* (If a Turk has blood up to his elbows, the Turk-convert must have it up to his shoulders) expresses the same idea as the proverb 'A Turk-convert is worse . . .'. It is also effectively used in Serbian and Croatian conversational discourse, mainly in its figurative sense. Based on the metaphor of blood as crime (see Mandić and Đurić 2016: 24), the proverb uses the brutal representations of 'blood up to the elbows' and 'blood up to the shoulders' as a source domain in order to explain the target domain, namely the 'guilt' of the Turk-convert.

This proverb is defined in its standard proverbial meaning in the vocabulary of modern Serbian slang, *Vukajlija*. Again, authority is introduced by calling upon folk wisdom, while the lexicographic definition contains a catalogue of Serb-converts who turned out to be the worst Serb enemies. The behavioural pattern is pathologized, and becomes a question for psychologists:

> The accuracy of our wise proverb has been justified many times during our turbulent history. The unconditional attachment to a new god or master and the merciless proving of loyalty is a sad and difficult topic from our past, from Turk-converts before the Kosovo Battle and Mihailo Latas[29] to Ustasha butchers[30], known with certainty as being of Serbian origin. Whether it is a manifestation of complexes, an opportunity for a new beginning, or a suppression of their own past at any cost is a question for psychologists.[31]

In September 2016, the Serbian yellow press daily *Informer* published an article about a quarrel between officials of the Serbian football club Partizan. The article title makes use of direct speech by Vuletić: 'There is no peace in Humska! Vuletić to Bjeković – if a Turk has blood up to his elbows, the Serb must have it up to his shoulders'. In this case the standard term *poturica* is replaced by the ethnic *Serb* denoting 'Serb Muslim'. The proverb is used by Vuletić in its figurative meaning and denotes a person who is changing his allegiances – in fact he is referring to his colleague Bjeković. The authority of the proverb, however, is backed in the discourse by the phrase 'well-known Serbian proverb':

> The president of the supervisory board of Partizan, Vladimir Vuletić, answered the roll call of Nenad Bjeković by citing the well-known Serbian proverb: 'I would answer to Nenad Bjeković by citing Ljubomir Simović: "If a Turk has blood up to his elbows, the Serb must have it up to his shoulders. No one trusts a Turk-convert". Let him recall his own interview from *Tempo* in January 1969', said Vuletić.[32]

Sloga, the united syndicates of Serbia, posted an article in September 2016 with the title 'Ako je Turčin krvav do lakata, poturica mora biti do ramena' (If a Turk has blood up to his elbows, the Turk-convert must have it up to his shoulders). The lead explains that it actually refers to domestic capitalists who are treating workers worse than foreigners: 'The workers in these companies do not have a problem with foreigners but with domestic bosses who put pressure on them in many different ways'.[33]

Conclusion

The question of conversion from Christianity to Islam, which is the central topic of the proverb 'A Turk convert is worse . . .', not only affects the relationship between Christians and Muslims on the Balkan peninsula but also contributes to the understanding of identity construction among Muslims and Christians. The national historiographies have frequently misused the representations of the Ottoman period to justify persecution and marginalization of the Muslim inhabitants in the new nation states. The ideological nucleus of the Balkan Christian discourses regarding the Muslims, who speak the same language, is actually based upon an essentialist view of identity, equating confessional denomination (Christianity) with national identity. This discursive order thus allows the domestic Muslims either to come back to the (Christian) fold or to continue living under the stigma.

In the case of Serbia, converting from Orthodox to another religion equates to stepping out of the Serbian community. This essentialist and exclusionary identity model means that any change of religion should be understood as self-betrayal and a national apostasy that can only result in violent and deviant behaviour. The betrayal trope thus structures this discourse type and provides a perspective for expressing nominations, attributions and arguments. By using the stigmatization strategy, the conversion to Islam in Serbian discourse is mostly evaluated as an act of cowardice, and driven by interests such as the desire to preserve one's fortune, to build a career, or to receive privileges. As Goffman (1991: 145–46) points out, stigma 'can be transmitted through lineages and equally contaminate all members'. Consequently, stigmatization is, in this case, attached to the whole community of the colingual Muslims. And this is the way to reproduce second-class citizens.

This chapter shows that the whole set of Serbian proverbs is based on the rejection of the Ottoman heritage and the condemnation of the conversions to Islam, and is also used for the stigmatization of the Ottoman past and domestic Muslims. The terms *Turčin* and *poturica* have come a long way from classificatory terms (like ethno-confessionyms) via apparent pejoratives beginning with modern nation building to figurative speech. The proverb 'A Turk-convert is worse . . .' is used in different literary genres in both literal and figurative senses. However, even when the proverb is used in figurative speech, interdiscursive relationships with its literal meaning are commonly established. So, the authority of 'folk wisdom', 'a well-known proverb', and 'science' is introduced. Whether or not it is used with a literal or a figurative meaning, the proverb retains its stigmatizing function to a greater or lesser degree.

Considering the very powerful Western discourse on Orientalism and the influence of the Habsburg Monarchy upon the Serbian elite in the eighteenth and nineteenth centuries, the Serbian case can be seen as leaning on Western and Central European traditions while adjusting them to the oral cultural patterns and the archetypal dichotomy of the hero-betrayer. If the use of ideologically loaded language and the national-confessional oppositions in the midst of the liberation fights was historically motivated and poetically justified, the contemporary use of these linguistic means is marked by (un)conscious reproduction of stigmatizing stereotypes and social discrimination.

Marija Mandić is a senior research associate at the Institute for Balkan Studies of the Serbian Academy of Sciences and Arts in Belgrade, Serbia. She holds a PhD in linguistics from Belgrade University, Faculty of Philology. From 2016 to 2018, she undertook a fellowship at the Alexander von Humboldt Foundation for the postdoctoral project 'Migration and Narration: The Case of the Muslims from the Western Balkans' at the Institute for Slavic Studies at Humboldt University in Berlin. She is working as co-investigator on the international project 'Probing the Boundaries of the Transnational: Imperial Legacies, Transnational Literary Networks and Multilingualism in East Central Europe (2018–2021)', based at the University of Oslo. Her latest monograph is *Discourse and Ethnic Identity: The Case of the Serbs from Hungary* (Munich: Otto Sagner Verlag, 2014).

Notes

The chapter is the result of the project 'Language, Folklore, Migrations in the Balkans' (no. 178010) funded by the Ministry of Science of the Republic of Serbia with support provided by a Humboldt Research Fellowship for postdoctoral researchers 2016–18 at the Institute for Slavic Studies of the Humboldt University in Berlin.

1. The Great Serb Migration included Serbian peasants, wealthy traders, craftsmen, and a large proportion of the ecclesiastical hierarchy (the Patriarch, bishops, priests, monks) fearing Ottoman revenge for siding with the Christians in the War of the Holy League (1683–99). The Serbian population fled en masse from the Ottoman territories together with the defeated Christian army (Ilić [Mandić] 2014: 67).
2. The Belgrade situation can be compared to other Balkan Orthodox capitals, such as Athens and Sofia. Muslims in Athens still do not have an official place to pray or a cemetery in which to bury their relatives (Sakellariou 2017: 512–13). In Sofia, there is one active mosque, the Banya Bashi Mosque, built in the sixteenth century, and the issue of a Muslim graveyard is not properly regulated (see https://www.blitz.bg/obshtestvo/iskat-tursko-grobishche-v-sofiya_news135212.html; last accessed 24 January 2018).
3. Bieber differentiates between three types of conversions to Islam: the first and most common are voluntary conversions for economic, practical or safety interests; the second type includes violent and forced conversions; finally, the third encompasses *devshirme*, the practice of taking male children from Christian families and bringing them up as Muslims in order to serve the state (Bieber 2000: 21–22).
4. The Shtokavian dialect zone includes modern-day Serbia, Montenegro, Bosnia and Herzegovina, and a large part of Croatia.
5. Delić (2016) presents a very complex and comprehensive analysis based on the corpus of twenty-one volumes of representative collections of oral epic poetry collected in modern-day Serbia, Montenegro, Croatia, and Bosnia and Herzegovina in the last three decades of the nineteenth century and at the beginning of the twentieth century. The corpus was created as a searchable database by Mirjana Detelić and Branislav Tomić and is available online (see Detelić and Tomić 2010). To this corpus, Delić added two earlier epic collections (from the seventeenth and eighteenth centuries). This large corpus enabled her to analyse songs referring to the period from medieval time to the nineteenth century, and to compare two perspectives: Christian and Muslim.
6. *Giaour* (also *Gawur*) is a Turkish term meaning 'infidel', and it was used in the Ottoman administration and in the colloquial discourse of the Muslims for non-Muslims or, more specifically, for Christians in the Balkans. Initially, it was employed as a term of contempt, but later came to mean a neutral non-Muslim (Björkman 1997; Detrez 2013: 44–45). In the epic songs of the longer verse called *bugarštice*, collected mostly in the eighteenth century, the main semiotic opposition is rendered as 'Turks vs Hungarians'. These two ethnonyms denoting the two largest ethnic groups engaged in the conflict apparently function as metonymic labels for confessional groups, i.e. 'Muslims vs Christians' (Delić 2016).
7. The epic epithet *silan* (mighty) is regularly used with other nouns and Christian names with the meaning of 'a powerful, great hero'.
8. The Epic Poetry Database allows searches for keywords, such as *poturica*, in all the epic songs in the corpus.
9. The epic term 'vlah' (Vlach) is a polysemantic one; it can signify social, professional, ethnic or confessional belonging (Petrović 2014: 176–87; Delić 2016).

10. The original version of *Gorski Vijenac* and its English translation *The Mountain Wreath* by Vasa D. Mihailovich, used in this paper, are published on the website Rastko; https://www.rastko.rs/knjizevnost/umetnicka/njegos/mountain_wreath.html; last accessed 11 September 2020.
11. Pavlović points out that ideological battles over Njegoš have never ceased, and draws our attention to the recent misuses of this poetic work for providing judicial and political argumentation, as in the case of the ICTY Hague Tribunal, when in the trial of Radovan Karadžić prosecutor Katrina Gustafson claimed that in *The Mountain Wreath* Njegoš 'celebrated the killing of Muslims, that is, converts' and called for 'the purification of our land from the infidels' (Pavlović 2016: 107); or when the initiative by the Montenegrin government to introduce a national holiday dedicated to Njegoš was opposed by the Montenegrin Muslim community and hence withdrawn (ibid.).
12. The gymnasium history textbook by Radoš Ljušić uses the following citations, among others: '*Memoaristi s početka 19. veka beleže da su ti muslimani, poturčenjaci, bili gori i nesnosniji raji od Osmanlija, pravih Turaka*' (Memoirists from the beginning of the nineteenth century note that those Muslims, Turkified ones, were worse and more unbearable to common people than the Ottomans, the real Turks) (Ljušić 2013: 246 cited in Miletić 2017a; translation into English by the author – MM).
13. A qadi is the judge of a sharia court.
14. I am grateful to Jovanka Đorđević, a scholar in modern Greek studies, who informed me of this usage. In colloquial Greek, the ethnonym 'Turk' is very often used in a derogative sense, and a child of a Muslim and Christian couple is called τουρκόσπορος (τουρκόσπερμα) 'Turkish semen' (Mandala 1993: 770). Greek-speaking Muslims who live in Greek Macedonia and other parts of Greece and Turkey are called Βαλ(λ)αχάδες or Βαλαάδες 'from Allah' (Tsetlaka 2015).
15. In Bulgarian, *Turska sila, bălgarska nevolja* (Turkish power, Bulgarian trouble), *Turčin i kuče edno e* (the Turk and dog are one the same), *Turčin vjara njama* (literally, 'the Turk has no faith', meaning you cannot trust a Turk); in Romanian, *față turcească* ('Turkish face', used for someone who casts a wicked or moody look), *turcul te bate, turcul te judecă* (the Turk is beating you, the Turk is judging you); and in Hungarian, *búsul, mint ki török rabságba esett* ('he bemoans as if he was a Turkish slave', used for a bad neighbour); *fejére telt a török átka* (the Turkish curse was over his head) (Endrődy 2004). However, in the South East European languages, there are also some neutral and positive stereotypes in relation to the Turks (ibid.), but that goes beyond the scope of this paper.
16. In linguistic scholarship, different terms are used for this type of discourse: *e-language, netlingo, e-talk, geekspeak, netspeak, weblish, NetSpeak, Netlish, Internet language, cyberspeak, electronic language, electronic discourse, electronic communication, interactive written discourse*, etc. (see Crystal 2006: 19; Popović 2009: 184). Some of the important features of e-discourse are: language mistakes (due to fast communication on the internet), conscious deviations from the standard language, creativity in language use (slang, neologisms, language games, etc.), expressive means (emoticons, fonts, gifs, photos, posters, etc.), many English insertions and loans, and onomatopoeiac words. This type of discourse is also determined by 'polyphony, distance, anonymity, the possibility to quickly join and leave conversations without many of the formalities considered necessary for non-virtual communication' (Popović 2009: 183 – translation into English by the author MM).
17. The basic subgenres are as follows: e-mail, chat, forum, posts and comments on social media, internet journal, video clip.

18. In the original: *Sivi Vuk*: Aj marš turci!Došlo je naše vreme!Nikad više Srbe ubijati nećete!!Bagro ljudožderska!Otpadu ljudske rase; *seherzada_begovica*: Turaka nema na nasim prostorima vec preko 100 godina. Za tih 100 godina neko vas jeste unistio, to se mora priznati kada se baci pogled na mape 'srpskih zemalja', a sad koje to bio, ne bih znala rijet!; *Vladimir Rus*: Zato ima Poturica, a Poturica gori od Turcina. Vi bi to trebali najbolje znati gospodjo ili gospodjice Seherzada; https://hercegbosna.org/forum/post1088622.html; last accessed 16 March 2018.
19. In the original: 'POTURICA GORI OD TURCINA, JEBACE VAM SRBI MATER KAD TAD !!!!!!!!!!!!!!!!'; https://m.facebook.com/paokpartizanfamily2010/posts/329259694113566; last accessed 15 March 2018.
20. In the original: – 'ALo majmuni, to sto je neko musliman nema nikakve veze! Ako nije antisrbin, ako voli Partizan, dobrodosao je na Jug i medju sve nas! Smrt fašizmu ziveo Partizan!'; – 'Jesi ti komunjara ili sta?'; – 'Ne, ja čovek, ja sam Srbin, volim Partizan, mrzim fašizam. Šta ti tu nije jasno?!'; – 'Pa onda reci da i mrzis komunizam'; same URL as in Note 19.
21. In the original: 'Ovih dana smo, takođe, po ko zna koji put svedoci da je "poturica gori od Turčina", i da u samoj Srbiji imamo nosioce mržnje prema srpskom narodu i kreatore umobolnog pokušaja da se narod koji je preživeo trostruki genocid u 20. veku sada proglasi genocidnim narodom, samo zato što se u građanskom ratu u bivšoj Jugoslaviji na vekovnim ognjištima i kućnom pragu branio od novih zločinaca i ponovljenih genocidnih namera'; https://naslovi.net/2015-07-06/glas-zapadne-srbije/dveri-pozivaju-na-protest-poturica-gori-od-turcina/15318169; last accessed 15 March 2018.
22. See https://www.in4s.net/pisani-manastirski-dokazi-tacijev-pradeda-je-bio-srbin/; https://www.kurir.rs/vesti/politika/302693/tacijev-pradeda-bio-pravoslavni-svestenik; https://www.srbijadanas.com/clanak/sok-tacijev-pradeda-bio-srpski-pop-10-02-2015; last accessed 15 March 2018.
23. https://www.facebook.com/zicer.org/posts/1020124251375275?comment_tracking=%7B%22tn%22%3A%22O%22%7D; last accessed 9 May 2020.
24. In the original: 'Nauka ga je odavno dala takozvanom psihologijom konvertita, narodna mudrost to izražava sa "Poturica gori od Turčina". Oni žele uspeh u stranci i preko nje, ali su s pravom, čak i bez osporavanja od strane vodećih ljudi stranke, nesigurni u svoj status u stranci . . . Zbog toga se neumorno dokazuju time što su "veći katolici od pape", verniji od starih pripadnika, čak i osnivača. Pa i veći protivnici svima koji nisu "njeni"!'; http://www.kolubarske.rs/sr/blog/bezkraja/5176/Poturica-gori-od-Tur%C4%8Dina.htm; last accessed 20 March 2018.
25. See http://blog.dnevnik.hr/cnn/2006/12/1621865608/poturica-gori-od-turcina.html; last accessed 20 March 2018.
26. In the original: 'Puno veći problem su osobe poput ove anonimne Zagrepčanke koje pokazuju zapanjujuću razinu bezosjećajnosti prema ženama koje misle drugačije . . . i koje svojim stavovima vlastiti spol dovode na razinu pokorne služinčadi koja je tu da šuti i trpi. Podsjeća me to na onu: "Poturica gori od Turčina"'; http://www.fizzit.net/vijesti-i-politika/komentari-i-kolumne/5128-kad-je-poturica-gori-od-turcina-odgovor-zagrepcanki-koja-brani-seksizam-matea-kovacica; last accessed 20 March 2018.
27. In the original: To je ključ za razumevanje stalnih nemačkih pritisaka da i mi postanemo geopolitički konvertiti. Kako narod kaže: "Poturica gori od Turčina". Nemačka je za nas sada gora od Amerike koja je čitavu stvar u Ukrajini zakuvala!'; http://www.novosti.rs/

vesti/naslovna/drustvo/aktuelno.290.html%3A533612-Dragomir-Andjelkovic-Berlin-go ri-od-Turcina; last accessed 20 March 2018.
28. In the original: 'Tohleto balkánské přísloví vzniklo v době, kdy osmanská říše ohrožovala Evropu jako takovou. Ujalo se i u nás, v české kotlině. Přeloženo do naší mluvy znamenalo, že přisluhovač jakéhosi režimu byl horší, než jeho představitel. Podíváme-li se např. na období protektorátu, je význam toho přísloví více než pravdivý. Bohužel!'; https://www.parlamentnilisty.cz/arena/nazory-a-petice/Josef-Jezek-Poturcenec-horsi-Turka-434955; last accessed 20 March 2018. See also the article which was published in the newspaper *Pravý Prostor* (Right Place, but now it is only available at the personal blog of Jan Hofirek: 'Poturčenec horší Turka aneb budeme poslouchat tureckého bašibozuka?' (A Turk-convert is worse than a Turk, or should we listen to Turkish humbug), which criticizes the Turkish ambassador to the Czech Republic for condemning the Islamophobia expressed in Czech Parliament but who, according to the article, has no right to criticize, since he is an official representative of a country pursuing a very intolerant policy towards minority groups; http://haiku-etc.bloger.cz/CO-NA-TO-RIKAM/POTURCENEC-HORSI-TURKA-aneb-BUDEME-POSLOUCHAT-TURECKEHO-BASIBOZUKA; last accessed 8 May 2020.
29. Omar Pasha Latas (1806–71) was born Mihailo Latas to Serbian parents in Habsburg Croatia. Initially an Austrian soldier, he later converted to Islam, joined the Ottoman army and became one of its best generals (Jelavich 1983: 349).
30. The Ustasha (*Ustaša*) was a fascist and ultranationalist Croatian organization most active between 1929 and 1945. Fronting the Nazi-backed Independent State of Croatia during the Second World War, the movement engaged in the mass murder of hundreds of thousands of Serbs, Jews, Roma, and antifascist Croats within the territory under their control.
31. In the original: 'Naša mudra narodna izreka čija je tačnost opravdana mnogo puta tokom naše burne istorije. Bezuslovno priklanjanje novom bogu ili gospodaru i nemilosrdno dokazivanje vernosti tužna je i teška tema naše prošlosti od poturica pre Kosovskog boja, preko Mihajla Latasa, do nekih ustaških koljača za koje se pouzdano znalo da su bili srpskog porekla. Da li je to bilo lečenje kompleksa ili prilika za novi početak i zaboravljanje i zatiranje sopstvene prošlosti po svaku cenu, pitanje je za psihologe'; https://vukajlija.com/ako-je-turcin-krvav-do-lakata-poturica-mora-biti-do-ramena/331739; last accessed 1 April 2018.
32. In the original, title: 'NEMA MIRA U HUMSKOJ! Vuletić Bjekoviću: "Ako je Turčin krvav do lakata, Srbin mora biti ramena!"' Main text: 'Predsednik Nadzornog odbora Partizana Vladimir Vuletić odgovorio je na prozivke Nenada Bjekovića, i to citirajući čuvenu srpsku izreku: - Nenadu Bjekoviću bih odgovorio citirajući Ljubomira Simovića: Ako je Turčin krvav do lakata, Srbin mora biti do ramena. Poturici niko ne veruje.' Nek' se podseti na svoj intervju iz *Tempa* iz januara 1969. godine - poručio je Vuletić za Žurnal'; http://informer.rs/sport/partizan/289637/nema-mira-u-humskoj-vuletic-bjekovicu-ako-je-turcin-krvav-do-lakata-srbin-mora-biti-ramena; last accessed 1 April 2018.
33. In the original: 'Radnici u tim kompanijama nemaju problema sa strancima već "domaćim" šefovima koji ih pristiskaju i mobinguju na raznolike načine'; https://www.facebook.com/joint.unionsserbianunity/posts/1091862114224592; and http://sloga.org.rs/zeljko-veselinovic-da-pokazemo-poslodavcima-da-ne-mogu-da-rade-sta-hoce; last accessed 1 April 2018.

References

Aleksov, Bojan. 2003. 'Poturica gori od Turčina: Srpski istoričari o verskim preobraćenjima', in Husnija Kamberović (ed.), *Historijski mitovi na Balkanu*. Sarajevo: Institut za istoriju Sarajevo, pp. 225–58.

———. 2005. 'Perceptions of Islamization in the Serbian National Discourse', *Southeast European and Black Sea Studies* 5(1): 113–27.

Anzulović, Branimir. 1999. *Heavenly Serbia: From Myth to Genocide*. London and New York: New York University Press.

Archer, Rory. 2012. 'Assessing Turbofolk Controversies: Popular Music between the Nation and the Balkans', *Southeastern Europe* 36: 178–207.

Aviv, Efrat. 2016. 'Millet System in the Ottoman Empire', *Islamic Studies*, 28 November. Available at: http://www.oxfordbibliographies.com/view/document/obo-9780195390155/obo-9780195390155-0231.xml; last accessed 23 March 2018.

Bakic-Hayden, Milica. 1995. 'Nesting Orientalisms: The Case of Former Yugoslavia', *Slavic Review* 54(4): 917–31.

Bazdulj, Muharem. 2017. 'Može li Srbin biti Musliman?' *Nedeljnik*. 5 January. Available at: http://admin.nedeljnik.rs/nedeljnik/portalnews/moze-li-srbin-biti-musliman-1/; last accessed 9 May 2020.

Bieber, Florian. 2000. 'Muslim Identity in the Balkans before the Establishment of Nation States', *Nationalities Papers: The Journal of Nationalism and Ethnicity* 28(1): 13–28.

Björkman, Walther. 1997. 'Kāfir', in *The Encyclopaedia of Islam*. Band 4. Boston: Brill. Available at: https://referenceworks.brillonline.com/browse/encyclopaedia-of-islam-2/alpha/k?s.start=80; last accessed 9 May 2020.

Buchanan, Donna (ed.). 2007. *Balkan Popular Culture and the Ottoman Ecumene: Music, Image and Regional Political Discourse*. Lanham, MD: The Scarecrow Press.

Crystal, David. 2006. *Language and the Internet*. Cambridge University Press.

Delić, Lidija. 2016. 'Kliče Miloš srpski pop'jevati: Konceptualizacija etnonima u usmenoj epici', in Dejan Ajdačić (ed.), *Srbi i srpsko*. Belgrade: Alma, pp. 50–71.

Detelić, Mirjana. 2005. 'The Place of the Symbolic City in Constructions of Nation and Religion: A Case of Balkan Folklore', *Enter Text* 5(2): 78–89.

———. 2008. 'Slavery in the West Balkans: History and Oral Tradition', in Wolfgang Dahmen, Petra Himstedt-Vaid and Gerhard Ressel (eds), *Grenzüberschreitungen: Traditionen und Identitäten in Südosteuropa. Festschrift für Gabriella Schubert*. Wiesbaden: Otto Harrassowitz Verlag, pp. 62–71.

Detelić, Mirjana, and Branislav Tomić. 2010. 'Epska narodna poezija.' Available at: http://monumentaserbica.branatomic.com/epp/; last accessed 9 May 2020.

Detrez, Raymond. 2013. 'Prenational Identities in the Balkans', in Roumen Daskalov and Marinov Tchavdar (eds), *Entangled Histories of the Balkans. Volume One: National Ideologies and Language Policies*. Leiden: Brill, pp. 13–66.

Đinđić, Marija. 2013. 'Turcizmi u savremenom srpskom književnom jeziku (semantičko-derivaciona analiza)'. Doctoral dissertation. Faculty of Philology, University of Belgrade.

Elbasani, Arolda, and Jelena Tošić. 2017. 'Localized Islam(s): Interpreting Agents, Competing Narratives, and Experiences of Faith', *Nationalities Papers: The Journal of Nationalism and Ethnicity* 45(4): 499–510.

Endrődy, János. 2004. 'Poturčenec horší Turka', *Navýchod* 4. Prague: Východoevropský klub studentů FF UK. Available at: http://web.archive.org/web/20160420152232/http://navy

chod.cz/articles.php?id=d431e5b4-8dc8-11df-aa30-00304830bcc4; last accessed 9 May 2020.
Filipović, Muhamed. 1990. 'Fundamentalisti, to smo mi' [an extended interview], *Borba*, 3–11 May. Belgrade.
Goffman, Erving. 1991. *Stigma: Notes on the Management of Spoiled Identity*. New York: Simon & Schuster.
Greenawalt, Alexander. 2001. 'Kosovo Myths: Karadzic, Njegos and the Transformation of Serb Memory', *Spaces of Identity* 1(3): 49–64.
Ilić [Mandić] Marija. 2014. *Discourse and Ethnic Identity: The Case of the Serbs from Hungary*. Berlin and Munich: Otto Sagner Verlag.
Jelavich, Barbara. 1983. *History of the Balkans: Eighteenth and Nineteenth Centuries*. New York: Cambridge University Press.
Jovanović, Miloš. 2009. 'Taming the Tavern: Social Space and Government Regulation in 19th Century Belgrade', *Godišnjak za društvenu istoriju – Annual of Social History* 16(3): 57–68.
Karadžić, Stefanović, Vuk. *Srpski rječnik*. [1818] 1987. Belgrade: Prosveta.
Kuusi, Matti. 1966. 'Ein Vorschlag für die Terminologie der parömiologischen Strukturanalyse', *Proverbium* 5: 97–104.
Ljušić, Radoš. 2013. *Istorija za treći razred gimnazije opšteg i društveno-jezičkog smera*. Belgrade: Freska.
Magarašević, Đorđe. 1983. *Putovanje po Srbiji u 1827 godini*. [First edition: 1882, Pančevo]. Belgrade: Prosveta.
Mandala, Maria. 1993. *Elleniko lexico*. Athens: Tegopoulos – Phytrakes.
Mandić, Marija. 2016. 'Unifying the Other: The Case of the March Violence in Kosovo and the Mosque Burning in Belgrade', *Ethnologia Balkanica* 18: 281–305.
———. 2017. 'Collective Narrative as an Argumentative and Legitimizing Device: The Narrative on the "Serbian" Origin of Bosniaks'. 27th ASEN Annual Conference 'Anthony D. Smith and the Future of Nationalism: Ethnicity, Religion and Culture', 27–28 March, London School of Economics.
Mandić, Marija, and Ljubica Đurić. 2016. 'Krvavi izrazi i psovke u savremenom srpskom jeziku', in Mirjana Detelić and Lidija Delić (eds), *Krv: književnost, kultura*. Belgrade: Institute for Balkan Studies SASA, pp. 17–42.
Masters, Bruce. 2009. 'Millet', in Gábor Ágoston and Bruce Masters (eds) *Encyclopedia of the Ottoman Empire*. New York: Facts On File, pp. 383–84.
McCarthy, Justin. 2000. 'Muslims in Ottoman Europe: Population from 1800 to 1912', *Nationalities Papers: The Journal of Nationalism and Ethnicity* 28(1): 29–43.
Mentzel, Peter 2000. 'Introduction: Identity, Confessionalism, and Nationalism', *Nationalities Papers: The Journal of Nationalism and Ethnicity* 28(1): 7–11.
Miletić, Aleksandar R. 2017a. 'Vidovdanska etika, poturčenjaci i milosnice. Veliki narativ Srbije u udžbeniku istorije Radoša Ljušića'. *Internet bilten*. 19 September. Available at: http://pescanik.net/vidovdanska-etika-poturcenjaci-i-milosnice/; last accessed 23 March 2018.
———. 2017b. 'Odgovor Čedomiru Antiću'. *Peščanik*. 3 October. Available at: https://pescanik.net/odgovor-cedomiru-anticu; last accessed 23 March 2018.
Milutinović, Zoran. 2008. 'Sword, Priest and Conversion: On Religion and Apostasy in South Slav Literature in the Period of National Revival', *Central Europe* 6(1): 17–46.
Norrick, Neal, R. 1985. *How Proverbs Mean: Semantic Studies in English Proverbs*. Berlin: Walter de Gruyter.

Olson, Laura J. 2017. 'Negotiating Meaning through Costume and Social Media in Bulgarian Muslims' Communities of Practice', *Nationalities Papers: The Journal of Nationalism and Ethnicity* 45(4): 560–80.
Pavlović, Aleksandar. 2016. 'Njegoš and the Politics of Reading', *Anzeiger für Slavische Philologie* 54: 107–22.
Pavlovic, Srdja. 2001. '*The Mountain Wreath*: Poetry or a Blueprint for the Final Solution? On the Margins of Alexander Greenawalt's article "Kosovo Myths: Karadzic, Njegos and the Transformation of Serb Memory"', *Spaces of Identity* 1(3). Available at: http://www.yorku.ca/soi/Vol_4/_HTML/pavlovic.html; last accessed 9 May 2020.
Petrović, Njegoš P. 1847. *Gorski vijenac*. Vienna (First Serbian Edition). Unabridged internet edition available at: http://www.njegos.org/petrovics/gvijenac.htm; last accessed 23 March 2018. Translated into English as *The Mountain Wreath* by Vasa D. Mihailovich. Unabridged internet edition available at: https://www.rastko.rs/knjizevnost/umetnicka/njegos/mountain_wreath.html; last accessed 23 March 2018.
Petrović, Sonja. 2014. *Siromaštvo u folklornoj tradiciji Srba od XIII do XIX veka: Prilog proučavanju narodne kulture*. Belgrade: Albatros Plus.
Popović, Ljudmila. 2009. 'Leksičke inovacije u elektronskom diskursu srpskog i hrvatskog jezika', in Branko Tošović (ed.), *Razlike između bosanskog/bošnjačkog, hrvatskog i srpskog jezika / Die Unterschiede zwischen dem Bosnischen/Bosniakischen, Kroatischen und Serbsischen*. Berlin: LIT Verlag, pp. 183–204.
Said, Edward W. *Orientalism*. (1979) 1994. Vintage Books Edition. New York: Random House.
Sakellariou, Alexandros. 2017. 'Fear of Islam in Greece: Migration, Terrorism, and "Ghosts" from the Past', *Nationalities Papers: The Journal of Nationalism and Ethnicity* 45(4): 511–23.
Samardžić, Radovan (ed.). 1982. *Istorija srpskog naroda* II. Belgrade: Srpska književna zadruga.
Sapir, Edward. 1929. 'The Status of Linguistics as a Science', *Language* 5(4): 207–14.
Sells, Michael. 2001. 'Kosovo Mythology and the Bosnian Genocide', in Omer Bartov and Phyllis Mask (eds), *In God's Name: Genocide and Religion in the Twentieth Century*. Berghahn Books, pp. 180–205.
Sollie, Siri Therese. 2012. 'The Exhibition of the Ottoman Heritage – from Collective Memory to the Museum Display', *Glasnik Etnografskog muzeja* 76: 19–41.
Todorova, Maria. 1997. *Imagining the Balkans*. New York: Oxford University Press.
———. 2004. 'Conversion to Islam as a Trope in Bulgarian Historiography, Fiction and Film', in Maria Todorova (ed.), *Balkan Identities: Nation and Memory*. New York: New York University Press, pp. 129–57.
Tsetlaka, Athanasia-Marina. 2015. 'The Rise of Greek Nationalism and the Greek-Speaking Muslims (*Vallaades*) in Western Macedonia', in Dimitris Stamatopoulos (ed.), *Balkan Nationalism(s) and the Ottoman Empire*. Istanbul: The Isis Press, pp. 89–100.
Vukajlija. Rečnik slenga, www.vukajlija.com; last accessed 9 May 2020.
Vukomanović, Milan. 2008. 'Images of the Ottomans and Islam in Serbian History Textbooks', in Christian Moe (ed.), *Images of the Religious Other: Discourse and Distance in the Western Balkans*. Novi Sad: CEIR and Kotor Network, pp. 17–38.
Waltman, Michael, and John Haas. 2011. *The Communication of Hate*. New York: Peter Lang.
Whillock, Rita Kirk, and David Slayden (eds). 1995. *Hate Speech*. Thousand Oaks, CA: Sage.
Wodak, Ruth, and Martin Reisigl. 2009. 'The Discourse Historical Approach (DHA)', in Ruth Wodak and Michael Meyer (eds), *Methods of Critical Discourse Analysis*. Thousand Oaks, CA: Sage, pp. 87–121.

Zadrożna, Anna. 2017. 'Reconstructing the Past in a Post-Ottoman Village: Turkishness in a Transnational Context', *Nationalities Papers: The Journal of Nationalism and Ethnicity* 45(4): 524–39.

Chapter 11

FROM BROTHERS TO OTHERS?

Changing Images of Bosnian Muslims
in (Post-)Yugoslav Slovenia

Alenka Bartulović

When asked about his feelings upon returning to his second home, Ljubljana, in 2015, Damir bitterly responded that he was always pleased to come back to Slovenia, since 'only here am I referred to as a Bosnian (Bosanc), only here can I be what I really am'. With his sarcastic comment, Damir exposed not only a deep critique of postwar Bosnia and Herzegovina, where Dayton 'trivision' (Jansen 2015) privileges the members of the three constitutive nations (Bosniaks, Serbs and Croats) and marginalizes the segment of the population with the civic and inclusive Bosnian identity (see Bartulović 2013), but also simultaneously recollected the discrimination that he encountered during the 1990s, when he, as a refugee, temporarily joined his Bosnian relatives who had migrated to Slovenia during the Yugoslav golden years. Together with the other approximately thirty thousand refugees from Bosnia and Herzegovina who sought out refuge in independent Slovenia at the outbreak of war in 1992 (Đonlić and Črnivec 2003: 16), Damir had to face the long-lasting but contextually adaptable legacy of othering Bosnians (and in many respects also other former Yugoslavs) in one of the most developed Yugoslav republics, which after the violent dissolution of the federal state became a praised example of the successful postsocialist transition. Damir remembered mostly negative aspects of his temporary stay in Ljubljana, and despite the fact that the extremely heterogeneous community of

Bosnians living in Slovenia had diverse experiences, it cannot be ignored that for decades the term 'Bosnian' in the Slovenian context has been burdened with negative connotations, evoking the imposed homogenization and cultural stereotyping of people who were not born in Slovenia or were descendants of the migrant families from other (former) Yugoslav territories. In various ways, this influenced the possibilities, everyday lives, and process of self-understanding and identification amongst people who even today are characterized as non-Slovenes. Declaring someone to be Bosnian did not, however, necessarily mean that the person was in fact Bosnian, since it usually (but not exclusively) denoted a Serbo-Croatian-speaking migrant regardless of his or her ethnic or religious background (see also Kalčić 2005: 158), yet it was one of the most offensive labels used to ridicule and marginalize the unadjusted subjects unable to grasp Yugoslav modernity.[1] This was also confirmed in conversations with my acquaintances and interlocutors who grew up in Ljubljana during the 1970s and 1980s[2] in the era when the number of migrants from former Yugoslavia, but especially Bosnia and Herzegovina, became prominent (see Dolenc 2005), gradually leading to a shift in public opinion, which, especially from the 1980s onwards, exposed the growing ethnic distance between Slovenes and their Yugoslav brothers (see Medvešek and Vrečer 2005: 294). Despite this, most of the interlocutors who admitted to having consistently used the term Bosnian in the derogatory sense, often replacing it with other similarly offensive labels, for example *južnjak* (southerner), explained that this had nothing to do with nationality or religious belonging (although the 'wrong' name and surname ending in –ić would always provide a helpful incentive); it had more to do with level of taste, education, and personal characteristics, as well as with mentality, cultural development, behaviour and etiquette. An interesting and highly unexpected aspect of this is that, at first glance, the religious belonging of Bosnians, hence also their predominantly Muslim identity, seems to be completely absent from this form of othering. This is even more surprising if we take into consideration the fact that the Slovenian schooling system has, in recent years, been recognized as one of the main ideological apparatuses for transmitting and nurturing the Slovenian variety of frontier Orientalism (Gingrich 1996; see Bartulović 2010).[3] Interestingly, the absence of Islam as a vehicle of the societal exclusion and marginalization of Muslims (later Bosniaks)[4] in Slovenia could also be noted in early sociological works analysing the status of the Bosnian community in Slovenia. This intriguing absence will be explored in the first section of this chapter, which is divided into two parts and examines the changing perceptions of Bosnians and, in particular, Bosnian Muslims in Slovenia, and also focuses on the transformation of the sociocultural cleavages between Slovenes and Bosnians that occurred from the late Yugoslav years through to independent Slovenia. As social scientists have often been recognized as proponents and reproducers of various social hierarchies in Yugoslavia (see, for example, Allcock 2000; Stefansson 2007; Archer, Duda and Stubbs 2016), the first part of the chapter analyses some of the most referential sociological and anthropological works focusing on Bosnians, primarily Bosnian Muslims or Bosniaks, in Slovenia from the 1980s onwards. The aim of the first section is to sketch and expose the changes of prevailing interpretative frames in scholarly analysis of the heterogeneous Bosnian community and forms of othering in Slovenia before and after the country's independence in 1991. This part will also outline the impact of the Yugoslav ideal of brotherhood and unity, as well as the urban-centric postwar politics of the country's modernization (Allcock 2000), which exposed especially the rural and Muslim populations as the main targets of developmental discourse. This hierarchization of urban and rural mentalities, which were closely related to Yugoslav Orientalism, I will argue, not only had an immense impact on the images of Muslims in socialist Slovenia but also continued to direct the stereotypization of Bosniaks in independent Slovenia, influencing their identification in the post-Yugoslav years. Secondly, using existing literature as well as ethnographic material from a case study exploring the music-making of young refugees from Bosnia and Herzegovina in Ljubljana in the beginning of the 1990s,[5] the analysis brings into focus the continuities and discontinuities in the presentation of Bosnians in Slovenia before and after the Yugoslav dissolution. Here, especially, the chapter looks more closely at how the process of changing attitudes towards Bosnian refugees occurred (at least among the younger generations of Slovenes) with the introduction of *sevdalinka*, the musical genre that gradually developed during Ottoman times and has since experienced various transformations and reinterpretations. This genre has often been described as a peculiar fusion of musical traditions, but it is predominantly known as the Bosnian urban song. Since it had been undervalued amongst the Slovenes before the 1990s, its popularization testified to the changing contexts and new interest in the former Yugoslav compatriots. To understand the complexity of the othering process of Bosnians in post-Yugoslav Slovenia, one should also look for manifestations of a specific internalization or rejection of the stigma amongst Bosnians in Slovenia. Therefore, in conclusion, the chapter illustrates how sevdalinka, as an ideologically burdened musical genre (see Kozorog and Bartulović 2016), was used to negotiate identities and contradict the stereotypization of Bosnians in Slovenia.

Rethinking Bosnians: Peasants at the Crossroads?

On the eve of the Yugoslav dissolution, Silva Mežnarić (1986) published one of the first and most referential sociological studies of the Bosnian community in Slovenia, which at the time comprised mainly economic migrants, although they were purportedly Yugoslav brothers and as such not officially considered a separate category or minority. From the 1960s onwards, Slovenia attracted a number of people from other Yugoslav republics to its developing industrial centres (see

Allcock 2000; Pezdir 2004; Kalčić 2005). However, the number of migrants in Slovenia varied significantly throughout the Yugoslav era, reaching its peak at the end of the 1970s and into the 1980s when the European labour market began to close down for Yugoslavs, making Slovenia one of the most attractive destinations for internal emigration (Dolenc 2005; Lamberger Khatib and Pezdir 2009: 118). As Isabel Ströhle emphasizes, the beginning of the second half of twentieth century was an era of Yugoslav developmental dictatorship, which (despite the rhetoric of egalitarianism) contributed to the intensification of the social differentiation process taking place from the 1950s onwards, and reinforced tensions between different regions as well as between urban and rural parts of the country (Ströhle 2016: 114–15; see also Allcock 2000). Immigration from rural areas was in fact strongly encouraged by state institutions with guaranteed jobs in industry, catering and tourism, plus various grants and vocational training opportunities (Kalčić 2005). Aided by her colleagues and students, who conducted interviews mainly with male workers in Slovenia and their families who remained in the rural areas of north-western Bosnia, Mežnarić produced an affected scholarly response to the distorted images of the then still Yugoslav compatriots. Although at first glance her work, suggestively titled *Bosnians: Where do Slovenes go on Sundays?*, exposed the importance of religious belonging and its impact on the prevailing gap between the predominantly Roman Catholic Slovenes and the majority of Muslim Bosnian migrants,[6] for the most part it highlighted alternative othering mechanisms, which were much more acceptable to Yugoslav authorities. Namely, she framed her discussion along the lines of urban-centric discourse on migration in Yugoslavia, thus joining the prevailing stream of Yugoslav scholars, particularly sociologists as well as sociologists and anthropologists from abroad interested in postwar Yugoslav modernization (see Simić 1971; Lockwood 1975). They were, in fact, preoccupied with the exploration of the migration process between the less and more developed parts of the country (Mežnarić 1986: 28), including rural–urban migration flows. Bosnia and Herzegovina was always classified as one of Yugoslavia's less-developed republics, characterized by the lowest rate of urbanization (Spangler, in Stefansson 2007: 62). As such, it was subsidized alongside Kosovo, Montenegro and Macedonia by FADURK, the Fund for the Accelerated Development of the Underdeveloped Republics and Kosovo, created in 1965 (Ströhle 2016: 113). Framing the developmental scheme in terms of the differences between republics instead of regions (Allcock 2000: 84), the Bosnians in Slovenia, especially those drawn from their rural environments by rapid industrialization, were stigmatized as the underdeveloped segment of the Yugoslav population. Thus, it is not surprising that Mežnarić openly rejects the term 'migrant worker' and embraces the category of partly proletarianized peasants (Mežnarić 1986: 20), which is evident in her titling one of the chapters in the book 'Peasants at the Crossroads'. In fact, in the synopsis of the book, she writes:

Supported by central planning policies, which pulled the rural population out of underdeveloped areas, emptying villages and food production capacities without, at the same time, creating employment and housing within the urban immigration zone, this developmental pattern generated a kind of floating workforce. This uprooted population nested around urban and semi-urban areas, waiting for their life chance. (Mežnarić 1986: 230)

Here, she clearly follows the conceptual dominance of understanding migration as well as modernization in Yugoslavia as a process of peasantization of the cities (see Simić 1971), highlighting the inability of villagers to adapt their lifestyles to the urban context. Although this trend, as Keith Brown (2001: 419) notes, was never unique to Yugoslavia (see also Jansen 2005a: 158), it became a prevailing model for explaining Yugoslav history from 1945; moreover, it became commonplace to interpret the process of modernization in terms of the hybrid lifestyles of the so-called peasant urbanite (Simić 1971), peasant worker (Lockwood 1975), or partly proletarianized peasants (Mežnarić 1986). These labels denote the ambivalent figure and, most of all, the liminal status of the new and not yet completely modernized inhabitants of Yugoslav cities who also retain the small-town mentality. Therefore, it logically follows that the Yugoslav variety of socialist modernization as well as the scholarly analysis of postwar Yugoslavia partly contributed to the hegemonic discourse that depicts Balkans as neither modern nor unmodern but rather 'both at the same time, continually undergoing a process of modernization' (Brković 2017: 14; see also Todorova 1999; Allcock 2000; Green 2005). Not surprisingly, Mežnarić follows this epistemological path by suggesting future directions for researching the migrations and integration processes of newcomers, namely the examination of so-called urban shock (Mežnarić 1986: 208), which she deems insufficiently researched. Yet what seems more obscured and intentionally ignored in her study, and in many others, on internal migration in Yugoslavia that emphasizes conflicts between urbanites and rural newcomers (see Mlinar 1965: 1294) is precisely the impact of the national and religious dimensions of identities on the marginalization of migrants.

Modernization of the Peasants, Peasantization of the Muslims?

It is interesting that in Mežnarić's interview in the periodical *Mladina* (Mekina 2015), she claimed that the book emphasized the differences between the three ethnic communities from Yugoslavia, which were homogenized under the name of Bosnians. The book's synopsis, written in English and intended for international audiences, depicts the content as an analysis of the 'ethnic diversification' and the 'rejection [of newcomers] by the indigenous population' (Mežnarić 1986: 229). However, even though sociology – especially from the 1960s onwards, when social stratification became one of the main areas of research (Archer

2014: 137–38) – was relatively bold in the socialist era, particularly compared to ethnology (see Rihtman-Auguštin 2001; Bougarel, Helms and Duijzings 2007: 15), Mežnarić skilfully meanders through the text without seriously considering religious or ethnic differences, and she also fails to examine what effect these differences have on Slovenes' perception of their Yugoslav brothers. The only evidence of acknowledging ethnic and religious differences (although here it is completely essentialized) can be found in the statistical data and in her students' fieldwork notes, where one, for example, writes about the unfamiliar and somehow exotic gender relations observed among Bosnian Muslims:

> Women down there [in North West Bosnia] . . . none of them work, they are quite different than ours . . . Here we see them [Bosnian men] on the streets, where they fight, harass women, and you come there [in Bosnia], and everything is quite domestic, they offer you bread, soured milk . . . What I find particularly interesting . . . is the rigid division of labour amongst genders . . . The man is working in Slovenia, the woman is at home tending the cows, caring for the children. (Mežnarić 1986: 92)

Here, it becomes obvious that certain cultural differences were detected, but even then, the predominance of the urban–rural and modern–unmodern dichotomy remains. The author frames Slovenia in urban imagery (for example 'they were fighting on the streets') while highlighting the rurality of Bosnia (emphasizing farming, domesticity, homemade products, etc.) and demonstrating the limited success of the socialist transformation.

Although there have been some debates and conflicting claims about socialism as an urban-centred system (Allcock 2002: 101; Jansen 2005: 160–61), it has been convincingly argued that the ideals of Yugoslav modernization openly blamed the peasant population for slowing social development, meaning that the socialist era was marked not only by agrarian reforms but also by a strong (political and ideological) alienation of the countryside (see Wairiner 1959; Allcock 2000, 2002). Moreover, the socialist transformation of Yugoslav society 'was equated fairly directly with rapid industrialization, and in relation to this the countryside was regarded both as a resource to be exploited and as a primary locus of "the class enemy"' (Allcock 2000: 126). Thus, the lower working classes together with peasantry often faced exclusion and deprivation (Archer, Duda and Stubbs 2016: 7). Despite calls for cross-confessional brotherly unity, Muslims similarly experienced a more subtle but long-lasting stigmatization and were, like the peasants, often perceived as the most parochial and unmodernized segment of the Yugoslav population (see Bringa 1995). They were a problem that should be dealt with (see Rexhepi 2017: 147), and this could be seen in the strong political action directed towards the emancipation and unveiling of Muslim women, as the practice of veiling has been heavily stigmatized as backward and peasant-like (see Mesarič 2013: 15).[7] In the framework of Yugoslav Orientalism, where varieties of frontier Orientalism (Gingrich 1996; Bartulović 2010; Baskar 2010;

Jezernik 2010) mixed with ideologically constructed and nurtured memories of underprivileged rayah, the Muslims represented an unwanted imperial legacy and were considered 'remnants of the "alien Ottoman yoke"' (Hajdarpašić 2008: 718). Furthermore, through the socialist reinterpretation of the Ottoman legacy, they were often blamed for the cultural, political and economic backwardness of the Balkan nations (see Todorova 1996; Lovrenović 2008), and despite the fact that the Communist Party in the 1950s and 1960s revised its policies towards the nations and nationalities, the idea that Muslims are guided by (religious) conservatism silently persisted (Hajdarpašić 2008: 728).[8] Hence, during socialism, both Muslims and peasants were given the same role in the Yugoslav imagination – they were depicted as an obstacle to modernization (Lazić 1995: 18). By avoiding sensitive topics and protecting the untouchable interethnic harmony, this process of rhetorical peasantization of Muslims provided a more acceptable means of othering in a country of purported brotherhood and unity, while also openly privileging urban spaces as epicentres of societal development, wherein peasants ought to be successfully transformed into members of the working class.[9] Without mentioning ethnic distances, simple ideas of an urban–rural dichotomy might offer an ideal interpretation of social conflicts, but they also serve to conceal existing Islamophobic attitudes in socialist Slovenia.

Exclusion from Europe: Post-Yugoslav Orientalization of the Bosnians

In the 1990s, the interpretative frame in the post-Yugoslav space shifted radically. The nationalization process gradually emphasized the Muslim vs Christian dichotomies, bringing the ideas of the clash of civilizations (Huntington 1997) to the forefront of public discourse. During the war in Bosnia and Herzegovina Bosniaks were mostly depicted as victims of brutal violence and ethnic cleansing, yet at the end of the twentieth century there was a noticeable change in public representations of Muslims. Muslims were regarded as a threat to Europe (Rexhepi 2015: 197). However, these opposing images of European Muslims often merged into one in Slovenia, which offered a temporary home to thousands of refugees from the war-affected areas. As Sabina Mihelj observes in her article on the media representation of (Bosnian) refugees, the mass media employed a number of different strategies, which put distance between Slovenes and Bosnians, and portrayed Bosnian refugees as an intrusion of the Balkans into Europe (Mihelj 2003: 165). Furthermore, she noted that the refugees were reduced to their culture and/or collective identity, and argued that

> by representing the refugees as culturally different, the media were playing a central role in hindering the integration of refugees into the host society. Moreover, the difference between the two collectives was often represented in terms of religion, i.e.

Christianity and Islam. Therefore, distancing the subject (as well as the addressee), i.e. Slovenians, from the object, i.e. Bosnian refugees, was not just a matter of instituting a difference between two nationalities but much more a matter of drawing a distinction between different civilizations and, inter alia, between Europe and the Balkans. (Mihelj 2003: 176)

Introduction of a clear boundary between the Christian West and the Islamic East was crucial for the newly independent Slovenia, which was struggling with the process of negotiating its position in Europe and eager to escape the stigmatized Balkan (see Lindstrom 2003). This Orientalization and ethnization of differences was, however, not only part of the media discourse; it could be traced elsewhere. For example, a similar focus on cultural and religious differences could be seen in Slovenian scholarly writings on Bosniaks, who, in fact, in the 1990s, because of the war, political discourse and the revival of Islam, became much more aware of their ethnic and religious distinctions (see Pezdir 2004; Kalčić 2005, 2007). Although these issues of ethnonational differences came to the forefront of public and scholarly discussions in the post-Yugoslav space, which often meant embracing ethnic bias or methodological nationalism as a dominant epistemological optic (see Bougarel, Helms and Duijzings 2007; Bartulović 2013; Jansen 2015; Archer, Duda and Stubbs 2016), academic approaches to this topic in Slovenia varied immensely. Some scholars, for example, joined the media discourse and used culturalist arguments to act as advocates of the national and religious rights of Bosnian refugees. Prominent Slovenian sociologist Peter Klinar, for instance, called for solidarity with the refugees while simultaneously warning against potential problems that the arrival of the newcomers might cause for both the refugees and Slovenian society:

> We have to remember that they are coming from an industrially developing country, but they have found shelter in more developed societies or even in societies on the scale of postindustrial development. Additionally, it should be noted that they are a Muslim population with a specific culture, about which many negative stereotypes are spreading in Western European countries. (Klinar 1992: 781)

According to Klinar, originating from less-developed places and belonging to the Islamic culture (ibid.: 784) could, therefore, hinder the permanent settlement of Bosniaks in Slovenia. Here, we are faced with the liminal phase when the dominant perspective of Bosnians as semi-rural and unmodernized Others began to assume evident overtones of Islamophobia and Balkanism. Socioeconomic divisions were in fact beginning to show more obvious overlaps with the ethnoreligious cleavages. On the other hand, many scholars (several of them anthropologists) turn to the question of the changing role of religion in the Muslim/Bosniak community during the breakup of Yugoslavia, while simultaneously offering a critical analysis of the emergence of more visible manifestations of discourses of Orientalism and Balkanism in Slovenia. Considering Slovenia's relatively small academic community, the number of papers, articles, theses and monographs on Islam and its perception in Slovenia is surprisingly high. This research focus could of course be interpreted as an obvious consequence of the growing general academic interest in Islam of recent decades, but it could also be viewed as a reflection of a need to explore and understand various interrelated processes in the former Yugoslav space, and their connection to the events taking place in the global arena: namely, religious revival and the nationalization process, global debates on the transformation of Islam and terrorism, and increasing Islamophobia (see Rexhepi 2017). Despite the fact that during the war in Bosnia the relatively high number of Bosnian refugees made the Slovenian Bosnian community even more heterogeneous (see Đonlić and Črnivec 2003; Cukut Krilić 2009; Bartulović and Kozorog 2017), Slovenian scholars largely focused on the religious and ethnic identities of Bosnian Muslims, who, as European Muslims, always incited more interest amongst the anthropologists working in Bosnia and Herzegovina than their Roman Catholic and Christian Orthodox neighbours (Bougarel, Helms and Duijzings 2007: 18–19). In the early 1990s, therefore, Islam was introduced as the most visible identity marker and the most obvious sign of ethnic difference between the Bosniaks and Slovenes.

Islam in Focus

Emphasizing the importance of the Bosniak religious identity, anthropologists focused on Islamic religious practices, particularly veiling, as the most visible sign of the re-Islamization process. In 2007, for example, Špela Kalčić published her doctoral thesis entitled 'I am not a Barbie Doll: Dress Practices, Islam and Identification Processes among Bosniaks in Slovenia'. In other works, Kalčić also noted that the Islamic dress practices and way of life in Slovenia were a silent but visible resistance of Bosniaks, who decided to practise their independent lifestyle to fight against the marginalization and humiliation they had experienced in Slovenia. She also confirmed that Slovenes were always looking down on Bosnian Muslims, describing stories of discrimination in socialist Slovenia (Kalčić 2009: 233, 239, 242). Although most of her interlocutors ascribe these negative attitudes to a deep-seated Slovenian aversion towards Islam, some emphasized the enduring prevalence of Balkanism and the legacy of the aforesaid peasantization of Muslims. As one of Kalčić's interlocutors remembered, she felt degraded in elementary school in the late 1980s, especially when a school counsellor advised her to continue her education at an agricultural high school because of her average grades. As a comparison, her schoolmate, with the same grades but a different name and surname, was encouraged to apply to medical school (ibid.: 233).

Taking into consideration the low standing of the farming professions in (socialist) Slovenia (see, for example, Černič Istenič 2011), the act of pressing Bosnian Muslims to work the land clearly demonstrated what was perceived as a suitable career path for the former Yugoslav brothers, being jobs that were not particularly attractive to locals.[10] Thus, we are once again faced with the notion of Muslims as belonging to the rural, apparently underdeveloped world, which did not completely disappear with the dissolution of Yugoslavia. In fact, with Slovenian independence and post-Yugoslav transformation, which also included a rise in unemployment, pauperization of the working class, and other socioeconomic turbulences, these feelings of alienation amongst Bosniaks grew even stronger (Kalčić 2009: 234). However, with the institutionalization of their activities, Bosniaks are trying to achieve the status of a recognized minority in Slovenia. An important role in connecting the community of Bosniaks was played by the Islamic community in Slovenia, yet many of the Bosnians, including some of the Bosnian refugees (Muslim and non-Muslim alike) who lived in Slovenia during the 1990s, felt alienated amongst the members of various Bosniak associations.

Reproducing the Urban–Rural Distinction in Exile

When interviewed, Bosnian refugees who came to Slovenia in the 1990s regularly stressed that their experiences with Slovenes were not as bad as those of their predecessors (see also Janko Sprajzar et al. 2004: 241). They usually argued that this was because they were, in fact, very different from migrant workers, who came to the country during the Yugoslav modernization. Thus, as might be expected, most of them could not relate to the Bosnian diaspora, emphasizing that their lifestyles, manners, appearance and mentality differed radically. In the interviews, some of them noted that they had much more in common with the Slovenes than with Bosnian migrant workers. By painting a negative picture of the Bosnian diaspora, they often position themselves in the contrasting role of educated and civilized urbanites: 'Well, this attitude towards southerners was probably left over from the time of Yugoslavia . . . Maybe because at that time the workforce that was coming to Slovenia from Bosnia was mostly non-qualified . . . And, of course, they were, I will not say, troublemakers . . . But when you look, usually they say: "See what the Bosnian did?"' (ibid.: 241, 242). Most of them did not even try to oppose these simple generalizations depicting people from other Yugoslav republics as primitive and sometimes even prone to criminal activities and violence: 'In recent years, Slovenia has welcomed a generation from the lower classes, for example construction workers . . . more or less uneducated, hailing from less developed areas and not very cultured. These people were very often involved in bar fights . . . generally, problematic; the southerners' bad reputation originates from that time' (Markotić 2009: 11–12). These passages clearly demonstrate that many Bosnian refugees completely distanced themselves from the migrants and Bosnian diaspora in Slovenia, internalizing the stereotypization of migrant workers as lazy, primitive, backward and uneducated. Faced with the stereotypes of their backwardness from Slovenes, a few of them even refrained from using their mother tongue in public. Unsurprisingly, many did not feel it was necessary to battle against these depictions. In contrast, other refugees felt differently and described the inner need to prove themselves as civilized and modern. In this process of fighting against imposed homogenization, they employed various tools and strategies. I will offer only a glance into these actions with a short ethnographic example related to the music-making of Bosnian refugees in Slovenia in the 1990s, which has been analysed in depth elsewhere (see Kozorog and Bartulović 2015, 2016; Bartulović and Kozorog 2017; Kozorog 2017). I will briefly examine the impact such discourses on the persistent othering of Bosnians has had on the identities of Bosnian refugees in Slovenia, as well as on the rehabilitation or enhancement of the urban–rural gap in exile.

The Power of the Displaced Sevdalinka

To contextualize the strategies used in the fight against the stigma, it should be noted that at the time of the dissolution of Yugoslavia, the popularity of pop and rock bands from the rest of the former Yugoslavia surged in Slovenia. In contrast, Dertum and Vali, the two best-known refugee musical groups based in Ljubljana, interpreted traditional songs – mostly sevdalinka. In the 1990s, this hybrid musical genre became a visible national symbol of Bosnia and Herzegovina, and was also appropriated by the Bosniaks as an expression of exclusive national heritage. Yet the genre's history has been turbulent; sevdalinka has been used as an argument in conflicting ideological positions throughout history (Peka Pennanen 2010; Kozorog and Bartulović 2016). While offering a new context for the transformation of sevdalinka, the socialist era shunned the genre, mostly because of its oriental influences (Peka Pennanen 2010: 83), yet in the 1990s it experienced a new life not only in Bosnia and Herzegovina but in the broader post-Yugoslav space. It was furthermore simultaneously used as a tool of identification and social criticism both within and outside the refugee community in Slovenia. When it entered the musical world of the Slovenes, who in the past had perceived the genre mostly as primitive eastern howling, it denoted resistance towards the dominant negative representations of the Balkans and former Yugoslavia in a newly independent country (Ceglar 1999). Within the refugee community from Bosnia and Herzegovina, sevdalinka prevented complete spatial marginalization of the refugees, and musical creativity allowed several youngsters to perform at the most renowned festivals and Slovenian concert venues (see Bartulović and Kozorog 2017). In its transformed and hybrid version, it was also a clear marker of the modernized urban identity of the Bosnians living in Slovenia. This was possible because both the public and academic discourses (see Karača

Beljak 2014) continuously emphasized that sevdalinka is an urban phenomenon, and as such it should be regarded as an intimate Bosnian urban song. These extraordinary repetitions also had an effect in exile, where sevdalinka was, through hybridization and experimentation, transformed into an acceptable musical form for part of the Slovenian public too.

The emphasis on the urbanity of sevdalinka overpowered the discourses of the many refugees involved in musical activities. The most evident illustration appeared in an article by Vali's band leader and ethnomusicologist Vesna Andree Zaimović entitled 'Bosnian Traditional Urban Song "On the Sunny Side of the Alps": From the Expression of Nostalgia to a New Ethnic Music in Slovene Culture' (Andree Zaimović 2001). She noted that during the war in Bosnia and Herzegovina, a number of so-called cultural immigrants among the refugees (artists, cultural workers, journalists and intellectuals) found their temporary home in Slovenia, and used sevdalinka, which she consistently defines as an authentic and traditional urban song, to combat negative and incorrectly based stereotypes about the traditional and present culture of Bosnia and Herzegovina. According to her, 'sevdalinka is a form of urban identification, which is why all those citizens who originate from such areas gladly accepted it. By promoting sevdalinka as such, they also propagated the urban spirit of B&H' (ibid.: 114). Like Bosniak interpretations of sevdalinka in postwar Bosnia and Herzegovina, where it was interpreted as a positive force (Peka Pennanen 2010: 86), Vesna Andree Zaimović opposed the predominant depictions of Bosnians in Slovenia, and used sevdalinka as evidence of Bosnian urban culture. While 'sevdalinka has become a well-suited medium for the propagation of the cultural values of B&H, which fights deep-rooted prejudices' (ibid.: 115), it is obvious that it has also become a mechanism for drawing boundaries between the so-called Bosnian urban and cultural refugees and the rural and apparently uneducated economic migrants and refugees. Even some interlocutors who actually tried to oppose such clear divisions could not embrace nor completely tolerate the lifestyle they encountered in the refugee centres, where they (sometimes even for the first time) met people from rural areas, and perceived them to be uneducated and uncultured. Some of them even claimed that the rural and uneducated population were in fact responsible for the retraditionalization and ethnonational radicalization of Bosnia and Herzegovina. This was a clear consequence of the nationalist exploitation of rurality (Jansen 2005a: 155; Stefansson 2007: 67). These feelings were intensified because the members of the bands also encountered disapproval when performing their version of sevdalinka. As a singer in one of the bands recalled, the older women from the village could not get accustomed to their sound or their rock image. Similarly, many younger refugee musicians confirmed that they had never listened to sevdalinka when they were still living in Bosnia and Herzegovina, often perceiving the genre as an outdated musical form that is more connected with the worldviews of the older generations, not cosmopolitan youth. Thus, in the new context it had to be transformed to suit a more urbanized taste. Many of the musicians from the two bands, including the former guitarist of Vali, admit they had an aversion to more traditional performances by a singer accompanied only by a loud accordion:

> I must admit that this classic form that many people still adore sounds a little bit peasant-like to me. Although sometimes you have really good musicians, listening to their performances is something that is, in a way, a little bit amusing or even funny. On the other hand it can also be repulsive. But if you are drunk, it can also be great (laugh). I'm more interested in this, let's call it jazzy, experimentation with sevdalinka. These variations are more pleasing to my ear, but of course we have different tastes, we grew up in different places.

The territorialization of musical tastes clearly reflects the importance of the rural–urban gap in the identification process of refugees from Bosnia and Herzegovina. Similar attitudes could be found amongst the new Slovenian audience who started listening to sevdalinka in the 1990s. A Slovenian musician in the conversation explained that he thought the band Dertum was legendary, because he shared with its members the same visions and approach to music: 'Musical closeness is really the most important for me'. While Bosnian refugees from both bands were extremely surprised by their popularity amongst Slovenes, members of the Bosnian diaspora rarely frequented their concerts. According to one member of the association of Bosniaks in Slovenia, they preferred to organize their own parties, where a more conventional approach to sevdalinka was nurtured. Youths from both refugee groups often interpreted these gatherings as a reflection of the relatively conservative attitudes towards music, which once again were contrasted with the attitudes and tastes of cosmopolitan urbanites, who were more open to different influences and mixing. In urban-centric discourses, 'purity was reformulated into backwardness, narrow-mindedness, and primitivism' (Jansen 2005: 157). Therefore, with the aim of fighting the negative stereotypes attached to Bosnians in Slovenia and of countering the nationalization of the genre, the new ideologists of the reinvented sevdalinka in Slovenia (intentionally or unintentionally) embraced the urban–rural dichotomy, pushed the importance of religious and national belonging aside, and nurtured the Yugoslav discourse of modernization as a crucial part of their identification process. So, while media and public representations (and in some ways even researchers) of the 1990s largely emphasized the homogeneity of the refugees by primarily focusing on culturalist ideas about the differences between the predominantly Muslim Bosnians and the Slovenes, some of the refugees themselves (as well as the Slovenes who frequented the concerts of the refugee bands) used the urban–rural and ideological divides to accentuate the internal heterogeneity of the Bosnian community.

Conclusion

The aim of this chapter was to explore the dominant perceptions of Bosnians and, particularly, Bosnian Muslims in Slovenia from the 1980s onwards. Therefore, it addresses the transformation of discourses in decades when Yugoslavia became increasingly divided on a socioeconomic as well as on a national basis, with the two becoming even more closely linked (Archer, Duda and Stubbs 2016: 3).

Although the Yugoslav sociology and public debate of the 1970s regularly stressed the importance of discussion on social equality (Allcock 2000: 186; Ströhle 2016: 115), arguments were often framed to fit the ascribed model of Yugoslav modernization, where a clear urban–rural dichotomy and marginalization of semi-rural Others were not only unproblematized but were in fact reinforced as the dominant framework of analysis. Avoiding the dangerous topic of national cleavages, many scholars have managed to interpret the distancing from Bosnians in Slovenia simply as a question of unsuccessful integration of newcomers into city life. Yet the implication of additional developmental and mentality obstacles between the Yugoslav brothers is nevertheless clearly illustrated in Mlinar's interpretation of life in Titovo Velenje:

> In the south-eastern part of the country, where the differences between life in the city and life in the countryside are more marked than in the rest of Slovenia, the problem of the adaptation and integration of newcomers in the urban community proves to be a much more difficult and long-lasting process, as it is, for example, in the case of the individuals from around Velenje. (Mlinar 1965: 1,275)

What becomes clear with analysis of the migrant community from Bosnia and Herzegovina in the last decades of Yugoslavia is the fact that Slovenes were far more likely to portray Bosnians as backward, uneducated, rural or semi-rural than as culturally radically different. Even though we can find traces of masked Orientalism and aversion to Islam, this view was dismissed in accordance with the ideology of brotherhood and unity. This image, however, experienced a transformation throughout the 1990s when scholarly attention was overpowered by interest in Islam. Despite the shift of the perceptions introduced by the nationalization process, religious revival, and the dissolution of Yugoslavia, it is obvious that urban-centric othering survived, not only amongst Slovenes but evidently within the Bosnian community in Slovenia and beyond. In fact, in postwar Bosnia and Herzegovina, the schism between urban and rural mentalities (regardless of the continuous process of blurring boundaries between rural and urban initiated by modernization and globalization) became extraordinarily strong during the traumatic war, where urbicide and revenge of the countryside became a common frame of interpretation for explaining the brutal war (see Baskar 1999; Bougarel 1999; Allcock 2002; Stefannson 2007). This was also highlighted by the Bosniaks, since the 'crystallization of Muslim nationalism in Bosnia during the war went together with the emergence of analyses interpreting the war as a confrontation between the "urban civilization" of the Muslims and the "barbarous and tribal minds" of the Serbs' (Bougarel 1999: 160). The post-Yugoslav years and nationalization process did not simply abolish this legacy of othering. Inequality, disparity in living standards, poverty, unemployment, and structural discrimination called for a culprit. In addition to a non-functional state (Bartulović 2013; Jansen 2015), the semi-rural Other remained, even in a deeply nationalized context, an easy target (see Jansen 2002, 2005a, 2005b; Stefannson 2007; Armakolas 2007; Bartulović 2013; Henig 2012). Remarkably, in independent Slovenia, rehabilitation of the urban–rural gap enabled the integration of the segment of refugees from Bosnia and Herzegovina, who became, through their musical activities and especially their hybridization of sevdalinka, lost brothers (and sisters). Focus on the specific microcontext of refugee creativity in the 1990s provides a surprising inversion, wherein brotherhood is established precisely in the years of the final death of the Yugoslav ideology of brotherhood and unity. Of course, this shifting and ambivalent attitude towards the Bosnian Muslims was nothing new, as Edin Hajdarpašić (2015) clearly testifies in his research on the nationalization process during the period from 1840 to 1919, which led him to develop a useful analytic category for Bosnian Muslims to encompass the claims of sameness and otherness: (br)other. This category captures the position of the Muslims, who were in fact both brother and Other to their Croat and Serb neighbours towards the end of the nineteenth century and into the twentieth century, but it can be also used in the late or even post-Yugoslav context. The acceptance of the refugees could be ascribed not only to their urban identification but also to other factors: their mostly atheistic orientation and secularism as well as their praise of cosmopolitanism and Eurocentric (reformulated Yugoslav) conception of modernity. This, however, provided additional arguments for the reinterpretation of the persistent categories of good and bad Bosnians or good and bad Muslims in Slovenia. Here, besides the clear Orientalistic discourses that have become prominent in recent decades in the Slovenian public domain and were most obvious in the discussion on the construction of the mosque in Ljubljana (see Bartulović 2010), elements of the rural–urban or the modern and parochial mentality recur. Yet, in the face of such endurance, it is remarkable how little attention has been devoted to the urban–rural dichotomy in the analysis of the othering process in Slovenia and beyond. Thus, to move past a one-dimensional interpretative framework obsessed with the simple Orientalist vision of Muslims, it is necessary to study the multiplicity and intersections of the othering mechanisms in different historical moments. I hope that this chapter prompts a deeper investigation into the entanglements of the different legacies of othering, and opens new avenues to a more complex understanding of discrimination and marginalization, as well as to the occasional romanticization of Muslims/Bosniaks in the post-Yugoslav space.

Alenka Bartulović is an assistant professor at the Department of Ethnology and Cultural Anthropology of the University of Ljubljana, Slovenia. She is the author of an award-winning book *'Nismo vaši!': antinacionalizem v povojnem Sarajevu* ['We're not one of you!' Anti-nationalism in postwar Sarajevo] (Ljubljana: Znanstvena založba Filozofske fakultete, 2013). She has published a number of scholarly articles and book chapters. Her research interests include the remembering process and identification in the Balkans, refugee studies, urban–rural relations, rural anthropology, gender studies, and construction of the Other. Her latest work explores urban–rural dichotomies in the Balkans, and artistic practices of Bosnian refugees in Slovenia.

Notes

This chapter is the result of two research projects I have been working on in recent years. The first, carried out in collaboration with Miha Kozorog, is on the musical creativity of Bosnian refugees in Slovenia in the 1990s, while the second aims to explore the power of rural–urban dichotomies on the identification process in the Balkans. The author acknowledges that the ongoing research project (Programme P6-0187(A)), 'Slovenian Identities in the European and Global Context', was financially supported by the Slovenian Research Agency.

1. Since private consumption was often perceived as the prime indicator of progress in Yugoslavia, the status was connected with the consumption of specific goods (Ströhle 2016: 114–15; see also Patterson 2011). The adjective 'Bosnian' could also relate to particular objects that, despite not having been made in Bosnia, could be proclaimed and laughed at for being Bosnian. Being said to wear Bosnian, Czech, or peasant shoes or other attire was a way to imply a lack of taste or a contentment with dated or out-of-fashion clothes of lower quality.
2. It should be emphasized that these findings cannot be generalized and that Bosnians were not always treated by Slovenes as a homogeneous group. Some of the interlocutors who grew up in the 1960s informed me that they did not encounter similar othering of their 'brothers' from Yugoslavia. Also, in rural areas, where the school classes were more or less ethnically homogeneous, the designated Others were usually pupils from the poor mountain farms.
3. Lessons dealing with the so-called Turkish incursions and narratives of suffering born under the sign of Ottoman oppression were mostly introduced through the subjects of history and literature (Bartulović 2010; Baskar 2010).
4. The term 'Bosniaks' was introduced as an official name for Bosnian Muslims in 1993.
5. My colleague Miha Kozorog and I conducted ten semi-structured interviews with musicians from the refugee bands and their fans. We were both, in certain ways, also involved in the musical activities of the refugees in the early 1990s.
6. It is interesting that most of my interlocutors, when asked about their interpretation of the book title, claimed that it reflects the religious distance between two communities and shows the difference in the holy days of Roman Catholics and Muslims. But the title is in fact a reference to different pastime activities. While many single men without their families expected sociality in the city centres during the weekends, Slovenes habitually spent their weekends hiking and enjoying free time outdoors and with their fami-

lies, mostly in the rural areas. In her recent interview in the periodical *Mladina* (Mekina 2015), Mežnarić confirmed that the title was in fact a quote from one of the interlocutors, who was surprised by the emptiness of the cities.
7. This political stigma has roots in the Balkans of the nineteenth century, since the process of de-Ottomanization in the newly independent states of the Balkans clearly demonstrated that modernization was often equated with Europeanization and Westernization, which in fact called for the denouncing of any associations with Islam.
8. It is interesting to note that there were also varying alternative perspectives on the Ottoman legacy in South East Europe, which have been explored by Edin Hajdarpašić (2008). Ambivalent approaches to the Ottoman legacy can also be detected in the work of Bosnian Nobel laureate Ivo Andrić (see Bartulović 2017).
9. The connection of Muslims with retrograded rurality disregards the achievements of the Ottoman Empire in the urbanization of the Balkans.
10. Looking at the professional profile of workers originating from Bosnia and Herzegovina even today, most of the men do construction work, while the women are mainly depicted as cleaners. This stereotypical image of Bosnian women in Slovenia is reflected in the fact that the Muslim name Fata (Fatima) has become almost synonymous with the Slovenian word for cleaner. Fata is often used as the unavoidable character in (Slovenian) comedies (sometimes directed by the Bosnians, for example Branko Đurić Đuro, who always emphasizes that Slovenes and Bosnians have a similar sense of humour because they both enjoy laughing at Bosnians).

Bibliography

Allcock, John B. 2000. *Explaining Yugoslavia*. Irvington, NY: Columbia University Press.
———. 2002. 'Rural–Urban Differences and the Breakup of Yugoslavia', *Balkanologie* VI(1–2): 101–25.
Andree Zaimović, Vesna. 2001. 'Bosnian Traditional Urban Song "On the Sunny Side of the Alps": From the Expression of Nostalgia to a New Ethnic Music in Slovene Culture', in Svanibor Pettan, Adelaida Reyes and Maša Komavec (eds), *Music and Minorities*. Ljubljana: Založba ZRC, ZRC SAZU, pp. 111–20.
Archer, Rory. 2014. 'Social Inequalities and the Study of Yugoslavia's Dissolution', in Florian Bieber, Armina Galijaš and Rory Archer (eds), *Debating the End of Yugoslavia*. Farnham, UK: Ashgate, pp. 135–51.
Archer, Rory, Igor Duda and Paul Stubbs. 2016. 'Bringing the Class Back In: An Introduction', in Rory Archer, Igor Duda and Paul Stubbs (eds), *Social Inequalities and Discontent in Yugoslav Socialism*. Abingdon, UK: Routledge, pp. 1–20.
Armakolas, Ioannis. 2007. 'Sarajevo No More? Identity and the Experience of Place among Bosnian Serb Sarajevans in Republika Srpska', in Xavier Bougarel, Elissa Helms and Ger Duijzings (eds), *The New Bosnian Mosaic: Social Identities, Collective Memories and Moral Claims in a Post-war Society*. Aldershot, UK: Ashgate, pp. 79–99.
Bartulović, Alenka. 2010. '"We Have an Old Debt with the Turk, and It Best be Settled": Ottoman Incursions through the Discursive Optics of Slovenian Historiography and Literature, and Their Applicability in the Twenty-First Century', in Božidar Jezernik (ed.), *Imagining 'the Turk'*. Newcastle upon Tyne: Cambridge Scholars, pp. 111–36.

——. 2013. 'Nismo vaši!': Antinacionalisem v povojnem Sarajevu. Ljubljana: Znanstvena založba FF (Zupaničeva knjižnica 35).

——. 2017. 'Postjugosłowiańskie interpretacje orientalizmu Ivo Andricia: niejednoznaczność osmańskiego dziedzictwa w Bośni i Hercegowinie', *Łódzkie Studia Etnograficzne* 56: 27–48.

Bartulović, Alenka, and Miha Kozorog. 2017. 'Gender and Music-Making in Exile: Female Bosnian Refugee Musicians in Slovenia', *Dve domovini: razprave o izseljenstvu* 46: 39–55.

Baskar, Bojan. 1999. 'Anthropologists Facing the Collapse of Yugoslavia', *Diogenes* 47(4): 51–63.

——. 2010. 'The First Slovenian Poet in a Mosque: Orientalism in the Travel Writing of a Poet from the Imperial Periphery', in Božidar Jezernik (ed.), *Imagining 'the Turk'*. Newcastle upon Tyne: Cambridge Scholars, pp. 97–110.

Bringa, Tone. 1995. *Being Muslim the Bosnian Way: Identity and Community in a Central Bosnian Village*. Princeton, NJ: Princeton University Press.

Brković, Čarna. 2017. 'Epistemological Eclecticism: Difference and the "Other" in the Balkans and Beyond', *Anthropological Theory* (November): 1–23.

Brown, Keith S. 2001. 'Beyond Ethnicity: The Politics of Urban Nostalgia in Modern Macedonia', *Journal of Mediterranean Studies* 11(2): 417–42.

Bougarel, Xavier. 1999. 'Yugoslav Wars: The "Revenge of the Countryside" between Sociological Reality and Nationalist Myth', *East European Quarterly* 32(2): 157–75.

Bougarel, Xavier, Elissa Helms and Ger Duijzings. 2007. 'Introduction', in Xavier Bougarel, Elissa Helms and Ger Duijzings (eds), *The New Bosnian Mosaic: Social Identities, Collective Memories and Moral Claims in a Post-war Society*. Aldershot, UK: Ashgate, pp. 1–35.

Ceglar, Miha. 1999. 'Balkan scena', in Peter Stankovič, Gregor Tomc and Mitja Velikonja (eds), *Urbana plemena – subkulture na Slovenskem v devetdesetih*. Ljubljana: Študentska Založba, pp. 75–82.

Černič Istenič, Majda. 2011. 'Medijska podoba kmetijstva in kmeta v Sloveniji', in Tanja Petrović (ed.), *Politike reprezentacije v Jugovzhodni Evropi na prelomu stoletij*. Ljubljana: Založba ZRC, pp. 76–99.

Cukut Krilić, Sanja. 2009. *Spol in migracija: izkušnje žensk kot akterk migracij*. Ljubljana: Založba ZRC, ZRC SAZU.

Dolenc, Danilo. 2005. 'Priseljevanje v Slovenijo z območja nekdanje Jugoslavije po II. svetovni vojni: Etnična podoba Slovenije skozi statistične podatke', in Miran Komac and Mojca Medvešek (ed.), *Percepcije slovenske integracijske politike, Zaključno poročilo*. Ljubljana: Inštitut za narodnostna vprašanja, pp. 35–87.

Đonlić, Minka, and Vesna Črnivec. 2003. *Deset let samote: Izkušnje bosansko-hercegovskih begunk in beguncev v Sloveniji*. Ljubljana: Društvo Kulturni vikend.

Gingrich, Andre. 1996. 'Frontier Myths of Orientalism: The Muslim World in Public and Popular Cultures of Central Europe', in Borut Brumen and Bojan Baskar (eds), *MESS, Mediterranean Ethnological Summer School, Vol II*. Ljubljana: Inštitut za multikulturne raziskave, pp. 99–127.

Green, Sarah. 2005. *Notes from the Balkans: Locating Marginality and Ambiguity on the Greek–Albanian Border*. Princeton, NJ: Princeton University Press.

Hajdarpašić, Edin. 2008. 'Out of the Ruins of the Ottoman Empire: Reflections on the Ottoman Legacy in South-Eastern Europe', *Middle Eastern Studies* 44(5): 715–34.

——. 2015. *Whose Bosnia?: Nationalism and Political Imagination in the Balkans, 1840–1914*. Ithaca, NY: Cornell University Press.

Henig, David. 2012. '"Knocking on My Neighbour's Door": On Metamorphoses of Sociality in Rural Bosnia', *Critique of Anthropology* 32(1): 3–19.
Huntington, Samuel. 1997. *The Clash of Civilizations and the Remaking of the World Order.* New York: Touchstone.
Janko Spreizer, Alenka, et al. 2004. 'Oblike ljudke in birokratske diskriminacije skozi pogled ljudi, ki jih uradno nikoli niso poimenovali za begunce', *Razprave in gradivo* 45: 218–47.
Jansen, Stef. 2002. 'Svakodnevni orijentalizam: doživljaj "Balkana"/ "Evrope" u Beogradu i Zagrebu'. *Filozofija i društvo: Journal of the Belgrade Institute for Social Research and Philosophy* 18: 33–72.
———. 2005a. 'Who's Afraid of White Socks? Towards a Critical Understanding of post-Yugoslav Urban Self-Perceptions', *Ethnologica Balkanica* 9: 151–67.
———. 2005b. *Antinacionalizam: Etnografija otpora u Beogradu i Zagrebu.* Beograd: Biblioteka XX vek.
———. 2015. *Yearning in the Meantime: 'Normal Lives' and the State in a Sarajevo Apartment Complex.* Oxford: Berghahn Books.
Jezernik, Božidar (ed.). 2010. *Imagining 'the Turk'.* Newcastle upon Tyne: Cambridge Scholars.
Kalčić, Špela. 2005. 'Changing Contexts and Redefinitions of Identity among Bosniaks in Slovenia', *Balkanologie* IX(1–2): 149–71.
———. 2007. *'Nisem jaz Barbika': Oblačilne prakse, islam in identitetni procesi med Bošnjaki v Sloveniji.* Ljubljana: Filozofska fakulteta.
———. 2009. 'To je moj džihad: O tem, zakaj so se nekatere Bošnjakinje v Sloveniji začele pokrivati', in Mirjam Milharčič Hladnik and Jernej Mlekuž (eds), *Krila migracij: Po meri življenjskih zgodb.* Ljubljana: Založba ZRC SAZU, pp. 217–46.
Karača Beljak, Tamara. 2014. *Zvučni krajolici: Pogled na vokalne fenomene Bosne i Hercegovine.* Sarajevo: Muzička akademija u Sarajevu.
Klinar, Peter. 1992. 'Mednarodni migracijski trendi in begunci iz Bosne in Hercegovine', *Teorija in praksa* 29(7–8): 773–84.
Kozorog, Miha. 2017. 'Doubly Excluded, Doubly Included, "Something In-between": A Bosnian Refugee Band and Alternative Youth Culture in Slovenia', in Miha Kozorog and Rajko Muršič (eds), *Sounds of Attraction: Yugoslav and post-Yugoslav Popular Music.* Ljubljana: Znanstvena založba Filozofske fakultete, pp. 73–97.
Kozorog, Miha, and Alenka Bartulović. 2015. 'The Sevdalinka in Exile, Revisited: Young Bosnian Refugees' Music-Making in Ljubljana in the 1990s (a Note on Applied Ethnomusicology)', *Narodna umjetnost* 52(1): 121–42.
———. 2016. '*Sevdah* Celebrities Narrate *Sevdalinka*: Political (Self-)Contextualization of *Sevdalinka* Performers in Bosnia and Herzegovina', *Traditiones* 45(1): 161–79.
Lamberger Khatib, Maja, and Tatjana Pezdir. 2009. 'Could I Ask You, My Brother, to Send Me a Little Something?', *Dve domovini* 29: 115–34.
Lazić, Mladen (ed.). 1995. *Society in Crisis: Yugoslavia in the Early 1990s.* Belgrade: Filip Višnjić.
Lindstrom, Nicole. 2003. 'Between Europe and the Balkans: Mapping Slovenia and Croatia "Return to Europe" in the 1990s', *Dialectical Anthropology* 27: 313–29.
Lockwood, William G. 1975. *European Moslems: Economy and Ethnicity in Eastern Bosnia.* New York: Academic Press.
Lovrenović, Ivan. 2008. 'Ivo Andrić: Paradoks o šutnji', *Časopis za kulturu, književnost i društvena pitanja* XIII(1–2): 1–36.

Markotić, Mirjana. 2009. 'Življenje nekdanjih beguncev iz BiH v Sloveniji'. Unpublished thesis. University of Ljubljana, Faculty for Social Work.
Medvešek, Mojca, and Natalija Vrečar. 2005. 'Percepcije sociokulturne integracije in nestrpnosti: nove manjšine v Sloveniji', in Miran Komac and Mojca Medvešek (eds), *Percepcije slovenske integracijske politike, Zaključno poročilo*. Ljubljana: Inštitut za narodnostna vprašanja, pp. 271–377.
Mekina, Borut. 2015. 'Dr. Silva Mežnarić: sociologinja migracij', *Mladina* 49 (4 December). http://www.mladina.si/171241/dr-silva-meznaric/; last accessed 10 September 2019.
Mesarič, Andreja. 2013. 'Wearing Hijab in Sarajevo: Dress Practices and the Islamic Revival in Postwar Bosnia and Herzegovina', *Anthropological Journal of European Cultures* 22(2): 12–34.
Mežnarić, Silva. 1986. *'Bosanci': A kuda idu Slovenci nedeljom?* Ljubljana: Krt.
Mihelj, Sabina. 2003. 'Negotiating European Identity at the Periphery: "Slovenian Nation", "Bosnian Refugees" and "Illegal Migration"', in Ib Bondebjerg and Peter Golding (eds), *Media Cultures in a Changing Europe*. Bristol: Intellect Books, pp. 165–89.
Mlinar, Zdravko. 1965. 'Prijateljski, soseski in sorodstveni odnosi v Velenju', *Problemi: Revija za kulturo in družbena vprašanja* 33/34: 1,271–294.
Patterson, Patrick Hyder. 2011. *Bought and Sold: Living and Losing the Good Life in Socialist Yugoslavia*. Ithaca, NY: Cornell University Press.
Peka Pennanen, Risto. 2010. 'Melancholic Airs of the Orient: Bosnian Sevdalinka Music as an Orientalist and National Symbol', in Risto Peka Pennanen (ed.), *Music and Emotions*. Helsinki: Helsinki Collegium for Advanced Studies Vol. 9, pp. 76–90.
Pezdir, Tatjana. 2004. 'Transnacionalne aktivnosti – primer migrantov iz Bosne in Hercegovine in njihovih potomcev v Sloveniji', *Časopis za kritiko znanosti* 32(217/218): 184–94.
Rexhepi, Piro. 2015. 'Mainstreaming Islamophobia: The Politics of European Enlargement and the Balkan Crime–Terror Nexus', *East European Quarterly* 43(2–3): 189–214.
———. 2017. 'Unmapping Islam in Eastern Europe: Periodization and Muslim Subjectivities in the Balkans', in Irene Kacandes and Yuliya Komska (eds), *Eastern Europe Unmapped: Beyond Borders and Peripheries*. New York: Berghahn Books, pp. 53–77.
Rihtman-Auguštin, Dunja. 2001. *Etnologija i etnomit*. Zagreb: Naklada Publica.
Simić, Andrei. 1971. *The Peasant Urbanities: A Study of Rural–Urban Mobility in Serbia*. New York: Seminar Press.
Stefansson, Anders. 2007. 'Urban Exile: Locals, Newcomers and the Cultural Transformation of Sarajevo', in Xavier Bougarel, Elissa Helms and Ger Duijzings (eds), *The New Bosnian Mosaic: Social Identities, Collective Memories and Moral Claims in a Postwar Society*. Aldershot, UK: Ashgate, pp. 59–77.
Ströhle, Isabel. 2016. 'Social Stratification and the Making of a Rural Underclass in Kosovo', in Rory Archer, Igor Duda and Paul Stubbs (eds), *Social Inequalities and Discontent in Yugoslav Socialism*. Abingdon, UK: Routledge, pp. 112–31.
Todorova, Maria. 1996. 'The Ottoman Legacy in the Balkans', in Carl L. Brown (ed.), *Imperial Legacy: The Ottoman Imprint on the Balkans and the Middle East*. New York: Columbia University Press, pp. 45–77.
———. 1999. *Imaginarni Balkan*. Beograd: Biblioteka XX vek.
Wairiner, Doieen. 1959. 'Urban Thinkers and Peasant Policy in Yugoslavia, 1918–1959', *Slavonic and East European Review* (December): 59–81.

Chapter 12

Exploring Religious Views among Young People of Bosnian Muslim Origin in Berlin

Aldina Čemernica

The arrival of over one million refugees to the countries of Western Europe in 2015 has intensified debates on Islam and Muslims across Europe. Germany accepted 890,000 refugees and was thus the country that received the highest number of asylum seekers (see 'Pro Asyl').[1] Many of them were from Syria, Iraq and Afghanistan. The refugee crisis put European solidarity to the test. Above all, the countries of Central Europe refused to receive asylum seekers for security reasons. At the same time, the Islamic religion and the culture of the Muslim newcomers were named as reasons for not accepting refugees from Muslim-majority countries.

However, one must think of the Bosnian war refugees who fled to Western Europe in the 1990s. More than a million people escaped the war in Bosnia and Herzegovina (1992–95) and fled to, or were relocated in, the countries of Western Europe. Germany received the highest number – between 345,000 and 350,000 – and many of these refugees were Bosnian Muslims. Despite their faith, the public responses to them in the receiving countries were positive because they were seen as secular and white Europeans. Studying people of Bosnian Muslim origin in the diaspora has become popular not only in the context of forced displacement and trauma but also in the discourses on Islam and Muslims since 2001.

In this chapter, I present some of the research results of my doctoral project on identity constructions among young people of Bosnian Muslim origin in Berlin. Interviews were conducted with interlocutors with a refugee background who came to Germany as refugee children or had parents who were refugees. While researching their identity constructions, I explored, among other things, the role religion plays for these people, and their attitudes towards their religion, as well as their understanding of the term 'religion'. In this context, the question of the concepts of 'Bosnian Muslim', 'German' and 'European' also plays a role.

Bosnian Refugees and Immigrants as the Focus of Research

Bosnia and Herzegovina has a large diaspora, with up to two million people living abroad.[2] Most of them are living in the neighbouring countries and the countries of Western Europe. According to the Federal Statistical Office in Germany 415,000 people of Bosnian origin were living in that country in 2018.[3]

Some intellectuals in Bosnia and Herzegovina are of the opinion that the Bosnian diaspora developed as a consequence of the war in Bosnia and Herzegovina, as a large number of people left the country permanently. Mass emigration continued after the war. The poor economic situation and the lack of prospects for young people forced thousands to leave. According to investigations by some organizations in Bosnia and Herzegovina, the number exceeds 150,000.[4]

There were some major waves of migration from Bosnia and Herzegovina in earlier periods. After the fall of the Ottoman Empire, hundreds of thousands of Bosnian Muslims emigrated from Bosnia and Herzegovina to Turkey. From the 1960s to the 1970s, guest workers (*gastarbeiter*) came from the former Yugoslavia, including Bosnia and Herzegovina, to the Federal Republic of Germany and other European countries. Thus, a significant number of people with a Bosnian and Herzegovinian background already lived in Germany, because many of the former guest workers chose to remain there. This was one of the reasons many war refugees from Bosnia and Herzegovina came to Germany. Their relatives in Germany provided the necessary documents to enable them to enter the country. In some cases, the relatives also provided accommodation to family members who had fled from Bosnia and Herzegovina.

Since the war in Bosnia and Herzegovina, numerous researchers have addressed the situation of Bosnian refugees and immigrants. The book *The Bosnian Diaspora: Integration in Transnational Communities* (Valenta and Ramet 2011) provides the first comprehensive insight into the situation and experiences of Bosnian refugees and immigrants in countries directly neighbouring Bosnia and Herzegovina (Serbia, Croatia) as well as in various European countries, the United States, and Australia.[5] Some editors in the volume (Halilovich, Povrzanović-Frykman, Coughlan) observe that the 'Bosnian migrant communities are heterogeneous in several ways' (ibid.: 14). This heterogeneity is not only a result of the war and the ethnic division in Bosnia and Herzegovina that influenced developments in the diaspora; it exists beyond ethnicity, as the social position of Bosnian migrants within the class hierarchy in the host society can play a crucial role, as can their different backgrounds (rural vs. urban). Some of the migrants from Bosnia and Herzegovina entered the host countries from 'above' and have managed to restore their former high socioeconomic position; 'others entered the receiving country from "below" and experienced difficulties in trying to improve their position within the class hierarchy of the host society' (ibid.: 15). The anthropologist Hariz Halilovich speaks in the context of heterogeneity about translocalism among Bosnian communities in Australia. His observation on Bosnian migrants in Melbourne showed that they still feel connected to their native places and try to preserve their local traditions and features: 'Thus, while attempting to preserve their culture and identity from back home, translocal communities in reality transform the identity of the original source of a particular culture and identity they imagine they are reviving and preserving' (Halilovich 2011: 77).

Many studies on Bosnian war refugees have examined the trauma caused by forced displacement and uncertain residence status in host countries. The latter was particularly the case in Germany. After their arrival in Germany, the majority of refugees from Bosnia and Herzegovina received a temporary protection status called *Duldung*, which involved many restrictions. Usually, the refugees could not work or study. Duldung also included a residency obligation restriction (*Residenzpflicht*), meaning that refugees were not allowed to leave their places of residence. The adults received no opportunity to integrate into society. There were no German language courses for them, and many spent long periods living in refugee hostels, so there was almost no interaction with the local population. The situation was especially confusing for children, who learned the German language and went to school and were thus integrated, but suffered under the restrictions and the possibility of deportation.

With the signing of the Dayton Peace Agreement at the end of 1995, refugees from Bosnia and Herzegovina were expected to leave Germany. A readmission agreement was signed between Bosnia and Herzegovina and Germany, and came into force in January 1997. It is estimated that of the 350,000 Bosnian refugees, some 20,000 were allowed to stay in the country with the help of various regulations enacted from 2000 onwards. Thousands of refugees from Bosnia and Herzegovina took advantage of the opportunity to emigrate from Germany to the United States, Canada, Australia, and countries of Western Europe. They did not want to (or could not) return to Bosnia and Herzegovina because either their native places had become ethnically homogeneous as a result of ethnic cleansing, or they had simply lost their property in the war (see Mihok 2001; Pfohman 2012; Čemernica 2017).

Debates on Integration and Muslims in Germany

Let us look at the current migration and integration policies in Germany, especially those affecting Muslims and refugees. Today, in light of the refugee crisis of 2015, also known as the 'long summer of migration', there seems to be an overlapping of the terms 'Muslim' and 'refugee'. The media is constantly reporting on refugees with a Muslim background. The populists and xenophobic groups have benefited from the refugee crisis, and gained more popularity because of it. They are cultivating a fear of refugees and a dichotomy between them and us (local population vs refugees). The question of identity is essential for them, and within this frame some present themselves as guardians of Christianity or of European culture.

In 2000, the German government officially stated that Germany was an *Einwanderungsland* (country of immigration). It was recognized that Germany had a large number of people with a migration background who had helped to build the German economy, and that immigrants were and still are a substantial part of German society. This does not mean that they have the same access to resources as Germans, but it is an ongoing debate and process. The debate also addresses the question of how to name people with a migration background. Part of the debate is also the question of who we are as a society, and what makes us German.

In this context, the word *Leitkultur* (guiding culture) became very popular. The concept was introduced by the political scientist Bassam Tibi. He understands the term to encompass a kind of value consensus that should be valid not only for Germany but for the whole of Europe, and for everyone living within Europe. He speaks of a concept based on the achievements of Occidental Europe. It is, so to speak, a European guiding culture that would guarantee a peaceful coexistence. The concept includes individual human rights, such as freedom of faith, secular democracy, recognition of pluralism, and mutual respect.[6] In 2000, the *Leitkultur* was introduced in public debate by some politicians. It generated a lot of media attention and has been present in debates about integration ever since. It is most commonly used to state what is expected from migrants in Germany. Often, these values are put in the context of people with Muslim background, for example by stating that wearing a headscarf or burka is not part of a European culture. Thus, the concept failed in its intention to be valid for everyone in society, regardless of whether a person has a migration background or not. The dichotomy of 'them vs us' has simply been perpetuated, as has the exclusion of Others. Critical voices also say that such a concept is unnecessary, because Germany has its Basic Law (the German constitution) with basic rights.

German scholars claim that from 2000 onwards we can perceive a shift in the vocabulary used to discuss the people with a Muslim background who once came to Germany as guest workers (the majority of whom were of Turkish origin). In the 1960s and 1970s, they were called *Gastarbeiter*, as it was expected they would return to their home countries after the termination of their employment contracts. Later, they were called *Ausländer* (foreigners). Since 2001, they have simply been known as Muslims (see Spielhaus 2011; Khorchide 2014). This shows a tendency towards a homogeneous view of people of Muslim faith without taking into account their diversity or the plurality of their lifestyles. Since 2015, there seems to have been a shift in the usage of the word 'refugee', because there is often an equalization of the terms 'refugees' and 'Muslims' in public debates.

The scholar of Islamic studies Riem Spielhaus criticizes the ongoing association of 'integration' with 'Muslim background', because Muslims are presented as problematic migrants who still need to be integrated (Spielhaus 2013: 5).

She also criticizes quantitative studies and surveys, which cannot satisfactorily provide insight or an explanation for the attitudes and feelings of people with Muslim backgrounds in Germany. If somebody states that he or she is a Muslim and a religious person, there is often no explanation of what that really means. The Islamic religion is most often reduced to visible signs, such as wearing a headscarf or going to a mosque, yet there are Muslims who, despite declaring themselves to be Muslim and religious, do not in fact adhere to the rules of the religion. There can be various reasons for declaring oneself a Muslim and constructing such an identity; for example, Islam can function as a cultural and ethical component for younger people:

> These new generations distinguish between practising religion and believing religion to describe their relationship with Islam. It is a part of the cultural legacy within the private sphere, with no direct influence on their social [or] public behaviour. Especially for those who are upwardly mobile, Islam is an ethic – a source of moral values giving significance to their lives but without implication for their practice. (Cesari 1998: 31)

Exploring Views on Religion

How do people of Bosnian Muslim origin fit into all these debates on Muslims? They are in a special position because they are people of Slavic origin and Islamic faith who are, in fact, part of Europe. There are many theses regarding the question of why ancestors of present-day Bosnian Muslims converted to Islam during the Ottoman rule. The maintenance of social status, opportunities for improved social standing, and similarities between the so-called Bosnian Church and Islam are just some of the reasons given. The ongoing debate on the question of conversion also shows that the process is seen as a very unusual and unique phenomenon on European soil. Thus, the status of Bosnian Muslims is quite confusing, because they are seen as some kind of aliens or Others. The question of the religious attitudes of Bosnian Muslims and the development of their religious behaviour and national identity is, therefore, the subject of numerous research studies, many of which focus on Bosnia and Herzegovina. A deeper insight into the identity and lifestyles of people of Bosnian Muslim origin in the diaspora is currently evolving, including in Germany.

The interviews showed that the young people of Bosniak origin in Berlin hold differing views on religion. While some strictly adhere to religious rules and describe themselves as religious, others who do not follow religious doctrine still see their faith as something important to them and describe themselves as persons of faith. It must be acknowledged that there were also people for whom religion did not play a crucial role.[7]

Functions of Religion

According to the Berlin-Brandenburg office of statistics Berlin had 3,75 million inhabitants in 2019. Around 535,998 Germans with migration background and 758,550 foreigners were living in the city. Among them were 16,739 people of Bosnian and Herzegovinian origin.[8]

In the 1990s, Berlin received 29,294 Bosnian refugees (Mihok 2001: 145). Many of them had to leave Germany after the war in Bosnia ended. There are several Bosnian associations in Berlin, although the migrants from Bosnia and Herzegovina there are not as well organized as in some cities in western Germany. When it comes to the religious institutions of Bosnian Muslims, the most important and prominent one is the Islamski kulturni centar Bošnjaka u Berlinu (IKB, or Islamic Centre of Bosniaks in Berlin). It was founded in 1989 and is dedicated to work in the fields of religious education, culture, humanitarian aid, and sports. The centre also provided help to war refugees from Bosnia and Herzegovina in matters of bureaucracy and accommodation, and assisted those who had to return to Bosnia and Herzegovina as well as those who emigrated to other countries. Many of my interlocutors visited the centre as children because their parents had gone there. Today, as adults, few of them go there frequently anymore. Those who follow religious rules are the ones most connected to the centre. The young people who are active there organize and take part in discussions and conferences addressing the identities of young Muslims in Germany, and they engage in interreligious dialogues among young people of different faiths. They are also represented on social networks such as Facebook through the public group the Udruženje omladine IKB-a Berlin (Association of Youth of the IKB Berlin).

One young woman who follows religious rules said that she learned to love her religion because as a child she had visited the centre with her parents, who were refugees, and saw many good and positive things in her faith: 'I try to be a good person with the help of my religion . . . I try to follow religious rules'. Because she wears a headscarf, she has experienced some discrimination in the form of comments on the street. Nevertheless, she has managed to organize her life well. It was her dream to become a midwife, and she recently completed her training for this job. She stresses the important role of language, and thinks that her excellent knowledge of German will open many doors for her. Independent of her experiences, she is comfortable in Germany, and feels she has assimilated into the different cultures well, which she describes as something positive.

Another young woman who practises her religion and wears a headscarf says that her family was not religious when they came to Germany as refugees. She turned to religion when she was fifteen or sixteen years old. After graduating from secondary school at the age of eighteen, she decided to wear a headscarf. She says that since then 'it has been a constant fight, but in the sense of self-reflection as a religious person'. Currently, she is enrolled in Islamic studies, but she admits her mother was disappointed with her decision, as she had wanted her to study law. The young woman had a traumatic experience early in life as a refugee child. She had lived in a derelict flat and was in constant fear of being deported. Being a refugee from Bosnia and Herzegovina was something that shaped her personality. While speaking about her country of origin, she became very emotional. When she was a child, her mother, a single parent who had to work, would send her to spend summer holidays with family in Bosnia. Therefore, she feels very connected to Bosnia and to her roots.

It can be said that the young women who wear headscarves are all quite self-confident. They are confronted with discrimination because they are visibly Muslim, but they have learned to deal with it. All of them are studying or working. It must be noted that these women are also the targets of some negative comments in Bosnia and Herzegovina from their family members who do not understand why they, as young women, wear the headscarf. They constantly have to explain that they see the headscarf as a part of their religion.

Religion is also seen as something that gives strength and helps to develop self-confidence. A young man who practises religion states: 'It is a part of me. But it was my personal choice, not something that was instrumentalized. It is something that enriches me, it gives me the strength to deal with people'. Many of my interlocutors do not regularly practise Islam; nevertheless, their faith seems to be important to them; as one young woman says: 'Faith is really important to me, but I don't practise it in a big way. I try, for example, to fast. Someone who believes and who has faith upholds certain principles, such as *"Nächstenliebe"* [love thy neighbour]'.

Dealing with religion can be challenging, especially when a job is sometimes incompatible with religious beliefs. An interlocutor who is a successful actor in Germany states: 'Religion shows me borders. I try to extend the borders and look at how compatible they are with Islam, the things I do, like acting. But then I think: "God loves me, he gave me this love and passion for acting, singing and dancing. This comes from him, so it must be OK"'. The interlocutor is speaking of personal borders in relation to his religion. He is aware of his religious obligations and is in constant need of finding a compromise for himself. So, religion is seen as a moral foundation and an instruction for social behaviour. In this sense, the recognition of God's existence is crucial, but practising religious rules is not a decisive factor.

Among the interlocutors there were also some who do not see religion as a constitutive part of their everyday lives, like the following young woman. She is unmarried but lives with a German and has two children with him: 'My grandparents were religious. I know some things, but I do not follow religious practices. . . . I cannot say with 100 per cent certainty whether or not there is a God'. In the case of this woman, the Islamic religion was not a substantial part of her life, nor does it influence her life decisions. She is highly educated and has a good job. She has had different boyfriends with different cultural backgrounds, but has decided not to marry a Bosnian. She mentions that her lifestyle might look unusual, since she is a Bosnian Muslim, but her parents and even her grandparents in Bosnia have never had a problem with it. Her parents wanted her and her brother to receive a good education, and to that end they allowed them to live an independent life, and to be with whomever they wanted.

Being Bosnian Muslim – German – European?

The concepts of Bosnian/Bosniak, German and European were not explicitly posed as a question during the interviews. The question of a national or regional identity is among the more difficult ones, especially when it comes to people with a migration background. During the interviews, some of the interlocutors mentioned that Bosnian Muslims and their understanding of religion differ from those of other Muslims in Berlin. In this case, it is important to stress that the young people of Bosnian Muslim origin have encountered and established friendships with Muslims in Berlin from other countries, thus they embrace the idea of Islam in Bosnia and Herzegovina as a kind of European Islam. This relates to the idea of culture as a social practice in which religion is a part of culture. Therefore, religion is interpreted in a way that promotes ethical and moral values but does not yet stand as disconnected from a modern way of life or progress.

But how does religion relate to the concept of a national understanding? A young woman who was born in Berlin states that she tries to follow the religious rules when she can, but she does not practise religion frequently. She tries to live morally (e.g. without drinking alcohol), but she does not wear a headscarf and has not experienced discrimination.

Only her name indicates that she is not of German origin. Nevertheless, she thinks that she can never truly be German: 'I was born and grew up here in Berlin. But I would never say that I am a German'. She states that she was raised the

Bosnian way, in the sense of a Bosnian mentality. When she thinks of Germans, she thinks of people who have a German heritage and name and who, among other things, belong to the Christian faith. Thus, she confirms the common ideas within the concept of a nation or ethnicity that many people share. Even if a person receives citizenship, it does not mean that he or she feels full acceptance as a member of a group under the label of 'nation'. Thinking in terms of categories still persists.

Some of my interlocutors said that they feel like Europeans: 'I perceive my identity in three senses: European – Bosnian – Berliner'. This young man demonstrates his connection to the idea of being a European. Different categories, like religion and nation, do not play a role here anymore. Feeling Bosnian means maintaining connections to the roots. Feeling like a Berliner expresses a regional connection, a devotion to a city that has become a new home. By doing so, he avoids identification with Germany as a whole. Berlin is considered a place where a large number of people of different origins and various lifestyles reside and contribute to the certain flair and identity of the city.

Conclusion

Some preliminary results of my doctoral project have been presented in this contribution. It is important to state that the examination of the attitudes towards Islam is only one of the topics of the research. There is much more that is important to the interlocutors: family, relationships, surroundings, opportunities (standing in society), discrimination, the Bosnian War of 1992–95 and forced displacement, problems within Bosnia and Herzegovina (ethnical division), and the ways in which these factors influence their relationships in Germany. Therefore, the concept is, in a broader sense, oriented towards Steven Vertovec's theory of super-diversity:

> The experiences, opportunities, constraints and trajectories facing newcomers and the wider set of social and economic relations within the places where they reside are shaped by complex interplays. To recap, these factors include: country of origin (comprising a variety of possible subset traits such as ethnicity, language[s], religious tradition, regional and local identities, cultural values, and practices), migration channel (often related to highly gendered flows and specific social networks), legal status (determining entitlement to rights). (Vertovec 2007: 1049)

Religion still plays an important role in the identity of Bosniaks or Bosnian Muslims, because it functions as a feature through which these people are categorized and seen as a group. The war in Bosnia and Herzegovina and the genocide of Bosnian Muslims marginalized them and reduced them to their religion even more. In this context, it is necessary to look behind the common idea of religious behaviour, and to question religious views among young people of Bosnian Muslim origin, in this case in Berlin. By doing so, we can perceive different concepts towards religion among these people, and can try to understand their perception of religion.

Aldina Čemernica is a PhD candidate at the Department of Slavic and Hungarian Studies at Humboldt University in Berlin, where she previously completed both her master's degree in Central and Eastern European cultures and her bachelor's degree in South Slavonic languages and literatures and German linguistics. She is currently completing her PhD thesis entitled 'Identity Constructions among Young Adults of Bosniak Origin in Berlin'. Her research interests include migration, transnationalism, self-positioning of young people with migration backgrounds, and constructions of symbolic and social boundaries. She currently works as a research associate for a member of the Berlin House of Representatives.

Notes

1. For more, see 'Pro Asyl: Fakten, Zahlen und Argumente'.
2. The Ministry of Human Rights and Refugees in Bosnia and Herzegovina states that 1.700.000 of their people and their descendants are living abroad. See http://www.mhrr.gov.ba/iseljenistvo/aktuelnosti/Informacija%20o%20iseljenistvu%20iz%20BiH_dec%202012.pdf; last accessed 18 September 2019.
3. https://www.destatis.de/DE/Themen/Gesellschaft-Umwelt/Bevoelkerung/Migration-Integration/Tabellen/migrationshintergrund-staatsangehoerigkeit-staaten.html; last accessed 18 September 2019.
4. The number 150,000 is given by the Institute for Youth Development (KULT).
5. Valenta, Marko, and Sabrina P. Ramet (eds). 2011. *The Bosnian Diaspora: Integration in Transnational Communities*. Farnham, UK: Ashgate.
6. For more see: Bassam Tibi, 'Leitkultur als Wertekonsens'. https://www.bpb.de/apuz/26535/leitkultur-als-wertekonsens?p=all.;%20last%20accessed%2022%20August%202017; last accessed 22 August 2017.
7. The interviews were conducted in either the Bosnian or the German language. Quotations from the interviews used in this chapter were translated into English by the author.
8. See: https://www.statistik-berlin-brandenburg.de/publikationen/stat_berichte/2019/SB_A01-05-00_2019h01_BE.pdf; last accessed 12 November 2019.

References

Printed Sources

Čemernica, Aldina. 2017. 'Refugee Stories among Young People of Bosnian Muslim Origin in Berlin', in *Der Donauraum – Zeitschrift des Institutes für den Donauraum und Mitteleuropa. Jahrgang 55 – Heft 3–4/2015: *Challenges and Opportunities of Migration in and from South East Europe*. Vienna: Boehlau, pp. 137–45.

Cesari, Jocelyne. 1998. 'Islam in France: Social Challenge or Challenge of Secularism?', in Steven Vertovec and Alisdair Rogers (eds), *Muslim European Youth: Reproducing Ethnicity, Religion, Culture*. Aldershot, UK: Ashgate, pp. 25–38.

Halilovich, Hariz. 2011. '(Per)forming "Trans-local" Homes: Bosnian Diaspora in Australia', in Marko Valenta and Sabrina P. Ramet (eds), *The Bosnian Diaspora: Integration in Transnational Communities*. Farnham, UK: Ashgate, pp. 63–81.

Khorchide, Mouhanad. 2014. 'Wir und die Anderen? Identitätskonstruktionen junger Muslime in Europa', in Wael El-Gayar and Katrin Strunk (eds), *Integration versus Salafismus: Identitätsfindung muslimischer Jugendlicher in Deutschland*. Schwalbach am Taunus: Wochenschau Verlag, pp. 49–64.

Mihok, Brigitte. 2001. 'Der politische Umgang mit den bosnischen Bürgerkriegsflüchtlingen in Berlin (1991–2000)', in Frank Gesemann (ed.), *Migration und Integration in Berlin*. Opladen: Leske + Budrich, pp. 145–61.

Pfohman, Shannon Colleen. 2012. 'A Comparison of the Situation of Bosnian Refugees in Berlin and Chicago: Perceptions of the Facilitating Factors and Obstacles Affecting Their Adaptation Process'. PhD thesis, Freie Universität Berlin. https://refubium.fu-berlin.de/bitstream/handle/fub188/3562/Printversion_Pfohman2014.pdf?sequence=1.; last accessed 13 January 2017.

'Pro Asyl: Fakten, Zahlen und Argumente'. https://www.proasyl.de/thema/fakten-zahlen-argumente/; last accessed 28 June 2018.

Spielhaus, Riem. 2011. *Wer ist hier Muslim? Die Entwicklung eines islamischen Bewusstseins in Deutschland zwischen Selbstidentifikation und Fremdzuschreibung*. Würzburg: Ergon.

———. 2013. 'Muslime in der Statistik: Wer ist Muslim und wenn ja wie viele?' Ein Gutachten im Auftrag des Mediendienst Integration. Berlin, June 2013. https://mediendienst-integration.de/fileadmin/Dateien/Muslime_Spielhaus_MDI.pdf; last accessed 24 August 2017.

Valenta, Marko, and Sabrina P. Ramet (eds). 2011. *The Bosnian Diaspora: Integration in Transnational Communities*. Farnham, UK: Ashgate.

Vertovec, Steven. 2007. 'Super-diversity and its Implications', *Ethnic and Racial Studies* 30(6) (November): 1024–54.

Internet Sources

http://www.bpb.de/apuz/26535/leitkultur-als-wertekonsens?p=all.; last accessed 22 August 2017.

http://www.mhrr.gov.ba/iseljenistvo/aktuelnosti/Informacija%20o%20iseljenistvu%20iz%20BiH_dec%202012.pdf; last accessed 18 September 2019.

https://www.destatis.de/DE/Themen/Gesellschaft-Umwelt/Bevoelkerung/Migration-Integration/Tabellen/migrationshintergrund-staatsangehoerigkeit-staaten.html; last accessed 18 September 2019.

https://www.statistik-berlin-brandenburg.de/publikationen/stat_berichte/2019/SB_A01-05-00_2019h01_BE.pdf; last accessed 12 November 2019.

Tibi, Bassam. 2002. 'Leitkultur als Wertekonsens'. https://www.bpb.de/apuz/26535/leitkultur-als-wertekonsens?p=all.;%20last%20accessed%2022%20August%202017; last accessed 22 August 2017.

Chapter 13

THE WEST, THE BALKANS AND THE IN-BETWEEN
Bosnian Muslims Representing a European Islam

Merima Šehagić

From 1992 onwards, the German government admitted more than 320,000 refugees from former Yugoslavia, most of whom were from Bosnia and Herzegovina, with Berlin alone taking upwards of 30,000. This was strictly subject to the condition that these displaced people were given not conventional refugee status but so-called *Duldung* status, which emphasized the temporal nature of the protection (Dimova 2006). Up to 250,000 of these refugees returned to Bosnia and Herzegovina between 1992 and 2005, either on a voluntary basis or, in most cases, because of the repatriation plan. Those who managed to settle in Germany have had to deal with the retraumatizing consequences of Duldung status – remaining unsure whether their stay will be prolonged for another six months, for another three years, or if they will receive a permanent residence permit after more than fifteen years of uncertainty.

Part of this German contextualization is the acceptance and overall perception of the integration of Bosnian Muslims into German society, which has been relatively positive. Governmental sources indicate that Muslims from Bosnia and Herzegovina are classified as European and unproblematic because of their seeming ability to integrate well. When compared with most non-European migrant groups, migrants from Bosnia and Herzegovina are said to have experienced less discrimination and stigmatization. This group was even considered to be a white refugee elite in certain host societies. The mainstream perception of Bosnian Muslim refugees as white Europeans, and their self-perception as whites in a white country, resulted in the underemphasis of their simultaneous position as Muslims in a white country. Therefore, by analysing different intersecting processes of racialization, this paper explores and simultaneously problematizes the somewhat idealized success story of Bosnian Muslims and their integration experiences in Western countries.

The German Case

It is important to first point out that a Bosnian Muslim population existed in Germany prior to the wartime migration wave. In 1990, approximately 660,000 people from socialist Yugoslavia were living in Germany; they were primarily 'guest workers' who had arrived in the 1960s and 1970s (Dimova 2006; Valenta and Ramet 2011). This has, of course, influenced the resettlement of the new wave of refugees, as it was assumed that these existing migrants would help to ease the process for the newcomers. Another point requiring consideration is the role that these earlier migrants, together with established migrant organizations, play in developing a framework for people from South Eastern Europe living in Western countries. The guest workers who came from socialist Yugoslavia might not have been part of a unified religious group, but they originated from the same country. Therefore, the migrant networks that were established in the 1970s were not necessarily religious – they were Yugoslav (Duranović 2012: 74). This means that a non-religious framework is created into which the new wave of Muslim refugees are initially placed, and on which their first experiences in the host country, as well as the expectations and perceptions of the host country, will depend.

In terms of the individual experiences and everyday life of Bosnian Muslims, numerous scientific works originally focused on the early phases of (often temporary) resettlement that related to traumatic experiences from the conflict in Bosnia and Herzegovina, and protection regimes in receiving societies. More recent studies, conducted with the realization of the permanent character of the Bosnian refugees, shifted their focus towards integration issues, changes in social status, and, in general, the difficulties of having to leave one's home country and start over in a new environment (Valenta and Ramet 2011: 7). In a way, this is self-explanatory, as we need more time to pass in order to be able to ask the different questions that arise once a more thorough understanding of the lives of former refugees has been attained. In addition to Rozita Dimova's research on Bosnian Muslims in Berlin, and people's experiences living under Duldung status, there are government publications available specifically related to the integration of Bosnian Muslims into German society. These sources indicate that Muslims from

Bosnia and Herzegovina are classified as European and unproblematic because of their seeming ability to integrate. According to the report 'Muslimisches Leben in Deutschland' (Muslim Lives in Germany) from the Federal Office for Migration and Refugees: 'As a community, Muslims from this region seem to be integrated well. There exists a high level of contact with Germans, and an interreligious and interethnic openness' (Haug, Müssig and Stichs 2008: 303).

One could also reverse this reasoning, because studies have implied that the integration of Bosnian Muslims into Western countries has been eased mainly because of their pre-existing European background and appearance, or invisibility. For example, when compared with most non-European migrant groups, Bosnian migrants often experienced less discrimination and stigmatization (Valenta and Ramet 2011: 10). They were even considered to be a white refugee elite in certain settings (Colic-Peisker 2005: 620). As Valenta and Ramet rightly point out, in no way do these perceived advantages imply that a European background gives Bosnians and Herzegovinians a migratory experience free of stigmatization and discrimination. The experiences of migrants can be very different, depending on, for example, which host society we are talking about. This is what makes the German case even more interesting. According to the European Union Minorities and Discrimination Survey, for migrants from former Yugoslavia, the experience of overall discrimination is highest for those living in Germany (Valenta and Ramet 2011: 11), yet the representations of Bosnian Muslims in Europe under discussion are rather contradictive to the actual experiences of discrimination and racism.

What follows in the next sections is theoretical considerations about Balkanism and constructions of whiteness, which help to challenge the existing public discourse of the Bosnian case. The latter will be addressed in a specific migrant framework, and then later in this text in relation to the racialization of Islam. The aim here is not to politicize the position of Bosnian Muslims in Europe, nor to assess whether or not their integration has been a success, especially as I consider existing discourses on integration to be problematic in the first place (I will not go into that further here). A thorough elaboration of this larger framework, however, and how the good migrant – or the good Muslim – is conceptualized is required for understanding the effects of this on the everyday life of Bosnian Muslims.

Muslims in Europe

How can we better understand the positive positioning of Bosnian Muslim migrants in Europe? Can we conclude that the geographic closeness of Bosnia and Herzegovina to countries like Germany, the Netherlands and Austria is key to their easier resettlement experience or, at least, representations of their experience? The simple answer to this question is that we cannot. I would like to discuss historical representations of peoples from the Balkans, to which Bosnian Muslims belong, in order to grasp the full picture – and, moreover, because this European belonging has been far from static in the past. This picture is centred around geographical imaginations of the West, of the Balkans, and even of the Orient. In her book *Imagining the Balkans*, Maria Todorova (1997) counters the typification of the Balkans and the ascription of nationalism to Eastern culture as somewhat savage. She elaborates on how the Balkans were geographically discovered in the late eighteenth century and stereotyped as the New Orient, but without tradition and past continuities. The typification of Balkan backwardness is connected to the idea that there is some sort of readily identifiable Balkan ethnic or racial type (Fleming 2000: 1218).

In the eighteenth century, travellers to the relatively unknown region described locations across the Balkans as sites of poverty and misery. Some of the peoples from the Balkans were perceived to resemble Asians rather than Europeans. This was not based on their general appearance but on ascribed characteristics, such as extreme sensibility (Bakić-Hayden 1995: 921). After the New Orient, the nineteenth century would see the Balkans redefined to distinguish between what was called 'proper' Europe and Oriental Europe. This opened the path for peoples within the Balkans to shift the imaginations of otherness to others; for example, Yugoslavs from the former Habsburg Monarchy distinguished themselves from the peoples who lived in areas that had formerly been part of the Ottoman Empire. Eastern Orthodox peoples perceived themselves as more European, and those who had a European Muslim identity in the Balkan region were thus perceived to belong to an Oriental Europe (ibid.: 922). We can detect similarities to the present in these earlier constructions of Europeanness, and the impact they have had on claims of sameness and ascriptions of otherness. When looking at Bosnian Muslims within the context of both this chapter and their developed self-perception, or in terms of the boundary-making between them as Muslims from Europe and other Muslims of non-European origin, we cannot deny the parallel in the way this too is connected with imaginations of the Orient versus a proper Europe.

Apart from the negative typification of the Balkans, the ethnic complexity of the region was often regarded as a frustrating factor, as it was neither fully Western nor fully Oriental. The relation between the Balkans and the rest of Europe is characterized with familiarity and, at the same time, distance. This resembles the West's relation to the Orient according to Edward Said's (1978) paradoxical notion of intimate estrangement, by which the Balkans are somehow the 'outsider within' (Fleming 2000: 1220). Even though scholars would likely not have come up with the notion of Balkanism without the previous existence of Said's Orientalism, it must be noted that these are two different things (Bakić-Hayden 1995; Fleming 2000; Todorova 1997). Within the framework of this chapter, however, it is not productive to go into further detail about the discussions on both the similarities and the distinctiveness of the two concepts. What is important is the changing ways in which the location of the Balkans in relation to Western Europe has been represented through different ages. From seventeenth-century representations of the Oriental to European Turkey and later a part of Europe, the Balkans still stands as 'Europe's resident alien' (Fleming 2000: 1229).

What is interesting about these spatial imaginations is a noteworthy shift away from distanced and more negative ideas when looking specifically at Islam in Europe. As mentioned before, the Bosnian community is often portrayed as different from Muslims of non-European origin: they have the seeming ability to integrate well into Western host societies. The spatial aspect of being both close to and far from the West is employed to promote social inclusion in the present, instead of the previous othering inherent to geographical imaginations of the Balkans. Furthermore, the mainstream perception of migrants from Bosnia and Herzegovina as white Europeans, and their own self-perception as whites in a white country, impact their position as migrants in a Western country, as does their early identity (re)construction and the practical aspect of their resettlement: being white means being invisible and, therefore, protected to a certain extent from experiencing otherness (Colic-Peisker 2005: 621).

Choosing, or claiming, the European white identity can be seen as a mechanism of advantageous self-identification or self-inclusion, which helps to create distance from the refugee status, which is needy and 'other' (Colic-Peisker 2005: 624). Moreover, it creates distance from the discussed Balkan identity, which refers to an unsettled and violent periphery of Europe (Ramet 1999). It seems this in-between position enables or privileges Bosnian Muslim migrants to claim Europeanness without ever achieving full belonging. The next section of this chapter addresses this privileged position, and its implications, in greater detail.

Constructions of Whiteness

Among academics, there is a kind of fear or apprehension when studying whiteness. A fear related to a possible fixed character of whiteness that might be produced when creating spaces to speak about whiteness (Ahmed 2007: 149). What we have to acknowledge, however, is that whiteness has remained a relatively underdiscussed and underresearched racial identity within white-dominated societies, while the category of 'non-white' has frequently been subject to debate. Moreover, the effect that this relative invisibility has had is the naturalization of whiteness (Bonnett 2015: 173) – or, to put it in other words, the underemphasis on whiteness is precisely what contributes to its fixed and unquestioned character. The perception of whiteness as static, ahistorical and aspatial also leads to the positioning of white (not merely in the putative sense) people as fundamentally outside the debates on racial identity politics (ibid.: 177). There are some distinct moral attributes of 'being white' that are removed from a social context and do not take history or geography into consideration. An example of one of these is being racist but not experiencing racism (ibid.: 180). This is especially interesting in the framework of this chapter. The attempts to destabilize the dichotomous and overgeneralizing positions of white vis-à-vis black have been partial because they attack certain mythologies of blackness yet leave whiteness undiscussed (ibid.: 179). Sara Ahmed (2007) offers us an insightful and promising take on the issue:

> We could say that any project that aims to dismantle or challenge the categories that are made invisible through privilege is bound to participate in the object of its critique. We might even expect such projects to fail, and may be prepared to then witness such failure as productive. And yet we can get stuck in this position, endlessly caught up in describing what we are doing to whiteness, rather than what whiteness is doing. (Ahmed 2007: 150)

What we do need, however, is 'a reconceptualization of whiteness as a diverse and mutable social construction' and an anti-essentialist perspective on white identity (Bonnett 2015: 186). Now that we have established an understanding of what it is not, or at least is no longer considered to be, let us start by defining what whiteness is. As Sara Ahmed (2007: 150) writes: 'Whiteness could be described as an ongoing and unfinished history, which orientates bodies in specific directions, affecting how they "take up" space. It is an effect of racialization, which in turn shapes what it is that bodies "can do"'.

Within the context of this chapter, whiteness is explored in relation to migration and the transition from being at home to becoming an outsider in a new host society; therefore, it is crucial we look at how intersections of categories of difference are shaped by temporal and spatial dimensions. This means that we recognize the transnational character of migrants and, thereby, understand that they hold different changeable positions within different places at the same time (Samaluk 2012: 373). What I want to point out here is the discourse of a racialized Europeanness, which was perceived to be increasingly synonymous to whiteness in the twentieth century, that travels across borders (Bonnett 2015: 176). For example, Barbara Samaluk's research on white privilege and disadvantage among migrants from Central and Eastern Europe illustrates how Europeanness can be utilized as a means to an imagined sameness, which in turn can affect self-positionality towards other minority groups. It is the process of migration that has made these questions of whiteness and Europeanness relevant.

Jon E. Fox's research on Hungarians and Romanians and their experiences of racism in the UK provides us with a similar scenario. The study shows how claims to whiteness help to define and defend East Europeans' position in a pre-existing and dominant racialized discourse. Through these claims, they are not only racializing themselves – the position also enables them to racialize others (Fox 2013: 1972). The study shows that whenever faced with direct challenges to their position as white members of society, Hungarians and Romanians explicitly claimed their whiteness (ibid.: 1876). We must consider that East Europeans are not yet part of the dominant society mainly because they are concentrated in the low-end sector of the economy. Therefore, reproducing a racialized discourse enables them to claim, at least symbolically, a sense of belonging to the dominant category of whiteness (ibid.: 1880). According to Fox, this is what racism does, it 'darkens others and whitens the self; if this does not actually improve the standing of East Europeans, it improves their perception of their standing' (ibid.: 1881).

Just as was explained in the previous sections on the Bosnian experience, putative whiteness and a closer (self-)positioning towards a European belonging does not imply being excluded from experiencing stigmatization or, in this case, racism. Whiteness merely eases the process of resettlement, especially in relation to those other 'less white' migrants, but it does not rule out racism (Fox 2013: 1872). Here, racism is understood as 'not a static disposition that resides in the individual, universally deployable across all situations; rather it is a dynamic and contingent social practice, a discursive strategy, an interpretative frame, a way of seeing and doing that is judiciously used for specific purposes' (ibid.: 1874). There is a resemblance in the positioning of Bosnian Muslims in relation to other Muslims of non-European origin. Claims to Europeanness, or whiteness, have placed not only Bosnian Muslims in dominant hierarchies but also those who are more distant from a European belonging. The main difference, however, between these studies on East Europeans vis-à-vis Bosnian Muslims is an important and yet undiscussed dimension in the framework of whiteness: religion, and more specifically, Islam. Can we speak of a racialized discourse when discussing the position of Muslims in Europe? The next section will clarify how and why this is indeed possible. It will also complete the complex scheme of intersections that Bosnian Muslims are part of: claiming Europeanness, similar to East Europeans, whilst simultaneously belonging to constructions of the Other within the frameworks of Islam in Europe, as well as those of Balkanism.

Racialization of Islam

Let me begin by sketching a picture of European representations in relation to the place Muslims are given, or permitted, within the discourse of European identity. According to Talal Asad, 'Europe is ideologically constructed in such a way that Muslim migrants cannot be satisfactorily represented in it' (Asad 2003: 159). What exactly does he imply with this, especially in the case of Bosnian Muslims, who were part of Europe even prior to the wartime migration wave? In the section about Balkanism, I have already addressed ascriptions of backwardness and tradition to that which is considered non-European in a conceptual sense. This line of thought simultaneously connects countering ascriptions of civilization and modernity to a proper Europe. As Asad explains, it is not merely these ascriptions and the legal rights and obligations that come with them that we look at when discussing the idea of a European identity. The discourse of European identity is connected to notions of inclusion and exclusion, where those who are included experience anxieties about those (i.e. the non-Europeans) who are excluded (ibid.: 161). And it is within this discourse that a representation of Europe, a narrative, is constructed in which Islam is excluded (ibid.: 165).

I will clarify this exclusion with an example that Asad uses about the position of Bosnian Muslims in Europe. He presents a fragment of an interview from 1995 with Tadeusz Mazowiecki, a former UN Special Rapporteur for the Commission on Human Rights in former Yugoslavia. Mazowiecki states that Bosnian Muslims are not a danger to Europe and that 'it bodes ill for us if, at the end of the twentieth century, Europe is still incapable of coexistence with a Muslim community'. Asad unravels the assumption of this statement: 'Bosnian Muslims may be in Europe but are not of it' (Asad 2003: 164). Even though these Muslims might not seem to fit within constructions of otherness of non-Europeans (Bosnian Muslims did not migrate to Europe and are not racially distinguishable from other white Europeans), they are still excluded from claims to Europeanness. As Asad concludes, this is because of the argument introduced earlier: 'Muslims are external to the essence of Europe' and cannot, therefore, be satisfactorily represented in it (ibid.: 165). It is interesting to connect these conceptualizations of European identity to the experiences of Bosnian Muslims in European host societies. As we have seen, there is a great need among the Bosnian Muslim diaspora community to (over)emphasize their Europeanness in Western host societies, with ideological constructions of European values at the centre. Apparently, there is a need to legitimize their place in Europe. Moreover, for Bosnian Muslims to be included or to establish a sense of European belonging, a Europeanization of the Islamic world is perceived to be necessary and desirable. The underlying belief is that these Muslim migrants need to assimilate into Europe's civilization (ibid.: 170).

There is, of course, a significant difference between being excluded from European representations on the one hand, and processes of racialization on the other. How these two intersect has to do with the ways Muslims are represented in Europe, however essentialist and unsatisfactory this may be. According to David Tyrer and Salman Sayyid, 'as seemingly non-racial, Muslims are represented as haunting, incorporeal, and incomplete subjects' (Tyrer and Sayyid 2012: 353). Owing to an assumed lack of shared symbolic grounds between Muslims and European host societies, the presence of Muslims is frequently represented as an awkward one that endangers the cohesive structure of the nation (ibid.: 354). The reason the identities of Muslims are problematized is that the emergence of a Muslim subject in a European context is deemed problematic, irrespective of an actual Muslim presence in society. The Muslim subject interrupts existing racialized governmentalities within a Western postcolonial racialized discourse, which in turn complicates the possibilities for population management (ibid.: 356). It is precisely because Muslims are deemed non-racial that the exercise of racialized governmentalities concerning Muslims is made impossible. Therefore, because Muslims are framed as unrecognizable, incompletely racial, and radically different, their 'excessive alterity needs to be properly racialized in order for us to have the correct knowledge frame and governmental techniques to deal with it' (ibid.: 359). This process of the racialization of Islam has been perfectly summed up by Tyrer and Sayyid as 'the paradox of a human population paradoxically racialized as being incompletely racialized' (ibid.: 364).

The idea exists that Islamophobia cannot be considered a form of racism, mainly because Muslims are perceived as non-racial (Tyrer and Sayyid 2012: 354). But we must not forget that the category of race was co-constituted with religion. For example, when we look at the relation of the race concept to religion in fifteenth- and sixteenth-century Spain, we can conclude that the making and shaping of race is grounded in the racialization of religious subjects (Meer 2013: 389). Even though the biological racism of the nineteenth century has taken up the dominant discourse of race and racism, we can conclude that it is more of an exception to Europe's oldest racisms – antisemitism and Islamophobia – which are actually culturalist (Modood 2015: 155). At the core of biological racism, we find the unequal treatment of people based on their physical appearance or other ascribed physical differences. Cultural racism builds further on this discourse and is based on the unequal treatment of those who differ culturally from the dominant society. Furthermore, according to Tariq Modood (ibid.), cultural racism implies a demand for the cultural assimilation from groups who also suffer from biological racism. I would like to add that within the scope of this chapter and the research project that is connected to it, I do not merely ascribe this dimension of cultural racism to those who also suffer from biological racism. This would significantly exclude the experiences of white Muslims, who do conform to a 'European' physical appearance. By acknowledging processes of racialization and the possible racist treatment of (putative) white Muslims in Europe, this chapter has aimed to contribute to academic debates on the racialization of Islam, while problematizing the naturalization of whiteness that seems to be (re)produced throughout these same debates.

To conclude, I would like to introduce an interesting study by Leon Moosavi on white converts to Islam, which connects the complex relationship between Muslims in Europe and the racialization of Islam, while at the same time deconstructing whiteness. There is a tendency to perceive whiteness and Islam as incompatible (Moosavi 2015: 1918), most probably because racism is usually connected to how non-white people experience being excluded members of society. Moosavi's research, however, shows us how whiteness can also be confiscated, and how throughout this process one's privileged position can thus be transformed. He calls this the re-racialization of white converts to Islam, because they are no longer considered to be white within a racial discourse where Muslims in a British context are perceived to be non-white (ibid.: 1922). It is the fluidity of race as a constructed concept based on the categorizing of bodies that makes such a process possible (ibid.: 1923). As Moosavi points out, an important aspect of re-racialization is that white converts are never completely re-racialized. They are still considered to be white to a certain extent, and therefore maintain privilege to a certain extent, but their whiteness becomes a polluted whiteness upon conversion (ibid.). Processes of re-racialization and the concept of a polluted whiteness are especially interesting in relation to the experiences of Bosnian Muslims in Germany, because they too are affected by the intersections of whiteness, or Europeanness, and the racialization of Islam.

This chapter has explored the different theoretical discourses that need to be connected in order to properly serve the case of Bosnia and Herzegovina. Following Sara Ahmed's lead, the questions that we should now be asking are: What is whiteness doing? What is Europeanness doing? What is the racialization of Islam doing? And what can we learn from the Bosnian Muslim case when researching processes of racialization?

Merima Šehagić is a doctoral fellow affiliated with the Berlin Graduate School of Muslim Cultures and Societies, where she studies the everyday experiences of Bosniaks in Berlin in relation to their complex positioning as white European and Muslim migrants within the framework of Islam in Europe. She completed a BA degree in cultural anthropology and development studies at Radboud University Nijmegen in 2013. She continued in the field of social and cultural anthropology for her MA studies at the University of Amsterdam, during which she conducted ethnographic fieldwork on the reconstruction of self of Bosnian Muslim women in Sarajevo who had survived wartime sexual violence.

References

Ahmed, Sara. 2007. 'A Phenomenology of Whiteness', *Feminist Theory* 8(2): 149–68.
Asad, Talal. 2003. *Formations of the Secular: Christianity, Islam, Modernity*. Stanford, CA: Stanford University Press.
Bakić-Hayden, Milica. 1995. 'Nesting Orientalisms: The Case of Former Yugoslavia', *Slavic Review* 54(4): 917–31.
Bonnett, Alastair. 2015. 'Constructions of Whiteness in European and American Anti-racism', in Pnina Werbner and Tariq Modood (eds), *Debating Cultural Hybridity: Multicultural Identities and the Politics of Anti-Racism*. London: Zed Books, pp. 173–192.
Colic-Peisker, Val. 2005. '"At Least You're the Right Colour": Identity and Social Inclusion of Bosnian Refugees in Australia', *Journal of Ethnic and Migration Studies* 31(4): 615–38.

Dimova, Rozita. 2006. 'From Protection to Ordeal: Duldung Status and Bosnians in Berlin' (working paper no. 87). Retrieved from Max Planck Institute for Social Anthropology. https://www.eth.mpg.de/pubs/wps/pdf/mpi-eth-working-paper-0087; last accessed 1 May 2020.

Duranović, Amir. 2012. 'Das religiöse Leben der "Gastarbeiter" aus Bosnien-Herzegovina in Deutschland in den 1970er und 1980er Jahren', *Südosteuropäische Hefte* 3(1): 67–77.

Fleming, Katherine. 2000. 'Orientalism, the Balkans, and Balkan Historiography', *The American Historical Review* 105(4): 1218–33.

Fox, John. 2013. 'The Uses of Racism: Whitewashing New Europeans in the UK', *Ethnic and Racial Studies* 36(11): 1871–89.

Haug, Sonja, Stephanie Müssig, and Anja Stichs. 2008. 'Muslimisches Leben in Deutschland' (Report No. 8). Retrieved from Deutsche Islam Konferenz. http://www.deutsche-islam-konferenz.de/SharedDocs/Anlagen/DIK/DE/Downloads/WissenschaftPublikationen/MLD-Vollversion.pdf?__blob=publicationFile; last accessed 1 May 2020.

Meer, Nasser. 2013. 'Racialization and Religion: Race, Culture and Difference in the Study of Antisemitism and Islamophobia', *Ethnic and Racial Studies* 36(3): 385–98.

Modood, Tariq. 2015. '"Difference", Cultural Racism and Anti-Racism', in Pnina Werbner and Tariq Modood (eds), *Debating Cultural Hybridity: Multicultural Identities and the Politics of Anti-Racism*. London: Zed Books, pp. 154–172.

Moosavi, Leon. 2015. 'White Privilege in the Lives of Muslim Converts in Britain', *Ethnic and Racial Studies* 38(11): 1918–33.

Ramet, Sabrina P. 1999. *Balkan Babel: The Disintegration of Yugoslavia from the Death of Tito to the War for Kosovo*. Boulder, CO: Westview Press.

Said, Edward. 1978. *Orientalism*. New York: Pantheon Books.

Samaluk, Barbara. 2012. 'Whiteness, Ethnic Privilege and Migration: A Bourdieuian Framework', *Journal of Managerial Psychology* 29(4): 370–388.

Todorova, Maria. 1997. *Imagining the Balkans*. Oxford: Oxford University Press.

Tyrer, David, and Salman Sayyid. 2012. 'Governing Ghosts: Race, Incorporeality and Difference in Post-Political Times', *Current Sociology* 60(3): 353–67.

Valenta, Marko, and Sabrina P. Ramet. 2011. 'Bosnian Migrants: An Introduction', in Marko Valenta and Sabrina Ramet (eds), *The Bosnian Diaspora: Integration in Transnational Communities*. Farnham, UK: Ashgate, pp. 1–24.

Conclusion

František Šístek

Three decades have passed since the demise of the League of Communists of Yugoslavia at its last 14th Congress held in Belgrade in January 1990. This event marked the beginning of the process of the violent break-up of the Yugoslav federation. According to the Dayton Peace Accords signed in December 1995 after three and a half years of war in that post-Yugoslav republic, which had declared its independence following a referendum in 1992, Bosnia and Herzegovina has essentially been run as an international protectorate. For a quarter of a century, the international community has been officially represented by the High Representative for Bosnia and Herzegovina, whose main task is to oversee the implementation of the Dayton Peace Agreement. Since 2009, the office of the High Representative for Bosnia and Herzegovina has been occupied by Valentin Inzko, an Austrian politician of Slovene origin. In fact, since 1995, most holders of this office have come from the countries of Central Europe. Wolfgang Petritsch, another Austrian politician with Slovene roots, served as High Representative from 1999 to 2002. The Austrian-born German politician Christian Schwarz-Schilling was High Representative in 2006 and 2007, and he was succeeded by Slovak diplomat and politician Miroslav Lajčák, who served until 2009. The longest-serving administrator of the Austro-Hungarian dominion of Bosnia and Herzegovina, Benjámin Kállay, ruled the occupied provinces for twenty-one years (1882–1903). It is at times tempting to make parallels between Habsburg and post-Dayton Bosnia and Herzegovina; however, as has been indicated especially in the chapters of this book based primarily on material from the post-communist period and the present, migration of Bosnian Muslims to the countries of Central Europe – accelerated by the war in the 1990s, which drove over two million Bosnians and Herzegovinians from their homes (more than half of them Bosniaks) – has proven to be a very important factor for the recent developments and transformations of mutual links, representations and transfers between the Bosnian Muslims and Central Europe. In January 2020, the 35-year-old lawyer Alma Zadić, representing the Green Party in the coalition government led by chancellor Sebastian Kurz of the Austrian People's Party, became the first Austrian minister not to be born in Austria, and also the youngest ever justice minister of Austria. Zadić, who is of Bosnian Muslim background, was born in the city of Tuzla and managed to escape to Austria with her family as a schoolchild during the war in her native land in the first half of the 1990s. The Central European perspective grounded in the notion of the postimperial legacy of the Habsburg Empire is obviously of limited practical use in this case, which should rather be interpreted in the wider context of migration and integration. In other countries beyond Central Europe with relatively sizeable populations of people of Bosnian and Herzegovinian origin and their descendants, other women of Bosnian Muslim origin with personal refugee experience have also entered national politics, notably: Alma Hadžialić, Sweden's minister of education from 2014 to 2016; Anesa Kajtazović, a member of the Iowa House of Representatives and first Bosnian American elected to public office in the United States; and Arminka Helić (Baroness Helic of Millbank), a member of the British House of Lords since 2014.

The complex realities of post-Dayton Bosnia and Herzegovina are, of course, very different from the challenges faced by the Austro-Hungarian administration during the four decades of Habsburg rule (1878–1918). The multiple links between Bosnia and Herzegovina (and Bosnian Muslims in particular) and Central Europe have a rich and fascinating history, as documented by many chapters of this book. But their contemporary phase is also very vibrant, regardless of whether we attempt to frame its particular aspects as continuities and transformations of a postimperial and postcolonial legacy, or to take a completely different approach. Nevertheless, we can certainly agree with Xavier Bougarel's conviction that taking into account the longue durée perspective from Habsburg times until the present is indeed necessary in order to fully understand the current situation of the Bosnian Muslims (Bosniaks). In particular, Bougarel believes that 'the positioning of the Bosniak political and religious elites vis-à-vis the international players currently present in Bosnia-Herzegovina can also be explained by certain expectations and political strategies that appeared in the Austro-Hungarian context and were used throughout the twentieth century with greater or lesser degrees of success' (Bougarel 2018: 2). The remarkable continuity and specific character of the Islamic Community of Bosnia and Herzegovina, as outlined in this volume by Zora Hesová, provides another telling example of a topic whose analysis must inevitably consider the longue durée perspective. The historical legacy of Habsburg rule in Bosnia and Herzegovina is also being reassessed and instrumentalized by the Central European countries in their foreign policies and economic and cultural diplomacy. Piro Rexhepi has recently argued that the 'resurgence and reconceptualization of the Habsburg Empire as a "successful" multicultural empire... converges with Austria's newfound post-Cold War role in promoting EU multiculturalism and integration in Bosnia–Herzegovina' (Rexhepi 2019: 479). Suitable portions of the Habsburg legacy in Bosnia and Herzegovina are also frequently appropriated, reinterpreted primarily as bilateral ties between particular nations (e.g. Czech contributions to the cultural development of the South Slavs) and instrumentalized according to particular present-day needs by other successor states of the Habsburg Monarchy (see Hladký et al. 2019).

The history of Austro-Hungarian rule over Bosnia and Herzegovina, which has played a formative role for the development of links and exchanges between the Bosnian Muslims and Central Europe, as has been ascertained numerous times by different authors of this volume, has in fact only begun to emerge in all its complexity in recent years. Despite the existence of a relatively extensive scholarly literature dealing with various aspects of the Habsburg 'civilizing mission', there is still an urgent need for deeper and truly comparative research of different linguistic, national and social milieux in order to grasp both the multiple shared and mutually exclusive viewpoints, ideas, representations, policies, stereotypes and scholarly approaches across Central Europe. Only then can we arrive at a more complex picture that more adequately reflects the multinational character of the Habsburg Empire and the history of what, in the opinion of many, amounted to the monarchy's only colonial experiment in the Balkans. During our discussions in the research phase of this project, for example, we realized that there is still no comparative survey of reactions and attitudes towards such a key and seemingly 'over-researched' event as the occupation of Bosnia and Herzegovina in 1878, as they were expressed in different national milieux and language sources of the Habsburg Monarchy. The existing studies dealing with the reception and representation of the occupation are usually restricted to one particular national environment. The same goes for the actual military campaign of 1878 and the often-violent establishment of order by the Austro-Hungarian army in the aftermath of the occupation.

The authors of this book have generally subscribed to the idea, presented in the chapter by Clemens Ruthner, that Bosnia and Herzegovina amounted to a Habsburg colony, if not in name then at least in practice. This enables the application of postcolonial perspectives for the postimperial period of the last century, which might hopefully shed new light on the history of Bosnia and Herzegovina in the short twentieth century, and on some of its present problems. We are fully aware that the concept of Bosnia and Herzegovina as a colony continues to be contested, regardless of the fact that it has been gaining popularity in recent scholarly literature, not just in English but also in German and other Central European languages.

Many topics insufficiently discussed in the present volume for reasons of space invite further research. As was noted in the Introduction, most researchers from Central Europe who have been analysing diverse aspects of the history and present of Bosnia and Herzegovina and its Muslims have focused either on the period of Habsburg rule or on the post-Yugoslav period and beyond. Relatively little attention has been paid to the exchanges and transfers between Bosnia and Herzegovina and Central Europe, or to Central European representations of Bosnian Muslims in the Cold War period. In this volume, certain aspects relating to the postwar decades of the twentieth century are partly covered in the chapters by Bojan Baskar, Alenka Bartulović and Zora Hesová. However, there is an obvious gap in scholarly literature on the topic of representations of Bosnia and Herzegovina and Bosnian Muslims in different countries of Central Europe. The socialist period in Yugoslavia was, among other things, marked by a significant boom in the tourist industry. The number of tourists visiting Yugoslavia from both sides of the proverbial Iron Curtain, which divided Europe from the late 1940s until the fall of the socialist regimes in 1989, was steadily on the rise during the postwar decades. Cities and towns such as Sarajevo, Mostar and Jajce, and many attractive historical sights and natural wonders within the Socialist Republic of Bosnia and Herzegovina, became regular tourist destinations. If conducted from a comparative perspective encompassing the different countries of Central Europe and their diverse language sources, research of travelogues, articles from the daily press, and other sources from the socialist period (including materials intended for tourists) would probably reveal a greater richness and diversity of perspectives than some might expect.

The metaphorical descriptions of socialism in Central, Eastern, and South Eastern Europe as a sort of 'fridge' or 'lid', which were especially popular in the literature on the region of the 1990s, essentially conceptualize the several decades of postwar development and modernization (flawed and enforced as it often was) in a reductive way as a static period void of internal dynamics. As citizens of a socialist federation, the Bosnian Muslims were recognized as an independent and equal South Slavic nation at the turn of the 1960s and 1970s. The specific geopolitical position of Yugoslavia between the two Cold War blocs also had an impact on the Bosnian Muslims: 'The Islamic Community of Bosnia–Herzegovina was frequently deployed to service Yugoslav ambitions in building nonaligned socialism in the Middle East and North Africa, in particular' (Rexhepi 2019: 485). In comparison with scholarly literature that, in one way or another, deals with the effects of modernization on Bosnian Muslims and Bosnia and Herzegovina under the four decades of Habsburg rule and its representations, we know relatively little from Central European sources about the representations of Bosnian Muslims, their changing identity, lifestyle or position in Yugoslav socialist society in the four Cold War decades. A more intensive examination of the images of

Bosnia and Herzegovina and Bosnian Muslims in Central Europe from the late 1940s until the end of the 1980s could also enable us to reconstruct the continuities and discontinuities in the development of older stereotypes of the Balkans, Muslims and Islam. In general, we seem to know incomparably more about Orientalist, anti-Muslim, and Balkanist images and stereotypes from the decades preceding the First World War than about similar stereotypical representations from the post-Second World War decades, which are closer to our time. Limited attention has also been paid to the place of Bosnia and Herzegovina in Central European cultures and memory in the postwar decades: the Bosnian-born Yugoslav writer Ivo Andrić winning the Nobel Prize for literature in 1961; the impact of translations of works by modern Bosnian authors such as Meša Selimović as well as earlier works by Andrić; and continuing interest in the Sarajevo Assassination of 1914 are just some of the topics worthy of further enquiry. Moving on to the post-Yugoslav period, reactions to the war in Bosnia and Herzegovina and its reflections in various sources across Central Europe as well as representations of Bosnian Muslims in the region after the 11 September attacks of 2001, which are often marked by fears of terrorism and Islamophobia, are still waiting to be thoroughly explored and evaluated.

Historian Diana Reynolds Cordileone summarized the transformation of discourse about the Bosnian Muslims during the Habsburg era as 'taming the Bosnian warrior', a process that 'involved a slow transformation of the image of a fierce enemy in 1878 into a picturesque and steadfast defender of the dual monarchy in the beginning of the Great War' (Cordileone 2010: 169). Other variations on the theme of Bosnian Muslims as 'our', 'good' Muslims (Gingrich 1998) discussed in this book include the transformation of the mutually hostile and distrustful 'Turks' and 'Schwabos' into 'Slavic brothers', detected in Czech sources from the period of Habsburg rule (Ljuca 2006, quoted in the chapter by František Šístek), the image of the tolerant Bosnian version of Islam as a possible model for the whole of Europe analysed here by Zora Hesová, and the contemporary conceptualizations of Bosnian Muslims as 'good' migrants able to integrate well into European societies, as outlined in the last chapter of this volume by Merima Šehagić. However, it would be too optimistic to believe that such images of the Bosnian Muslims have been dominant in contemporary Central Europe. These largely positive representations (if we forget for a moment their somewhat paternalistic overtones) clearly coexist side by side with significantly darker, simplified images of a dangerous, threatening figure of a Muslim in present-day Central European discourses. Even 'our' Bosnian Muslims are frequently constructed with a stress on the 'adversarial aspects of the relationship with the Other' (Karim and Eid 2014: 218), simply because they, too, are Muslims. It has often been pointed out that Muslims in general tend to be seriously misrepresented in the West as a uniform and essentially alien community automatically linked with actual violence or its looming possibility. The monolithic vision of Muslims as 'potential terrorists' representing a permanent 'security threat', expressed in Central Europe not only by anonymous commentators on the internet but also by many politicians, journalists and opinion makers, can hardly be understood as a direct and uninterrupted continuation of ancient negative images of Muslims from the time of the Ottoman–Habsburg wars. Under scrutiny, these stereotypical representations usually reveal themselves as regional and national variations of a wider Western or global Islamophobic discourse. Nonetheless, such images and their simplistic logic sometimes curiously resemble the black-and-white representations of the cruel and evil hereditary enemy of Christendom, the 'unspeakable' Turk from the early modern age, analysed in the very first part of this book.

František Šístek is a research fellow at the Institute of History, Czech Academy of Sciences, and an associate professor at the Institute of International Studies, Faculty of Social Sciences, Charles University in Prague. He graduated in history from Central European University in Budapest and earned his PhD in social and cultural anthropology at the Faculty of Humanities, Charles University, Prague. He has focused on former Yugoslavia and representations of the South Slavs and the Balkans in Central Europe, national identities, images and stereotypes of the Other, and competing interpretations of the past in South Eastern Europe. His monographs include *Narativi o identitetu: izabrane studije o crnogorskoj istoriji* [Narratives of identity: Selected studies in Montenegrin history] (Podgorica: Matica crnogorska, 2015) and *Dějiny Černé Hory* [A history of Montenegro] (Prague: NLN, 2017).

References

Bougarel, Xavier. 2018. *Islam and Nationhood in Bosnia-Herzegovina: Surviving Empires*. London: Bloomsbury.

Cordileone, Diana Reynolds. 2010. 'Swords into Souvenirs: Bosnian Arts and Crafts under Habsburg Administration', in Reinhard Johler, Christian Marchetti and Monique Scheer (eds), *Doing Anthropology in Wartime and War Zones: World War I and the Cultural Sciences in Europe*. Bielefeld: Transcript Verlag, pp. 169–89.

Gingrich, Andre. 1998. 'Frontier Myths of Orientalism: The Muslim World in Public and Popular Cultures of Central Europe', in Bojan Baskar and Borut Brumen (eds), *Mediterranean Ethnological Summer School*. Piran: Institut za multikulturne raziskave, pp. 99–127.

Hladký, Ladislav, et al. 2019. *Czech Relations with the Nations and Countries of Southeastern Europe*. Zagreb: Srednja Europa.

Karim, H. Karim, and Mahmoud Eid. 2014. 'Re-Imagining the Other', in Mahmoud Eid and Karim H. Karim (eds), *Re-Imagining the Other: Culture, Media, and Western–Muslim Intersections*. New York: Palgrave Macmillan, pp. 217–31.

Ljuca, Adin. 2006. 'Turci a Švábové, nebo slovanští bratři? Český pohled na bosenské muslimy v letech 1878–1918', in Mirjam Moravcová, David Svoboda and František Šístek (eds), *Pravda, láska a ti na 'Východě': Obrazy středoevropského a východoevropského prostoru z pohledu české společnosti*. Prague: Fakulta humanitních studií Univerzity Karlovy, pp. 122–34.

Rexhepi, Piro. 2019. 'Imperial Inventories, "Illegal Mosques", and Institutionalized Islam: Coloniality and the Islamic Community of Bosnia and Herzegovina', *History and Anthropology* 30(4): 477–89.

INDEX

A
Adler, Alfred, 159–60
Adriatic coast, 44, 47
Al Andalus, 21, 162, 165
Albanians, 2, 22, 43–45, 179
Algeria, 118
Anatolia, 44, 142
Andrássy, Gyula (Julius), 52, 63–65, 77
Andrejka, Jernej de, 52
Andrić, Ivo, 145, 210n, 240
annexation of Bosnia and Herzegovina (1908), 52, 80, 107, 111–12, 132, 141
antemurale christianitatis (bulwark of Christendom), 28–41
anti-Islamic discourse, 94, 126, 240
anti-Ottoman struggles in the Balkans, 122
anti-Ottoman war of 1876–78, 124. *See also* Russo–Ottoman War (1877–78)
Arabs, 36
Asia, 124, 142, 228
Auersperg, Rudolf, 64
Austria
    Anschluss (1938), 157
    defence against Ottomans, 29, 34
    expansion into South Eastern Europe, 64
    hereditary lands, 30
    parliament (*Reichsrat*), 64, 126, 130
    Republic of, 6–8, 16, 24, 37–38
Austria-Hungary, 63–144
    break-up (1918), 141, 149
    imperialism, 82, 149
    Joint Ministry of Finance, 93
    media, 68 (*see also* Habsburg Empire)
    rule in Bosnia and Herzegovina (*see under* Habsburg, rule in Bosnia and Herzegovina (1878–1918))
Austronostalgia, 159–61
Austro-Slavism, 125
Azapagić, Mehmed Teufik, 109

B
Baden, Ludwig von, 34
Balkan peninsula, 2, 9, 28, 184
Balkan Wars (1912–3), 100
Balkanism, 146, 172, 201, 227, 231, 240
Balkans, 4, 7, 13, 15, 19, 24, 34, 36, 44–45, 59n, 63–64, 77, 79, 110, 122–24, 134, 136, 142, 162, 172, 174, 198, 200–1, 221, 229, 240
Ban Kulin, 55
Banja Luka, 46, 159
Bašagić, Safvet beg, 54
Beck-Rzikowsky, Friedrich von, General, 67
begs, 96–97, 101n
Belgium, 123
Belgrade, 43, 55, 152, 236
Berlin, 23, 157, 160, 182, 214–26
Bethlen, Gábor, 33
Bićanić, Rudolf, 158
Bihać, viii
Bijeljina, 96
Bismarck, Otto von, 63
Bocskai, István, 33
Bogomils, 96, 99–101n, 135, 151, 162
Bohemia, 28–41, 121–44, 146

Bohemian Crown Lands (Bohemia, Moravia, Silesia), 12, 16, 28–41, 125, 128, 130
Bosna, river, 67, 128
Bosnia, vii, 9, 43, 44–45, 70–71, 123, 137, 139–40, 148
Bosnia and Herzegovina, 1–24, 42–242
   church (medieval), 135
   Condominium of, 18, 53
   diaspora, 194–242
   economic exploitation, 79, 84, 86n
   identity, 10, 48, 54, 84, 151, 152
   language, 45, 54, 59n, 114
   mentality, 222
   nation, 53, 56, 92
   Ottoman conquest, 43, 135
   postwar/post-Dayton (after 1995), 5, 194, 205, 236–37
   provincial diet, 83
   provincial government, 53, 93, 111, 114
   refugees, 23, 194–210, 214–37
   society, 67, 79
   war (1992–1995), 1, 21, 23, 180–81, 194, 200, 207, 214, 222, 225–26, 236
Bosniaks, 8, 45, 48, 50–51, 57, 68, 97, 104, 127, 179, 181, 194–210, 214–23
Bosnian Muslims, 1–24, 30, 38, 42–242
   identity, 121, 134, 141, 214–34
   images and stereotypes, 63–75, 92–103, 121–44
Bosnians, 43, 45, 84, 127, 142
   diaspora community in Slovenia, 194–213
Bošnjak, 54, 100
Bratislava, 31
Brno, 137
Brod (Bosanski), 54
(br)other, 14, 141, 208
brotherhood and unity (Yugoslav socialist ideal), 196, 208
Bruner Dvořák, Rudolf, vii–viii
Bruner Dvořák, Jaroslav, viii
Buda, 30
Budapest, 83, 111
Budin Eyalet, 30
Budovec, Václav of Budov, 32, 35
Bulgaria, 22, 47, 174
Bulgarians, 37

Burián, István, 112
Byzantium. *See under* Constantinople

C

Caliphate, 108–9, 112
Calvinoturcism, 33–34
Canetti, Elias, 161
Carinthia, 37
Carniola, 37
Catholics (Roman)
   Bohemia and Moravia, 31–32, 36
   Bosnia and Herzegovina, 9–10, 15, 18, 42–62, 66–67, 79, 84, 97, 107, 111, 131–33, 135, 158, 202
   Slovenia, 197 (*see also* Croats)
Čaušević, Mehmed Džemaludin, 57, 112–13, 115
Cazin, vii–viii
Central Europe, vii, 1–24, 28–30, 33, 37–38, 65, 71, 81, 126, 133–34, 146, 149, 185, 214, 236–37, 239
Čermák, Jaroslav, 123, 136
Charles V, Duke of Lorraine, 34
Charles V Habsburg, Holy Roman Emperor, 29
Christendom, 2, 35, 37, 98, 241
Christianity, 33, 38, 51, 201, 217
Christians, 36, 42–43, 45, 50, 57, 65, 67, 70, 83, 93–95, 98–99, 111, 123, 139, 170–85
   Balkan, 67, 122
   Bosnian, 108, 149
   converts to Islam, 170–85
Chotek, Sofia, viii
'civilizing mission', 2, 68, 76–91, 93, 96, 121, 125, 137, 238
clash of civilizations, 200
colonialism (Bosnia and Herzegovina as Habsburg colony), 13, 17–18, 36, 76–91, 132, 238
collective memory, 37, 71, 122, 128
Communist Party (Yugoslav), 200, 236
Congress of Berlin (1878), 52, 63, 64, 77, 107, 110, 113
Congress of Vienna (1815), 64
Constantinople, 28, 42, 65–66. *See also* Istanbul

Comenius, John Amos (Komenský), 33–34
Confino, Jacques, 166
conversion, religious, 22, 44, 53, 111, 123, 132–134, 170–193, 233–34
Croatia
  discourse on Muslims, 141, 146–47, 174, 182–83
  Kingdom of Croatia (also Croatia-Slavonia), 18, 29, 37, 54, 93–96, 99, 123, 146, 148
  national identity, 38, 156
  nationalism, 97, 174
  Ottoman-held, 47
  Republic of, 6, 38, 215
Croats, 5, 10, 14–15, 17, 29, 45, 48–58, 71, 126, 131–34, 136, 145, 153, 167n, 179, 208
cultural style, 21, 155–69
Curipeschitz (Kuripešić), Benedict, 43
Cyrillic alphabet, 93
Czech
  economic expansion to South East Europe, 4, 125
  language, 12, 121, 129
  national identity, 38, 123
  relations with Bosnian Muslims, 121–22, 141, 238
  representations of Bosnian Muslims, 2, 11, 20, 38, 121–44, 149
  settlers in Bosnia and Herzegovina, 130
  society, 121, 124, 125, 141
Czechs, 19–20, 80, 126–27, 142
Czech Republic, 3, 6, 8, 16, 37–38, 130
Czechoslovakia, 129, 132

D
Dalmatia, 47, 64, 71, 123, 156
Daneš, Jiří V., 132
Danube, 7, 30, 34, 96
Dayton Peace Agreement (1995), 194, 216
de-Islamization, 126
de-Ottomanization, 126, 172, 178, 210n
Dinarics, 162
Doderer, Heimito von, 161
Dojmi, Lovro D. di Delupis, 156, 159, 167n
Đozo, Husein ef., 115–17

Drina, river, 10, 59n, 131
Dubica, 123
Duldung, 216, 225–27
Dyk, Emanuel, 130, 132–33
Džabić, Fehmi ef., 111–12

E
Eastern Question, 64
Economic crisis (1873), 65
education
  in Habsburg Bosnia and Herzegovina, 2, 18, 53, 92–103, 131
  in Slovenia, 195
Egypt, 115, 118
electronic discourse, 179–181
emotional regime, 163
epic poetry, South Slavic, 175–76
Erlich, Vera Stein, 21–22, 155–169
ethnic cleansing, 200, 216
ethnography/ethnology, 34, 51, 160, 163, 165, 184, 199
ethnoreligious communities of Bosnia and Herzegovina, 15, 48–59, 67, 84, 121, 131, 139, 157
Eugene of Savoy, 34
Europe, 38, 46, 86, 123, 126, 131–33, 200, 225–34
Evans, Arthur, 47

F
Ferdinand I Habsburg, 28–29
fez, 115, 135–36
Filipović, Josip, general, 17, 66–68
Filipović, Muhamed, 174
Filipović, Seidalija, 56
First World War, viii, 13, 56, 83–84, 141, 172, 240
France, 46, 63, 123
Francis Joseph I, 63, 65–66, 109, 114–15
Franciscans, 43, 66, 71
Franz Ferdinand. *See under* Sarajevo, assasination of Franz Ferdinand (1914)
Foča, 137

G
Gajret, cultural association, 55, 58
gastarbeiter (guest worker), 15, 215, 217–18

Gennadios, Patriarch of Constantinople, 42
German language, 17, 20, 35, 130, 132, 167, 216, 220, 238
Germanization, 123
Germans, 38, 127, 142
  colonists in Bosnia and Herzegovina, 132
Germany, 8, 24, 46, 64, 79, 85, 149, 157, 182, 214–27
Gingrich, Andre, 11–12, 38, 122, 142, 146, 148
Gradaščević, Husein Kapetan, 64
Great Britain, 63, 150–51
Greece, 47
Goražde, 137, 156–57

H
Habsburg
  administration in Bosnia and Herzegovina, 53, 109–12, 130, 133
  army, 70, 85, 109, 125–27, 129
  discourse on Bosnia and Herzegovina, 69–70, 137
  dynasty, 4, 29, 31–34, 38
  imperial politics, 77, 125, 130, 137
  legacy, 1–24, 107, 162, 237–38
  Monarchy (Empire, state), 1–24, 29, 34, 38, 64, 71, 86, 105–6, 113, 115, 118, 127, 129, 130–31, 133, 135, 142, 150, 158–60, 167, 178, 185, 237–38
  myth, 18, 82, 161
  rule (era) in Bosnia and Herzegovina (1878–1918), vii, 1–24, 56, 59n, 69, 71–72, 77, 82–84, 92–93, 97, 105, 107, 113, 121, 125, 130, 132, 137, 140, 147, 158, 237–40
  wars with Ottoman Empire, 16–17, 28–41, 99, 122, 241
Hadžiabdić, Refik Muhamad, 108
Hadžialić, Alma, 237
Hadžiselimović, Omer, 149
Hajdarbašić, Nurudin, 138
Hajdarpašić, Edin, 9, 13–14, 100, 141, 146–47, 208
Hájek, Max, 130, 132–33
Handjar, SS Division, 116

Handžić, Mehmed ef., 110, 115
Harant, Kryštof H. of Polžice and Bezdružice, 35
Helić, Arminka, 237
Herkalović, Tomo, 48
Herzegovina, 9, 70–71, 136, 147, 150, 156
Herzegovina uprising (1875–6), 77, 124
Herzegovina uprising (1881), 125, 129
High Porte. *See under* Ottoman, Porte
High Representative for Bosnia and Herzegovina, 236
Higher Sharia College, Sarajevo, 114–15
Holy Roman Empire, 34, 36
Holtz, Georg Freiherr vom, 68
honour killing, 128
Hořica, Ignát, 126–27
Hungary, 6, 8, 28–32, 35–38, 47, 83, 108, 122
Huttary, Josef, 124

I
Illyrian movement, 177
intelligentsia, 135
Inönü, Ismet, 152
Ireland, 146, 149
Inzko, Valentin, 236
Islam, 1, 4, 8, 10, 18, 23–24, 35–36, 38, 46, 51, 56–58, 67, 97, 104–21, 123, 132, 136, 138, 152–53, 162, 173–74, 177–78, 184, 201–2, 207, 214–23, 225–34
Islamic Community of Bosnia and Herzegovina (ICBH), 19, 104–20, 237, 239
Islamic
  dress, 202, 219–221
  judicial system, 113–114
  officials, 111–12, 114
  practice, 105, 118
  reformism, 115–17
  schools, 105, 114–16, 118
  tradition of Bosniaks, 105–6
Islamization, 105, 124, 130, 174, 177
Islamgesetz, 4, 113
Islamophobia, 3–4, 8, 37–8, 174, 177, 200–2, 217, 233, 240–41

Istanbul, 19, 42–43, 46, 52, 77, 107–8, 110–11. *See also* Constantinople
Izmir, 44

J
Jagić, Vatroslav, 59
Jahoda, Marie, 157–58
Jajce, 159, 239
Janissaries, 42, 68
Jászi, Oszkar, 161
Jerusalem, 109
Jews, 21, 36, 46, 66, 108, 127, 151, 155–169
Jovanović, Stephan von, 66
Jurišić, Nikola, 34, 43

K
Kaiser. *See* Francis Joseph I
Kajtazović, Anesa, 237
Kállay, Benjámin, 18, 53–54, 56, 81, 84, 93, 97, 111–12, 130, 132, 236
Kamenica, 137
Kara Mustafa Pasha, Grand Vizier, 34
Karadjordjević, Alexander, King of Yugoslavia, 57, 112
Karadžić, Radovan, 180
Karadžić, Vuk Stefanović, 175–76
Karčić, Fikret, 105, 109, 114, 116
Karić, Enes, 117
Kavazović, Husein ef., 117
kebap, 130
Kingdom of Serbs, Croats and Slovenes, 55, 57, 149
Kisch, Egon Erwin, 161
Komárno, 31
König, František, 130, 132–33
Köprülü, Fazil Ahmed, Grand Vizier, 33
Kosovo, 9, 64, 197
    battle (1389), 183
    war (1997–99), 181
Krajina (region)
    Bosnian, 10
    Croatian, 50 (*see also* Military Frontier (*Militärgrenze*))
Kroeber, Alfred, 161–62
Kostajnica, 123

Kőszeg, defense (1532), 30
Kuba, Ludvík, 121, 134–36

L
Lajčák, Miroslav, 236
Lamberg, Josip de, 43
Latin language, 10, 35
Latin script/alphabet, 51, 93, 131
Léger, Louis, 45
Leitkultur, 217
Leminger, Jindřich, 125–26
Lika, 57
Linz, 68
literature, 121–54
Ljubić, Josip (Ild Bogdanov), 51
Ljubljana, 194–95, 208
Long Turkish War (1593–1606), 30
Louis II Jagiellon, 28–29

M
Macedonia, 22, 163, 174, 197
Maglaj, battle (1878), 66, 126, 128–29
Magyars, 93
mahalla, 43, 47
Malečková, Jitka, 4, 149
Martić, Grgo, 48
Mazowiecki, Tadeusz, 232
Mažuranić, Matija, 48
Mahmud II, sultan, 44
Mehmed II, sultan, 42–43, 98
Mehmed IV, sultan, 33
Mehmed ağa, Ottoman envoy to Prague, 32
memoirs, 63–75, 121–44
Metaljka, 137
Mexico, 21, 160–61, 163, 165, 167
Mežnarić, Silva, 196–99, 210n
migrants, 2, 23, 194–243
Military Frontier (*Militärgrenze*), 31, 65. *See also:* Krajina
millet, 16, 42–62, 173, 175
Mioče, 137
Mitrinović, Čedomil, 58
Mlada Bosna (Young Bosnia), 56, 58
Mladić, Ratko, 180
modernity discourses, 71, 104

modernization, 19, 50, 65, 85, 115, 117, 131, 142, 145, 195–200, 203, 206
Mohács, battle (1526), 28, 36
Mollinary, Anton, 71
Montenegro, 7, 22, 46, 123, 125, 131, 136–37, 176–77, 197
Moravia, 12, 29–35, 37, 122, 137
Mostar, 95, 111, 136–37, 156, 239
mufti of Bosnia, 108–9
Muhammad, prophet, 36, 106, 110, 113, 138
Munich, 134
Mušić, Ivan, 66
music, 134, 204–6
Muslim National Organization (*Muslimanska narodna organizacija*), 112
Muslims, 38, 44, 52, 58, 66, 95, 98, 100, 116, 124–25, 129–30, 138–40, 170–93, 217
   Balkan, 3, 43, 121–24, 171, 175
   European, 225–35
   personal names, 94, 101n
   religious identity, 71, 195, 202
   Slavic, 104, 124, 171–73, 180–81, 218
   stigmatization, 170–93, 227
   women, 138, 199

N

nationalism, 42–62
Neruda, Jan, 123
Nikola, Prince of Montenegro, 124
Njegoš, Petar II Petrović, 175–77
Noir, Franz, 69
Novak, Vjenceslav, 12, 20, 145–54
Nové Zámky, 31, 33
Novi Pazar Agreement (1879), 107, 113

O

occupation of Bosnia and Herzegovina (1878), 17, 50, 52, 63–93, 104, 106, 117, 121–25, 129, 132, 141, 238
   resistance, 63–75, 80, 128
Omerović, Mustafa Hilmi ef., 108–9
Orientalism (E. Said), 11, 14–15, 20, 22, 82, 97, 139–40, 146, 148–50, 163–65, 172, 178, 185, 227, 240
   discourse, 36, 123, 125, 201, 208
   French painting, 124
   frontier (A. Gingrich), 11, 38, 122, 145–54, 195, 199
   nesting (M. Bakić-Hayden), 172
   style, 162
   Yugoslav, 196, 199
Orthodox Christians, 9–10, 15, 18, 42, 47, 49, 52–54, 56, 58, 79, 84, 97, 107, 131, 133, 135, 138, 140, 158, 179, 181, 202, 227
   rebellions against Ottomans, 65
   refugees, 65 (*see also* Serbs)
Osijek, 30
othering, 194–213
Ottoman
   administration, 43
   architecture, 138
   army, 80, 138
   Empire, 11, 32–3, 35, 38, 43–45, 48, 52, 59n, 63–65, 71, 76–77, 82, 97–98, 100, 106–7, 111, 113, 137–38, 150, 152, 166, 173, 176, 183, 215, 229
   expansion (conquest) of the Balkans and Central Europe, 9, 16, 29–30, 36, 122, 145, 170
   legacy/heritage, 106, 170–93, 200
   Porte, 32, 65, 107
   religious tolerance, 98
   rule (era), 44–45, 50, 54, 147, 150, 172, 182, 196, 218
   society, 35
Ottomans, 13, 29–30, 33–34, 37, 42, 45–46, 56, 63, 107, 122, 131, 145

P

pan-Slavism, 177
Palacký, František, 148
Palestine, 109
Pařík, Karel, 114
Paris, 134
Peace of San Stefano, 63
peasants, 15, 197–202
Pešina, Tomáš P. of Čechorod, 35
Petritsch, Wolfgang, 236
Philipovich von Philippsberg, General. *See under* Filipović, Josip

Plaschka, Richard, 66
Pljevlje, Mufti of, 72
Prague, vii, 5, 32, 34, 128, 134, 148–49
Preradović, Paula von, 161
Prophet. *See under* Muhammad, prophet
proverbs, 170–85
Poland, 37
Popp, Leonidas, 67

Q
Qur'*an*, 44, 66, 105–6, 133

R
racialization, 225–35
Raška, 45
raya (Christian population under Ottomans), 47, 52, 68
Redfield, Robert, 161
refugee crisis in Europe (2015–16), 4, 8, 16, 214
regional identities, 50
reis-ul-ulema, 104–20
religion, 42–62, 104–20, 214–24
Renan, Ernest, 44
Renner, Heinrich, 76
Rivet, Charles, 57
Rogatica, 108
Romanija Mountain, 156
romanticism, 140
Rosegger, Peter, 161
Rosenberg, Petr Vok of, 31
Rosenberg, William of, 31
Roth, Joseph, 161
Rüdiger, Ernst von Starhemberg, 34
Russia, 64
Russo–Ottoman War (1877–78), 63, 77

S
Said, Edward, 11–12, 146, 228
Salafism, 105
Samokovlija, Isak, 156–57, 159, 166
San Stefano, Treaty of, 78
Sandžak of Novi Pazar, 45, 77, 108, 137
Šarac, Sulejman ef., 112
Saracens. *See under* Arabs
Sarajevo, 45–46, 48, 55, 82, 85, 107, 109, 114–15, 135, 137, 151–52, 239

assassination of Franz Ferdinand (1914), viii, 80, 161, 240
Austro-Hungarian occupation (1878), 67, 69, 127
Nazi occupation, 156
Sava river, 34, 65
Scheufler, Pavel, vii
'Schwabo', 121, 127, 136, 141, 240
Schwarz-Schilling, Christian, 236
schools, 92–103
Second World War, 10, 21, 115–16, 129, 134, 164
secularity, 117–8
secularization, 142
Selimović, Meša, 240
Sephardim. *See under* Jews
Serbia, 6, 22, 51, 54, 59n, 66, 108, 125, 137, 146, 166, 170–93, 215
Serbian
anti-Ottoman uprisings, 175
language, 133, 176
nationalist discourse, 95, 97
press, 181–84
Serbo-Croatian language, 54, 130, 195
nationality, 132–33
Serbs, 5–6, 10, 14–15, 17, 37, 43, 45, 47–58, 66, 71, 83, 127, 131–34, 136, 138, 145, 146, 149, 151, 170–93, 208
discourse on Muslims, 141, 170–185
sevdalinka, 194–213
sharia, 19, 43, 108, 110, 113–14
Slavs
of Austria-Hungary, 63
of Bosnia and Herzegovina, 127
collective identity, 38, 125, 132, 134, 138, 142, 149
folk culture, 137
in Habsburg army, 126
language, 51
press, 131
solidarity, 122, 121–44, 148, 240 (*see also* South Slavs)
Slavonia, 30, 44, 46, 57, 71
Slavonski Brod, 95
Slavophiles, 5, 20, 121–44
Slijepčević, Pero, 56
Slovakia, 6, 8, 31, 37

Slovenia, 5–6, 37–38, 156, 194–213
Slunj, 64
Smederevo, 43
Sokollu Mehmed Pasha (Mehmed-paša Sokolović), 47, 97
Sokolović, Makarije, 47
South Eastern Europe, vii, 28, 63. *See also* Balkans
South Slavs, 4, 43, 57, 78, 84, 122, 124, 134, 142, 238
Spaho, Fehim, 55
Spaho, Mehmed, 55
Srebrenica, 180
Sremski Karlovci, 7
Štampar, Andrija, 156
Statut (Statute for Autonomous Administration of Islamic Religious Waqf and Educational Affairs, 1909), 19, 112–13
Stefanović-Vilovsky, Theodor von, 68
Stein, Benno, 157, 159–60
stigmatization. *See under* Muslims, stigmatization
Stolac, 70
Styria, 37
Şükrü, Ahmed Efendi, 108
Suleiman I, sultan, 28, 31, 43, 97–99
Sulevic, Kašpar Zdeněk Kaplíř of, 34
Supek, Olga, 160–61
Šuško, Dževada, 106
Suppan, Arnold, 77
Švabo. *See under* 'Schwabo'
Szabo, Gjuro, 161
Szigetvár, 31

T
Tartars, 33
terrorism, 15, 202, 240–41
textbooks, 92–103
Thallóczy, Lajos von, 84
Thessaloniki, 44, 46
Thirty Year's War (1618–1648), 30, 32
Thököly, Imre, 33
Todorova, Maria, 13, 146, 172, 228
travelogues, 76, 121–44
Travnik, 64, 136

Treaty of Berlin. *See under* Congress of Berlin
Trebinje, 54, 150
Tržac, 64
Tschuppik, Karl, 161
Tunisia, 108, 118
Turkey (before 1922). *See under* Ottoman Empire
Turkey, Republic, 115, 152–53, 215
Turkish
  cruelty, 35, 147
  language, 33, 43, 45, 51
  legacy, 138
  motifs in Central European folklore, 37, 122
'Turkish threat', 28–29, 30, 34–38
'Turkish/Ottoman yoke', 35, 99, 172, 200
Turks, 2, 28–41, 43, 45, 48, 70, 96, 121–44, 170–85, 217
  images and stereotypes, 10–11, 16, 28–41, 93, 98, 121–44, 149, 172, 240
  Ottoman, 28, 34, 36, 124–25
Tuzla, 109, 237

U
uprising against conscription law (1882), 109
urban/rural dichotomy, 23, 194–213, 216
Una river, 65

V
vakuf, 110–12, 114
Valoušek, František, 121, 134, 137–40
Velc, Ferdinand, 139
Velenje (Titovo), 207
Velika Kladuša, 64
Vienna, 21, 63, 83, 86, 107–8, 112, 126, 156, 158–60, 163, 176
Vienna, First Siege of (1529), 30, 37
Vienna, Second Siege of (1683), 12, 33–34, 37, 99, 122
Vinaver, Stanislav, 151–52
Vis, island, 156
Visoko, 159
Vlachs, 43, 48–49, 176
Vratislav, Václav V. of Mitrovice, 35, 39n
Vrbas River, 51

W

waqf. *See under* vakuf
Werfel, Franz, 161
West, Rebecca, 20, 145–54
Westernization, 99
White Mountain, battle (1620), 32
Whiteness, 24, 214, 225–35

Y

Young Czech Party (*Mladočeši*), 126
Young Turk Revolution (1908), 112
Yugoslav Muslim Organization (JMO), 55–56, 58
Yugoslavia, 6, 8, 10, 16–17, 19, 22, 57, 79, 80–81, 106, 112, 115, 117, 146, 149, 151, 153, 157–58, 161, 164, 176, 194, 196–98, 201–2, 204, 208, 215, 225–26, 232, 236, 239
family life, 155–69

Z

Zadić, Alma, 237
Zagreb, 21, 55, 155, 157–58, 160–61, 182
Zenica, 127
Žepče, 128
Žerotín, Bedřich of, 31
Žerotín, Karel the Elder of, 34
Zionism, 157, 159
Zrinski, Nikola, 31, 34
Zvěřina, František Bohumír, 124

www.ingramcontent.com/pod-product-compliance
Lightning Source LLC
Chambersburg PA
CBHW071154070526
44584CB00019B/2790